HASIDIC
WILLIAMSBURG

HASIDIC WILLIAMSBURG

A Contemporary
American Hasidic Community

George Kranzler

JASON ARONSON INC.
Northvale, New Jersey
London

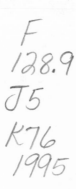

F
128.9
J5
K76
1995

For credits, see Acknowledgments on page 313.

This book was set in 10 point Schneidler by TechType of Upper Saddle River, New Jersey, and printed by Haddon Craftsmen of Scranton, Pennsylvania.

Library of Congress Cataloging-in-Publication Data

Kranzler, George, 1916-
    Hasidic Williamsburg : a contemporary American Hasidic community /
George Kranzler.
        p. cm.
    Includes bibliographical references and index.
    ISBN 1-56821-242-9
    1. Jews–New York (N.Y.)–Social conditions. 2. Hasidim–New York
(N.Y.)–Social conditions. 3. Williamsburg (New York, N.Y.)–Social
conditions. 4. New York (N.Y.)–Social conditions. I. Title.
F128.9.J5K76 1995
305.892′407471–dc20   94-12972

Manufactured in the United States of America. Jason Aronson Inc. offers books and cassettes. For information and catalog write to Jason Aronson Inc., 230 Livingston Street, Northvale, New Jersey 07647.

This book is dedicated
to my dear wife,
whose infinite patience and love
enabled me to devote more than a decade
to this study of the hasidic community of Williamsburg.

꘍꘍꘍ꘌꘌꘌ

Contents

Preface

*H*asidic *Williamsburg* recounts the dramatic emergence of this unique community in the face of major crises. It is the story of the loyalty of its members to their Rebbes and their teachings, and to the milieu they created in this old Jewish neighborhood in Brooklyn, New York.

This account presents the findings of a decade of research into the survival and life-style of Hasidic Williamsburg as a functioning community. It furthermore updates the results of my longitudinal study of the processes of social change in this major center of Orthodox Jewish life since before World War II. In *Williamsburg: A Jewish Community in Transition* (1961), I reported the transformation of this moderately Orthodox Jewish community and its rise to prominence after the influx of large numbers of refugees from Nazi persecution and the Holocaust, and of Orthodox residents from other neighborhoods who liked its educational and other institutions. It concluded with a report on the radical decline of the community and the serious threat to its survival, and the imminence of its collapse, echoing the fate of similar Jewish neighborhoods in New York.

Hasidic Williamsburg portrays the desperate struggle and relentless efforts of its leaders, foremost among them the Rebbe of Satmar and other prominent Hungarian hasidic rebbes, to stem the progressive disintegration of the Jewish neighborhood. It presents their valiant attempts to provide the vital resources for its survival in the face of persistent poverty and other grave problems, and to develop programs that would secure the future of this unique hasidic community.

Hasidic Williamsburg concludes with the assertion that at the beginning of the '90s its inhabitants are hopeful of being able to weather the present crisis and to continue to function as one of pluralist America's viable religious communities.

≫≫≫≪≪≪

Introduction

Hasidim navigate secular worlds while living a life apart.
New York Times, May 2, 1989

At the end of *Williamsburg: A Jewish Community in Transition,* I raised a number of questions about the future of the Jewish community of Williamsburg as significant changes threatened its survival in the '60s. The major threats were:

1. The outmigration of the wealthier and upwardly mobile elements and of the younger Orthodox families [even among the newcomers who had preserved the community's viability since before World War II].
2. The replacement of the older, mostly Irish, Italian, and Slavic non-Jewish population in the marginal areas by growing numbers of Hispanics, especially Puerto Ricans, whose numbers increased from 9 percent to 29 percent of the Brooklyn population in the '50s. This resulted in tension, occasional friction, and crime, such as thefts, robberies, break-ins, and personal attacks.
3. Most serious was the insecurity created at the end of the '50s and in the '60s by the accelerating outmigration of a number of hasidic and nonhasidic groups to other, more attractive Jewish neighborhoods with better facilities. They took with them their institutions and organizations, which had been a major source of the attraction of Williamsburg for Orthodox Jewish families, those who had remained since before World War II as well as those who had settled there since the war.

When the Satmar Hasidic Community, headed by its famous rebbe, Rabbi Yoel Teitelbaum, which had become the largest and most powerful group in Jewish Williamsburg, was faced with the dilemma of whether to stay or leave the neighborhood, I wrote (1961): "The question naturally arises what will happen to the Jewish Community of Williamsburg if and when the Satmarer Rebbe will move to a suburban area, as planned" (p. 209).

I concluded: "It remains to be seen whether there will be adequate serious concerted efforts on the part of the interested pressure groups to save Jewish Williamsburg as one of, if not the most important orthodox Jewish community in the country" (p. 210).

In *From Suburb to Shtetl* (1979), Egon Mayer quotes this final sentence from the Postscript of my book, and concludes: "With the benefit of hindsight on our side, it can be stated with certainty – but not without some sadness – that the concerted efforts of the interested groups never materialized and Jewish Williamsburg is no longer the most important orthodox Jewish community in the country. Boro Park is" (p. 34). Mayer continues by pointing out that the "pillars of the community" had left Williamsburg for Boro Park and other communities, and he leaves little doubt that this meant the end of Williamsburg as a major Orthodox Jewish community.

However, this researcher has found that at the end of the '80s, as a result of the decision of the late Rebbe of Satmar and the leadership of his community to stay and fight for the survival of the hasidic neighborhood, Williamsburg lives, thrives, and is actually larger and more viable than at any other time in its history. In spite of continuing problems, it is a community with a future because of the loyalty of the *hasidim* to their leaders, regardless of difficulties and disadvantages. They have succeeded largely thanks to their determination and concerted efforts to meet their problems head-on and to overcome their difficulties, providing for the welfare of the population themselves, and increasingly turning to the younger generation whose participation in all realms of community life has been a crucial factor in the community's survival. Thus, the decision of the Rebbe of Satmar to remain and fight for the neighborhood was the turning point that prevented the disintegration predicted as far back as the '30s (see my 1961 report, p. 14).

Of equal importance for the preservation of the neighborhood was the election of the present Rebbe of Satmar, Rabbi Moshe Teitelbaum, the nephew of the Old Rebbe who died childless in 1979. Although already 65, he yielded to the pleas of the heads of the Satmar community that he assume the heavy burden of heading the worldwide movement of Satmar. He gave over his own community of Szigeter *hasidim*, with its network of institutions, to his son. The crucial step was his decision to move his residence from Boro Park to a new mansion built for him on Bedford Avenue in the heart of Williamsburg, opposite the identical one that had been built for his uncle and predecessor, which still belongs to the widow of the Old Rebbe.

More than a decade after assuming this prestigious position, Rabbi Moshe Teitelbaum has the vast majority of the *hasidim* of Satmar behind him. Some of the most ardent followers of Rabbi Yoel have not yet been able to accept the demise of their "Holy Rebbe," who had been one of the greatest scholars and hasidic sages of the world. But the present Rebbe's organizational talents and ability to work with the older as well as the younger generations have secured him a place that is second only to the superstatus of his great uncle. The survival of Satmar and of Hasidic Williamsburg was well served by having a strong leader like Reb Moshe Teitelbaum, who has the wisdom and capacity to continue the religious, educational, and sociopolitical policies of the former Rebbe. Since he assumed power, he has successfully maintained and further expanded the empire of Satmar. He has directed the network of institutions and organizations so that they have been able to accommodate the exploding populations of Hasidic Williamsburg, Boro Park, Monsey, New York, and Monroe, New York's Kiryas Joel, as well as the other worldwide centers of Satmar. He has successfully maintained the full scope and requirements of the Hungarian hasidic life-style and is thus largely responsible for the development of the three-generational community of Williamsburg unique in the contemporary Jewish world. For, in most Orthodox, as well as in nonreligious Jewish and non-Jewish, communities the younger generations prefer to strike out for new neighborhoods, communities closer to their age and orientation. In contrast, the middle-aged and younger generation of Satmar *hasidim* prefer to remain in Williamsburg where, as one of their spokesmen put it, "There is not a generation gap."

> The only generation we are missing is the one that was lost in the concentration camps, in the gas chambers, and the suffering of the post-Holocaust period. Our youth is more intensely hasidic than their elders, not only in their wholehearted acceptance of the hasidic appearance and conduct, but also in their religious, scholarly, and ideological orientation.

This loyalty of the younger generations of the hasidic community starkly contrasts even with that of the youth of Jewish Williamsburg in its prime, which was an outstanding Orthodox Jewish community. Many of the children of the earlier religious population left the neighborhood to settle in other communities, such as Boro Park, Crown Heights, and Queens, which offered a better physical and social environment for themselves and for their children.

The young of Hasidic Williamsburg prefer to remain close to their parents, to their Rebbe, and to the institutions in which they were raised. They want their children to grow up in the same milieu that molded them in their early years. To have this intensely hasidic atmosphere they are willing to accept disadvantages and inconveniences such as inadequate housing and lack of facilities and services available elsewhere.

This strong commitment of the younger generation and the cohesiveness of the hasidic community have made it possible for their leaders to fight for the survival of their neighborhood and to launch a multipronged attack on the most pressing problems that have plagued Jewish Williamsburg since the '60s. It has enabled them to cope with the continued outmigration of the upwardly mobile, the housing shortage, and the departure of major groups and their institutions, which had been "the pillars of Williamsburg's attraction" and which Egon Mayer (1979) mentions as a sign of the disintegration of the neighborhood (p. 34).

This positive attitude of the younger generation toward hasidic life in Williamsburg is also responsible for some of the most important changes wrought in the past decade, particularly in the realms of social and economic mobilization and reorganization. The very appearance of life in the streets of Williamsburg seems youth oriented, as one of the interviewees stressed: "Go out into the streets and you will see that almost 90 percent of the people are young." Although this figure is obviously an exaggeration, it indicates the crucial role that the young and middle-aged play in the life of the community.

The concentration of the young on trade and business is responsible for their dominance of life in the streets of Williamsburg and in such centers of New York's trade and manufacturing as the Lower East Side and Mid-Manhattan. They are unashamed of their hasidic appearance and conduct. Though many of them could well afford to move to other, higher income Orthodox neighborhoods, most prefer to stay close to their families and to their rebbe, regardless of the sacrifices they must endure in terms of comfort and convenience. It is this spirit of commitment to be found in all the generations that has made the new hasidic community of Williamsburg a thriving center of American hasidic life.

* * *

Most of the direct quotes of statements by residents of the community are the author's translation from the original Yiddish or an admixture of Yiddish and English that is the common vernacular of the people in Hasidic Williamsburg.

>>> 1 <<<

Residential Patterns:
The Jewish Triangle

The major premise of *Williamsburg: A Jewish Community in Transition* (1961), the first volume of this longitudinal study of the Jewish community of Williamsburg, had been the assertion that economic, ecological, and mechanistic views of the determination of the structure of a community were unfounded. That study demonstrated what Walter Firey had first pointed out in *Land Use in Central Boston* (1947). He claimed that the spatial organization of a community is largely the product of valuational factors originating in the historical and cultural background of its population. Thus it also supported Robert M. MacIver's (1941) claim that "social systems are directly and indirectly the creations of cultural values . . . and every change in valuations on the part of social groups registers itself in institutional change" (p. 465).

Concordant with this view, *Williamsburg: A Jewish Community in Transition* argued that in spite of serious disadvantages, such as inadequate, antiquated housing, lack of playgrounds, shopping, and other vital facilities and services, the Jewish community of Williamsburg was not disintegrating like other, similar Jewish neighborhoods in Brooklyn, New York. Its religious milieu and its religious and educational institutions and organizations kept a large number of its old-time residents in the neighborhood. It even attracted new Orthodox Jewish refugees from the countries of Nazi persecution and the Holocaust. Through years of crises, such as the construction of the Brooklyn-Queens Expressway through the very center of the neighborhood, economic depression, the increasing influx of large numbers of ethnic and racial minorities and the ensuing friction and blight, the solidly entrenched religiocultural values kept a large portion of the pre- and post–World War II population in Williamsburg. Yet their numbers continued to fall due to the accelerating outmigration of the upwardly mobile and younger elements. This trend was further aggravated by the loss of large chunks of the marginal areas to Hispanics, blacks, and other minority groups during the '50s and '60s. Consequently, serious doubts about the future of the neighborhood plagued even those who had been most sanguine

1

about the ability of the Jewish community of Williamsburg to weather the threats to its survival.

This study of the new Williamsburg, undertaken a generation later, attempts to further substantiate the original assertion of the crucial impact of the religious values of its population on the structure and dynamics of the same community in its changed composition. In fact, it proposes to submit further evidence for the impact of religious values on the spatial arrangement and essential makeup of the hasidic community as it stemmed the process of disintegration of the neighborhood and created a new, larger, and thriving center of American Hasidism in Williamsburg.

It is still primarily a lower-class neighborhood in which over 50 percent of the population have incomes below the national poverty level (14 percent according to a 1986 census) and in which close to 40 percent depend on some form of government assistance, according to the head of the community. This latter figure may in fact increase substantially as a result of the economic downturn since the beginning of the '90s. However, this figure does not seem too high if one considers that a 1983 follow-up study of Robert and Helen Lynd's classic *Middletown* (1929), done by Theodore Caplow and his associates, found that about 50 percent of the present Middletown population receives some form of direct or indirect public assistance. Yet the general appearance and outlook of Williamsburg have improved significantly during the '80s. The streets are hustling and bustling with young *hasidim* engaged in some trade or business. Most of them are satisfied and happy to remain in Williamsburg, confident that the community will be able to handle whatever problems and difficulties may evolve. This upbeat, affirmative attitude is the key to the future and continued growth of the hasidic enclave in Brooklyn in the shadow of the Williamsburg Bridge.

In expansion of the original assertion of the crucial role of the value system in the mode and quality of a community, this study emphasizes the converse of Egon Mayer's "symbolic return" to the East European shtetl in the developments he traces in the concentration of Jewish life in Boro Park in *From Suburb to Shtetl* (1979). It is true that the Hungarian type of *hasidim*, such as those of Satmar, Pappa, Vishnitz, Klausenburg, and the others, chose to make Williamsburg an "island in the city," as Israel Rubin called his book on Satmar (1972), to allow for maximum integration within relative isolation from the sociocultural values and life-style of the urban society around them. Yet, theirs is not an Amish-like separation from technology and other rudiments of contemporary civilization. On the contrary, it is giving the lie to those like the Jewish social scientist and former Williamsburger who, when interviewed in 1986, remarked, "It is beautiful what they (the *hasidim*) have done. But Hasidism in America in this time and age is an anachronism. It is extraterritorial and has absolutely no future."

In fact, Hasidic Williamsburg has demonstrated the positive dynamics of ideological, as well as physical, growth, and has created a new type of American Hasidism that emphasizes being a part of the mainstream. As the director of the powerful ODA government office in Williamsburg remarked in an interview in *Minority Business Today,* published by the U.S. Department of Commerce (1985):

"Our primary mission was and continues to be providing assistance to Hasidic entrepreneurs . . . [enabling them] *to effectively compete within the American economic mainstream*" (italics mine; p. 13).

This Americanization of the *hasidim* is not only true for the spirit of enterprise that characterizes the dynamics of life in Williamsburg, it is equally true in other realms, such as their participation in the general, as well as the Jewish, political life. It is significantly in evidence in the emphasis of the hasidic community on self-help and on a maximum of independence, contrary to the popular image of the shtetl that had been shaped by centuries of suffering, persecution, privation, poverty, and inequality.

This radical change is the expression of the spirit of America at its best, in Boro Park, in Flatbush, in Monsey, New York, in Kiryas Joel in Monroe, New York, as in Williamsburg itself. But in the hasidic community of Williamsburg, in the homogeneity of its milieu, it emerges more powerfully because of the superficial contrast to the ultra-Orthodox life-style of its men and women, many of whom still bear the marks of the Holocaust and of its aftermath. Here the emphasis is now on youth in public life. The members of the third generation, who lack many of the inhibitions of their elders, are enthusiastically vying for their place in the American supermarkets of economic, and other, opportunities – in spite of limitations imposed on them by their hasidic garb, language difficulties, and other educational and cultural differences. One of the prominent heads of the Satmar community expressed this new attitude of the young when he spoke of his own grandson as typical of the new generation of young *hasidim* born in Williamsburg.

> This is the spirit of America. I learned the same trade my father had plied in Hungary, and I taught it to my son when we came here over 30 years ago. My grandson, like his friends, does not want to work in a factory or a shop like us. Many leave the Beth Medrash after they get married, and try to set up a business of their own. At first they struggle, and quite a few don't make it. But like my grandson and his study companions who started a new venture, they work hard. Eventually, they hope, they will succeed, while remaining faithful to their hasidic upbringing and while they continue their talmudic studies before and after work.

A highly perceptive and intelligent man who takes pride in his daily perusal of the *New York Times,* this leader of the Satmar community smiled and, with a twinkle in his eyes, he concluded: "Only in America!" At the same time he made a point of emphasizing that his grandson and his contemporaries have at least as good if not a better religious education than those who had grown up in the East European shtetl.

Of course, scholars, like Daniel P. Moynihan, Nathan Glazer, and Egon Mayer, stress that the general rise of pride in ethnicity in Midcentury America is largely responsible for this type of "Americanism." While this pride in their ethnicity is probably real for the hasidic community as well as for others, all of whom happily take advantage of new opportunities that developed since the '60s, it does not tell the whole story behind the spirit that pervades the new Williamsburg. The attitude of independence and self-help in Williamsburg goes far beyond the usual participation in government-sponsored programs for minority groups, as important as they may be. The very essence of Satmar, often to the chagrin of the broader Jewish community, is its independence, its refusal to affiliate for the sake of financial and other gains. This attitude made it possible for the Old Rebbe of Satmar to promulgate what is perhaps the strongest opposition to the Zionist state in Israel for treating religion as a matter of private concern. This attitude of independence is also responsible for his refusal of any form of affiliation or financial support for his educational institutions, which constitute the largest single Jewish educational system in the U.S., in order to avoid any form of influence, obligation, or supervision that would clash with his rigorous standards and values. This spirit of independence, expressing itself in numerous other realms of the communal life, blends well with the American emphasis on self-determination, independence, and pulling oneself up by one's own bootstraps. It has produced the glorious success story of two hundred years of immigrant absorption and cultural pluralism in this country, as nowhere else in the world.

HISTORICAL BACKGROUND

Williamsburg: A Jewish Community in Transition (1961) analyzed the developments that changed the nature of this Jewish neighborhood through three major phases:

Phase I: 1938, characterized as Williamsburg
Phase II: 1939–1948, characterized as Refugeetown
Phase III: 1949–1960, characterized as Hunksville

This volume of my longitudinal study reports on the most recent phase, Phase IV: 1961–1990, New Hasidic Williamsburg.

This period was initiated by the decision of Rabbi Yoel Teitelbaum, the charismatic head of the large community of Satmar Hasidim, to remain in Williamsburg and fight the processes of progressive blight and disintegration when other hasidic as well as nonhasidic groups moved to Boro Park and other urban and suburban religious Jewish communities, taking their institutions with them. The strenuous efforts of his and other Hungarian hasidic groups produced an amazing turnabout contrary to the expectations of students of Jewish community life in the U.S. who had all but written off the once thriving Jewish community of Williamsburg and come to doubt the viability of a hasidic community in the midst of secular urban America. By the end of the '80s, it had regained its old vigor. It had become a community in the true sense of the word meeting crisis after crisis and learning to cope with new problems as they develop.

What follows is a brief summary of the historical background of the Jewish community of Williamsburg, taken from my 1961 report, *Williamsburg: A Jewish Community in Transition*.

Williamsburg, formerly spelled Williamsburgh, was named after a Colonel Williams who surveyed the territory between Wallabout Bay and Bushwick Creek in the early nineteenth century. In 1851 Williamsburgh became an incorporated city; and in 1855 it was merged into the then still independent City of Brooklyn.[1]

The Williamsburg[2] of the present study refers to the Jewish community living in the area bounded by Wythe Avenue, Brooklyn Broadway and Heyward Street, and centered along Bedford, Lee, Marcy, and Division Avenues and their cross streets. This is the only neighborhood that showed some gain in population and increase in average income during the 1920s and early 1930s, when the rest of Old Williamsburg went into a steep decline as a residential area, losing up to 50 percent of its population.[3]

From the very outset this particular neighborhood west of Broadway had been a choice location for the higher social strata of Brooklyn. Bedford Avenue was the seat of the most exclusive[4] clubs of the borough, and of the Seneca Club, headquarters of the powerful Kelly machine of the Democratic party. Wealthy industrialists and professionals owned houses in the once tree-shaded side streets. Most of the trees and the social elite are gone. They left Williamsburg in the years before and after World War I, when Jewish elements began to settle there in larger numbers. Up to that time only the wealthiest Jews (of German extraction) had resided there, and had established congregations in some of the large churches sold by the Christian owners because their members had left the neighborhood. Even a reform congregation had been formed then, the first in Brooklyn.[5] This Jewish reform temple, Beth Elokim, located at 274 Keap Street, lost its function when these high-income Jews moved on to better neighborhoods. In 1921 the building was sold to a congregation of Orthodox Russian and Polish Jews who had begun to settle in Williamsburg in large numbers in the years after World War I, and who subsequently effected a complete change in the character of the community.

In the beginning of the 1920s Williamsburg became really Jewish Williamsburg as an Orthodox community of the moderate Ashkenazic Russian Polish type. By 1930, the formerly predominant non-Jewish population had shrunk to an estimated third of the approximately 20,000 people who lived there,[6] and those who remained withdrew mostly to the outer zones of the section. Consequently, the district turned into a typical lower- and low-middle-class Jewish neighborhood, in which workers, employees, and small businessmen replaced most of the higher class Jewish and non-Jewish population. Numerous synagogues were established throughout the section, the largest in former church buildings. Hebrew schools and organizations were formed, and many of the clubhouses, beginning with the exclusive Hanover Club on Bedford Avenue, were taken over by Jewish organizations. Soon Williamsburg became one of the neighborhoods that attracted those elements that had outgrown the Jewish immigrant communities of the Lower East Side, Old Williamsburg, (east and south of Broadway), Brownsville, and the East Bronx socially and economically.

One of the oldest members of Jewish Williamsburg described the change in the communal pattern in these words:[7]

I was one of the first Jews who lived in this neighborhood. When I moved here fifty years ago this was a very ritzy section, and only the very rich resided here. Walking down Hewes Street from Bedford Avenue was like walking into a park, with trees and well-cared-for gardens on both sides of the street. Imagine this, once my son saw a Jew with beard and *peyes* on Taylor and Lee, and the Christian children were running after him, throwing stones and calling him names. He was amazed and disturbed and came running to me for an explanation.[8] It's quite different now. Every second man wears a beard and the children on Lee Avenue are Jewish and most of them have a *yarmulkeh* and go to a *yeshivah*. But it took a long time for all this to happen. When I came here, Williamsburg was still a *"midbar,"* a desert, for Jews. By the beginning of the First World War there were already different kinds of congregations, and the Hewes Street and South Fifth Street synagogues were located in the huge church buildings. But Williamsburg became really Jewish after the war, when the richer Jews moved to Flatbush and Crown Heights, and the plain people moved here from the East Side and other neighborhoods of "Greene." The stores in the streets changed owners and carried Jewish merchandise, foods, and religious articles. For us who had known Williamsburg before, this was a wonderful change. But, of course, it was never as Orthodox or as "fanatical" as it is now. We had no "Glatt Kosher." And most of our children went to the public schools, even though the Yeshiva Torah Vodaath was founded in the late '20s and attracted students from everywhere. There were movies all over, which are practically all gone. And there were dance halls and poolrooms for the young. But still there were really *"baale-battishe"* Jews living here and many *talmidei hachomim.* Their huge *seforim-shrank,* libraries, which now gather dust in the siderooms of the *shuls,* were all used then. It was a really fine Jewish life here in Williamsburg.

The impressions of this old-timer are borne out by the data. Jewish communal life in Williamsburg flourished during the 1920s. It declined only in the 1930s, after the crash and the depression had affected many of both the lower- and higher-income groups, and when the richest elements and the younger generation moved to better neighborhoods, or sections where they would not be bound to the Orthodox life pattern that dominated Jewish Williamsburg, though to a considerably lesser degree than it has in the community's later development.

Toward the end of the 1920s and during the 1930s the moderate hasidic Galician and Polish Jews began to settle in Williamsburg in larger numbers. They organized their *shtieblach,* small makeshift synagogues, in stores, basements, and flats. A few even had their own Rebbes, though all of them were of minor stature, compared to the famous hasidic leaders who came to Williamsburg during the late 1940s. This new element soon made itself felt. Though not as extreme as the later newcomers, they brought a warmer, more intensely religious spirit to Williamsburg, which until then had been dominated by the more restrained, formal, and rational spirit of the Ashkenazic Russian-Polish Jews of the earlier years. The large parochial school that they founded grew by leaps and bounds and developed in a few short years into a major institution with a national reputation, replacing the Hebrew schools commonly associated with the Ashkenazic type of congregation. The pattern of customs and mores that had satisfied the Orthodoxy of the earlier elements did not meet their hasidic standards. Gradually many of the practices accepted before their influence was felt (especially in the social realm) were no longer considered proper for the Proper Williamsburger. More intensely Orthodox youth movements displaced the moderate general organizations. Due to their relatively low economic status during the difficult years, it was a long time before members of the hasidic group assumed some of the community leadership held by the Russian-Polish group.

When the first German and Austrian refugees began to settle in Williamsburg, the depression of the 1930s was still effective; but soon afterward, the beginning of the war in Europe changed everything. Both the old and the new elements were able to take advantage of the boom. The diamond industry, in particular, brought to New York by Belgian refugees, most of them Orthodox, benefited the Jewish population of Williamsburg, and raised the community's standard of living, and with it the amount of money available for commercial projects. Although a good many of the wealthier Jews moved to better neighborhoods, they were easily replaced by new leaders from the ranks of both the old and the new population. The latter increased by the day, as new elements from the countries overrun by the Nazis immigrated into the United States.

The Orthodox of the middle and lower classes were attracted to Williamsburg because it was a community with the right spiritual climate in which to settle and bring up their children. During those years the Orthodox institutions of Williamsburg grew and developed to larger proportions than could ever have been anticipated even by the optimists among their founders. Their effect on the young, and the general rise in Orthodox standards introduced by the increasingly predominant Czechoslovakian, Polish, and Hungarian hasidic newcomers, intensified the already Orthodox community pattern further.

With the end of World War II, the inmates of the Displaced Persons camps, the concentration camps, and the internment camps, as well as their more fortunate comrades who had found temporary haven in every corner of the world, flocked to the United States. Williamsburg again was most attractive to those seeking an intensely Orthodox atmosphere. The earlier groups of newcomers had adjusted themselves into the community's existing institutions, congregations, and organizations, and had risen within the framework of these organization, especially those who had brought with them their own spiritual leaders. The Hungarian groups especially, which until the 1940s had played a minor part in the communal life of Williamsburg, gained by this wave of immigrants, and they quickly formed their own strong religious centers of the extreme hasidic type to which they had been accustomed in their old homelands. Among their new leaders were famous hasidic Rebbes who not only brought their own followers with them, but also attracted a considerable following from among the earlier groups.

The influence of these extreme groups grew rapidly and attracted many of both the younger and older elements among the natives and earlier immigrants. On the other hand quite a few of those who were unwilling to go along with the intense form of communal life introduced by the newcomers, moved away as quickly as they could find accommodations in other, less extreme Jewish neighborhoods.

Others, especially of the original Russian-Polish group, voiced their open resentment and created occasional conflicts or tensions. Since both groups agree on the theoretical principles of the Jewish faith and the application of the laws of the Torah to actual life situations, and their differences are only a matter of the degree to which they adhere to this application, there could not be any serious conflict between the more or less Orthodox factions. By their numerical and spiritual strength, the new Hungarian elements were able to impose a large part of their extreme pattern of practical Orthodoxy on communal life, in the synagogue, on the local economic scene, and in the social structure and general valuation.

By the end of the 1940s, when the frenzy of the postwar phase and its subsequent brief regression had subsided into a more normal situation, many of the newcomers had worked their way into influential positions in the community by virtue of their economic and social adjustment. By 1949, there was no longer any question that the extreme hasidic newcomers, led by world famous hasidic Rebbes, had replaced the majority of the former leaders. They took the initiative in many areas of religious and practical life that had previously been neglected for lack of funds, courage, or zeal on the part of a leadership that lacked the unifying and organizing power available to the hasidic leaders. Numerous religious institutions were established. New businesses were built up and made popular far beyond the immediate community. Trades that had been plied by Orthodox Jews since the years of the early immigrants were taken up by the newcomers. Within a short time they were able to establish large communal centers in the heart of Williamsburg. Consequently, Williamsburg became the hub of this extreme Orthodox type of religious activity. Despite the fact that many of the original residents and earlier refugees and Displaced Persons moved to better and more moderate Jewish neighborhoods, housing conditions became even worse than during the war years. Rent and real estate prices rose to twice the level of comparable neighborhoods.[9]

More than any other realm, the religious and cultural life of the community was affected by this intensification of the customs and mores. A holiday in Williamsburg became a sensation for strangers, and an experience unparalleled even for those who had known hasidic life in Europe. "I have never seen or heard of anything like this at home," remarked an old-timer critically, as he viewed the all-night spectacle of the Simhat Torah celebration on Bedford Avenue. He thought of his hometown, which had never seen busy streets like Bedford Avenue blocked off for hours while thousands of Jews, young and old, in hasidic garb or in the most fashionable American clothes, joined in dancing through the wee hours of the morning. He did not doubt that there was a similar or even more intense form of religious experience in the old European courts of the hasidic Rebbes. To find it in the setting of a modern metropolis, and shared by such a variegated multitude of Jews who only 20 years ago were thousands of miles apart, physically and spiritually, was something that might impress even the most critical observer. These high spots of communal life in Williamsburg impress themselves even more strongly on the youth and the adults who are prepared for it by the intensity of the religious attitude throughout the year, and in the daily routine of their private and social life.

Since the middle of 1952, a new turn of events has ushered in a different, and perhaps final, phase of the Jewish community of Williamsburg. The long projected Queens-connecting highway, blueprinted to cut through the very heart of the neighborhood, is finally being undertaken. Ten of the most populated blocks will have to come down. The houses have already been taken over by the city, and their inhabitants given notice of eviction. At this point the tenants have to make a decision as to whether to stay on in Williamsburg, and pay the exorbitant rent that is now charged by landlords because apartments are at a premium in the blocks not touched by the project, or move out of the neighborhood into different Jewish sections.

Since most of the hasidic Rebbes are staying on, at least for the time being, more than half of these tenants intend to stay. One of them, a German Jew with a thorough education, both secular and religious, who gave up teaching in favor of a lucrative export business and could afford a better neighborhood, remarked wistfully:

> My wife looked for an apartment in Crown Heights. But I was wishing all along to myself that she would not succeed. I'd gladly pay the $110.00 for the six rooms on Bedford Avenue, knowing that my children will be able to continue their schooling, and grow up here. And I myself have the ideal set-up of a *kehillah* with friends who spend their spare time in the study of Torah, and who can be an example of true Judaism to me and my family. What else could I wish for, neighborhoods where my wife and I play bridge? No siree, for me Williamsburg is good enough, as it is. What will happen later, we shall see.

He expresses the waiting attitude of all those who are worried about the effect of the highway on the neighborhood, but are willing to hold out at any price, for as long as possible. Others are moving away. Much of the building-up process has temporarily stopped because of the uncertainty. The years to come will show whether the presence of the famous Rebbes will be able to block the almost certain ruin of the neighborhood as a residential area.[10] Low-cost housing projects are planned for Williamsburg several years after the completion of the highway. It will be interesting to observe the clash of these purely ecological projects with the valuational structure of the community in the present composition.

This is how things stood when I penned my postscript to *Williamsburg: A Jewish Community in Transition* at the end of 1960. This volume, turning to the new Williamsburg, takes over at the nadir of the history of this unique Jewish neighborhood in Brooklyn. It describes the forces and analyzes the factors that affected the radical changes responsible for the emergence of a stronger, more viable, and vigorous hasidic community with a strong future as a functional member of contemporary pluralistic American society.

THE STUDY AREA: THE JEWISH TRIANGLE

The study area of Williamsburg lies south of the Williamsburg Bridge and extends more than a mile inland from the waterfront of the East River. It is comprised of a

120-block area, bounded by Brooklyn Broadway, Flushing Avenue, Kent Avenue, and Whythe Avenue. It has about 9,000 dwelling units, according to the 1970 Census. This is about 1,000 less than recorded 10 years earlier in the residential core. Its 111 industrial buildings are located primarily in the marginal areas, along the waterfront, the old Brooklyn Navy Yard, in the Williamsburg Bridge Corridor, and at the southern end. A large portion of the old, blighted area was designated as a Williamsburg Urban Renewal Area (WURA) in the late '60s at the northwestern boundary. Much of it was used for the construction of five large public high-rise projects that are described in detail later in this chapter. Numerous blocks in the marginal areas have been torn down. The houses were abandoned, razed, or destroyed by fire and vandalism, like in so many other old neighborhoods of Brooklyn and elsewhere.

Large sections of these stretches of wasteland were assigned to the New York City Partnership for the construction of low-cost housing for low- and middle-income residents in the mideighties by the New York City Housing Authority. By 1990 lots were made available to both the Jewish and non-Jewish elements in the neighborhood, as actual construction is gradually undertaken and financed by funds that are largely derived from the sale of abandoned houses and land owned by the city.

A large segment in the center of the Jewish core, located in the blocks adjoining the mansion of the Rebbe of Satmar, which had been purchased by the administration of the Satmar school system, has been the subject of protracted legal controversy. A determined group of the political leaders of the Puerto Rican residents tried to stop the construction of a large new building to accommodate the exploding student population of Satmar schools and its faculty. After years of costly court proceedings, the state supreme court decided that there was no merit to the claim of the Puerto Rican residents that the *hasidim* were receiving preferential treatment in the distribution of the land.

The population of the entire study area, one of Brooklyn's densest neighborhoods, according to preliminary figures of the 1990 U.S. Census, was 35,792, comprised of 17,819 females and 17,973 males. The most significant aspect of these figures is that 50.7 percent are less than 20 years old. There was an increase of 14 percent in the total population since the 1980 Census, but there was a 77.8 percent increase in the number of persons less than 20 years old. A study made by the Primary Health Care Center pointed to the abnormally high birthrate of 23.2 live births per thousand in 1989, for example, for the immediate area, in contrast to 15.9 per thousand in the United States as a whole, as a major reason for this leap in juvenile population. The excellent *South Williamsburg* study done for the local office of the Opportunity Development Association (ODA) in 1977 and updated in 1982 estimates that the actual population is considerably higher than the figures from the U.S. Census. They point out that a high percent of the residents are non-English-speaking members of various ethnic groups. (According to the 1991 Primary Health Care Center study, over 22 percent of the immediate area does not speak English at home, and almost twice as many speak English poorly.)

This accounts for the relatively high percentage of the area's population not reached or improperly tabulated by the Census takers. The preliminary Census figures, however, confirm the ODA estimate of a 14 percent annual growth of the population in the tracts overwhelmingly populated by *hasidim*. The Primary Health Care Center study also ups the ODA's 1982 estimate of seven to eight children per family to eight to ten in 1990.

These extraordinary figures of the high birthrate are also confirmed in the small sample study of hasidic women in Williamsburg reported in chapter 7, and in the figures recorded by the director of the Yeled Shaashuim Recovery Home for Mothers, in Kiryas Joel, the exurban branch of Satmar near Monroe, New York, and by the Puerto Rican manager of the largest public high-rise project in Williamsburg. According to him the average Puerto Rican family in the mideighties had 2.4 children, while the average hasidic family had 7.4 children.

Consequently, most estimates of the current hasidic population of Williamsburg range between 40,000 and 57,000. Therefore, we can reasonably speak of a hasidic population at the end of the '80s of 40,000 men, women, and children, most of whom belonged to fifteen larger and smaller Hungarian hasidic subcommunities. Yetev Lev, the congregation of Satmar, the largest and most powerful of the hasidic communities of Williamsburg, had a membership list of over 10,000 men by the mideighties. The others belonged to the congregations of the Rebbes of Klausenburg, Pappa, Tzelem, Vishnitz, Spinka, Krasna, and others. There are also still a few small nonhasidic congregations in the community, but they are only remnants of what had been the most powerful of the synagogues of the pre– and post–World-War-II era. Their already limited membership is rapidly diminishing due to natural attrition and to the continuing departure of many of those who had spent a lifetime in the old Williamsburg. In the words of one of their prominent members, "We no longer feel at home here." Like the rest of his family he has reluctantly moved to Flatbush after 65 years of active participation in the life and affairs of the Jewish community in Williamsburg.

Much of the zonal structure that had been central to the discussion of the residential patterns in my previous report, in the decades before and after World War II until 1960, is no longer relevant. The new Williamsburg of the '80s and '90s is trying to cope with the realities of a housing crunch and shortage of apartments, especially for the hundreds of young couples marrying annually who want to remain in Hasidic Williamsburg close to their Rebbe and their families. So much has changed during the intervening decades–progressive blight, accelerating outmigration, the construction of the Brooklyn Queens Expressway and the large public high- rise projects, the constant efforts at renovations and new construction projects and programs initiated by the hasidic community with the help of federal, state, and city funds, and private enterprises.

All of these factors have thoroughly altered the lines in the zoning map from my 1961 report. The northern, northwestern, and northeastern, as well as the southern, marginal areas are the location of light, and some heavy, industries. Minority groups, which now constitute approximately 30 percent of the population (25 percent Hispanic, 5 percent blacks and other racial or ethnic groups) are still concentrated in the north, northeast, and southern marginal areas, in addition to those who occupy about 50 percent of the units in the public high-rise projects. Division Avenue is generally considered the dividing line between the Jewish and Hispanic sections of the neighborhood. This line of demarcation, however, is no longer valid, as the hasidic community, forced to expand, is acquiring and reconstructing segments of Division Avenue and its extension into Harrison Avenue to meet the constant demand for more adequate housing. Generally, the areas occupied by Hispanics and other ethnic groups are among those in the poorest condition due to economic depression and the departure of much of the industry that had provided jobs for its largely unskilled population (cf. any of the several studies of New York's minority groups, e.g., Daniel Patrick Moynihan and Nathan Glazer's *Beyond the Melting Pot* [1970], Ida Susser's *Norman Street* [1982], and Jonathan Riemer's *Canarsie* [1985]; see also the statistics of the 1975 U.S. Labor Department study *Profile of Puerto Rican New Yorkers* [1975]).

Most of the positive changes in the appearance and composition of the zonal structure of the neighborhood have come from the intensive efforts of the hasidic community of Williamsburg to alleviate the heavy pressure for adequate housing for its large families through renovation and new building projects. Though not proceeding fast enough to keep pace with the acceleration of its veritable population explosion (doubling every 12 years), there is visible progress everywhere. Much of the area has been rehabilitated by individual and communal reconstruction and beautification projects, with the help of federal, state, or city funding. More recently private efforts have led to the development of middle-range to luxurious condominium complexes, such as Kent Village constructed on Kent Avenue along the navy yard, an area much of which had been off-limits to the Jews of the old Williamsburg. Leaping real estate prices and the general economic downturn of the beginning '90s are slowing down this process of upgrading the housing of the neighborhood, but it is progressing steadily. This progress starkly contrasts with the situation in the adjoining areas occupied primarily by Latinos and blacks, where real estate prices and rents are much lower. Deterioration and neglect run rampant, except for the renovation and reconstruction work undertaken by Los Suros, the Southside United Housing Department Federation. This organization is under the leadership of the Catholic clergy of the neighborhood churches. Hispanic and other political leaders, and different groups and organizations dedicated to the improvement of life for the Latino population.

The efforts of the hasidic community to find territory for more expansion are naturally directed toward the marginal strips and corridors where whole blocks have been destroyed by vandalism and neglect, and the areas cleared by WUR that have not been used for public housing projects.

There are three types of renovation and reconstruction programs. Some are community initiated or sponsored. Others are public housing projects, that is, developed with the help of federal, state, and New York City programs. The project initiated by former Mayor Edward Koch, the New York City Partnership, established in 1985, is one such program. It plans to support the construction of 450 homes for low-, moderate-, and middle-income families with the help of Cross subsidy funds. It will also rehabilitate blighted blocks "in a program that will go a long way to rebuilding the neighborhood and add greatly to the stability of the community" (Koch 1985). The third type of construction is carried out by independent developers like those who built the Kent Village complex and are working on additional innovative projects. Bedford Gardens and Clemente Plaza are managed by private companies. Though other public high-rise projects, such as Taylor-Whythe, have some larger apartments on each floor, Bedford Gardens units are most sought after because they have been designed with the large hasidic families in mind. Their rents are considerably higher than the large apartments in the neighboring public high-rise projects. In February 1991, in response to the increasing economic crisis adding to the difficulties of many of the hasidic families, even those of middle income, a tenants organization was formed to block recently announced further steep increases in the already expensive rents.

Increasingly, private efforts are behind the renovation or total reconstruction of houses and, in some cases, whole blighted blocks in marginal areas, transforming them into attractive streets. Some of the higher-income residents of the neighborhood have combined apartments or houses, torn out the inside, and reconstructed them according to the needs of their large families; often they spruce up the outside as well as the inside. As a result of these private and communal efforts, some of what were once the most drab and dreary marginal side streets have become desirable, attracting especially the middle-aged and younger couples who are intent on remaining in the neighborhood, close to their families and their Rebbe. These spruced up streets range from the waterfront to Marcy and Harrison Avenues. The houses have been dressed up with porches and marble fronts reminiscent of the life-style of Boro Park and Flatbush. Hasidic children now play on the sidewalks of blocks that had once been totally avoided because of the presence of bars and other undesirable stores and establishments in the immediate vicinity. Private developers have also undertaken to renovate apartment houses at the upper end of Division Avenue and on adjoining streets that had been almost totally abandoned by Jewish residents since the '60s.

Even Bedford Avenue, always the center of the best residential area of Williamsburg since the nineteenth century, and the seat of prominent community leaders and organizations, had suffered from deterioration and blight. It, too, is now going through a process of thorough rehabilitation, as the result of a combination of private efforts, government programs, and communal projects. Though progressing slowly, some of what were once among the finest apartments and mansions and clubhouses of the elite of pre-World-War-II society have been primed for renovation. Part of the larger hasidic subcommunities, such as those of Satmar, Pappa, Tzelem, and others, are being rebuilt with the help of funds derived from the sale of the large, planned apartments, for which lots were drawn years ago.

Indeed, Bedford Avenue is still the heart of the New Hasidic Williamsburg, as it had been in the glorious pre-World-War-I years, and in the subsequent pre- and post-World-War-II eras. It is the location of the mansion built for the Old Rebbe of Satmar as well as of the one built for the New Rebbe of Satmar across the street. At the very hub of the Jewish Triangle, between Keap and Rodney Streets, Satmar has built a beautiful, large, new building to house Yeshivas Vayoel Moshe, which accommodates twenty-four classes of boys between the ages of 4 and 6. Its large cafeteria/auditorium is a popular hall used for weddings and other festive occasions. At the end of the '80s, another large new building was begun. The Yeshiva of Satmar was built behind the mansion of the New Rebbe on land that had been purchased from WUR, and accommodates fifty-four more classes of Torah V'Yiroh, thus adding a new class every two months. As noted, construction was delayed for more than two years when the Puerto Rican leadership went to court to stop it, claiming unjust preference of the hasidic population. Finally, in November 1990, the presiding judge threw out their case as "without merit." Since then, the construction of this vitally needed school building, plus housing for the staff, is proceeding at full speed. This decision was confirmed by the appeals court in February 1991.

Opposite the earlier *yeshivah* building of Vayoel Moshe is the impressive large structure of the former YMHA, once a favorite social and health center for the entire neighborhood. In 1985, after serving as the location of a number of organizational offices, it was acquired by the Spinker Yeshiva, and its large halls and rooms are filled with classes, from nurseries to postgraduate seminars. The houses at the northwest end of Bedford Avenue before it crosses Division Avenue, once the location of elegant homes that had seriously deteriorated, have been remodeled and elegantly refronted. Similarly, the smaller, cheaper blocks at the southern end of Bedford Avenue, before it becomes the center of the thoroughly blighted Bedford-Stuyvesant area, have been renovated and are now prime real estate. One side has been taken over by the subcommunity of the Rebbe of Pappa. Its formerly limited headquarters has been expanded and a large new synagogue was added, with a beautiful new front, around the next corner. They have renovated the entire block and converted the buildings into a school housing nursery, kindergarten, and elementary students, in addition to the main *yeshivah*, which is in the former building of the elementary division of the old Torah Vodaath, before it was moved to Flatbush.

Much of the reconstruction and beautification work along Bedford Avenue and the other thoroughfares and side streets of the Jewish Triangle was done with the help of the Neighborhood Preservation and other urban revitalization funds. These were obtained through the strenuous efforts of the community of Satmar, directed by ODA, the local office of the U.S. Department of Commerce and Small Business. It spearheaded a number of the most valuable projects and campaigns of Williamsburg to gain access to federal, state, and New York City programs on behalf of the hasidic population. One of the important projects created and directed by ODA is the Primary Health Care Center, located on a side street off Bedford Avenue, which has been adding divisions and staffs of specialists every year. In 1985, for example, it treated 40,000 cases of various types of illnesses and handled the health-care needs of the men, women, and children of the hasidic population. In 1990 it was moved to a large, new facility near the ODA headquarters on Heyward Street, enabling its staff to further expand its services to the neighborhood.

Equally important is another institution that had started as a division of the Primary Health Care Center of ODA. Pesach Tikvah, the Gate of Hope, is the first mental health institution for *hasidim* as well as other Orthodox Jewish men, women, and children. It, too, started in a large renovated facility off Bedford Avenue, and has also been moved to a larger building several blocks farther south in an area that is increasingly being used for the expansion of the overcrowded Jewish Triangle. There is ample room for further extension of its services, which include day-care centers, full-time centers, and a new division for family services and which are used by Orthodox Jews from all parts of New York.

In stark contrast to many of the renovated community and private buildings on Bedford Avenue is the once magnificent structure of the Hewes Street Shul, the anchor synagogue of the old Polish-Russian Jewish population of pre- and post-World-War-II prominence. Its towers still stand out above the other new or rebuilt synagogues, but it shows signs of the serious neglect it has suffered since its members left the neighborhood. Its shell is now used by Beth Chanah, the large girls school of the Klausenburger Hasidic Community. Similarly, the once thriving, busy center of Agudath Israel next door and the still larger former synagogue building of Young Israel at the hub of Bedford Avenue, were converted into school buildings after their organizations had been decimated by natural attrition and the outmigration of their members.

These and similar positive and negative changes in the profile of the neighborhood in the center of the Jewish Triangle as well as in the deteriorating marginal areas are characteristic of the transformation of Williamsburg that seemed to herald its doom in the '60s. Thirty years later the indomitable spirit of the hasidic community has succeeded in blocking the process of further decline and disintegration.

Just as effective as the renovation and construction program in changing the residential profile of the new Williamsburg is a dramatic increase of business establishments. The old shopping areas on Lee Avenue, parts of Division and Bedford Avenues, and Roebling Street have been spruced up or provided with new fronts, including many that had been boarded up for years. More significant is the fact that numerous businesses are springing up in the cross streets throughout the entire neighborhood – in basements, on rebuilt first floors, in abandoned houses or factories at the very edges of the marginal areas of the Jewish Triangle. They have radically changed the character of the old, formerly tree-lined, quiet residential areas.

Equally important is the development of numerous light industrial establishments run by *hasidim* in the marginal areas of Williamsburg from Brooklyn Broadway and Division Avenue in the Williamsburg Bridge Corridor, along Whythe and Kent Avenues and, on the other side, north of the bridge and south of the Jewish Triangle, beyond Flushing Avenue. They attest to the spirit of enterprise that is changing Williamsburg from what it had been before. Electronics, appliances, high technology, automotive, photo, and computer lines have partially replaced the the once-dominant and still-popular garment and textile factories. Lumber and construction companies have taken over some of the buildings left behind by the Schaefer Brewery and other heavy industry that have moved elsewhere or gone out of business along the navy yard and the East River. New ladies' garment and children's and infants' wear stores are mushrooming everywhere. A growing number of jewelry, gold and silver, and shoe stores are opening up in the main avenues and side streets and are adding luster to the local scene. It remains to be seen what impact the hard-hitting economic decline of the beginning '90s will have on the thriving businesses and trade of hasidic entrepreneurs, some of whom have already been forced to dismiss large numbers of hasidic employees.

THE PUBLIC HOUSING PROJECTS

Major changes in the residential profile of Williamsburg were wrought by the construction of five large housing projects in the '60s and '70s. The three older ones are managed by the New York Housing Authority. The two newer ones, Bedford Gardens, funded by New York City, and Clemente Plaza, federally funded, are now managed by private companies. (See Table 1.1)

The projects replaced large groups of blocks that had been in a state of severe deterioration in the northwest area. They were part of the Urban Renewal Area's residential segment, between Bedford and Whythe Avenues, except the first, the Jonathan Williams Plaza, which is located in the very center of the Jewish Triangle. Like most public housing projects built midcentury, they stand out not only because of their high-rise towers – some as high as twenty-two floors. Their construction

TABLE 1.1
Williamsburg's Major Housing Projects in the '60s and '70s

Project	Source of Funding	Year Completed	Number of Units	Population
Jonathan Williams Plaza	state	1963	577	1,650
Independence Towers	state	1968	744	2,077
Taylor-Whythe	federal	1974	525	2,024
Bedford Gardens	city	1975	640	2,000 (approx.)
Roberto Clemente Plaza	federal	1976	534	3,000 (approx.)
Total			3,020	10,751

*Source: New York City Housing Authority, 1984 Special Tabulation of Tenant Characteristics

contrasts starkly with most of Williamsburg's antiquated housing stock, which consists of pre-World-War-I brownstones and pre-World-War-II apartment houses, except for the once elegant homes and social clubs of the old elite on Bedford Avenue, most of which date back to the nineteenth century. Though different in style, the projects have blended into the changing setting of the neighborhood as renovation and new construction alter the appearance as well as the old zoning structure of Williamsburg.

Originally, the announcement of the construction of the public housing projects was a major source of alarm, accelerating the departure rate of the older, as well as some of the more recent, residents of the Jewish community in the '50s. The impact was similar to the effect of the urban renewal of old neighborhoods to provide housing for lower income and minority residents in New York City and elsewhere. The flight was precipitated by the fear of a massive influx of large numbers of minority groups who occupy 85 percent of all housing projects under the authority of the New York Housing Department, and their impact on the security and life-style of the old Jewish and Italian communities so vividly described by Jonathan Riemer (1985) in *Canarsie*. In retrospect, the worst of these fears did not materialize, as about 50 to 60 percent of the units in the projects are occupied by whites, mostly *hasidim*, with the exceptions of Bedford Gardens, where they rent about 70 percent of the units, and Clemente Plaza, where Hispanics constitute about 55 percent of the tenants as a result of the supreme court decision for the equal distribution of the units between Hispanic and hasidic residents. Recent efforts by the Latino organizations to have a larger portion of the apartments assigned to them were rejected by the court.

At any rate, it seems obvious that the relative calm and degree of cooperation on the official boards and committees that have been organized by the neighborhood are a direct result of the determined efforts of the Old Rebbe of Satmar not to run away, and to take a strong stand against deterioration and the waves of friction and crime that were rampant in the '60s and '70s. But, although to a lesser degree, they persist in the '80s and '90s as evidenced by occasional outbreaks of hostilities, muggings, and robberies. According to police records, 1,500 such incidents were reported in 1989 in Williamsburg and in the marginal areas, though some of the more serious infractions were committed by elements from other neighborhoods, like the murders of an elderly rabbi on the way to the early-morning services and of a young girl on the way to extracurricular school activities.

But by and large, cooperation between the leadership of the hasidic and nonhasidic populations in the official bodies, and with the local police, and the intensive efforts of the *Shomrim*, a volunteer civil patrol organization, and a privately financed patrol supplementing the public housing police, have resulted in providing what the leaders and members of both populations consider a relatively high degree of safety. According to the official police statistics and the crime index statistics of the New York City Housing Authority, Williamsburg has become "one of the safest neighborhoods" in New York City. This is also the opinion of a number of Jewish and non-Jewish people interviewed. In 1987, for example the Puerto Rican manager of the largest housing project stated unequivocally that in his opinion Williamsburg was the safest place for anyone to live in New York City. The same opinion was voiced by a member of the janitorial staff of another housing project, a black man, and by an Irish saleswoman working in a store in mid-Manhattan. Both stressed that they prefer living in Williamsburg, where they feel more secure than in the neighborhoods where their families reside.

Yet, there is still the feeling of mutual distrust, as voiced by the Puerto Rican project manager. It has taken him years of strenuous effort to eliminate most of the friction in his large building complex. But he has 24-hour guards and TV surveillance of elevators and other communal areas. Typical of the more positive attitude is the statement of the assistant manager of another housing project, who said: "The *hasidim* here have come out of their shell, and there is some friendly interaction, especially among the women with small children in our playgrounds in summer." Similarly, a middle-aged hasidic woman who has lived on the tenth floor of another project for more than twelve years, stated:

> The Hispanics and blacks in our building are friendly and cooperative, unlike those who lived here when we moved into our apartment. It took years of complaints and serious efforts of the management and the tenants to get rid of the troublemakers, drug addicts, and other hostile elements. Once, when we were away, a Puerto Rican neighbor told us that she had chased away some youngsters who had been tampering with our door locks. Generally, we feel secure and protected here.

Another project manager told us what we had heard voiced by a number of other officials, as well as private individuals: "Hispanics and Jews still don't love each other, but they have come to respect one another." An official of the *Shomrim*, the volunteer citizens patrol, stressed that the Hispanic neighbors are often helpful in spotting car thieves in the streets. And a project official summarized the interactions among his tenants as follows: "We have come a far way. If a Hispanic would call for help, his hasidic neighbors will come to his aid." However, some of the hasidic tenants express misgivings about the conduct of their Hispanic neighbors. As one of them said: "I'll move out as soon as I can afford it. I don't want my children to see how their teenagers and young adults are carrying on around here, especially in summer."

In general, the description in an article in the May 1975 issue of the *National Geographic* about Jewish Williamsburg, "The Pious Ones" by Harvey Arden, is still valid. The *hasidim* and their non-Jewish neighbors live "back to back," rather than side by side. There is, however, inspite of occasional incidents of friction or crime, mostly by outsiders or residents from the marginal areas, a noticeable degree of improvement in the relationships between the hasidic and Latino populations, as stressed by the head of the Seneca Club, the old local headquarters of the Democratic Party, at the end of the '80s.[11]

On the positive side, the five large public housing projects have provided housing for low-income residents at a relatively inexpensive cost. In 1987, rentals for low-income residents ranged between $250 and $450, on the average. They went as high as $500 for the few larger apartments, when available, depending on the income and size of the family. In Bedford Gardens, built with the large families of the *hasidim* in mind, the very large five bedroom apartments cost $600 and up in 1987. But the private management company in charge is constantly attempting to further raise the already high rentals, to the consternation of many of the residents who, especially since the onset of the economic downturn in the beginning of the '90s, have organized to fight a sizable new hike.

About 62 percent of the five housing project units are occupied by whites, most of them *hasidim* and Orthodox nonhasidic Jews. All of the projects are overapplied, as all of their managers emphasize. There is a very small turnover among the over 3,000 units, which are distributed according to a key established by the New York Housing Authority. Some preference is given to tenants who are already living in the project and whose households have outgrown the size of their unit, which happens constantly. Most of them, however, have to wait a long time for the chance to get more appropriate housing. Income is checked annually to make certain that tenants with higher incomes than the limits set by the Housing Authority do not remain in apartments provided specifically for low-income families, except in Bedford Gardens, whose units were designed for middle-income tenants. The average annual income in the projects is around $10,000 (See 1984 *Special Tabulation of Tenant Characteristics* of the New York Housing Authority.) Several managers reported that they are flooded with applications, and most managers receive calls from people who would like to apply for vacancies if and when they come up. "I have on the average between 200 and 300 calls a day," stated the manager of the largest project, indicating the great interest and need for the type of housing the projects are providing for the neighborhood.

Obviously, the public housing projects can accommodate only a small percent of the apartments needed by the hasidic community, which grows by approximately 500 couples each year. If one adds to this the fact that, as borne out in the small sample survey of hasidic women in 1989/1990, the average hasidic household includes between seven and eight children, the housing crunch is clearly seen to be a permanent problem, getting more serious every year. The public housing projects can do little to alleviate it significantly.

One additional problem faced by the Orthodox Jewish tenants of the projects is that a majority of their units, especially the larger ones that many of the hasidic families require, are located higher than the sixth floor. The largest family of one of the projects, as the manager pointed out, which has eleven children, lives on the nineteenth floor. Since Orthodox Jews do not use elevators on the Sabbath and other holidays, they have no choice but to walk up and down the long flights of stairs as often as two or three times a day. Some of the Jewish project tenants have established private prayer services in homes volunteered by some of them, which they use on Friday evenings. But this does not solve the problem, since morning and afternoon services require regular synagogues for the reading of the weekly portions of the Torah. This is a particular problem for the *hasidim* who want to pray with their Rebbe, and who attend his communal meals and inspirational gatherings such as those held on Friday nights, or the *Seudah Shlishit*, the Third Meal of Sabbath. One middle-aged *hasid* tenant, when interviewed on how he handles this problem, especially in view of his large family, stated unequivocally, "If one has to, one walks. I and five of my older boys walk at least three times up and down the twelve flights of stairs on a typical Sabbath." Consequently *hasidim* benefit only moderately from vacancies, except for the elderly who are given preference for the units on the lowest floors, and newly married couples.

One of the most effective forums within the public housing projects is a tenants' association which meets regularly and elects officers to act as spokesmen for the various tenant groups and present their problems and concerns. They work closely with the project management. Each of the projects has one or more *hasidim* representing the interests of the Orthodox tenants. One Orthodox young man, who is the vice president of the project association, has been elected to the citywide tenants council. He takes particular pride in his contribution to the peaceful and constructive collaboration among all elements in the huge project and the management.

Each project has a community center with facilities for social, recreational, and cultural activities, though there are almost no programs dedicated to acquainting the various groups with the cultural and religious backgrounds of the others. Generally, there is almost no mixing of the various groups in any of the activities sponsored by the management, except in senior citizens clubs and in a health and diet workshop in one of the projects, in which hasidic women participate regularly. On the playgrounds and in the miniparks of the projects, too, the children of each group play separately. In summer, mothers with their small children and baby carriages meet on the playgrounds, except in Bedford Gardens, where older counselors take care of the hasidic boys and girls in the well-equipped play areas. Otherwise most of the hasidic youngsters rarely use the playgrounds, except perhaps on long Friday afternoons when they ride their tricycles and bicycles, unless there is the chance of friction with the youngsters of the minority groups who may be found there most of the time. In the newest and largest project there is a special room set aside in the community center on Sabbath and holidays as a study hall for the young hasidic boys. For the elderly, the ubiquitous benches are favorite meeting places. But here, too, hardly any of the hasidic men and women mix with other Jewish or non-Jewish tenants.

The project managers publish periodic newsletters, which are devoted to announcements of interest and concern to all of their tenants. The halls and offices of each project have large bulletin boards and spaces for general and special tenant group announcements in English, Yiddish, and Spanish. They are effective means of bringing current project news and urgent communications to the attention of the tenants. Educational, welfare, or social program announcements are prominently displayed in the halls and on the large bulletin boards. The management offices in four of the five housing projects – Bedford Gardens is managed by a private company whose office is located in Manhattan – are hubs of much activity. They serve as nerve centers for all communications and for official and unofficial interaction among the various groups of tenants.

Curiously, the largest and once most beautiful of the housing projects built in the Williamsburg neighborhood, the Lindsay, which had been designed for mostly middle-income residents, has almost no hasidic or nonhasidic Jewish tenants. It is located a few blocks farther southeast, outside of the Jewish Triangle, beyond Brooklyn Broadway. Initial efforts made to attract leaders and members of the Jewish community, such as offering cheaper rentals to rabbis and prominent community leaders, failed. The hasidic groups rejected all attempts to get them into the Lindsay. The problem was not simply that it was situated on "the other side of the tracks," far from the centers of their community life. More important was the fact that a large well equipped swimming pool was located in the very center of the project, visible from each of the apartments in the complex. This well-intended amenity was the real reason behind the hasidic rejection of the Lindsay: they and the other ultra-Orthodox Jews did not want to expose their children to the social life, swimwear, and activities going on around the pool.

In retrospect, the five public housing projects in Jewish Williamsburg have not caused the serious problems originally feared, although they did attract large numbers of Latinos and other minority groups in the '70s. It took, however, years of adjustment and concerted efforts to control friction and crime, and to effect the current relative calm and cooperation in spite of lingering distrust and not infrequent incidents.

Summarizing the present situation, an editorial in *Der Yid* (1990), in reaction to accusations of differential treatment of *hasidim* by the local police, cited a speech made by Rabbi Hertz Frankel, the spokesman of Satmar and the entire hasidic community of Williamsburg, made at a special New York City Council hearing about the situation in Williamsburg: "There is not another neighborhood in New York like Jewish Williamsburg in which Jews live as peacefully with their neighbors, including blacks and Latinos. It is only outside agitators who are trying to make trouble and stir up incidents of hostility and friction."

ETHNIC MINORITIES

The introduction to this chapter emphasizes that the Irish, Italian, and Slavic non-Jewish populations of the old Williamsburg had almost completely been replaced by Hispanics (about 25 percent) and blacks (about 7 percent). Though many of the earlier groups of Puerto Ricans who had flocked into the neighborhood's fringe areas since the midfifties have moved to other locations, they have been replaced by a new wave of Puerto Ricans and other minorities. Prominent among the newer groups of Latinos are Dominicans, Haitians, and Ecuadorians. As in most Brooklyn neighborhoods, Hispanics are largely non-English speaking young adults, few of whom are highly skilled (see U.S. Labor Statistics, *Profile of Puerto Rican New Yorkers,* Regular Report 46. New York: U.S. Dept. of Labor, July 1975). Their average income level in the five public housing projects in Williamsburg is slightly higher than that of the whites (see Table 1.2). They have suffered much from the departure of heavy industries along the East River waterfront in the '60s and '70s. They have a higher percent of unemployed and people on welfare than the white and black tenants.[12]

But the educational level and occupational skills of the Latinos are rapidly rising, according to local school officials in Williamsburg. Their children are filling the local public and parochial schools, and many are doing quite well. Latinos have also become increasingly active in local political life, in the Seneca Club, and on local community boards. Generally, they are vying for their fair share of public programs, government assistance, and funds. The heads of the local Catholic churches are providing guidance and leadership to improve their lot from that of the most deprived among the ethnic groups of Williamsburg and other neighborhoods.

The leadership of the hasidic community has established a relatively good working relationship with the responsible Latino leaders. They are serving together on a number of official community bodies. But until the formation of the aforementioned New York City Partnership for the construction of new housing, and more recently the Community Alliance for the Environment against the planned erection of a city garbage recycling plant in the Brooklyn Navy Yard, there seemed to be little substantial collaboration.

Though the *National Geographic's* characterization of the hasidic-Hispanic interrelationship is still valid, there seems to be a gradual improvement, as some of the

TABLE 1.2
Average Income of Tenants in Three Williamsburg New York City Housing Projects – 1984

Project	White	Black	Puerto Rican	Other	Total
Jonathan Williams	$ 9,775	$ 9,514	$ 9,055	$ 9,135	$ 9,129
Independence	$ 9,677	$13,253	$11,440	$ 9,545	$10,350
Taylor-Whythe	$ 7,924	$ 9,051	$ 8,223	$10,755	$ 8,179
All New York City Projects	$10,038	$10,142	$ 8,968	$10,160	$ 9,821

TABLE 1.3
Percent of Families on Welfare in Three Williamsburg New York City Housing Projects – 1984

Project	White	Black	Puerto Rican	Other	Total
Jonathan Williams	5.3%	6.7%	11.5%	–	7.8%
Independence	3.7%	6.7%	10.9%	–	4.9%
Taylor-Whythe	11.1%	15.0%	15.3%	6.7%	12.5%
All New York City Projects	7.6%	26.2%	33.5%	24.4%	25.2%

Source: New York City Housing Authority, Research & Development. Special Tabulation of Tenant Characteristics (January 1984).

women interviewed in the public housing projects commented. But most of the activities on the playgrounds and in the miniparks of the projects and elsewhere show little mixing of the two groups even on the youngest level. A number of government agencies and organizations in the predominantly Hispanic sections, such as Los Suros, El Puente, and others, are making strenuous efforts to improve the quality of life, health, and socioeconomic conditions in South Williamsburg, though they are frequently stymied by the transitory trends among the young adults.[13]

THE HASIDIC COMMUNITY

The hasidic community of Williamsburg is estimated at 40,000 men, women, and children, according to a study done for the local ODA in 1982. It consists of fifteen to twenty mostly Hungarian-type hasidic groups. Each of these has been established by followers of a hasidic Rebbe or by one of the descendants of one of the famous religious leaders of the East European hasidic movement. They usually take their names from the towns in eastern Europe where the particular Rebbes had established their main residence. More than half of the Williamsburg groups are branches of larger hasidic sects, each of which has its own *bet hamidrash*, a synagogue, study hall, and in many cases a school or study group attached to it. In recent years most of the larger ones have established their own summer camps and an increasing number have established bungalow colonies for their members in the Catskill Mountains.

The largest of the subcommunities is Yetev Lev, the congregation founded by the famous Rebbe of Satmar, Rabbi Yoel Teitelbaum, who had started his own hasidic movement in the Carpatho-Russian town of Satmar (Satu Mare) in 1932. After his escape from a concentration camp in Bergen-Belsen and a brief sojourn in Israel, he settled in Williamsburg in 1947, where a number of his followers had preceded him, and where Rabbi Levi Y. Grünwald, the so-called Tzelemer Rebbe, had in a number of ways introduced the life-style of Hungarian Hasidism. Until his death in 1979, the Old Rebbe of Satmar was revered as one of the most charismatic leaders of the contemporary hasidic world, and as a scholar of the highest rank recognized by all, including the famous scholars of the nonhasidic Lithuanian *yeshivot gedolot*, the most elite of talmudic academies. He commanded a personal following in the hundreds of thousands, many more than he had ever had in the old world after his rise to renown as a Rebbe. He was also, as previously mentioned, the most outspoken leader of the opposition to Zionism and to Israel as a secular state. Yet on his occasional visit to the Holy Land and to London he was welcomed by huge crowds everywhere and treated like royalty. At the end of the '80s, the regular membership of his congregation, Kehilath Yetev Lev, named for a famous scholarly treatise by his grandfather, was over 10,000 men and their families.

The educational system of schools for boys and girls, founded by Rabbi Yoel Teitelbaum soon after his arrival in Williamsburg, grew to become the largest single Jewish school network in the U.S., comprising over 19,000 students from nursery to *kollel*, the Institute of Advanced Talmudic Studies. It has over 2,000 students in Israel, more than 1,000 in its schools in England, and another 1,000 in Belgium, Brazil, Argentina, and Austria. The school population at Satmar institutions in Williamsburg doubles every seven years. In 1986, it added eleven new classes for a total of 7,000 boys and girls in its twenty-five subdivisions. Kehilath Yetev Lev, the congregation of Satmar, has an annual budget of $2.5 million, and it doubled its membership in the past decade thanks to the close to 500 young couples who are getting married each year and who want to remain in Williamsburg.

Incidentally, Satmar also has the largest number of synagogues and school buildings of any group in Boro Park and Monsey, New York. The exurban branch of Satmar, Kiryas Joel, in Monroe, New York, named after its founder Rabbi Yoel Teitelbaum, already had over 1,000 families in 1990, and its school buildings are packed with close to 4,000 boys and girls, from nursery to the *kollel*. Leaders of this community expect it to reach a total population of 10,000 before the end of the decade. These figures indicate the size of the Satmar community and its preeminent position in the hasidic community of Williamsburg and far beyond.

Kehillat Yetev Lev, the Satmar congregation, is run by a group of older leaders and an increasing number of middle-aged and young businessmen and scholars who are entering all ranks of the informal and formal structures and institutions and organizations of the community. In fact, as we shall see throughout the subsequent chapters, these so-called *avreichim*, the middle-aged and young activists, are increasingly becoming the dominant element in all branches of Satmar. This new wave of leadership was one of the major factors behind the decision of Rabbi Yoel Teitelbaum, the Rebbe of Satmar, to remain and fight the progressive disintegration of the Jewish neighborhood, as it is the central factor behind the radical turnabout and rise of the new Williamsburg as a major center of contemporary American hasidic life.

In retrospect, the major motivation of Satmar to concentrate in Williamsburg was the need for a location that was conducive to maximal sociocultural isolation from unwanted influences as well as to participation in the economic and political life of the American mainstream. Williamsburg provided the desirable optimal combination of these two: a total milieu for the ultra-Orthodox hasidic life-style and all available options for the enterprising bent on succeeding in the open market of free competition.

Four reasons are primarily responsible for the concentration of the *hasidim* in their own enclave, rather than blending into mixed religious neighborhoods like Boro Park:

1. In the first place, *hasidim,* like other Orthodox communities, must live close to their synagogue, to their *bet hamidrash*, the house of study, and a *mikvah*, a ritual bath, all of which are part of their daily lives. Their religious scruples do not permit the use of a car or other means of transportation on Sabbath and holidays.
2. The stores and shops in the neighborhood cater to all their general and specific needs, such as food, clothing, and various kinds of religious articles, which

stores in other vicinities do not carry. Their health services, physicians, drug stores, even their barbers and tailors are trained to accommodate the special requirements of the Orthodox life-style.

3. It is vital for *hasidim* to have their own types of social, educational, and welfare organizations in order to provide for the full range of functions in all phases of life, from birth to the grave, and beyond. Only a close-knit, compact community like Williamsburg, which is structured to accommodate the intensely religious beliefs, customs, and laws of its population, such as those that regulate the interrelationships between men and women, can provide for all the needs of the hasidic life-style of such a large and constantly growing population without causing stress and strain in all realms of interaction.

4. Most important of all for the hasidic community is their desire to live close to the hallowed person of their Rebbe, to pray with him, especially on Sabbath and the holidays, and to attend the regular and special services, gatherings, and meetings at which he provides the guidance and inspiration that are essential to their beliefs and life-style. Foremost among them are the so-called *tishen*, the shared meals, and the *farbrengen*, the inspirational gatherings, which are central to *Hasidut*, the body of hasidic beliefs and individual and collective conduct.

On the regular or special occasions of being in the presence of and looking up to their charismatic leader, *hasidim* feel that they are being deeply affected. Their whole being is elevated to a level far beyond the routine life of worries, sorrows, and the pressures of their daily existence. Their very being feels hallowed by their proximity to the lofty plane on which the Rebbe functions and to which he elevates the spirit of those ready to follow him. This unique experience of Hasidism permeates every phase and facet of the communal life and creates the type of milieu that *hasidim* desire for themselves and for their children.

This intense spirit of Hasidism-in-action requires the kind of setting that mixed neighborhoods can hardly provide. *Hasidim* want their boys and girls to walk in streets that are saturated with the experiences that pervade their life-style, that come with their hasidic garb, and to witness the conduct of their fellow *hasidim* at all times. They want their boys to study at institutions that educate them to a life of devotion to Torah study, to learning that expresses itself in the streets as well as in the homes. The hasidic education will guide them, their thinking, and their conduct as they grow up, marry, and mold their individual and collective life to the ideals of their elders and forebears. They want their girls to grow up in an environment in which their mothers conduct themselves according to the strict guidelines of *tzni'uth*, modesty, which they will not find even in the Orthodox communities of Boro Park and Flatbush, as one father complained after a visit to Thirteenth Avenue on a hot summer afternoon. Yet the women and girls wear elegant and not infrequently expensive clothes as they parade their baby carriages up and down Bedford and Lee Avenues. Almost without exception they wear long stockings, *sheitels,* wigs, and long-sleeved dresses, even in the stifling heat of sticky Williamsburg summers, without raising an eyebrow or a snicker from passersby.

The result of this milieu is the three-generational community in which the young and single as well as the married want to live close to their parents, Rebbes, and the institutions that have molded them. It is here that the young women want to be "just like our mothers," as the tastefully dressed wife of a young *hasid* put it.

For this total effect the hasidic community is willing to make supreme efforts and endure great sacrifices. Williamsburg is thus quite different from other Orthodox, even hasidic, communities that include a variety of religious and nonreligious, hasidic and nonhasidic, as well as non-Jewish, elements. According to Egon Mayer (1979), Boro Park, for example, has priced its young out of the neighborhood with its sky-high real-estate and rocketing rentals. Only a central force such as the loyalty of the *hasidim* to their Rebbe and to his community fosters the kind of cohesiveness lacking in most other neighborhoods. In contemporary Jewish, as well as in non-Jewish, communities, even the most religious, the young are expected to strike out for greener pastures, literally as well as symbolically, as an expression of their upward mobility.

Naturally, this cohesiveness combined with the constant growth in Williamsburg are pushing rental and real-estate prices even higher than in comparable neighborhoods in New York. This creates considerable hardships for young couples as for families whose expanding households require more space than the average Williamsburg apartment provides. As one worried father complained wistfully, it is almost more difficult to find a good apartment than a *choson,* a groom, for one's daughter. The resultant pressure is one of the primary concerns of the community leadership in its efforts to initiate even more construction and renovation. Not even the creation of Kiryas Joel, the suburban branch of Satmar in Monroe, New York, at an annual cost of $10 million per year, as the Rebbe of Satmar stressed, has alleviated the housing shortage significantly, in spite of the great advantages it offers to those who can afford to live there, and who are willing to accept the sacrifice of traveling to and from New York, a distance of approximately 45 miles (or a commuting time of 90 minutes), which is still the greatest source of jobs and business opportunities for most.

SUMMARY

As a result of the determined efforts of the hasidic community of the new Williamsburg, the rapid decline and looming disintegration of the Jewish Williamsburg neighborhood has been reversed, despite a number of crises during the past three decades. The process of renovation, reconstruction, and new building is everywhere in evidence, though not proceeding fast enough to alleviate the pressure of the constantly expanding population. Undoubtedly, Williamsburg is still predominantly a lower-class community – more than 35 percent of its residents had incomes below the poverty level at the end of the '80s, and this rate has risen to over 50 percent, according to a recent analysis of the U.S. Census figures in a report of the local Primary Health Care Center.

But the general profile of the Jewish Triangle, even in the midst of the serious impact of the present recession, is one of a moderately thriving, expanding community with the emphasis on youth and on a solid future. The area is going through various phases of beautification of the residential and shopping zones. The streets are filled with the hustle and bustle of a busy economic and social life as never before, not even during the best years of the post-World-War-II era. The new developments have largely changed the old zonal structure, and have replaced it with a more fluid, more homogeneous organization, as a corollary to the expansion, reconstruction, and new building of residential and some industrial facilities in the blighted marginal areas.

Thus, in the very configuration of the residential patterns, the new Williamsburg evinces the strength of its value orientation and its determination to translate its hasidic spirit into a strong community life. It has learned to cope effectively with everpresent outer and inner problems on all levels of life – physical, economic, and sociocultural.

⇒⇒ 2 ⇐⇐

The Economic Revitalization of the Hasidic Community of Williamsburg: The Spirit of Enterprise

Since the beginning of the '60s observers of the American Jewish scene have been predicting the impending doom of the Jewish community of Williamsburg's status as one of the foremost Orthodox Jewish communities in this country. A number of crises, such as the accelerating exodus of the young and of the older, more affluent residents to other neighborhoods in and around New York, the galloping blight and disintegration of large blocks of streets, and the invasion of significant numbers of members of ethnic minority groups, threatened its survival. In my postscript to *Williamsburg: A Jewish Community in Transition* (1961), I had pondered the fate of the neighborhood if the massive outmigration of the Orthodox as well as of the less religious elements continued unabated.

The gloomy scenario of the collapse of the Jewish community of Williamsburg, treated as a fait accompli by many (see, e.g., Egon Mayer's *From Suburb to Shtetl* (1979) did not materialize, primarily because of the decision of the hasidic community of Satmar and other Hungarian hasidic groups to make a stand and fight for the survival of Jewish Williamsburg. Led by Rabbi Yoel Teitelbaum, the famous Rebbe of Satmar, they rejected the mass exodus to Boro Park and other Orthodox communities made even by some of the smaller hasidic groups. Motivated by their loyalty to their Rebbe, they conscientiously set about marshaling their forces and resources in a determined effort to cope with the most serious threats and to meet the constantly growing needs of their mostly lower-class population.

Thirty years later, in spite of continuing major and minor crises, the hasidic community of Williamsburg is larger, more vibrant, and more viable than at any time in its history. Its concerted efforts have assured the survival of the area and provided a sound basis for the continuity and future of its three-generational community, in spite of persistent housing shortages and the fact that more than one third of the population lives below poverty level.

Yet nowhere more than in the economic sphere can even the casual visitor to the new Williamsburg observe the significant changes that have transformed the very appearance and atmosphere of the neighborhood. Even the once sleepy side streets that cross the four main avenues from east to west have come alive. Shoppers mix with local residents, craftsmen, workers, and the stream of young mothers who push their baby carriages along the busy streets. They frequent the old and new stores that have opened on the first floors of private buildings and in rehabilitated basements. By themselves, neither the heavy flow of commercial traffic, nor the loading and unloading of delivery trucks are unusual in thriving neighborhoods that combine commercial and residential functions. And the large thoroughfares, like Bedford Avenue, that serve as main arteries of the industrial traffic for Brooklyn and Long Island, had always connected Williamsburg with the outside world of business.

What is different now and characteristic of the spirit and life-style of the hasidic community is the fact that the trucks, vans, forklifts, and dollies are frequently handled by young or middle-aged *hasidim.* They are dressed in overalls or work uniforms that do not hide their long, dangling *tzitzit* and their *peyot* under their work caps. In the old Williamsburg, there had also been some menial workers; they were soda men, glaziers, and shoemakers. Yet, hasidic truck drivers, auto mechanics, or construction workers, foremen and contractors, which are a common sight in the '90s, would have raised eyebrows and provoked curious comments. Hasidic bus drivers, truck drivers, and the handlers of other commercial vehicles and equipment as well as hasidic craftsmen and shopkeepers bear vivid testimony to the new spirit of Williamsburg, a spirit that has engendered the lively commercial bustle without interfering with their ultra-Orthodox life-style.

This transformation of the old, sleepy, declining residential neighborhood is reflected in the new look, which was largely produced with funds from various neighborhood preservation and beautification programs made available with the help of the local office of the ODA, a branch of the U.S. Department of Commerce and Community Services Administration. Grants from federal, state, and urban agencies enabled the residents to spruce up their houses and stores. Sidewalks were repaired and bright, new street lights were installed in the main streets. New trees replaced the old, mostly dead nineteenth-century elms that had lined the avenues. New front gardens were planted. Renovation and weatherization are everywhere in evidence. New construction is replacing much of the old inadequate pre-World War I housing stock, as detailed in chapter 1.

The most important element of this new look is the emphasis on youth, on the young people who have become prominent in almost every sector of commercial, organizational, and religious life. Typical of the pride of the hasidic community in this aspect of their new life-style is the comment of a middle-aged woman who, when asked to compare the Williamsburg she had known 20 years ago with Williamsburg today, said: "Our *yunge Leit,* the young people, are taking over the old stores, start new businesses, and have become the leaders in many activities of our *kehillah.*" The *hasid* in charge of running the transportation system for the constantly expanding educational network of schools affiliated with Satmar said: "I have only two men close to 40 working for me. All the others are in their twenties and thirties." And the man who heads the school system pointed out:

> Young people, our *avreichim*, young married scholars, workers, and entrepreneurs, have become the most potent force in our organizational work. They carry much of the burden, and are constantly expanding the scope and range of our activities, as most of our leaders and activists are getting on in years. They are ill or showing the wear and tear of the years of suffering in the Holocaust, of the escape, and of the adjustment and rebuilding their life in this country.

In fact, that the new Williamsburg has become a three-generational community is the very source of its strength. It is now a place in which the young want to remain and continue the traditions and life-style of their elders. Their religiosity and education are on an even higher level than they had been in the small towns of Hungary and Romania, from where most of the Williamsburg *hasidim* had come to these shores.

This emphasis on the young, on the rejuvenation of life in Williamsburg, expresses itself most poignantly in the realm of the economic transformation, in the choice of careers, in the types of trades or enterprises that have become popular. They are quite different from the economic patterns described in my earlier report (1961). In the first place, it must be stressed that the young of today confront the same problems their elders did when it comes to dealing with the outside world because of their strict adherence to the ultra-Orthodox life-style, from their hasidic garb, beard, and *peyot* to the rules of conduct that restrict their social life and their dealings with outsiders. Obviously, this is not very conductive to success, which so often requires being part of the crowd, joining in the mainstream of American business and professional life. Nevertheless, a small number of *hasidim* have penetrated the walls of discrimination, moving into jobs that require little visibility and limited contact with the public that might resent their appearance and conduct. As a spokesman of the Satmar community put it: "Not more than 10 percent of our *yunge Leit*, our young people, are working for the government in such offices as social security, the post office, or even the banks or welfare agencies where they have to face the broader public. For they are not always willing to bear with their being and looking different."

A few hasidic scholars work in universities. Some are professors, others work in laboratories where they are accepted for their contributions; but they do not take part in the academic life. Their refusal to mix socially prevents their full participation in the American blend of professional and social life. *Hasidim* will hardly take part in business luncheons, executive conferences, or the almost obligatory get-togethers with customers over drinks at bars, restaurants, and nightclubs. Yet, these are essential to successful advancement on all levels, regardless of the quality of the work they produce.

As long as they won't make any concessions, such as eating in places that serve nonkosher food, keeping their heads uncovered, or shaking hands with women, their chances of doing business or conducting negotiations for deals are severely limited, even if there is no outright anti-Semitism involved. Some progress has been made in this respect in the past decades in offices that permit Orthodox Jewish employees to wear *yarmulkehs*, skullcaps, and similar concessions to young religious people who have demonstrated their capabilities. They are advancing in the professional world or in corporate or government bureaucracies, frequently as a result of court decisions, and of the general spread of nondiscrimination in the job market. One young man, a psychiatrist, put it this way:

> Ever since I have come back from my religious studies in an Israeli *yeshivah*, I have never taken off my *yarmulkeh*, not at medical school, nor in the hospitals in which I worked; and not on the job as administrator of a hospital unit. They consider me just as another of those crazy guys around here. My colleagues wear jeans and T-shirts, just like their patients. To tell the truth, I am still one of the best-dressed doctors around here. And my beard is practically a status symbol.

Yet besides his skullcap, this young doctor looks like every other college Joe since the 1960s. He does not present the appearance of the *hasidim* who wear their gabardines, beards, and long *peyot* everywhere and all the time, who are not accepted in many academic and professional environments. There are some notable exceptions, those who have made a name for themselves based on their work in laboratories or in clinics, as instructors, clinicians, or practitioners.

There is, of course, a deeper reason why young *hasidim* do not even aspire to enter the professions or other types of careers to which the majority of young, well-educated American Jews have flocked, especially since World War II. This is the almost exclusive concentration on religious education from nursery school to advanced talmudic studies, which often continue for years even after marriage, with only a minimum of time allotted to the required secular studies. Boys rarely attend classes in secular studies after their *bar mitzvah*, while hasidic girls receive mostly vocational training once they have completed the required general studies. This enables them to take jobs as teachers, bookkeepers, secretaries, computer programmers, or sales personnel before and after marriage, and in between having children. They do so mostly in order to help prepare for their wedding, or to supplement the income of their husbands; for, due to its large size, the average hasidic family increasingly requires a two-check income, especially in the early years of the marriage.

Furthermore, the cost of living for *hasidim* is much higher than that of the typical American household because of high rent, higher cost of kosher food, and the high cost of nonpublic education. This holds true even though the typical hasidic family does without much that is standard for the general American life-style, especially in the areas of leisure and entertainment activities. Lacking a thorough secular education and degrees, the hasidic self-made man must pull himself up by his own bootstraps as a craftsman or entrepreneur, unless he enters one of the increasing number of careers as religious functionaries, rabbis, or educators. Most must start small, work hard and long hours. They hope to advance and prosper after long, lean years and much frustration and the ever-present danger of failure, which incidentally has increased considerably since the beginning of the economic downturn in the beginning of the '90s.

In *Williamsburg: A Jewish Community in Transition* (1961) I quoted a pre-World War II refugee who had been a successful businessman prior to his emigration from Germany. After years of unemployment, failures, and disappointments, he had worked his way up to the position of foreman at a leather goods factory by sheer stamina, hard physical labor, and dedication to the interests of the boss. He induced the owner to hire several of the Hungarian hasidic newcomers. Though they caused him some problems because of their ultra-Orthodox conduct, which exceeded his own Orthodox standards of religiosity, he retained them and was quite satisfied with their attitude and work. After little more than half a year, the newcomers had learned enough of the trade and decided to strike out on their own. They did quite well and branched out into new, related lines. "They had the guts," he commented, "the resolve and the resources to do what I had often considered but never dared do because I had a growing family to support and send through school." This case is typical of what was to become the pattern for many of the newcomers who had no formal education or commercial experience. After they became thoroughly familiar with a trade, several formed partnerships and set up shops or businesses of their own. One of the prominent leaders of the hasidic community of Williamsburg spoke in these terms about the difference between his generation and that of his own grandson:

> I had learned my trade in my father's shop in the small Hungarian town. And when we came here I trained my son to become an equally competent craftsman. The attitude of my grandson and his friends is quite different. When I offered to train him, too, and eventually take him also into my shop that can use more help, he rejected my offer. He and his fellow students who have recently married have a different view than we. They don't want to spend years in a shop learning a trade from "the ground up." They scouted around for some venture that seemed promising and that would not require tremendous resources to start with. They took the plunge knowing full well that they took a chance and the likelihood of failure and hard years of struggle were awaiting them, since they had absolutely no knowledge, education, or commercial experience. They are still struggling, but the prospects of their breaking through and building up a successful business are improving daily. We, I and my son, did not have the courage and the opportunities were not available then, as they are now. Within a few years they have achieved what took us decades of hard, physical labor. With the help of the Lord, they hope to broaden their trade into a lucrative enterprise.

A third characteristic illustration of this new trend among young *hasidim* after the conclusion of their advanced talmudic studies was offered in an interview with a *hasid* still in his late thirties. Together with one of his fellow scholars he had started a small electric appliances store in the basement of a house in a side street, off Lee

Avenue. Eventually, they branched out and began dealing in computer hard- and software in a second building. Now they do a thriving business, especially in the computer line, as attested to by the head of a New York hospital, who said: "Our hospital staff buys all their computer hard- and software from a business in Williamsburg. Also my personal friends buy from this hasidic firm what they need. They are reliable and cheaper than the big firms with whom they had dealt before." When questioned about technical details, one of the hasidic owners with beard and *peyot* smiled and admitted frankly, "I know nothing about the technical aspects of computers. All I do is I buy and sell; and if necessary, I consult the companies with whom we deal. They are only too happy to provide technical guidance to us and to our customers." While directing the busy traffic of people delivering shipments of merchandise, and customers purchasing and picking up large packages, he said:

> You see, I have no formal secular education beyond the basics I learned in the first year of high school. But I have no difficulty communicating with my suppliers or customers, as you can see. The same is true for many of my friends and contemporaries who have started a business of their own. Some have failed. Quite a few are struggling. But others, like my partner and I, have achieved a good measure of success, with the help of the Lord, even without having a secular education. Already I have bought a house for my family in Kiryas Joel, and my partner, one right here in Williamsburg. Both of us are very active in *Hatzoloh* and in a number of other community organizations. Yet, we still make time for our daily Torah study before we start work in our business every morning. We are satisfied to operate on a lower margin, and try to satisfy our customers. That is what counts.

It was hasidic businessmen like this one whom an older Williamsburg *hasid* had in mind when he said in a conversation, after the conclusion of the services in a synagogue attended mostly by second- and third-generation American young professionals, lawyers, physicians, or officials in social security and other government services: "Our *yunge Leit* have no college education like your people here. But I am willing to bet quite a few of our *yunge Leit* make out better than your professionals. And they have large families to feed, clothe, and send to *yeshivot.*"

Though this remark may be somewhat exaggerated, it points up the pride of the older *hasidim* in the spirit and achievements of the younger generation. Though they have little secular education and limited commercial know-how and experience, obviously, they have no problem communicating. They master the English language adequately and read the *New York Times* and trade magazines, as one proud mother pointed out whose four sons and several sons-in-law are engaged in some phase of a furniture wholesale business. This knack of hasidic storekeepers to master the intricacies of their trade became first apparent to this writer when he visited a ladies clothing store in the heart of the garment district in New York. It was run by two middle-aged *hasidim*. They had started in a loft of an old building on Eighth Avenue. Now they own the entire corner and have combined its three stores into one whose large area is divided into various departments. Lines of expensive cars were parked outside, and groups of well-dressed women and girls kept coming in and leaving with large packages. Obviously they were finding what they were looking for, here at the edge of one of the busiest commercial neighborhoods of Manhattan, in the early evening hours. The owners and their employees, men and women from the hasidic community, moved easily among their higher-class customers. They referred frequently to famous fashion magazines, which were everywhere on display. One of the owners proudly showed me an article about their business in the latest issue of a high-gloss fashion magazine. In the mid-eighties the two hasidic owners, who continue to wear the traditional kaftans, beards, and *peyot*, expanded their business to several other locations, including one on Thirteenth Avenue in Boro Park and another in Miami Beach, all apparently doing quite well.

These anecdotes highlight the most significant change in the economic patterns of the new Williamsburg. The middle-aged and young *hasidim* in their black garb, beards, and *peyot* are able to deal successfully with higher-class clientele as well as with their own people, with their employees as well as with their suppliers. This counters all expectations and reverses the experiences of earlier generations of immigrants for whom acculturation and outward as well as internal assimilation were the sine qua nons of success. This new generation of hasidic entrepreneurs has managed to blend into the mainstream of American commercial life, despite the handicaps posed by their appearance, language, and sociocultural isolation.

It stands to reason that this breakthrough has not happened over night. It is largely the result of strenuous efforts of the community leadership and its organizations to create a milieu that would afford their young a fair share of opportunities. Crucial to this process is the local office of the ODA, which provides access to training and job opportunities, and technical assistance in dealing with the various federal, state, and city agencies. The staff of technical advisers, specialists, and counselors has succeeded in tapping vital resources, developing channels for funding and financing, and business procurement in governmental and private sectors of commercial life. They have successfully cultivated political connections and technical expertise that have produced changes and opportunities not thought possible even a decade ago.

Foremost among these notable achievements that benefit the entire American hasidic community is the official designation of the *hasidim* as a "Disadvantaged Minority." It took more than 10 years of applying intense legal and political pressure to overcome open resistance, technical and legal obstacles, even after the first partial opening of the closed doors in 1974. In a formal ceremony, in July 1984, in the presence of high government representatives and political figures from the U.S. Department of Commerce and the White House to New York state and city officials and heads of other ethnic minority groups, the hasidic community achieved this important recognition. It enables its members to benefit from the programs that are available to other ethnic and racial minorities.

The record of the work of the ODA in the decade and a half of its existence of helping untrained and inexperienced *hasidim* establish themselves or expand their businesses and trade is very impressive. Incidentally, as one high government official pointed out, it provides valuable evidence for the effectiveness of the federal programs that evolved from the War on Poverty and on Inequality, which have benefited the needy of the Jewish community as well as other disadvantaged groups. The hasidic community has particularly benefited from the support of the Minority Business Development Association (MBDA), as evidenced in the brief summary of the achievements of the local ODA that appeared in *Minority Business Today* (1985). The article presents an interview with its dynamic director, Rabbi Tzvi Kestenbaum, whose efforts were largely responsible for this major breakthrough on behalf of the local and wider hasidic community.

First and foremost, the ODA's officers have systematically located funding sources for training and job development. They guide and sponsor the establishment of new business ventures by *hasidim*, most of whom have neither the technical know-how nor the skills and experience necessary to start new careers in business, having spent most of their youth at religious studies. Hence they are limited to trades and commercial ventures that do not require intensive formal education.

Yet, inspite of these handicaps, the ODA reports that between 1974 and 1985 it helped 2,500 *hasidim* start their own businesses. It processed for them close to $50 million in loan applications. It prepared $31 million worth of procurement bids for federal, state, and city agencies in 1985, to which *hasidim* had no access prior to their designation as a "disadvantaged minority." Most important of all, the ODA has established the Small Business Investment Company, chartered by the Federal Small Business Administration. Its officers work with hundreds of clients, directing their efforts, providing access to funding, management help, and other technical assistance. They search for avenues to establish new business ventures. The MBDA program has assisted them in engaging in international trade with countries such as Japan, China, Korea, Italy, Portugal, Spain, Romania, and various Latin American countries. The ODA has also been the prime mover in the establishment of the Williamsburg Merchants Association, which has been one of the main forces in the improvement of the appearance and security of the neighborhood.

These efforts of the ODA and other community organizations continue unabated and are achieving results that have been praised by visiting government officials, such as the late U.S. Secretary of Commerce Malcolm Baldridge and by his successor Robert A. Mosbacher, by Governor Cuomo and Mayor Dinkins and his successor Mayor Giuliani, and other prominent federal, state, and city political figures.[1] All these officials commented favorably on the determination of the hasidic community to overcome their social and economic disadvantages and enter the mainstream of American business.

Some outsiders have criticized the propriety of these efforts by the hasidic community to draw on governmental resources, on programs and projects designed to help disadvantaged and discriminated minority members individually and collectively, for their needy. In response, one has only to think of the findings of the update of the classic *Middletown* studies of Robert and Helen Lynd, especially Theodore Caplow's (1982) volume *Middletown Families: Fifty Years of Change and*

Continuity, which points out that "at least fifty percent of Middletown families received public assistance in one form or another, either directly from federal agencies or from local agencies to which the federal government was the major contributor" (p. 27). Similarly Gregory J. Duncan, in "Welfare Use in America" (1986), reports that "according to a 1986 Report on The Use of Welfare more than one of every four Americans has lived in a family that needed welfare assistance during a 10 year period."

It seems, therefore, that it is quite appropriate for the *hasidim* of Williamsburg and elsewhere to avail themselves of the same type of direct and indirect assistance. They are further justified by the fact that Hasidic Williamsburg has what is probably one of the highest birthrates in the U.S., and the largest number of children per household. Most of all, the officials emphasize, the criticism is unwarranted in view of the fact that, by all official and unofficial estimates, one-third of the hasidic population in the community has incomes below the 1985 poverty line of $10,000 for a family of four. And in families in which both husband and wife work, the joint income is considerably less than the typical $30,000 indicated in a special report of a study done by the U.S. Census in 1984 and 1986.

This need of public assistance is further underscored by the fact that about one-third of the hasidic population consists of the elderly who are unable to work or young scholars and businessmen or tradesmen at the beginning of their family and career building. They have a modest income and live on the most basic level, as the manager of one of the large public housing projects pointed out: "Many of the hasidic families here crowd their six or more children into one room. They sleep in triple bunk beds or on matresses stored in the closet during the day. They cannot afford to pay for the extra rooms or for the larger apartments set aside in the project for the large-size families." In his project the average middle-aged hasidic family has between seven and eight children, while the average Hispanic family has between two and three children. According to a 1986 article in the *New York Times,* the average income of the Jewish family in Williamsburg was $9,000, whereas it was $7,000 for the average Hispanic family, a figure that takes into account the areas adjoining the Jewish Triangle, which have a concentration of low-income Hispanic families. The 1980 Census estimated the median income at $8,406, compared to a median income of $16,818 for all of New York City. In one of the Williamsburg public housing projects the average white, mostly Jewish family had an income of $8,226, the average black family, $9,593, and the average Hispanic family, $10,787. While the Jewish population of this project is not representative of the entire hasidic community, it is indicative of the one-third poor or needy, who are uppermost in the minds of the community leaders, and who are the recipients of direct or indirect help from the growing number of social welfare organizations and projects.

The seriousness of this situation becomes even more evident when we consider the cost of providing for the basic needs of a typical hasidic family, such as keeping its young clothed. In my earlier study (1961), I indicated that during Phase I, until World War II, the cost of a set of clothes for the average adult was about $70; in

Phase II, 1939–1945, it was about $100; and in Phase III, 1949–1960, it was about $125. The same set of clothes in the mideighties ranged from $750 to $850, and is still rising in the '90s. Even if we consider the high rate of inflation since 1960, the life-style of the *hasidim* requires considerably more than the average department store outfit of the average American.

The proprietor of a popular shoe store in the heart of Jewish Williamsburg pointed out that the average hasidic family among his customers has to purchase at least eight pairs of shoes for its children, at a cost of several hundred dollars. In his store, the average family spends between $500 and $800 per year on shoes for children. Similarly, in 1985, girls' dresses ranged between $52 and $85 for the middle of the line in a popular children's clothing store. The proprietor, himself a *hasid*, estimates that the typical family among his customers spends about $500 per child on underwear, pajamas, dresses, and coats or jackets. If one adds the cost of adult clothing one realizes that the $20,000 on which the low-income earners must exist hardly suffices to make ends meet. Hence, it is not surprising that the average large hasidic household cannot do without some form of government support or private help, as both the owner of the shoe store and the proprietor of a local drug store emphasized. A majority of their customers must draw on Medicaid or similar programs to cope with the constantly rising costs of maintaining their families. This situation has been further aggravated in the '90s by the growing economic crisis and the rising joblessness among *hasidim,* as well as the rest of the work force.

Yet, it must again be stressed that, as every visitor to Williamsburg realizes, the women and children one sees in the streets are generally well dressed. Only when the boys are of school age do they switch from toddler and small children's outfits to the black hasidic clothes, which are equally expensive. When questioned about the generally beautiful outfits the hasidic children wear, and the equally stylish clothes of the women, a young hasidic woman, cited several times in this report, commented: "We don't go to the movies or to the theater. Nor do we eat out in expensive restaurants, or employ baby-sitters, under normal circumstances. So we lavish attention on our homes and on our clothes. We take pride in being well dressed, within the limits of our budgets and the restrictions of the hasidic life-style." Her 16-year-old niece, also quoted several times in this report, who got married a year after the interview and has three children at the beginning of the '90s, stressed that she makes all her own clothes with the help of patterns she buys in a store. "At Beth Rachel we have been taught to sew, and not to show off with our clothes. I am not proud of those of our girls who have jobs uptown and are trying to compete with the Fifth Avenue look of the women they see there." She herself took a job as a nursery-school teacher soon after her graduation from high school. She stopped working when she gave birth to her first child. Her husband, a bright young *kollel* scholar, will continue his advanced talmudic and rabbinic studies as long as possible, even though it means that the young couple will have to do with much less than those families in which the husband leaves his studies soon after marriage to take a job or start a business. When asked if she wants more children while her husband was still studying, the young woman said: "Yes, as many as my mother and grandmother, who had ten and eleven, respectively."

When asked whether she was satisfied with life in Williamsburg, she replied enthusiastically: "I love it. Life is not so ostentatious as in Boro Park or Monsey. If I will be able to afford it, I might perhaps want to have a house in Kiryas Joel, like my uncle and aunt. There you have even less outside influences than here in the city."

In spite of this generally typical attitude of the young women, one finds periodic admonitions in *Der Yid*, and on large posters on empty walls in the streets, which warn against excesses in fashion, especially in summer clothes, and against the fashionable long wigs that have become part of the Orthodox environment in Boro Park, Flatbush, and Monsey, New York.

In the lower-income range of Jewish Williamsburg there is, of course, much less emphasis placed on the tokens of conspicuous consumption. Even a skilled craftsman, like the bookbinder who in 1986 was making about $500 per week, emphasized when interviewed that though he could not plead poverty, yet, with six children in school he had little left over for luxuries. He had to depend on a reduction in tuition and on some form of government support when sickness or other emergencies struck. "I must have a large apartment for my growing family. My wife is pregnant, and I am the sole provider for the increasing needs of the household. And, you know, one cannot skimp on food, medicines, and clothes."

This response is typical of most of the work force of Jewish Williamsburg, except for the 6 to 10 percent successful businessmen and entrepreneurs. These are able to afford the more affluent life-style now increasingly in evidence, such as the renovations that add porches, balconies, and marble fronts to their houses and similar elements of what some Williamsburgers call the "Boro Park style."

Almost half of the *hasidim* are blue-collar and white-collar workers. They are machine operators in factories, clerks in stores and offices, mechanics in repair shops and construction companies. The white-collar workers are secretaries, bookkeepers, sales personnel, or among the lower levels of the managerial ranks. They handle from the simple to the sophisticated mechanical power tool equipment that has become part of the Williamsburg street scene as well as that of the other neighborhoods where *hasidim* have established their production centers. They are locksmiths, carpenters, electricians, and auto mechanics. An increasing number have become insurance agents, financial managers, real-estate agents, and brokers. Some work with stockbrokers, or at similar sorts of financial institutions and organizations. Some work in various realms of the jewelry and diamond business. As pointed out before, about 10 percent work in government agencies.

Table 2.1 shows the typical breakdown of one relatively new congregation of younger and middle-aged *hasidim*, the average of whom is in his mid-to-late thirties or early forties. The youngest has three children. The older members typically have six or seven and expect to have more.

Table 2.2 presents the occupational background of a congregation of older *hasidim*, whose average age is 55, and average household has six children.

TABLE 2.1
Occupational Distribution of a Small Congregation of Young and Middle-aged Hasidim

Number of Men*	Percentage	Occupation
7	12.5%	entrepreneurs (manufacturer, wholesale trade, import and export)
10	18.0%	small business owners
16	28.5%	business employees
8	14.5%	skilled craftsmen
6	10.7%	semiskilled craftsmen
4	7.2%	teachers
3	5.0%	ritual functionaries
1	1.7%	post office employees
1	1.7%	*kollel* scholar
56	100%	

*Average number of children: 6; average age: 35

TABLE 2.2
Occupational Distribution of a Congregation of Older Hasidim

Number of Men*	Percentage	Occupation
1	3%	factory owners
1	3%	store managers
7	20%	businessmen
17	48.6%	business employees (sales office)
2	6%	retired blue-collar workers
8	23%	white-collar workers
36	100%	

*Average number of children: 6; average age: 55

Both of these congregations are typical of what one finds on practically every block in the Jewish Triangle. In both, the majority of the members are either owners or employees in a business setting. Conspicuously absent are professionals, the sort of career that is the goal of most young Jews, as it is in the nonhasidic Jewish communities. The bulk of the members in both hasidic congregations are business employees, or skilled and semiskilled craftsmen. They are sales personnel or work in offices. They have become quite competent in handling computers and advanced bookkeeping equipment. Quite a few work for large hasidic enterprises, such as 47th Street Photo or Crystal Clear Co.

At least 15 percent of the younger and middle-aged men in these congregations and in the hasidic work force in general are employed in some aspect of the diamond, jewelry, gold, and silverware businesses. At least 25 percent of the middle-aged and younger *hasidim* have established businesses of their own. Some of these are rapidly becoming prominent in the organizational structure as well as in the economic life of the hasidic community. As serious budget cuts are limiting the support that the young would-be entrepreneurs had counted on for help to get off the ground, they are turning elsewhere for new lines of business that require less government support, such as insurance, travel bureaus, financial management, real estate, and so forth, as reflected in the frequency of the appearance of advertisements for these sorts of businesses in *Der Yid*.

One segment of the occupational distribution that is still growing is that of skilled and semiskilled craftsmen, as more younger *hasidim* are learning to handle all types of equipment and machinery; much of this kind of work has been spawned by developments in computer and laser technology. One middle-aged *hasid*, when asked about his new enterprise – he gave up his job of delivering medical equipment when his wife gave birth to their tenth child – stated proudly: "I started a new sign-making shop with state-of-the-art computerized equipment. I learned to do things in my place, at the fringe of Jewish Williamsburg, that none of my competitors has been able to produce before." He started several new lines and spoke about plans for national distribution. He was already doing well enough to be able to give his two oldest daughters jobs in his shop, instead of having to send them out of the hasidic neighborhood for work. "I feel like a different person," he said. "I have developed skills and am building up my own trade." This sense of achievement provides a brighter outlook for the future, though he had previously never handled any machine more sophisticated than his stationwagon and a delivery van. Incidentally, having met this *hasid* again a while later, I was told of the forthcoming marriage of his eldest and the engagement of his second daughter to a young *kollel* scholar, both of whom will depend largely on his support, which prompted him to look for new avenues by which to increase his income. He is now happy to be a sales representative for a computer software company, having gained confidence in his understanding and ability to handle and deal with most aspects of the computer line.

Similarly, many of the younger *hasidim,* though having spent most of their time on talmudic study in a *yeshivah,* are becoming quite adept at handling light and heavy mechanical and other equipment and sophisticated machinery, such as computerized bookkeeping, metal casting, and processing machines. They drive heavy lumber and other trucks, and do not mind their role until they know enough, earn enough, and can gather the resources to start their own trade or business, at which point they will hire menial workers, as some said frankly.

One interesting aspect of this orientation toward menial work is the fact that, unlike in earlier times and in other communities, this trend has not led to the development of a proletarian attitude like that found among the masses of East European Jewish immigrants since the turn of the century. Although, as in the two congregations analyzed in the preceding pages, as many as 25 percent are blue-collar workers, they are first and foremost *hasidim* who are looking forward to the time when they will be able to establish their business, if possible. Incidentally, this new attitude is also different from that of many of the German and other refugees who came to the U.S. in the '30s and '40s. Quite a few of them had been well-to-do businessmen or entrepreneurs before Hitler had driven them from their native countries, but they either lacked the courage or were simply unable to start a business of their own again, in spite of their rich experience and considerable know-how. Instead they looked forward to the time when their children would enter academic and other professions of higher social status and make up for their own loss of the social rank they had enjoyed in their "golden era" in their old home.

In contrast, the young and middle-aged *hasidim*, having spent their youth in religious studies, and having grown up in solid community-oriented homes in the hasidic spirit and life-style, are not open to union radicalism. They do not feel this need of the old Jewish working masses. They may suffer some of the pressures, even some of the exploitation that features so prominently in the once-popular Yiddish folk literature, in the plays, short stories, and novels of some of America's foremost writers of the past generation. They want to be and to remain part of the hasidic community. They hope to educate their children in the intense Orthodox spirit in which they have been raised. They want them to marry into *baale-battishe* hasidic families, and become Torah scholars or choose a *baale-battishe* career. Above all, they aspire to a better socioeconomic life that will afford them the means to become contributing members and activists in the expanding networks of social, religious, and welfare organizations and institutions. This does not take away from the fact that they are plumbers, carpenters, locksmiths, electricians, and repairmen who wear work uniforms and handle construction jobs. They have beards and *peyot* and take pride in their skills, and quite a few earn a decent living. "We make as much as your government employees or doctors," said one of these middle-aged *hasidim*, who started his own notion business on the Lower East Side and is quite satisfied with his trade, which affords a relatively good living and a decent life-style for his growing family. He has an extensive library for his talmudic and hasidic study before and after work. No radical socialist ideas will take root where such a state of mind prevails, though the first years were rough ones. He struggled and had to work overtime to make ends meet and give his young children a good education, something that is uppermost in his mind, second only to his reverence for and enjoyment of living near and praying with his beloved Rebbe.

Of course, a major source of employment, especially for the young scholars of the advanced talmudic and rabbinic research institutions, are the constantly growing hasidic educational systems for boys and girls in Williamsburg, Boro Park, Monsey, Monroe's Kiryas Joel, and other hasidic centers. There is a constant need for teachers, supervisors, administrators, and personnel from bus drivers and cafeteria managers to maintenance workers, as ever new schools are added to accommodate children from day-care centers to the institutes of advanced religious studies. In contrast to the *yeshivah* teachers of the earlier pre- and post-World-War-II period who were poorly and irregularly paid, and who had to look for other work during the summer months, today's *yeshivah* teachers, once they have proven their competence over a two-year trial period, are given regular twelve-month positions. They receive fringe benefits, not least of which are free tuition for their children and special consideration in the food stores, such as the butcher shop of the Satmar community. Hence, today's hasidic *melamdim* are no longer the proverbial schlemiels of the old Hebrew schools who could not find any other means of sustenance or used teaching as a temporary job while they went to school or trained for better-paying work. Typical of this new attitude in the hasidic community toward the teachers and their needs are such plans as that for the construction of adequate housing for the staff adjoining the building of a large new *yeshivah* on the land behind the mansion of the new Rebbe, or the arrangement of bungalows for the teachers' families during the summer months, when the classes above primary school move to the summer camps in the Catskills and are taught by their regular, year-around *melamdim*. Small wonder that a large number of the teachers in the boys' and girls' schools, as well as the administrators, are relatively young or middle-aged. Most of them are products of the schools of the hasidic community. Hence, a job in the *hinuch*, the field of education, has become a prime occupational goal for the students of the advanced institutes who want to dedicate themselves to lifelong study and dissemination of Torah knowledge.

A number of similar occupations have also opened up as a result of the growing need for religious functionaries at all levels of the elaborate social organizations that are mushrooming with the growing needs of the exploding population. Besides the usual ritual slaughterers, the *shohtim*, the butchers and kosher supervisors that have always had their place in every religious Jewish community, the hasidic community trains capable young scholars to become *poskim* and *dayanim*, religious judges, or arbitrators, to adjudicate not only matters of ritual law, but also a broad spectrum of civil and business matters. Teams of middle-aged *dayanim* sit at regular announced hours in the *bet horo'oh*, or the court of the hasidic rabbinic organization on Division and Bedford Avenues. A number of these bright, still relatively young scholars and judges have made a name for themselves as experts in difficult divorce or desertion cases. Others excel in matters of personal conflict or business disagreements that are elsewhere brought before the public courts. One of the prominent nonhasidic rabbis still left in Williamsburg, whose once vibrant congregational building has been converted into an Orthodox girls' school, when questioned about crucial differences and changes in the religious life of Hasidic Williamsburg, said:

> Our *yeshivot* never really focused on producing *poskim*, rabbis who are competent to judge not only questions of *kosher* and *treifoh*, chicken or meat, but who devote themselves systematically to dealing with the daily problems that confront a functional Torah community. We were educated on the model of the classic Lithuanian

Yeshivah whose major goal was to produce *talmidei hachomim*, Talmud scholars above all else, to perpetuate the chain of the scholarly tradition that had been destroyed in the Holocaust. Our *yeshivot* succeeded in training the American *lamdan*, outstanding theoretical scholars. Relatively little attention was paid to the applicability of the theoretical subject matters studied, except for those advanced students who wanted to become rabbis. These devoted some time to the mastery of the sections of the *Shulhan Aruch*, the code of religious and ritual laws, required to get *smihah*, the rabbinic ordination.

There is now some shift toward producing specialists in various areas of practical *halachah* in our *yeshivot*. But there is no comparison to the systematic training of the hasidic *yeshivot*, which initiates every student since early youth into multiphased branches of the vast *halachic* literature. Thus they produce *poskim*, expert judges who are competent to handle all matters of vital concern to a community like Williamsburg.

Indeed, life in Williamsburg and other hasidic communities has little use for the polished orators, pulpit artists, and social directors who dominated and still are partially predominant in even the Orthodox synagogues in the U.S. in the past half-century. It demands *poskim*, judges who are not only scholars, but who have mastered the full range of the halachic literature in all realms of the individual and collective life, not only in questions of ritual concern.

Increasingly one finds in *Der Yid*, the official organ of Hasidic Williamsburg and elsewhere, ads that congratulate superior young *kollel* scholars for having earned the higher level of rabbinic ordination, the *Yodin-Yodin*. This qualifies them to function as judges in a broad range of civil matters usually not handled by the average rabbi. It must, however, be stated that in the past few years a growing number of outstanding young scholars in nonhasidic *yeshivot* are also spending additional years on intensive study to acquire this distinction of higher ordination, both in Israel and in the U.S.

There are now an increasing number of occupations that offer careers to the graduates of the hasidic *yeshivah* system besides those of teachers, rabbis, *dayanim* (judges), and *shohtim* (slaughterers). Among these are *sofrim*, scribes, who produce and check *mezzuzot*, the parchment scrolls that are attached to doorposts; *tefillin*, the parchment scrolls that are in the leather phylacteries worn by males during the morning prayers; and *sifrei Torah* and *megillot*, the large and smaller parchment scrolls of the Torah, and of the books of the Bible, such as the Purim story. They write *ketubot*, marriage contracts, or *gittin*, divorce documents, all of whose prices have risen tremendously. The average Torah scroll now ranges from $20,000 to $30,000. There is now STAM, the organization of officially recognized scribes, which checks and certifies the professional qualifications of scribes. The number of certified *sofrim* has thus increased in proportion with the demand and the price paid for this painstaking work. Yet, there is a still greater demand for scribes, especially in the cities outside of New York which have to be satisfied with the rare visits of traveling *sofrim*. There are also now a number of places in Williamsburg and other communities where *hasidim* have taken up the trade of producing *tefillin, taleisim*, and *tzitzit*, which were formerly imported from Eastern Europe or Israel.

An equally significant source of careers for young *hasidim* in their own community and in other hasidic neighborhoods is the network of religious, ritual, social, and economic organizations and institutions. As the head of Satmar has said:

> We thought we would have to go outside to find effective administrators and workers for our offices. Yet here, right among our young, we discovered the kind of talents, the dedication to the needs and the needy, and the resourceful men and women who master not only the technical difficulties of this work. They have the spirit, as well as the devotion, the *mesirat nefesh*, that makes up for some of the lacking broader education. They exceed all expectations and make us real proud of our *hinuch*.

By taking on these careers, young and middle-aged *hasidim* have moved into the front ranks of the leadership of the hasidic community of Williamsburg. Nevertheless, the majority of the young choose a career in business, making their social work their avocation rather than their vocation. Fortunately, they have a number of outstanding role models among the middle-aged, the *avreichim*, and among the older generation, too, who have made their mark in business, and built enterprises that have gained nationwide recognition. Increasingly one meets *hasidim* in all of the various commercial centers throughout New York, not only in the diamond and jewelry centers around Forty-seventh Street in Manhattan. They have become a familiar sight in their dark gabardines, black hats, beards, and *peyot* outside of Williamsburg and the Lower East Side. One meets them in the heart of the garment and fur centers of Manhattan. They work and own factories in Long Island and other industrial centers and walk about in their hasidic outfits without much reaction. They have replaced the old American Jewish shop and store owners of the earlier decades whose children have flocked to the professions rather than, as earlier immigrant generations, take over the businesses built up by their fathers.

One has only to visit the stores of the largest and most famous of the hasidic businesses, the Forty-seventh Street Photo Company, whose advertisements fill the conspicuous centerfold of the *New York Times Sunday Business* section. There one finds hundreds of young hasidic men and women waiting on elegant clientele, some of whom have probably never encountered *hasidim* in their, to them, outlandish outfits. They handle the store traffic expertly, and are polite and competent. Not surprisingly, 47th Street Photo, owned by a former Williamsburg *hasid* now living in Boro Park, handles over 10 percent of all business done by Sony in the U.S. retail trade. There are a number of other similar electronics, photo, and computer wholesale and retail companies owned or run by *hasidim* in New York and elsewhere. They attest to the ability of the younger generation of *hasidim* to enter realms of business, trade, and crafts, and to acquire skills and expertise, in spite of their concentration on religious studies until years after marriage.

A growing number of these hasidic businessmen have chosen various lines of export and import, especially in clothing, crystal, and china. They have become exclusive agents for a number of European and Far Eastern products, as one finds in some trade magazines, and as is reflected in the ads of *Der Yid*. Typical of one of these lines of merchandise pursued by *hasidim* is that of imported clothes. For example, there is a store of childrens' clothes in a converted basement in the heart of Williamsburg whose exclusive boys clothes from France and England were featured in the *Spring Children's Wear* section of the *New York Times*; it is the only place where these are available in the U.S. The owner, a hasidic woman dressed in her modest hasidic clothes, travels twice a year to Europe to handpick her imports. Her basement shop has become a favorite for mothers who are looking for elegant clothes for their children.

Another hasidic woman from Williamsburg runs her crystal and lamp wholesale store in an old factory building just outside the Jewish neighborhood. Twice a year she travels with her husband to Italy, Spain, and Portugal. Her husband, who has his own gold and silverware wholesale business, accompanies her to the sources of elegant crystal and marble, while she assists him in the choice of the merchandise he imports mainly from Portugal. Both provide merchandise for wholesale and retail stores in New York and in other large cities of the U.S., such as elegant chandeliers or lamp bowls. Similar export and import businesses have been built by *hasidim*, many of them in their thirties and forties, in the best spirit of American enterprise, without yielding an iota of their ultra-Orthodox life-style.

The most significant transformation of the economic scene in Williamsburg itself has been the expansion of retail and wholesale shops and stores into the formerly quiet side streets. Almost every edition of the weekly *Der Yid* announces the opening of a new store, a new shop, or a trade office in one of the cross streets that stretch from Brooklyn Broadway to Whythe and Kent Avenues along the waterfront, areas that had once been off-limits to the Jewish population. There are now new business centers, such as the plaza above Bedford Gardens at the confluence of Bedford Avenue, Rodney and Keap Streets. Even more significant is the expansion south and southwest into the formerly blighted areas that range all the way to the blocks cleared for the sprawling Pfizer Drugs and Chemicals Corporation. A former public school building on Throop Avenue has been turned into one of the largest of the Satmar *yeshivah* centers for the intermediate boys division.

Once totally extraterritorial, the entire area between the Jewish residential core and the Throop Avenue Yeshiva building is gradually being acquired for commercial, industrial, and residential purposes. At the western end of this area, for example, a large factory building has been renovated and converted into a school building for two hasidic girls' schools. Similarly, a large factory complex that had stood empty for years has been renovated and converted into condominiums to accommodate the flood of newly married hasidic couples. Most of these reasonable apartments range between $450 and $750 a month. A number of new bus stops have been added in this marginal section adjoining the Jewish Triangle to the private and public bus routes that serve the hasidic population from Williamsburg to Boro Park and vice versa. There are always young hasidic men and women or children waiting at these corners in streets that had been purely industrial and far removed from Jewish traffic. Some institutions, such as Pesach Tikvah, a hasidic mental health facility, have moved their headquarters into this area.

Interestingly enough, a large number of the new stores that have opened in Williamsburg are devoted to infant and childrens' wear and adult clothes. In an informal shoppers survey of eighty women conducted in summer of 1985, most of the people who come from as far as Flatbush and Boro Park are interested in shopping for clothes for their children and for themselves. The respondents indicated that they preferred to visit Williamsburg stores rather than fancier and considerably more expensive stores in Manhattan. Among them are not only *hasidim* who naturally would prefer to shop in a setting closer to their life-style, for religious and social reasons. There are also well-to-do patrons from the suburbs, and even from out of state. One well-dressed Baltimore woman stated openly that she used to come to New York to do her shopping for herself and for her grandchildren at Bloomingdales and Saks Fifth Avenue. But she has since learned that she gets equally stylish and frequently better quality clothes at more reasonable prices in Williamsburg. It is not that she cannot afford the higher prices, but "it goes against my grain," as she put it, to spend more for something than it is worth.

At the initiative of the local ODA, about 120 retailers have joined an active Williamsburg Merchant Association, of which only two retailers are not Jewish. According to a 1983 survey conducted by an official of ODA, only about half of the merchants' stores had been in existence 25 years or more. Between 20 and 30 percent are 10 years old. And 28 percent had been started within the past 10 years. By 1987, their number had increased dramatically. Although some do not survive the keen competition, the majority seem to do well, judging by the improvement in appearance and the traffic of customers in the main shopping streets, which is considerable at all hours of the day, even during the hot summer months. Likewise out of date is the elegantly printed Minority Hasidic Vendors Directory, also compiled by the ODA, listing the 272 hasidic firms that qualified for government contract procurement as members of a disadvantaged minority, following the official designation of *hasidim* as such in July 1984. By 1988 the number of qualified hasidic enterprises had risen considerably higher, as evidenced by the recently established *Business Directory Yellow Pages,* which is updated and published every year in Williamsburg. It reflects the unabated growth of local retail, wholesale, and manufacturing establishments. Although clothes are still dominant, there is a marked increase in electrical appliances stores, in linens, in silver and jewelry stores, in furniture stores, and in a variety of food lines, these include kosher health foods, which did not exist for the ultra-Orthodox market but are now available in great variety, and new dairy products, yogurts, cheeses, wines, juices, liqueurs, condiments, candies, and cookies and cakes of all kinds.

Also on the increase are the number of services, reflected in the number of ads in *Der Yid.* There are automotive shops, insurance agencies, real-estate agencies, financial management, and brokerage firms. There are also a growing number of medical services, specialists, and legal experts who emphasize their religious orientation and ability to communicate with the hasidic populace. New stores specialize in handbags, pearls, shoes, and hats, and in baby carriages and baby furniture, reflecting the baby boom in the hasidic community. The weekly Yiddish newspaper carries ads for elegant ladies clothing and fashionable wigs, catering specifically to the women who cover their hair after marriage. At the same time, the *Yid* carries warnings by the rabbinic authorities against wearing the type of clothes and *sheitels*, wigs, that serve to enhance rather than mute the attractiveness of the wearers, as mandated by the required modesty of the hasidic women in their appearance in public and in their social conduct. Obviously there is a great awareness of good quality and fashion among the women of Williamsburg, concomitant with the relative rise in their income, and it enhances their ability to express their individuality in their clothes, as one of the younger women put it, when questioned about it.

There is also now an increase in stores that sell clothes for hasidic youngsters and adult males, both summer and winter garments, and for weekday and Sabbath wear. The typical hasidic outfit consists of a *bekeshe* or kaftan, longer or shorter coats, which range in price from, for a simple one, about $125 to, for a silken one, between $250 and $400. A *shtreimel*, the fur hat, either a low, flat one, or a *kolpik*, the high one, ranges from $800 to $2,000, depending on the quality of the fur and the workmanship. The small, round, velour hats, or the large, broad ones, ranged from $75 to $200 on the average, at the end of the '80s. A new feature, attesting to the resourcefulness of the *hasidim,* are rain-*shtreimels*, advertised regularly in *Der Yid,* and all-weather covers. The regular suits of *hasidim* that have longer jackets than those of the normal store suits, cost from $250 to $450, depending on the quality of the material and the workmanship. Of course, at the beginning of the '90s the cost of the hasidic outfits has risen considerably, commensurate with the general rise of men's and ladies' wear due to inflation; and this is causing further hardship for the low-income workers and the growing number of unemployed who lost their jobs due to the general recession that has hit the business community.

One group of advertisements in *Der Yid* that seems to reflect a trend is for companies that renovate, rebuild, or refurbish houses and homes, and for appliance companies. As I have already suggested, the women of Williamsburg lavish much attention and love on their homes. This was expressed by a hasidic woman in her mid-thirties, when interviewed in her apartment in one of the high-rise public projects: "Our parents and many of our older brothers and sisters came here from the concentration and DP camps with little more than the rags on their backs. Now, after years of privation and hard work, we want to live like others and enjoy our homes. Where else can a woman like myself express her sense of beauty and esthetics!"

This frank attitude conveys the trend among the younger women to try to create a more pleasant environment than the one in which they grew up. The vast majority of the homes and apartments of Hasidic Williamsburg, except for the 5 to 10 percent belonging to those who have been successful in business and can afford a grander life-style and have decorated their houses in the style one finds in Boro Park and Flatbush, are furnished simply. Most cannot afford more of a display of luxuries than the everpresent large bookshelf packed with the standard talmudic, halachic, and hasidic literature, and a china closet containing the usual silver candlesticks, *menorah, etrog* box, and other ritual vessels and bowls necessary for the proper celebration of Sabbath and the holidays. Most other available space is used for bedrooms and sleeping facilities for their large families.

This is what some of the middle-aged and younger women are trying to get away from, if they are fortunate enough to be able to afford it. The woman with whom we spoke showed us what she had done to her apartment since she had moved into it several years earlier. Much of the equipment had been old and unsatisfactory. She had most of the appliances taken out, and replaced them with the type that the average American housewife cherishes. The large living room was bright and well furnished. Yet here too, a large, glass-enclosed bookcase, which contained an excellent library typical of the scholar who has spent years on advanced talmudic studies, took up the center wall. The apartment had four bedrooms, one large one and three smaller ones, all tastefully furnished. The bedrooms for the older children had a small built-in desk with a typewriter and shelf for books. Some of these were school texts, in both Hebrew and Yiddish, and some were the type of English books for Jewish children that have been published in recent years for all ages.

This middle-aged woman herself had a good religious and secular education at a Bais Yaakov school for girls and has a broader perspective on the type of education she and her husband want to give their children. It requires a wider range of reading than the average Satmar home in which the parents have had a more limited secular education. Yet both this woman and her husband are staunch *hasidim* and very active in the second largest of Williamsburg's hasidic girls' schools. After years of struggle and heavy financial pressure, her husband has successfully developed a children's clothing business. The woman is happy that she has the time and the ability to be of assistance to him by scanning trade magazines and catalogs and can suggest the type of merchandise that in her opinion will go over well with the buying public. But she emphasizes that her share in the business is secondary to her primary duties and interests as a mother and housewife: "My home is my castle as I have been taught by my mother. I want my husband and children to enjoy it. We are not fancy like the homes in Flatbush or Monsey. But our apartment is clean and bright. It teaches our children how to live properly."

Indeed, her apartment is a far cry from that of her parents, who had raised eleven children. Asked whether she wanted to remain in Williamsburg or live elsewhere, she emphatically stated that she loved the life in Williamsburg, and would not want her children to grow up in another, less intensely hasidic environment. She wants a larger family, like most of her friends. But she hopes to be in a position to maintain her present comfortable life-style, with the same amenities that her husband's and her work afford them.

This attitude on the part of many of the younger couples makes furniture and appliance stores and renovation companies among the busiest in the new Williamsburg. Shopping seems to be a major outlet for these young women, as for the women in general; one sees them pushing their baby carriages along the major business streets, holding on to several toddlers at the same time. It is one of the few outlets they have from their busy schedule of handling the endless household and child-care chores.

An increasing number of the members of the hasidic population are fortunately in the position to be able to rent bungalows in the bungalow colonies that most of the larger hasidic congregations have established in the Catskill Mountains. The women spend the hot summer months there while the children above the third grade live and study in well-appointed summer camps nearby. The husbands spend the weekdays working at their jobs in the city and return to their family for the weekends. Incidentally, this is one of the by-products of the hasidic revival of Hasidic Williamsburg – they have saved the "Jewish Mountains" from total ruin. Although there are still many empty and bankrupt hotels, the better ones have been taken over by hasidic *yeshivot* for their boys' and girls' camps. Others have become centers of bungalow colonies. What is new is the opening of numerous stores in the mountains. Most are branches of stores from Williamsburg and other hasidic centers, which provide the hasidic population with the type of foods and other necessities their orthodox life-style requires. They have garages, medical services, even a center where teams of expert *dayanim*, judges, and *poskim*, rabbinical ritual authorities, meet regularly as announced in advance in the weekly *Der Yid*. *Hatzoloh*, the superb medical emergency volunteer corps, has a number of stations in the Catskill Mountains whose teams are available at all times and work closely with the local police, physicians, and hospitals. A large number of vans, cars, and buses commute daily from the city to the mountains and back, in addition to the regular bus services.

Thus, Hasidic Williamsburg is making sure that their families are properly taken care of and retain the same spirit and environment in their summer residences in the bungalow colonies as they have in the city. Daily study classes are held in the mountains for the adults during the time they spend there. And the children have a felicitous mix of study and leisure activities under the guidance of their regular *yeshivah* staff or special teachers. Thus they perpetuate and further reenforce the total spirit of the hasidic ideology during summer vacation as it is during the regular school year.

SUMMARY: THE ECONOMIC REVITALIZATION

The effectiveness of the efforts of the leadership of the hasidic community of Williamsburg to stem the collapse of the neighborhood and to cope with the most serious problems facing them emerges boldly from the record of the economic revitalization. Counter to pessimistic predictions, it developed new economic patterns that enabled its members to overcome serious handicaps and difficulties inherent in their life-style. Quite a few succeeded in business by sheer hard work and ingenuity. By the end of the '80s *hasidim* had become part of the mainstream of American business, exemplifying the spirit of free enterprise and competition.

Instead of following the masses of earlier residents of Jewish Williamsburg who left the neighborhood during the '50s and '60s, the hasidic community, led by the Rebbe of Satmar and his associates, undertook a multiphased attack on the most pressing problems threatening the survival of the community. Foremost among these were the economic depression, critical housing shortage, unemployment, and poverty, especially among the elderly survivors of the Holocaust and post-Holocaust experience. Williamsburg was able to come through because of the loyalty of the followers of the Rebbe of Satmar and the other hasidic leaders. They were willing to overlook serious disadvantages of remaining in Williamsburg in order to be close to their Rebbe and the milieu he had created, though other neighborhoods, such as Boro Park and Monsey, New York, offered "greener pastures" for their efforts to rebuild their lives.

First and foremost, the leadership of the Jewish community explored various methods of locating private and public resources to help them mount an intensive campaign of renovation and construction to meet the urgent need for adequate housing for the large families of its growing population. The most strenuous efforts were devoted to developing a sound basis for the survival and economic future of the neighborhood. Drawing on city, state, and federal programs, the community organization searched for avenues that would allow their mostly low-income members to gain access to the opportunities that were available to members of other ethnic and racial minorities.

After a decade of political and legal negotiations, they succeeded in achieving a major breakthrough when, in July 1984, the hasidic community was officially designated a disadvantaged minority. This prime requisite helped its members overcome numerous obstacles inherent in their strict adherence to their ultra-Orthodox life-style. Their hard work and spirit of enterprise enabled many of the *hasidim* to break into new lines of business and trade, and contributed to the process of economic growth and the revitalization of the entire neighborhood, though more than a third of the population is still living below the official poverty line.

It is particularly the middle-aged and younger native American *hasidim* who, despite their lack of formal education, skills, and experience, turned to business and trade rather than to the academic and professional careers chosen by the majority of the nonhasidic American Jewish youth. Aided by various training and counseling programs initiated by the local office of the ODA, hundreds of young and middle-aged *hasidim* have benefited from government resources and programs and qualified for various funding and procurement opportunities available to the members of other American ethnic and racial minorities.

At the same time, an elaborate network of social and welfare programs has developed a sound basis for meeting the many needs of the elderly and poor, for the young and indigent, by pooling the resources and manpower of the entire community. It is particularly in this realm that the active participation and initiative of the young on all levels of the community structure have produced excellent results. They have become a major factor in the progress of various social, religious, and cultural, as well as commercial and political, projects, in spite of growing pressures from government cuts in aid and the intensifying economic crisis of the beginning '90s.

Williamsburg *hasidim* have increasingly become part of American business life, without compromising their ultra-Orthodox life-style. They have established themselves in a number of commercial and trade areas inspite of their lack of formal education. Jewish Williamsburg is still primarily a low- and low-middle-income neighborhood. Yet, indications of the economic revitalization are in evidence everywhere. Less than a generation after predictions of doom and disintegration of Jewish Williamsburg, the prospects of a sound socioeconomic future for the three-generational hasidic community are promising. It remains, however, to be seen whether the economic crisis of the early '90s will seriously impede or reverse the level of progress achieved by the end of the '80s.

➽ 3 ❮❮❮

Patterns of Education: Jewish Education with a Future

INTRODUCTION

In *Williamsburg: A Jewish Community in Transition* (1961), I stressed that the educational system is an expression of the character of a community and of its central values. Hence, any changes in the community's structure are reflected in corollary changes in the way it brings up its young.

The 1961 study described the transformation of the educational patterns of the Jewish community of Williamsburg since the years before World War II. It highlighted the gradual changeover from the once prevalent typical Hebrew schools, *Talmud Torahs*, and Yiddish folk schools, with a total of about 1,200 boys and girls, to Orthodox day schools and *yeshivot*, particularly Yeshiva and Mesifta Torah Vodaath, with 826 students. Thus, a grand total of little more than 2,000 boys and girls received some form of Jewish education, from the minimal Sunday school to the all-day parochial schools of the late '30s and the early '40s. The majority of Jewish children attended public elementary and high schools.

Over the next 20 years, the older, moderately Orthodox residents left the neighborhood and were replaced by intensely Orthodox Jewish newcomers from other neighborhoods and cities, and by waves of immigrants from the countries of the Nazi occupation, war, and the Holocaust. They chose to settle in Williamsburg because of its increasingly religious Jewish atmosphere and excellent educational institutions, and in spite of limited housing and inadequate facilities and services. Consequently, the day schools and *yeshivot* grew by leaps and bounds, while the public schools experienced a commensurate loss of their large Jewish student population. (Between 1940 and 1950, the Jewish student population of P.S. 16 and 122, the two major local public schools, dropped from 89.3 percent to 75.9 percent.) They were replaced by growing numbers of children from other ethnic and racial minority groups, particularly Puerto Ricans who flocked into the neighborhood and into the adjoining areas during the '50s and '60s, and again in the '70s, as in other Brooklyn low-income neighborhoods.

The *yeshivot* for boys and Bais Yaakov elementary and high schools for girls, combining intensive secular with religious education, flourished. At the same time, some of the heads of the Hungarian groups chose to start their own schools, rather than send their young into the existing Orthodox day schools. First was the Tzelemer Rav, Rabbi Levi Y. Gruenwald, the head of Congregation Arugath Habosem. His example was followed by the Klausenburger Rav, and by the leadership of the Viennese Congregation Adas Yereim. Last, but not least, Rabbi Yoel Teitelbaum, the illustrious Rebbe of Satmar, decided to create an educational system of his own that would represent the religious, ritual, and social values and the life-style in which his followers had been reared and which differed significantly from the educational patterns of Williamsburg's mostly Lithuanian type of *yeshivot* and girls' schools.

The crises of the '50s and '60s accelerated the outmigration of many Jewish residential groups, who took their institutions with them to their new neighborhoods. Progressive blight and deterioration of the already inadequate housing and other facilities, the influx of minority groups, and growing friction threatened the very survival of the Jewish community in Williamsburg and with it the educational system that had flourished in the post-World-War-II era.

As we have already seen, the decision of the Rebbe of Satmar and his community, by then the dominant hasidic group, to remain and fight for the survival of the neighborhood in spite of the serious problems confronting it, was the turning point that initiated the gradual emergence of the new Williamsburg and its growth into an even larger, more vital, and more prosperous hasidic community. Since changes in the structure and dynamics of a community are reflected in its educational system, this revitalization of the Jewish community of Williamsburg resulted in the remarkable growth of its hasidic schools for boys and girls into what, by the late '80s, had become the largest single Jewish education system in the U.S.

This growth is particularly significant at a time when the world of education in general is in the throes of crisis, and when Jewish leaders and educationists are bemoaning the failure of the once glorified Hebrew schools and *Talmud Torahs* that had dominated the educational scene of the broader American Jewish community in the first half of the century and beyond. Even the Orthodox Jewish day school and *yeshivah* movement, which had grown from roughly 4,000 to close to 100,000 boys and girls since World War II in 463 elementary and high schools, and another 5,000 in *yeshivot* of advanced talmudic studies[1] is experiencing some decline because of socioeconomic and other factors. Only in the large, mostly Orthodox communities, is there again a significant growth of the elementary classes. This trend is also suggested by Helmreich (1982) when he indicates that in his sample of the alumni of one large *yeshivah* the average family has four children, while the general American Jewish community has dwindled down to 1.8 children per household.

Hence the rapid expansion of the hasidic school system and its retainment rate of 98 percent are indicative of the perpetuation of the hasidic community and its life-style, which had been considered doomed as an anachronistic relic of the world destroyed by the Holocaust, and which would vanish with the death of the last survivors in this country.

Yet, as the leaders stress over and over again, at the end of the '80s, more than half of the current hasidic community in Williamsburg was American-born. It has become what is probably the only large three-generational Jewish community anywhere. More important still, the third generation, in the words of the head of the Satmar schools, is more learned, and in the case of the girls, even more pious than their parents and grandparents had been, both in Europe and in the U.S. At the same time, as we have seen, the members of the third generation consider themselves very much a part of the American mainstream in some of their crucial values.

The key to this American success story is largely the hasidic educational system, started more than 40 years ago by the newly arrived heads of the major hasidic groups, particularly Yeshiva Torah Y'Yiroh, or United *Talmud Torah*, established by Rabbi Yoel Teitelbaum, the Rebbe of Satmar. He guided and nursed it along from its inception in 1947 until his death. His successor, Rabbi Moshe Teitelbaum, continues his predecessor's central concern for the *yeshivah*. He personally directs and supervises every phase of its growth. Thus, the Satmar school system reflects the full scope of the hasidic ideology and its application in the collective and individual life-style of the community. It defies many of the basic principles of the current secular and Orthodox Jewish educational philosophy and methodology, true to the fierce independence that characterizes the spirit and work of the Old Rebbe of Satmar, regardless of the tremendous cost and investment of the community's strongest efforts and resources.

In 1990, the Satmar United *Talmud Torah* and *yeshivah* system for boys and girls had about 8,500 students in fourteen buildings in Williamsburg. Its 1990 budget was over $20 million. At the current rate it is doubling its student population every 7 to 8 years; new classes are added every few months. In the fall of 1987, twelve new classes for boys and eleven for girls were opened to accommodate the broadening stream of new students. New buildings will be added in Williamsburg, Boro Park, Monsey, New York, and in Kiryas Joel in Monroe, New York, the locations of the largest Satmar communities. Altogether, there is a total of over 18,000 boys and girls in the Satmar schools in the U.S. and about 35,000 throughout the Jewish world, in the institutions of Satmar in Israel, Europe, especially in London and Antwerp, and in Latin America.

If one adds the students of the *yeshivot* and girls' schools of the other major hasidic subcommunities of Williamsburg, such as those of Pappa, Klausenburg, Tzelem, Vishnitz, Spinka, Kashau, Krasna, and Adas Yereim, to mention only the larger ones, there are now close to 14,000 youngsters, from children in the day-care centers and nurseries to the scholars of the *kollels*, who in 1994 are receiving an intense Jewish education. This is in stark contrast to the barely 2,000 boys and girls who received some form of Jewish education in pre-World-War-II Williamsburg. It provides the most striking indication of the nature of the radical transformation of the neighborhood, and the educational quotient of its Jewish future.

The same two factors that were crucial to the developments of Hasidic Williamsburg discussed in the preceding chapters are also responsible for the success of the educational systems of the hasidic community. In the first place, it is the devotion and loyalty of the *hasidim* to their leaders and their willingness to mold their total existence to the ultra-Orthodox life-style that they have created in the midst of an American cosmopolitan milieu through a maximum of sociocultural isolation. Obviously, this process requires a great deal of character strength, disregard of ridicule, and ignoring of the media that homogenize American life everywhere else. It disavows the tendency of the newspapers to view the acculturation of newcomers and their blending into the environment as vital for optimal success and acceptance. It involves sacrifices and supreme efforts to assure the perpetuation of this religious philosophy and life-style through education of the young. Furthermore, it rejects the very basis of socioeconomic success that even the most Orthodox day schools provide by offering a thorough secular education in addition to their religious program. The underlying hasidic philosophy was espoused in an article in *Der Yid*, (July 26, 1989) that discussed the job opportunities for the graduates of the hasidic girls' schools. Its emphasis was on the central belief that "He who gives life, will provide the means for its sustenance," and admonished the parents not to let their daughters look for jobs in unfriendly or dangerous environments.

The second major factor responsible for the phenomenal growth of the hasidic schools is the rejection of birth control in any form, except in cases of serious medical problems. As a result, the hasidic community has one of the highest birthrates in the world. As we have already seen, the average household in Williamsburg has between seven and eight children, according to the local health authorities, and between eight and nine in Kiryas Joel, the suburban Satmar town near Monroe, New York, according to the director of *Yeled Shaashuim*, the recovery home for women and their newborns. The consequence of this conscientious reproduction rate is a veritable population explosion, what with from 400 to 500 young couples joining the hasidic community of Williamsburg annually. Therefore, the decline of the student population that is currently plaguing the public schools, many of which had been expanding to accommodate the baby-boom generation's children, does not exist for hasidic schools. What's more, the rate of growth is increasing even more rapidly as the children of the *Avreichim*, the large native American middle generation who are now in their thirties and forties, are filling new classes and buildings as soon as they are opened.

The strong commitment to the hasidic ideology, spirit, and life-style and the high birthrate are the best assurances of the continuity and growth of the new Williamsburg and its schools for boys and girls. It also foreshadows a rising level of knowledge and devotion to continued study of Torah, which could not have been anticipated anywhere in the nonhasidic and hasidic Orthodox Jewish world since the destruction of the concentrated Jewish centers of Eastern Europe in the Holocaust.

DIFFERENCES BETWEEN THE HASIDIC SCHOOLS AND THE ORTHODOX NONHASIDIC DAY SCHOOLS AND *YESHIVOT*

To understand the character of the hasidic schools, it is necessary to point out a number of important differences that distinguish them from the now widely acclaimed Orthodox Jewish day schools and the *yeshivot* that have emerged as a major force on the American Jewish educational scene, especially since World War II. Before going into any detail, however, it must be stated that both types of Orthodox school systems share basic goals and central values, and in the course of the move toward the right in the '70s and '80s the mutual impact has diminished the differences stressed here.

By the end of the '80s, hasidic schools had over 100,000 male and female students in their approximately 500 institutions, from the day-care centers of the preschools to the *kollels*, the institutes of advanced talmudic studies.

From the very outset, it must be stressed that there is a strict separation of boys and girls even at hasidic day-care centers and nursery schools; most Orthodox day schools in the large religious Jewish communities, especially those in the smaller towns, teach boys and girls together, at least until the first grade. Depending on their position on the religious spectrum of day schools, which ranges from ultra-Orthodox to modern Orthodox day schools, boys and girls are taught together in many religious and in all secular, or "general," studies. In the more liberal modern day schools girls are even sharing the study of Talmud with their male classmates on the junior and senior high-school levels. Most Orthodox day schools have always kept at least the higher phases of intensive Hebrew studies separate, even where the small size of the student potential and the prohibitive cost required a degree of compromise on the lower levels.

Naturally, no such compromises are made in the larger Orthodox Jewish communities that have separate day schools for boys and girls, such as Bais Yaakov, and which follow their own curricula, which differ significantly from those of the *yeshivot* for boys. No compromise whatsoever is made in hasidic schools, no matter the size of the hasidic community. It may as well be pointed out here that the creation of girls schools in the Satmar and similar Hungarian communities came about only after a long period of intense debate and even controversy. Even some among the more "liberal" *hasidim* objected strenuously to the creation of girls' schools altogether because of the rabbinic injunction against teaching girls Torah as conducive to *tiflut*, moral deterioration. In the East European *shtetl*, especially in the Hungarian communities, girls learned all they had to know as future homemakers from their mothers and grandmothers.[2]

While the movement of Bais Yaakov schools for girls succeeded in overcoming strong objections in the largely hasidic communities of Poland, girls' schools were not permitted in the Hungarian hasidic towns where the need to stem the tide of secularization and assimiliation were not as obvious. Hence, it took much pressure and the decision of the ultimate authority, Rabbi Yoel Teitelbaum, the Old Rebbe of Satmar, to permit the establishment of the Beth Rachel schools for girls to avoid having the hasidic girls enter the flourishing elementary and high schools of Bais Yaakov in Williamsburg and elsewhere. But since then they have grown rapidly and as of the beginning of the '90s they even have slightly larger classes than the Satmar boys' schools.

Significant differences in the curriculum of the Hungarian hasidic girls' schools separate them from other Orthodox girls' schools.

In the first place, all religious studies in both the boys' and girls' schools are conducted in Yiddish. This language presents no difficulty to their students because Yiddish is the language spoken at home throughout the hasidic community of Williamsburg as well as in the streets, though most hasidic Jews are quite competent in their use of conversational English. There had been considerable use of Hungarian in the streets of Williamsburg in the decade after World War II, which caused some of the older American Jewish residents to call the neighborhood "Hunksville." Now it is only rarely that one hears even older *hasidim* speaking Hungarian. In contrast, there is little or no Yiddish spoken in the nonhasidic Orthodox day schools. Most classes are conducted in English or modern Hebrew. Only the lectures of the *roshei yeshivah* in the advanced classes of the higher divisions of the *yeshivot* are given in Yiddish. Most of the discussion and conversation among the students themselves is, however, carried on in English, or in Israel in Hebrew, with an admixture of the classic Yiddish terminology indigenous to Talmud study.

There is little essential difference in the basic subject matter covered by both the hasidic and nonhasidic day schools and *yeshivot,* from learning to read and become familiar with the *siddur,* the prayer book, to carefully studying the *Humash,* the Old Testament, and its commentaries, and the Talmud, from simple text perusal to advanced research in the "Sea of the Talmud" commentaries, novellae, and more than a thousand years of detailed exegesis. Similarly, both types of *yeshivot* delve into the vast literature of ethical and moral classics. In contrast, however, Satmar's Beth Rachel and other hasidic girls' elementary and high schools do not use the standard Hebrew texts, including the *Humash,* the Five Books of Moses, in the original language. All of the religious subjects are taught with the help of Yiddish workbooks and original texts created by a staff of experienced educators, such as the head of Beth Rachel High School Hebrew Studies Department. There is a growing book-shelf of new texts in Yiddish that provide a thorough foundation in the basic ritual, ethical, and practical aspects of Jewish religious life, such as concern the observance of Sabbath and the holidays, and family life. But the most important factor of classroom instruction in the hasidic schools is the oral transmission of the contents and spirit of the subject matter from teachers to students to avoid the study of Torah in the original Hebrew texts.

Related to the rejection of the teaching of Torah in Hebrew is another difference that derives from the rejection of the modern State of Israel by the Rebbe of Satmar and his *hasidim.* Most of the day schools and *yeshivot* increasingly expect their graduates to spend some time on advanced study in Israeli institutions. For example, 80 percent of the senior class of a girls' high school spent at least one year at teachers' institutes, women's institutes of higher religious study, and colleges, which are proliferating yearly, or at *kibbutz* institutes. This has become the pattern as much for women as for the older *yeshivah* students.

Not so in the hasidic schools of Satmar and similar Hungarian hasidic communities. Neither the study of modern conversational Hebrew, nor of the geography and history of the land of Israel, which are standard in most day schools, are taught in Beth Rachel and the other hasidic girls' schools. Nor do their graduates, like most of those of Bais Yaakov high schools, which have their own seminaries in Israel for American girls, intend to pursue postgraduate studies in Israel. They generally go to work and expect to get married as soon as possible. Even the introduction of a twelfth grade and of a teachers' training course, which some of the other hasidic girls' high schools in Boro Park, for example, are advertising, have gone beyond the discussion and planning stage.

Another major difference, mentioned previously, is the lack of emphasis on intensive secular studies, which is standard in other day schools. Most students of the hasidic *yeshivot* for boys end their study of required general studies courses soon after *bar mitzvah*, though as well known and substantiated by the ongoing research and the 1986 Report of the Institute of Social Research, workers with only elementary education have a poverty rate five times higher than those with some college education.

In contrast, the hasidic girls' high schools have a good general studies department that concentrates mostly on vocational courses, beyond the required health science, English, history, mathematics, and social science study. As a result, hasidic girls are able to take jobs as secretaries, bookkeepers, teachers, computer programmers, sales personnel, and seamstresses. They work before marriage, in order to help their parents and to save up for the costs of their wedding and setting up a home, as well as after. Most, according to the findings of a survey of a small sample of women, intend to look for mates who are capable and willing to spend years after their marriage on talmudic and rabbinic study at a *kollel* while their wives go to work to help defray the regular household expenses, beyond the limited help both sets of parents and a small fellowship provide.

But, as one of the leaders of the hasidic community stressed, in spite of the rising costs of living in Williamsburg the number of women with children who go back to work after giving birth is getting smaller in proportion to the increase of young and middle-aged *hasidim* who are successful in establishing themselves in business or in a trade. In fact, as indicated in the preceding chapter, a goodly number of hasidic women help their husbands in business, at least in the early years. Furthermore, a growing number are able to establish their own businesses in basements or on the stoops of their homes, or in the regular commercial or industrial sections near Williamsburg, or in Manhattan, Long Island, and the other centers of New York's business and trade.

Though the differences between the hasidic and nonhasidic boys' schools are not as radical as those of the girls' schools, there are a number of major and minor points in the emphasis, structure, subject matter, and organization that do set them apart.

Variations in the formal structure of the systems, though minor, indicate a different educational philosophy. Hasidic *yeshivot* start their students on text study much sooner than the nonhasidic day schools and *yeshivot*. The typical day school is geared to the general public-school pattern of permitting young children to acquire reading readiness. Only gradually are they introduced to serious text study in line with the insights of developmental psychology. Hasidic *yeshivot* start much sooner, leave less time for play and maturation, and have a longer school day. They place a great deal of emphasis on memorization and on covering ground – though recently some of the nonhasidic *yeshivot* have begun to emulate the approach of the hasidic schools, starting their students on serious study at an earlier age and placing more emphasis on quantity, rather than on a gradual, integrated approach. Hasidic *yeshivah* students generally learn more at the expense of in-depth understanding and analysis. I already pointed this out in my discussion of the educational patterns in post-World-War-II Williamsburg in *Williamsburg: A Jewish Community in Transition* (1961). The students of the Tzelemer Yeshivah, the first of the hasidic *yeshivot*, showed evidence of mastering the basic texts much sooner. But those students whose parents wanted them to acquire more of an in-depth approach transferred to Mesifta Torah Vodaath, which follows a moderate Lithuanian model.

The school day of the hasidic *yeshivot* starts at 8:00 A.M. for the youngest students, at 7:30 for the primary grades, and at 6:30 for the junior and senior high-school divisions. Special classes for advanced and gifted students start at 6:00 A.M. All classes start their day with morning prayer services. Only the advanced classes have an early study session prior to the morning services. All students eat breakfast and lunch at a staggered schedule in the large cafeterias. The food for all Satmar boys' and girls' schools is prepared in a central kitchen and shipped to the individual schools in special containers. All boys, except those between the ages of 7 and 14 who devote an hour and a half or more to secular studies, spend most of the school day on their religious studies. They return home at 6:00 P.M. for supper. Students of the junior and senior high-school divisions return for an evening session of review and preparation for next day's study. On days when the regular or special examinations are given, the older students come as early as 5:00 A.M. to the *yeshivah,* for final intensive review sessions.

More important is the fact that unlike the public schools and most day schools, hasidic *yeshivot* of Satmar and the other systems do not have the standard summer break, which historically goes back to the agricultural nature of the schooling schedule. The younger classes meet in their regular *yeshivah* classes for a limited program of morning study. From fifth grade up, the students of both the boys' and girls' schools spend the summer in well-equipped summer camps, with their regular, year-round teachers. There they study on a more relaxed schedule and with some time allotted to leisure and regular camp activities. Two shifts of teachers are with them all the time. One shift teaches them regular subjects. The second shift supervises their activities, including the evening programs, and sleeping in the student bunks. Similarly, the instruction in the higher *yeshivah* classes during the regular school year is divided between two shifts of teachers, one which is responsible for the morning session until 2:00 P.M.; the second is in charge of classes until the end of the evening schedule. Hasidic *yeshivah* teachers, unlike those of the earlier Hebrew schools, day schools, and nonhasidic *yeshivot,* have twelve-month positions. They are not forced to look for other jobs during the summer, like the *melamdim* and Hebrew school teachers of old. Their families are housed in adequate staff quarters or bungalows, which is an important fringe benefit for the teachers who otherwise would have to rent a place in the Catskill Mountain bungalow colonies, like most of all but the poorest of the Williamsburg *hasidim,* at considerable expense.

Another important difference between the educational system of Satmar and other *yeshivot,* is the fact that all boys above the age of 15 study at the Mesifta division in Kiryas Joel, the exurban branch of Satmar in Monroe, New York, regardless of whether they come from Williamsburg, or from the *yeshivot* of Monsey, New York, Boro Park, and other branches. Approximately 500 young men studied there in 1987, away from home, in an ideal, total hasidic setting, far from the distractions of the city life, close to the Rebbe of Satmar, who spends much of his time in Kiryas Joel. By 1991, their number had nearly doubled. In fact, most Mesifta boys remain in Kiryas Joel until they are ready to start training for a profession, a trade, or business, and getting married. A good many of them continue their advanced talmudic studies and rabbinic training at one of the three *kollels,* if they qualify. The first *kollel* of Satmar was established 20 years ago. Before that, the Rebbe of Satmar had objected to the institution of a *kollel,* which had been introduced in the U.S. by the surviving famous *Roshei Yeshivot,* the heads of the Lithuanian type of advanced institutes of talmudic research after World War II, first and foremost among them Rabbi Aaron Kotler. There, their best young scholars would spend years after marriage in continued study on a small stipend and, if possible, supported by the parents of their wives and their own parents.

In contrast, Rabbi Yoel Teitelbaum urged his older disciples to leave the *bet hamidrash* to find work, train for a job, and get married as soon as possible. In fact, many a time he would personally intervene with his more successful *hasidim,* asking them to train his older *bachurim* and employ them, if possible. But as the hasidic community of Williamsburg and elsewhere began to expand, and with it the need for competent teachers, rabbis, *dayanim,* judges, and *poskim,* authorities in various phases of the halachah, the ritual codes of Law, he established the first of his *kollels.*

In 1987 close to 300 young married students were spending long hours on intensive study in these institutions, under the guidance of superior older scholars, in two large centers in Williamsburg. Their number has increased considerably since then. Periodically, *Der Yid,* the hasidic weekly, publishes lists and congratulatory greetings from their colleagues, friends, and families upon their successful completion of a series of in-depth examinations and ordination, the *semichah.* Not infrequently, one also finds large congratulatory announcements in *Der Yid* when some of the outstanding young scholars of the *kollel* have achieved the still higher level of ordination, the so-called *Yoreh, Yoreh, Yodin, Yodin* title that entitles the awardees to function as judges in religious, personal, and business matters.

Thus, there is now a cadre of highly trained and experienced middle-aged scholars who man the courts set up by the Williamsburg hasidic community in Williamsburg itself and in other hasidic neighborhoods. Quite a few of these still relatively young *dayanim* have earned a fine reputation for their competence in various areas of the religious life of the community. Every week *Der Yid* publishes a list of the *dayanim* and the schedule of the sessions when they are available to the public. During the summer when much of hasidic life has shifted to the Catskills, the *dayanim*, the judges of the *Beth Horo'oh* court, announce the schedule of their sessions in central locations of the mountains. There is also a *bet din*, a central community court, which meets regularly in a large hall on the main floor of the building of the Central Rabbinical Organization, on Division and Bedford Avenues.

On a recent visit to the two *kollel* centers of Satmar in Williamsburg, this writer found the large halls crowded with young scholars seated around long rows of tables studying, debating, and consulting the extensive library, whose packed bookshelves take up every inch of wall from floor to ceiling. The *kollel* scholars discuss halachic problems with the older scholars in charge. They are joined by members from the hasidic community who have taken a break from their work to study on their own or with one of the scholars. Periodically, the *kollel* scholars present their research findings to the heads of the *kollels* or to invited prominent scholars, rabbis, and heads of talmudic academies. They also publish a Torah journal in which they present discussion of classic talmudic and current halachic problems that arise as the hasidic community must cope with the advancement of science and technology, for example, that may have a bearing on the Orthodox life-style.

Perhaps the most significant difference in the approaches of the hasidic and nonhasidic *yeshivot* relates to their educational philosophy and practical goals. The famous Lithuanian type of academies, after which most American nonhasidic *yeshivot* are modeled, focus on mostly theoretical study of the vast talmudic litera-ture, with little concern for the application and applicability of the subject matter studied. In fact, concentration on the study of the more esoteric realms of the Talmud is a hallmark of the higher levels of the advanced academies. Their research deals with some realms of the *halachah*, the ritual laws, that will have to remain theoretical until the coming of the Messiah and the rebuilding of the Holy Temple. There are two favorite methods of advanced study. In the one, the scholar ranges across vast realms of talmudic or halachic problems, and the discourses attest to his knowledge and research. The other, more recently favored method, which has become characteristic of Lithuanian scholarship, is in-depth analysis that concen-trates on specific textual treatment, issues, and problems of talmudic discussion. It is little concerned with covering ground. Rather, it prefers delving into seemingly insignificant minutiae, allowing the elite scholars to construct their theories that resolve apparent contradictions in the talmudic and halachic texts and codes, such as the Code of Maimonides.

Only those advanced *yeshivah* students who are interested in pursuing a career in the rabbinate, or who want to earn the rabbinic ordination as a conclusion of their *yeshivah* education, devote time to the systematic study of the tractate *Hullin* and those parts of the Code of Law that are assigned by the heads of the *yeshivot* as requisites for the awarding of the *semichah*, the rabbinic ordination. Historically, the heads of the famous talmudic academies in Europe did not get involved in practical rabbinics and depended on local rabbis in the towns in which their schools were located to deal with the regular ritual or religious problems of the community. This focus on producing *Bnai Torah*, scholars, was held up to the students of the large major American *yeshivot*: "We want a generation of *baale-battim*, laymen, who are competent businessmen or professionals who have devoted years to intensive study of Torah and will continue to do so in their spare time." This was the favorite statement of Rabbi Sh. F. Mendelowitz of Torah Vodaath, one of the foremost educators in the world of American *yeshivot*. Only Yeshivat Isaac Elchanan, the rabbinic institution of what later became Yeshiva University, put more specific emphasis on educating and producing practicing rabbis as well as scholars and teachers.

In contrast, the Hungarian hasidic *yeshivot* emphasize the application and the applicability of their students' education throughout their entire school career. From the very outset, once they are past the primary level, their students are oriented toward *halachah*, the vital daily application of the ritual and religious laws, as an integral part of the daily schedule. Younger students are taught *halachah* at least half an hour each week. From fifth grade on they devote ever more time of the afternoon session to this subject. The administration of the *yeshivah* determines what areas of the practical *halachah* the teachers are to concentrate on. Of course, the focus is on the most important phases of the ritual life, such as *tallit, tefillin, mezzuzah,* and *Shabbat* and the holidays. The study of the *Tur* and of *Yoreh De'ah,* basic halachic texts, which those interested in a rabbinic degree pursue in the nonhasidic *yeshivot,* are part of the daily halachic study of the average student in the hasidic *yeshivah.* The goal is obviously the halachic education not only of rabbis and *dayanim,* or *poskim,* the professional authorities in the religious and ritual laws, but of the masses of hasidic *baale-battim,* who are made thoroughly familiar with the language and literature of the laws that are to guide their life. It must be stressed, however, that there has been an increasing emphasis on halachic study among the higher level students of the nonhasidic *yeshivot* in recent years. In fact, quite a few are producing specialists in various areas of the religious laws among the scholars of the advanced institutes of talmudic and rabbinic research, in the *kollels.*

In addition to the basic religious studies, hasidic education emphasizes the study of *Hasidut,* the classic and contemporary literature and philosophy formulated by the famous disciples of the founder of the hasidic movement, Rabbi Israel Baal Shem Tov. Hasidic schools also teach the classics of Hungarian hasidic literature and the works of outstanding contemporary hasidic thinkers and leaders, foremost among them Rabbi Yoel Teitelbaum, the Old Rebbe of Satmar, and his forebears. Their phenomenal scholarship covered the full range of the talmudic and halachic literature. The Satmar Rebbe also wrote a number of treatises, commentaries, and elucidations on the basic philosophy of Hasidism, and the esoteric kabbalistic works on which they were based.

The study of *Hasidut* in the hasidic *yeshivot* starts with daily 20-minute lectures by the regular class teachers. Subsequently, time is set aside every day for guided and independent study throughout the years of attendance at a hasidic *yeshivah.* Regular and special occasions, such as the annual gathering of all students above the elementary level on Lag B'Omer, in Kiryas Joel, Monroe, New York, are addressed by the present Rebbe of Satmar, Rabbi Moshe Teitelbaum. He elaborates on the hasidic ideology at all gatherings, such as the Friday evening *tishen,* or at the *seudah shlishit*, the third Sabbath meal, and the *melaveh malkehs*, the communal meals on Sabbath and the holidays. Then there are specialists, like the middle-aged scholar whose daily classes in *Hasidut* are attended by hundreds of young and old men alike, before and after work. These regular and special classes inculcate the moral and ethical, as well as the mystical, teachings of the philosophy of the hasidic movement in the hearts and minds of the listeners.

On the other hand, students of the hasidic *yeshivah* are also exposed to the famous classics of the ethical literature that are part of the curriculum of the nonhasidic *yeshivot*. All Orthodox students study the *Mesillat Yesharim, The Path of the Righteous*, by Rabbi Moshe Chaim Luzzatto, the eighteenth-century Italian thinker, talmudist, and kabbalist, for instance. In fact, a staff of eighty *menahalim ruchanim*, spiritual counselors and administrators, are devoting much of their time to teaching and discussing the general moral and ethical philosophy that is an integral part of the major contributions of the great scholars since the Middle Ages in all divisions of the Satmar school system.

In general, it is quite obvious that while there are significant differences there is much more that the hasidic and nonhasidic schools have in common. What they particularly share is their growing emphasis on learning more and on intensive study, on love of Torah, and on translating the fruits of their studies into the daily life of the Orthodox Jewish community.

TEACHERS AND ADMINISTRATORS

An indication of the care lavished on the education of their young by the Rebbe of Satmar and the leaders of his community is their treatment of the teaching and supervisory staffs. A major part of their $10 million annual budget is devoted to developing and maintaining a staff of competent teachers and supervisors, as well as of experienced administrators, many of whom are products of their own schools. The majority of the approximately 600 teachers and administrators are quite young, in their late twenties and thirties. On a visit to a number of Satmar schools, this writer encountered only a few older teachers and supervisors. The same applies to the administrators, and to the close to 200 executives, service managers, and the maintenance personnel who handle the plants and the transportation system for the fourteen buildings of Satmar. Computers, electronic equipment, intercoms, beepers, all the latest in technological tools are very much in evidence and are constantly used for communication among the various levels of the staffs and services.

As pointed out before, teachers and administrators have twelve-month jobs since they spend the summer months with their classes in the *yeshivah* summer camps. Their families are also accommodated at the same camps. Similar benefits are also available to the teaching staffs, such as price reductions in products at the communal stores, like meat and *matzot*. Even more important is the fact that teachers do not have to pay tuition for their children, which is a major savings since most have large and still growing families. Unlike many of the older *melamdim*, the teachers of the *yeshivot* and *Talmud Torah* who taught because they could not find other gainful employment or who used teaching as a means of sustaining themselves while they prepared themselves for other professions, hasidic teachers seem wholeheartedly devoted to *hinuch*, education. It allows them to spend all their time on Torah study. Most come from the *kollels*. After passing a carefully scrutinized tryout period, they are hired for one year on a temporary contract, constantly guided and supervised by colleagues and administrators. Generally, as one teacher put it in an interview: "We teachers have a great deal of input in the running of the school, not only of our classes. We are not employees who have no say in what is going on and how we are treated. This gives us not only a greater sense of responsibility, but an important feeling of self-worth." They receive some insurance coverage and a pension plan. Detailed instructions to teachers on their duties and rights are indications of the strong concern of the heads of the community for their staffs and their families.

One of the projects that had been temporarily halted when the Puerto Rican community leaders tried to block the use of the land bought by the Satmar community, in the area behind the mansion of the Rebbe of Satmar, but which has since been resumed, is the construction of a large new *yeshivah* building with facilities for fifty-four classrooms. The plans of this project called for the construction of residential buildings for the staffs. Unlike the *melamdim* who not infrequently had to go on strike to receive their long overdue paychecks, today's hasidic school teachers receive higher salaries and are paid regularly, even though the administration is beset by difficulties raising funds for the educational budgets. Yet, even if a regular teacher is paid between $5,000 and $7,500 a year for half a day's work, since most teach only either the morning or the afternoon and evening sessions, it is barely enough to pay the monthly rental, which ranges from $450 to $650 for the modest, small apartments in Williamsburg, and the expenses of maintaining a frequently large and growing household, even if the fringe benefits are considered. Thus, even at this time when teachers are more adequately rewarded, they rank among those with the lower incomes in the community.

In 1990 there were about 600 teachers and administrators in the boys' and girls' schools of Satmar. Twelve principals, eight for the boys' and four for the girls' schools, administer the various divisions. As pointed out before, they have a great deal of independence in their handling of the school's affairs, although all divisions are under the close personal supervision of the Rebbe of Satmar. In fact, the Rebbe himself, as had been the custom of his uncle and predecessor, meets periodically with all of the teachers and discusses issues, methods, and general goals with them. Four times a year he visits all of the schools connected with Satmar and examines the classes of the Williamsburg, Boro Park, Monsey, New York, and Kiryas Joel *yeshivot*, which had a total of 12,500 students at the end of the '80s, and whose student bodies have since grown even more as a result of the leaping population figures of the community. Regular examinations of all individual students are conducted by a staff of eight *farherers*, examiners, who are personally responsible for the progress of all schools and classes.

The average size of the classes in the boys' schools is twenty-five, and thirty to thirty-five in the girls' schools. The morning sessions are devoted to the in-depth study of the same tractate of the Talmud in all boys' classes from the fourth grade up. Students between the ages of 7 and 14 spend part of the afternoon on secular subjects. Otherwise, the boys devote the entire school day to their religious studies. As pointed out before, members of the older classes return to the *yeshivah* for an evening session of review and preparation for next day's studies, under the guidance of the teachers who are in charge of the afternoon and night program. Also the large nursery and kindergarten classes are taught by two teachers. All boys' classes, including those of the nurseries and kindergartens, are taught by male teachers, as it is against the hasidic customs to have women instruct male students. This injunction led to a much publicized decision by a court that rejected the suit of the school administration of Kiryas Joel to have female bus drivers who hauled the boys to and from the yeshivah replaced by male drivers. As a result the Kiryas Joel school administration had to hire private transportation, though they are legally entitled to this public service.

Experienced rabbis and male and female educators are in charge of most of the girls' schools, but the actual classroom instruction, except for some teachers in the secular studies department, are women, many of them products of the Satmar school system.

As could be expected, in view of the length of the school day and the packed schedule, there are occasional problems of restlessness and even some aggressiveness among the boys. But the constant supervision and attention of the staff provide a great deal of personal guidance; and they are prepared to work with the parents if there are real problems. Girls, remarked one administrator of the girls' division, are naturally better behaved and their considerably more limited program allows for greater personal freedom and creative expression. As a result, this administrator emphasizes, boys have greater knowledge. "In fact," he said, "they know how to learn more than most of their fathers and grandfathers even in Europe. But the girls have more *yir'at shomayim*, fear of Heaven and depth of piety." This is indeed a remarkable record for the hasidic schools in the American environment, where Hasidism was considered doomed as an anachronistic relic of a world that had been consumed in the fires of the Holocaust.

SPECIAL EDUCATION

Though not a major problem, the need for special education for physically and mentally handicapped youngsters on all age levels is something that the directors of the hasidic schools have to deal with. They do have special classes but, whenever possible, the procedure is to mainstream these unfortunate boys and girls as soon as they reach a level on which they can function together with other children their age unless it would cause them or others in the classes undue emotional and mental stress. Special-education teachers instruct small classes or groups in their own *yeshivah* buildings. An attempt was made to place a number of special-education girls in an unused section of a neighborhood public school, but it failed when the media, which generally do not deal fairly with the hasidic community (as evidenced by a meeting with the representatives of the press, and another with a New York City Council committee, late in 1990) blew the case of the "wall" all out of proportion, causing a great deal of friction.

In order to avoid unnecessary provocation, a wall had been put up to set off the section of P.S. 16 in which the girls' groups were to be instructed. As a result of the instigation by radical political interests, the PTA leaders of the mostly Hispanic parents initiated a strike against the school until the wall was removed. Though legally entitled to the service, the administration of the Satmar schools decided to abandon the project and bring the girls' groups back into their own buildings, where they do not have to face physical threats, and are instructed by special-education teachers provided by the public-school board of education. Groups of children with learning problems between the ages of 6 and 10 are taught in specially equipped classrooms by qualified teachers of the Satmar division for disabled children. One group of nineteen more severely disabled students between the ages of 6 and 14 is transported to the unused section of the large new building at the edge of the Jewish Triangle that houses a middle school as well as the local school board. There they have the proper facilities and are instructed by qualified public-school specialists, but they have no contact whatsoever with the other students taught in this building.

Chush

The Jewish Center for Special Education, in Hebrew the *Yeshivah Limudei Hashem*, or *Chush*, as it is commonly known, is a special school established by the hasidic community in 1976 at the urgent request of parents of children who, though of average intelligence, suffer from learning difficulties and needed special attention in order to grow up as functional members of the community. A friend of the hasidic community, the owner of the Kedem Wineries, donated one of the buildings of the complex the company occupies adjoining the navy yard, to house the vitally needed facility. Currently, over one hundred students, schoolboys of all ages, are taught by specially trained teachers and receive the full attention of therapists and psychologists equipped with up-to-date diagnostic and therapeutic instruments. Unfortunately, only the nursery classes benefit from funds made available from government sources. The rest of the budget has to be raised by the parents and by the hasidic community. A group of devoted teachers works with the children, many of whom would otherwise have been institutionalized, their emotional and learning problems further aggravated. The concerted efforts of the Hebrew and general studies teachers, and of the specialists, have produced remarkable results. They take special pride in the fact that over 25 percent of the students of the higher classes have achieved a functional level of learning, that they have been mainstreamed into regular classes of the hasidic *yeshivah*.

More recently a special division for vocational training of these disabled children has been added on the high-school level. Also, a new division has been set up on the nursery level, which also includes some girls, to provide early help to the youngsters before their emotional and learning difficulties have deteriorated. Recently, a new school for girls with learning difficulties was organized, Beth Pesel Rivkah Special Academy for Girls, which has classes for early elementary and junior high school students and a prevocational high school division.

It is not surprising that the success of *Chush* has been widely recognized. It is supervising similar programs in other Orthodox Jewish communities in Montreal, Cincinnati, Cleveland, and even in London. It is one more example of the innovative and creative approach of the hasidic community of Williamsburg.

Pesach Tikvah

Since the mideighties, the Satmar community has had a day-care center facility and a service center for the mentally ill, under the supervision of the New York State Department of Health and in conjunction with the Woodhull Hospital, in an area not too far from the Jewish Triangle. It started out as one of the departments of the Primary Health Care Center, the major health facility of the hasidic community directed by the ODA. Now its day-care facility serves mentally ill or handicapped Orthodox Jewish men from all over New York. Organized by one of the leaders of the hasidic community, Rabbi Chaim Moshe Stauber, it is directed by qualified social workers, psychologists, and several consulting psychiatrists. The mostly young adult and middle-aged patients learn to handle simple tasks, such as packaging and stuffing envelopes, for which they receive minimal pay and a sense of achievement. *Pesach Tikvah* also runs a residential home for girls. In 1987 this facility, which is located in the very center of the neighborhood, had fifteen patients. In response to the increasing demand, a second such residential facility for teenage girls was planned and a suitable home purchased. At the end of the '80s, *Pesach Tikvah* expanded its services to provide counseling and therapy for outpatients.

Soon the urgent requests for care from the nonhasidic as well as from the hasidic community prompted the acquisition of larger facilities. Hence, only a few years after its establishment, *Pesach Tikvah,* the Gate of Hope, has moved to a larger building farther southwest, in the adjoining area whose razed or dilapidated blocks have been a major target for the hasidic community's vital expansion. These services of *Pesach Tikvah* are very important in view of the fact that public institutions are frequently not equipped to handle the communication problems and special needs of mentally ill patients from the Orthodox Jewish community, hasidic and nonhasidic alike, not to mention that they provide a haven from friction and ridicule, which these patients would surely encounter in racially mixed wards. Thus, *Pesach Tikvah* functions as a vital addition to the network of services established by the hasidic community that has been widely adopted and is recognized far beyond Williamsburg for its approach to a widespread problem.

Dor Yeshorim

The Institute for Genetic Disorders further bears testimony to the farsightedness of the hasidic community and its dedication to meeting the needs of its entire population. The Orthodox Jewish and hasidic communities, no less than the broader society, need to respond to the risks of genetic disorders and related health hazards. *Dor Yeshorim* was organized to provide vitally needed information to the general public and to institute active prevention programs, medical consultations, and care by qualified medical specialists for the hasidic and general community in Williamsburg, and beyond. It offers free testing for Tay-Sachs disease, which occurs with some frequency in religious Jewish circles, as well as for a number of other genetic disorders and diseases to young couples about to marry.

Some of these conditions have been traced back to the brutal treatment of the Jews during the Holocaust, and to the stress and strain of its aftermath, the years in the DP camps and temporary holdovers until the older generation of the *hasidim* was able to reach the safety of the U.S. *Der Yid* and other Jewish publications in nonhasidic as well as in hasidic communities throughout the country carry frequent notices, advertisements, and articles aimed at enlightening their readers about the risks and lifelong burdens that may evolve out of ignorance and lack of attention to these sorts of problems. A comment by one of the cooperating physicians of Williamsburg, for example, drew attention to the fact that some of the physical and mental disorders suffered by hasidic women may be due to their having ten or more children by the time they are in their forties, some giving birth far beyond the usual birth age limit, which is about 45 for the broader population.

ADULT EDUCATION

One indication of the effectiveness of the hasidic educational system and of the resultant attitude of the hasidic community toward continued, lifelong study of Torah is the rapid increase of large classes for men in the early mornings before services and at night, after the evening services. One class, for example, meets in the large *bet hamidrash* of the central Satmar synagogue and has over 500 regular participants every morning and hundreds of others attending the evening class. Significantly, these popular classes are not attended only by the older generation, but by the young and middle-aged men who have graduated from the yeshivah and the *kollels* of Satmar and the other hasidic *yeshivot* and who are determined to maintain their high level of knowledge to fulfill the *mitzvah*, the divine command of daily Torah study. In the two buildings occupied by the *kollels* of Satmar, there are a number of different-sized halls that are filled at all hours by alumni and by other *Bnai Torah*, the young and middle-aged Torah scholars, who want to progress further in their mastery of the Talmud, the *halachah*, and *Hasidut*, who either learn in groups or independently, or are guided by known *talmidei hachomim*, scholars.

Similarly, in the study halls of all the branch synagogues established by Satmar throughout the neighborhood, such study classes are meeting regularly, especially in the morning and evenings before and after services. Two of these adult education classes have proven particularly attractive, and regularly draw large crowds. One such class is taught by an outstanding talmudic scholar. A second huge class is taught by a specialist in broadening and deepening the study of the *Humash*'s weekly portion of the Torah. A third such popular attraction is the class taught by an eminent scholar who lectures on various topics of the classic and contemporary literature of Hasidism, to groups of all ages. Furthermore, there are daily study classes set up throughout the morning and afternoons for retired senior citizens. Also, classes for other special groups are announced frequently in the pages of the weekly *Yid*.

Incidentally this increase in daily Torah study classes in the hasidic communities coincides with a similar trend in Orthodox Jewish communities everywhere. The most famous of the now popular daily study programs is the so-called *Daf Yomi*. It was introduced more than 60 years ago at a world conference of Agudath Israel in Vienna by one of the famous luminaries, the Chief Rabbi of Lublin, Rabbi Shapiro. He proposed that Torah Jews everywhere study the same page of the Talmud, so that they could partake in the study and discussion groups wherever they found themselves. His proposal was well received and study groups were initiated. But it took until the past decade or so to make the daily *Daf Yomi* a major project. It is now constantly setting up new study groups that meet every day in synagogues and study halls to cover the two sides of a page of the same tractate of the twenty-two-volume Talmud. Every 7 years these groups celebrate the conclusion of this vast program. At the last *siyum*, in 1990, over 20,000 nonhasidic, as well as hasidic Jews participated in a mass gathering at Madison Square Garden. The further expansion of this type of mass study is evidenced by such complementary ventures as the *Dial-A-Daf* telephone transmission of lectures by noted scholars, which has many hundreds of subscribers in the Jewish communities of this country, Canada, and beyond. There are also a number of other tapes proliferating that aid the mass study of all realms of biblical, talmudic, and ethical topics for those who are homebound or otherwise unable to partake in classes.

As a result of this proliferation of Torah tapes and cassettes on most topics of traditional and contemporary scholarship in the hasidic as well as in the nonhasidic communities, the larger Jewish communities have established circulating tape libraries. These have been multiplying, each collection expanding by leaps and bounds, echoing the current rise of active participation in the worldwide Torah study movement by the lay community as well as the *yeshivah* world.

Incidentally, although the study of Torah by women is not generally acceptable according to the hasidic tradition – we have already seen that it took some doing for girls' schools to be accepted by the Hungarian hasidic communities – there are clear indications that even in Williamsburg the attitude is changing. Every issue of *Der Yid* announces regular and special lectures for girls and married women by outstanding women educators and by noted orators on topics relating to the daily life-style and to the cycles of laws and issues and themes related to Sabbath and holiday observances. Other classes for women deal with ethical and moral questions discussed in the classic and hasidic tradition. Regular classes are offered to girls and brides that explain the requirements of personal purity, of marital life, and of proper conduct at home and in public.

More recently, the topics of these increasingly popular lectures for women have been extended beyond the purview of religious and moral guidelines to include more secular issues. Programs dealing with mental health problems, or with the raising of children, especially those with psychological and emotional problems and learning difficulties, are becoming more common.

PUBLIC AND PAROCHIAL SCHOOLS IN WILLIAMSBURG

In addition to the Jewish educational system, the public and Catholic schools in Williamsburg reflect the radical transformation of the neighborhood since World War II, particularly in the last two decades. From having a heavily Jewish student population in the '30s and '40s, the public schools that are left, Public School 16 and the Middle School on Heyward Street, as well as the one larger Catholic school, are now filled by the children of the ethnic and racial minorities, mostly Hispanics, some blacks, and a growing number of Asians, and a small number of whites. The Middle School on Heyward and Lynch Streets, for example, has about 75 percent Hispanics, 20 percent blacks, and a few white students. At the end of the '80s, its approximately 800 students filled only half of the relatively new building. The other half is occupied by the offices and facilities of the superintendent of School District 14, to which all schools of Williamsburg and the adjoining areas belong. Similarly, there are now only about 800 students in the large building of P.S. 16, which takes up a long city block in the very heart of Williamsburg. The administration and staffs of both public schools are still partially Jewish, though their number is steadily decreasing. They are gradually being replaced by non-Jewish teachers and administrators who are white, Hispanic, and black.

Perhaps most symbolic of what has happened to the public school system in Williamsburg is the fate of Eastern District High School, in the very hub of the Jewish neighborhood. Once one of the largest and finest high schools in Brooklyn, with a significant Jewish student population and teaching and supervisory staff, its diminishing mostly Hispanic and black student population was transferred to a brand new building in nearby Bushwick, once a mostly lower-class old Jewish neighborhood southeast of Williamsburg. The huge building, one of the most prominent in the area, which fills a large city block between Harrison and Division Avenues, has been purchased by the hasidic community of Satmar and converted into the central elementary and high school of Beth Rachel, its girls' school, from Grade 1 to Grade 11. Not far, the day-care centers and the nursery and kindergarten classes fill two more buildings along Harrison Avenue. A total of over 3,000 girls fill every room in the former Eastern District High School building, and the overflow classes are housed in temporary buildings in the large school yard. The huge auditorium/cafeteria has been renovated to accommodate in addition to the needs of Beth Rachel the growing number of weddings of more than 500 young couples getting married every year in Williamsburg.

The student population of the large Catholic school, which had once been crowded to capacity by the children of the Italian, Polish, and Irish residents who lived in and around the old Jewish neighborhood until just after World War II, is now mainly composed of Latinos, especially the children of the large group of immigrants from the Dominican Republic, who are very religious. Most of them and other Latinos and blacks are residents of the large public high-rise projects and the areas adjoining the Jewish Triangle, from which the two remaining public schools also draw their students.

The principals of both the public and parochial schools stress that while their populations had gone through periods of change during the '50s and '60s, they have now stabilized, as Hispanics and blacks have become more affluent and show less of a tendency toward transience than the older residents. The principal of the Catholic school emphasized the strong religious and cultural interests of the parents in her school. They prefer sending their children to parochial school to avoid the problems and dangers of public-school life. They are active in the PTA and in local community affairs. This positive attitude was also reported by the administrators of the public schools. Though there is a bilingual program at P.S. 16, the principal reported that parents are anxious to have their children enter regular classes and become competent in English to avoid isolation and its adverse psychological and social effects.

The principals of the three non-Jewish schools interviewed described their students as coming mostly from the marginal areas, except those whose families reside in the five public high-rise projects and who pass through the streets of the hasidic neighborhood on their way to school. Yet, there is almost no contact, no exchange of cultural information between the two major population groups and their youngsters. There is also no mixing of the boys and girls on the large playgrounds of the large projects, whose residents are more or less evenly divided between *hasidim* and other minority groups. Neither the schools nor the projects themselves feature any form of cultural interchange. But there is little of the open hostility and friction that were rampant in the '60s and '70s, when the hasidic population was fighting for its survival and its right to remain. The principals confirm that their Hispanic students have come to respect the *hasidim* and are very much aware of the active self-defense and citizens' volunteer patrol in the neighborhood, which is always on guard and has significantly cut down on the waves of break-ins, theft, and personal attacks, which had been plaguing the neighborhood since the '60s.

The principals also agree that the *hasidim* have improved the appearance and general security of Williamsburg. "Without doubt," one of them said, "they have made it one of the safest areas in all of New York." One of the principals, who prides himself in keeping in touch with the people of the neighborhood where his school is located, attested to the generally good interrelationship between the *hasidim* and the other residents. Yet, like the other administrators, he confirms that except for the occasional use of the auditorium by the community of the Hasidim for large public functions, there is no official or unofficial contact. The exception is one group of severely disabled hasidic boys who are taught at his school by special-education teachers from the public-school system; but they have no opportunity to meet or interact with the rest of the school population.

There is, however, one important exception to this lack of collaboration. Although there are almost no Jewish children in the public schools, there are now three *hasidim* elected to and active on the local school board. For it has always been the policy of the hasidic administration to be represented on all local community boards, not only those which directly affect the hasidic community's interests. As was confirmed even in an article in the *New York Times* (July 4, 1987), they take seriously their obligation to safeguard the welfare of the entire neighborhood. Hence, they worked strenuously to have their representatives elected and, as confirmed by the school administrators, they are actively and constructively involved in all discussions and proceedings of the school board.

In retrospect, the success of the hasidic school systems has not only reshaped their own community, providing for their youth and their future. It has also transformed the remaining public and parochial schools into extraterritorial institutions. For the bulk of their students, except for those who come from the five public high-rise projects, come from the adjoining areas that are heavily populated by various ethnic and racial minority groups. Though there are still a number of teachers and supervisors left of the once mostly Jewish educational staffs, their number is constantly being reduced.

For better or worse, the sociocultural self-imposed isolation of the hasidic community of Williamsburg extends to its two school systems. But there is an air of mutual respect and cooperation wherever possible. It is only in cases when outsiders step in, such as the protest against the "wall" at P.S. 16, when the media, local politicians, and vested interests responded out of all proportion, that the positive collaboration on the board and among the administrators is disturbed.

SUMMARY: JEWISH EDUCATION WITH A FUTURE

The metamorphosis of Williamsburg from a disintegrating old Jewish neighborhood into a vibrant, expanding hasidic community, despite the most adverse conditions, is epitomized by the large hasidic educational school systems of Satmar, Pappa, Klausenburg, Spinka, Adas Yereim, and other smaller ones. Satmar alone, in the four decades of its existence, has developed the largest single financially and otherwise independent Jewish school system in the U.S. that differs significantly from most of the Orthodox day schools and *yeshivot*. Designed to perpetuate the Hungarian hasidic philosophy and life-style, it has educated a generation of native American hasidic men and women whose children are now filling new classes and schools as soon as they are opened. It has developed staffs of competent educators who mold their students in the spirit of Hasidism, loyal to their Rebbes and their teachings, and steeped in the tradition of Torah study as a lifelong practice, to be continued long after they have left their institutions and regardless of the professions they choose to enter. Their boys and girls affirm their faith in the viability of their traditional values and take up the challenge of translating their lessons into their daily life in the new Williamsburg.

Above all, the hasidic educational system has reared masses of learned and learning men and women. While partaking in the mainstream of American economic and political life, they are thoroughly imbued with the importance of perpetuating Torah and education, as well as *Hasidut* in their individual and communal life-style. From the ranks of these elite young scholars has come a generation of competent rabbis, *dayanim*, and *poskim*, who have proven their ability to cope with not only religious and ritual problems. They are demonstrating their keen understanding of the challenges of guiding a large, diverse community according to the ultra-Orthodox framework of the *halachah* and the hasidic tradition in the radically changing setting of modern-day urban America. To the three-generational hasidic community of Williamsburg its schools are the key and guarantee of its perpetuation and its future in this country and elsewhere in the contemporary Jewish world.

➤➤➤ 4 ⬅⬅⬅

The Structure of the Family:
No Generation Gap

[The family] more profoundly than any other organization exists only as a
process and we can understand it only through a study of the changes which
occur within it in the life history of each individual [group].

Robert M. MacIver, *Society*

My earlier study, *Williamsburg: A Jewish Community in Transition* (1961), described the
decline of the traditional family in the pre-World-War-II period, a trend observable
in other Jewish immigrant ghettos as well. It went on to trace the return to a more
intense traditional Jewish life-style as a result of 1) the influx of large numbers of
Orthodox residents and of groups of Orthodox refugees from Nazi persecution and
war, 2) improved economic conditions, 3) the rapid growth of day schools for boys
and girls, and 4) the impact of Orthodox Jewish youth organizations in the
neighborhood. Finally, it reported the continued intensification of the religious
life-style and with it the resurgence of the traditional family structure thanks in part
to the departure of less religious residents, the massive influx of Hungarian-type
hasidim, and the galloping blight of the area since the '50s. Soon the less religious
elements were followed by many of the more Orthodox elements, especially young
newly married couples who wanted to escape not only the deteriorating physical
conditions, but the increasingly intensive hasidic life-style of the neighborhood.
They moved to ecologically and socioeconomically preferable communities that
would not impose such stringent standards on them and on their families, thus
loosening their ties to their kin and their old associates, and to the spirit of Jewish
Williamsburg.

Those who remained in Williamsburg were bonded by the strong religiocultural
values of the neighborhood, as evidenced, for example, by the drop of juvenile
delinquency from a pre-World-War-II high of 15 percent to less than 5 percent, in
spite of the increasing influx of minority groups with one of the highest delinquency
rates in the city, and a further drop to close to 1 percent in the '80s.

The crises of the '50s and '60s, which threatened the very survival of Jewish

Williamsburg, and the subsequent establishment of the hasidic community in the sociocultural isolation of the Jewish Triangle produced a trenchant example of the impact of the total milieu and its valuational basis on the structure and dynamics of all facets of the family as the central institution of the community. The prime factors behind these transformations were: 1) the religious and sociocultural climate of the community, 2) the demographics, 3) the educational system, 4) the changing economic patterns, and 5) the dynamics of the hasidic family. All of these factors are closely interrelated and it is virtually impossible to discuss one without constant reference to the others.

Naturally, the religious milieu of the hasidic community of Williamsburg created by its sociocultural isolation, by its effective educational system, and above all by the ideology and spirit of Hasidism and the loyalty to the Rebbe and his teachings, is the major force molding and constantly reinforcing the traditional family structure and dynamics. It fends off the very forces that have been responsible for the gradual erosion of the traditional family's foundations and its interpersonal relations since pre-World-War-II Williamsburg, as in other Jewish and non-Jewish immigrant communities. This milieu is equally effective in eliminating many of the tensions and valuational conflicts not only between parents and children, but also between the children and their outside associations, which were still many during the '40s and '50s.

The most significant difference between the new Williamsburg and the Jewish community of the preceding phases is the attitude of the young and middle-aged who left the neighborhood. They moved to better, socioeconomically upward bound communities with superior facilities and services because they sought a more "tolerant," less intensely Orthodox setting. Though the young of the post-World-War-II period were much less inclined to leave behind the Orthodox life-style of their parents than those of the previous periods because of the impact of their day-school and *yeshivah* education and of the Orthodox youth movements, they did not want to remain. They moved to other religious urban and suburban communities. Many of them played an active role in bringing the spirit and life-style of the Orthodox Williamsburg in which they had been reared to their new homes. But, as pointed out in my previous study (1961), a goodly number left because they had begun to feel increasingly out of place in the midst of the massive build-up of the Hungarian hasidic community with its significantly more stringent life-style than the one in which they had been educated.

"It's just not our world any more," said a young woman, the wife of a middle-aged professional who came back to Williamsburg frequently as long as her parents lived there, until they too moved to Boro Park, like most of their friends and neighbors. Viewing the ubiquitous hasidic garb and mentioning the prevalent use of Yiddish in the streets all around her as she was interviewed, she said pointedly:

> It is just not our type of *Yiddishkeit* any more. I don't want my children to grow up here and be turned off from *Yiddishkeit* altogether, like many of my former girlfriends and members of their families. Nor do I want my children to adopt the hasidic life-style

that is in now, like the son of friends of ours for whom nothing his parents do is good enough. In my opinion they are as Orthodox as anyone who has gone through *Torah Vodaath* and Bais Yaakov in the days when we lived here.

This comment of a sincerely religious former Williamsburger highlights the reasons why many educated professionals with an equally superior Jewish education left Williamsburg for more moderately Orthodox Jewish communities such as Boro Park, Flatbush, Queens, Monsey, New York, and others like them in and around New York. The deterioration of the already poor physical living conditions served as additional impetus, or as an excuse, to leave the neighborhood.

The opposite reaction of the hasidic youth, especially those to be married, who insist on remaining in Williamsburg despite its obvious disadvantages, is the very source of the strength of the hasidic community and of its ability to overcome the negative physical and environmental conditions. This reaction is due, above all else, to the impact of the centrifugal role of the hasidic family and the strength of its cohesiveness. A spokesman for the Satmar community put it pithily:

> *Williamsburg has no generation gap,* except for the generation that perished in the concentration camps. Our youth is as genuinely hasidic as their parents, if not more so. There is no doubt that the young men will want to wear *kapottes* and *gartels,* beards, and *peyot.* Nor is there any question in my mind that the young women growing up here and going through our schools will cover their hair all the time and wear *sheitels,* wigs, after they are married. They are proud to don modest clothes, regardless of fashions, fads, heat, or cold. They will marry young and want to have large families just like their parents. Most of all, they will want to live near the Rebbe, his schools, and institutions. That is the key to our survival as a hasidic community.

In a nutshell, he touched the vital bases of the effectiveness of the hasidic milieu of the new Williamsburg as a result of its education and intergenerational role models.

In contrast, as pointed out before, the young of the earlier phases of Jewish Williamsburg were caught in internal and external conflicts because they attended public schools. In the higher grades especially, they encountered ideas and ideologies that were contradictory to what their mostly immigrant parents and their community believed. They associated with fellow students and friends whose life-styles were different from their own, and who would question, if not mock, the quaint old-worldishness of their parents, their homes, and their conduct. They felt the growing impact of the media, although TV was then not yet considered part of their world. They went to the theater and movies, which were not yet treated as *treifoh,* contradictory in spirit and content to the religious ethos of the community.

The boys and girls who attended day schools or *yeshivot* spent a good part of their school days on secular studies. Thus, they were required to become familiar with literature, scientific theories, philosophies, and political ideologies that differed from, and sometimes out-and-out contradicted, the basic beliefs and postulates they had absorbed in their intensive religious studies. Many belonged to organizations, even religious ones, some of whose activities, such as coed parties and dances, are proscribed by the ultra-Orthodox milieu of Hasidic Williamsburg. Similarly, the long summer vacations, whether spent in a summer camp, in bungalow colonies, or working in hotels in the Catskills, exposed them to life-styles and ways of thinking and acting that undermined what their parents and teachers had worked so hard to inculcate in them the rest of the year.

The parents themselves, most of whom were immigrants, had neither the education nor the knowledge, leisure, and competence to effectively counteract these influences that questioned, perverted, or even destroyed the very foundation of their guidance and teachings. The inevitable result was tension and open conflict, which were harmful to the cohesiveness of the family. They provoked emotional, intellectual, and spiritual traumas, which hurt the social welfare of the young as well as the old, and destroyed much of the inner strength and solidity of the community. Ultimately, it seriously impaired the discipline and mutual trust that are basic to the traditional family.

The intensive educational system and the religious climate of Hasidic Williamsburg effectively prevent most of these types of tension and conflicts that were so harmful to the perpetuation of the religious beliefs and life-style of the Jewish community of pre- and post-World-War-II Williamsburg. The sociocultural isolation conscientiously created by the former Rebbe of Satmar and the other hasidic leaders has proven most effective in warding off what has become the most powerful and insidious factor in the demoralization of contemporary youth. One has to think only of the amount of time children spend watching TV programs, very few of which are genuinely educational.

The militant stand the hasidic community has taken against TV, which they call the *treifeneh keileh*, the forbidden, immoral instrument, that swamps the viewers with experiences of "immorality, violence, and adultery," the three strongest prohibitions of the Jewish Law, has succeeded in removing it from all hasidic homes, as a glance at the low rooftops of the Jewish Triangle will show, cleared of the ubiquitous antennae forests covering the adjoining areas and, indeed, the rest of the U.S. The weekly *Der Yid* and other Yiddish publications, such as the *Light* and the *Jerusalem Guardian*, replace the regular daily newspapers in their homes. If they listen to radio, it is mostly to Jewish or Yiddish programs, especially those that feature hasidic music, such as the popular hasidic singer Mordechai ben David, himself a *hasid* and a scion of a noted Ger Hasidic family.

The considerable number of records and tapes by Orthodox hasidic and nonhasidic musicians provides the entertainment that takes the place of TV and pop music. A growing number of radio programs and audiotapes, which provide learning as well as moral and emotional guidance, many of them specifically directed at women, and more recently at Orthodox children, further reinforce the battle against the media blitz in the hasidic community. Hasidic businessmen read the *New York Times* and other commercial and trade publications, which they require to stay informed of developments in their fields of interest. Younger *hasidim*, like most of their elders, read almost no books in English except for those that are required in their secular studies. These have all been carefully screened, and passages that violate the religious views have been crossed out or removed. Not even the large number of fiction and nonfiction books in English or Yiddish that have appeared in the past 30 years, written expressly for Orthodox youth, are much in use, as a glance at the local bookstores indicates. One Williamsburg store has a shelf in the backroom filled with Orthodox Jewish youth publications. But they are mostly requested by teachers of the day schools looking for collections of stories and similar reading materials for the classroom and not, as one said pointedly, for her own enjoyment. This negative attitude toward Orthodox Jewish literature is in marked contrast to the strong emphasis on such books by the second largest hasidic movement, that of Lubavitch, with its large headquarters and publication center in Crown Heights. It has been publishing magazines and books for women and children of all ages, many of which are translated into Yiddish, Hebrew, Russian, German, French, and Italian, and are much in demand throughout the Jewish world.

Only in the past few years have an increasing number of booklets, workbooks, and various types of readers for children in Yiddish been written and introduced into the hasidic schools. A special publication organization was set up by the Old Rebbe of Satmar to make certain that proper texts for the boys' and girls' schools are produced by some of the gifted educators and administrators and made available. This cultural isolation has effectively maintained the spirit of the hasidic community, and with it the traditional family structure of the new Williamsburg. The boys and girls have no outside associations that would influence them and create the friction so frequently found in other Jewish communities.

Even their leisure time, including their vacations, are as pointed out before, spent in the same type of environment, such as the hasidic *yeshivah* summer camps. Throughout the year the hasidic *yeshivot* organize special programs, such as regular, mutual visits of the various branches of Torah V'Yiroh schools for boys in Boro Park, Monsey, New York, or Kiryas Joel. There are gatherings, such as the one arranged annually for all but the youngest Satmar *yeshivah* students in Kiryas Joel, on the *yahrtzeit*, the anniversary of the death, of the late Rabbi Yoel Teitelbaum, the Old Rebbe of Satmar, where they are feted and addressed by the present Rebbe. This is in addition to the regular hasidic gatherings, such as the Sabbath and holiday *Farbrengen*, gatherings at the Rebbe's *tish*, attended by fathers and sons, or the Saturday night *melaveh malkehs*, communal meals, and similar gatherings for hasidic women and girls. These hasidic encounters provide entertainment and the inspirational framework for the hasidic youth in their crucial formative years. Hence, there is little opportunity for outside influences or for the wrong role models to interfere with the respect and love for their fathers and mothers and what they stand for.

Important for the preservation of this attitude and inner discipline is the fact that at no time do hasidic parents become the pals of their children, as do the sophisticated moms and dads of the generation nourished on Drs. Spock, Gesell, and Ginot in the typical suburban Jewish and non-Jewish homes. Thus, there is no lowering of the barriers of respect and discipline, which in the '60s led to the permissiveness and eventual revolts of the Woodstock generation and their experimentation with drugs, sex, and alcohol, and perversions of traditional values and norms. For better or worse, the hasidic boys' life is harnessed early to the structures and strictures of the *yeshivah* and the life-style that make them grow up prematurely, depriving them of most opportunities for extended play and gradual maturing that have become part of the contemporary progressive education scene.

As is to be expected, there is a measure of aggressiveness developed early in the talmudic discussion and a level of rambunctiousness. It was in these terms that one outside visitor described the free-wheeling dancing, singing, and jumping he viewed at the Simhat Torah festivities. What he saw was the pushing and crowding forward at the festive table of the Rebbe, when everybody was trying to get hold of a morsel, *chap shirayim*, of the food sanctified by the blessing of the Rebbe. This is endemic to the hasidic life-style and expresses love, respect, and utter reverence rather than what the "objective" spectator perceived. It is this same spirit that has led to violent demonstrations in New York and in Jerusalem and which has been referred to as "excesses" of the "fanatic ultra-Orthodox" by the general Jewish and non-Jewish press. It is evident, too, in the storm and fist fighting outside of the police headquarters in Williamsburg or Boro Park or Crown Heights, which erupted, for example, when a hasidic Jew was seized and forced to violate the Sabbath, and which, like similar minor incidents, was blown out of all proportion by the media. One of the hasidic school administrators, when questioned about this in connection with the long hours of incessant study, said:

> There is no question that the boys will be more aggressive, less pliable and also less pious than girls. Boys will be boys, whether in jeans and T-shirts or in dark hasidic garb. But there is simply no comparison to the behavior of other teenagers. There is little chance that boys in long, black *kapotes*, *peyot* swinging from their temples, will be misbehaving in a manner even vaguely reminiscent of what teachers and administrators face in the public schools. There is a strong feeling of *derech eretz*, respect and discipline, fostered by the *yeshivah*, family, and the community milieu. The close association with their teachers and older students, and the constant awareness and personal guidance stressed by the Satmar Rebbe in his regular talks to the faculties of his boys' and girls' schools, provide the controls and norms that characterize all phases of the hasidic life-style especially in the *heder* and in the *yeshivah*.

This administrator of both boys' and girls' schools, with years of experience, emphasized that hasidic students, too, must have a chance to let off steam and vent their pent-up emotions and restlessness. Though frowned upon by the hasidic administration, some youngsters engage in scribbling graffiti, which includes threats against the heads of other hasidic movements. They even engage in fist fights, as when a group of Lubavitcher *hasidim* disregarded warnings and marched through Williamsburg on Simhat Torah as they do every year, visiting Jewish neighborhoods, singing, dancing, and presenting special holiday messages from their Rebbe. On another occasion, graffiti on the sidewalks of Williamsburg threatened the leader of the Belzer Hasidim when he visited the U.S. and New York, calling him by his first name "Berel." There was also the incident of the defacing of two synagogues in Williamsburg by *yeshivah* students protesting the mistreatment of demonstrators upholding the holiness of the Sabbath in Jerusalem.[1] Generally, however, the hasidic youngsters are well disciplined, harnessed by the rigorous schedule of the *yeshivah* life and buoyed by the spirit and inspiration of their hasidic experience. Thus, they are able to cope with the external and internal pressures of growing up. Early marriage, and the consequent avoidance of dating and its tensions and temptations, challenges and pressures, are crucial strategies of prevention and sublimation, which work for the strength of traditional family life in the hasidic community. Not surprisingly, there are instances of mental illness, separation, and divorce among these young men and women who generally marry early, when they are not able to cope successfully with the plethora of problems involved. In the past few years, a number of official organizations and private groups have been established in Williamsburg, Boro Park, and elsewhere to help those in need of assistance and guidance in these matters. Most of this work is done within the frame of the hasidic community since outside help that is ignorant of the hasidic mentality and the exigencies of the hasidic background would be of little value.

Such problems have been increasing since the end of the '80s and the beginning of the '90s, when serious economic difficulties have added further pressure to the already stressful situations of young married couples. And there are reports of battered hasidic women winding up in special shelters established for religious wives in New York, outside of the hasidic community itself. When questioned about it, a counselor to Orthodox couples in trouble remarked: "You know that there is a tremendous increase of friction and break-up of marriages because of the stronger "me-attitude" of young people in the broader society, and inevitably in the hasidic community as well, though at an incomparably lower rate."

Despite the presence of these problems and occasional excesses, the young of the hasidic community generally seem happy and satisfied. They do not question parental authority, and the dynamics of their family life has few of the worries that beset the average American family, especially since the '60s, whose parents have little in common with their children, except for a shared visit to a ball game or watching popular programs on TV or videos.

In addition to the pull of their feelings of loyalty to the Rebbe and his institutions, young couples are eager to remain. Obviously, they like the atmosphere and life-style around them in the neighborhood. Such was the suggestion of the young woman questioned as to her plans following her imminent marriage.

> Even if we could afford to live in Boro Park, where rents and houses are double and triple what they are here, I dislike the showing off with clothes, not only on holidays, but even on weekdays. My friends who live there tell me that you are not judged by who and what you are, but by the size and price of your chandelier, your car, jewelry, and the *sheitel* you wear. Here, in Williamsburg, I will be near my parents and other relatives on whom I can call for help and advice all the time. And as an inexperienced new housewife I will need plenty of it. My *choson*, my groom, has his close *haverim* here with whom he studied for years in the *Bais Hamedrash*, and with some of whom he will continue to learn in the *kollel* after we're married. I, too, have many friends here, and

classes and other activities that will keep me busy and happy during the time that I can spare from taking care of my home.

That is all that I want, to be near the Holy Rebbe, and near to our family, and friends. My _chosson_ and I want to continue to live in the simple, _ehrliche_, sincere way in which we have been brought up here, without having to strain ourselves to live up to the high standards and luxuries that young couples in Boro Park and Flatbush must to be accepted. We want to have children, just like our mothers and grandmothers. And we want them to grow up in the same way that we were raised. I only hope that we will soon find an apartment here that we can afford and that is not too far from the center of the neighborhood.

This young woman, barely 18 years old, had never dated before she met her future husband. Her remarks highlight the crucial role of the _yeshivah_ and of the girls' school education in developing such an unquestioning, enthusiastic attitude toward the traditional family and in the rejection of conspicuous consumption. Her ideal, like that of almost all of the young women interviewed, is to work and help support her husband so that he will be able to devote a few more years to his advanced talmudic studies. As she emphatically put it:

> Since I was a child, I dreamt of marrying a _talmid hacham_, a scholar, and of having children who would study seriously to become Torah scholars like their father and grandfathers. And I don't care how hard I will have to work now, and both of us when my husband will be ready to enter a trade or start some venture of his own. This is our wish, and we will do our best to make it come true, with the help of the Lord.

It takes a powerful education to produce this type of teenager, instead of the common caricature of a JAP, the Jewish American Princess, from other communities whose ambitions have been shaped by the media, by magazines like _Seventeen_, _Vogue_, and their imitators, in print or on the screen, with frequently disastrous results for their social and mental stability. Chances for the survival of the marriage of simple hasidic teenagers, like the bride we interviewed, are infinitely better than marriages in the broader community where separation and divorce threaten more than a third of all marriages. These marriages are also not characterized by the patterns of unhappiness, infidelity, and gross perversion that fill the media images of the life-style of married couples at the end of the century. This is true not because the hasidic young women are ignorant but because of their strong convictions. The picture is not quite as gloomy in the Jewish community as in society in general, as a recent study by Calvin Goldscheider points out. According to his findings in _Jewish Continuity and Change_ (1986), American Jews are still distinctive in their patterns of family life, marriage, and child rearing. He emphasizes, however, that this is "not because they fail to integrate into American culture, and not because they suffer from discrimination, and _not because they continue to live by the Jewish value patterns_" (p. xiii, italics mine). In contrast to this analysis of the American Jewish family, the hasidic family and its outer and inner cohesiveness are definitely based on the intensively religious Jewish and hasidic values in Williamsburg, as borne out by the testimony of the young bride and most other young women interviewed. They all credit their education at home and in school for this attitude.

The large size of the average hasidic family, seven to eight children per child-bearing-age household, has already been discussed. It is, of course, the result of the stringent injunction of the Jewish religion against any forms of birth control and abortion, except in cases of serious medical problems. As pointed out, the large hasidic family is crucial to the structure of the new Williamsburg. It is also central to the changing patterns of the family as it has evolved since the hasidic community decided to remain and build its unique life-style in sociocultural isolation from the influences of the outside world and its secular values and norms.

The resultant demographics of the hasidic community are as much a cause as a corollary of the powerful hasidic education system and other interrelated factors of the milieu and spirit of the young and middle-aged *hasidim* who have become the largest and increasingly most active element of the Williamsburg population. This is in marked contrast to the inverted pyramid model of the broader Jewish community. The attitude of the hasidic women in particular is different from that of the typical suburban Jewish women who are active in the movements for women's liberation, equality, self-realization, and self-fulfillment. Nor do they project the sentiment of the quintessential Jewish Mother who glories in the professional and social success of her children. Nor do the hasidic women follow the popular trend of limiting the number of their children, which has led to the well-known decline of the Jewish birthrate to 1.8 for the average household, far below zero population growth.

The education and molding of the attitude of the young of the hasidic community, especially the willingness of their teenager girls to marry early and have a large number of children, inevitably tie them to the kitchen and to the house for most of their married life, regardless of the pain and sacrifices involved. When questioned, they stress that they consciously choose these limits on their personal wants and interests, as a result of their education at home and at school. They emphasize the focus on these values in their background. They have been taught to find satisfaction in their home, in the raising of their children, and in their husbands' scholarship. They focus on faith, piety, and work for the collective rather than their own welfare, as one woman put it.

> I have already four lovely children and I hope to have more, just like my saintly mother, of blessed memory, who died too young to enjoy the *nahas* from her children and grandchildren because of her suffering in a concentration camp. My children make up for anything I might miss that other women enjoy. I worked for two years until my husband left the *kollel* and went to work. Some day, with the help of the Lord, eventually we will be able to live without straining and skimping on ourselves to give the children what they require. Thank God, we have what we need because we have higher values and goals than luxuries, going out, and attending the movies and eating out at fancy restaurants. Our *kehillah* has so many social affairs, banquets, luncheons, *melaveh nalkehs*, bazaars, and teas. They provide more than I would want of entertainment and leisure, with my limited time between taking care of the home, my husband,

and my children. We have a chance to dance all we want at *chassenehs*, weddings, in the right spirit and way. When my husband and I have a quiet evening, we like to discuss things. We plan, or just talk. That makes both of us feel close and happy, though he and I have to work hard.

There can be hardly a more vivid and thoughtful description of the ideal of the family life, of the husband and wife relationship, and their separate and shared involvement in the community's affairs. This woman has met and worked with other women and men who have different values and ways of entertainment and satisfaction. But, as she emphasized, she neither admires nor begrudges them their life-style. Her home is spotless, and she and her children are neatly dressed. Her husband has an old stationwagon he requires for his work. And occasionally, on free Sunday afternoons or on *Hol Hamoed*, when he does not work, like most Hungarian *hasidim*, he takes his family on trips to visit his wife's relatives who live in Monsey, New York and in Kiryas Joel, in Monroe, New York. They cannot afford a bungalow in the mountains yet; but if and when their business plans materialize, they hope to join the wife's sisters who live in Monsey, New York, but have a bungalow in a colony near the *yeshivah* camp which their oldest son will attend. "We have air-conditioning in our house, and my husband does not have to be alone during the week, like others who *valgern* themselves, who have to prepare their own food or eat out, which even in the summer cafeteria for husbands is not too cheap for a working man with a limited income."

The same woman is not ashamed to point out that she has taken advantage of the various opportunities for financial help and other relief on occasion when it was necessary. Most recently, she said, she was happy, after she gave birth to her youngest child, to be able to spend close to 2 weeks in the *Yeled Shaashuim* Rest Home for *Kimpetuerins*, the rest home for women after giving birth. It is a beautiful, comfortable place, the former mansion built for the Old Rebbe of Satmar before his death, where mothers and infants receive care until they are ready to go home. "I am fortunate to have several sisters and sisters-in-law living near enough to help and to take care of my children while I am away. But there are a number of groups in Williamsburg that send volunteers, women and school girls, to homes where the mothers are too weak or otherwise unable to take care of the home and the family."

She is also not embarrassed to report that though her husband makes a decent salary as a carpetlayer, she is happy to have the facilities of the well-staffed and well-equipped ODA Primary Health Center available when she or the children are ill or require medical or dental or other care.

Especially in the early years we couldn't possibly have afforded to go to regular doctors and specialists, the way they charge nowadays. And if it had not been for the WIC [Women, Infants and Children] Program of ODA on Heyward Street, I would have had it much harder to take care of the new additions to our family, while trying to meet all the other new costs that the birth of each new child, God bless them, brings. This aid is what these programs have been set up for, and there is no reason why we should not avail ourselves of them. We are not poor and don't want charity. We work hard for everything we own. But there are times and special situations when we, like everybody else, need a little help from the outside, since our family cannot help us financially, though we are all there whenever anyone of us needs something. My husband, like everyone in our *kehillah* here, gives much more than his due share of *tzedakah* and *hesed*, in charity projects, from packing food packages and delivering them every week to the homes of needy. We always have guests at our *Shabbos* table, so that our children will grow up knowing that *Hachnossath Orchim*, help feeding the poor and needy, is a must in our life as *ehrliche Yiden*, good Jews.

So, I don't feel bad at all to utilize some of the government programs that ODA and others make available to us, just like the working people in other ethnic communities. Some day, we hope, we won't even have to do this any more, with the help of the kind Lord.

This perceptive wife of a working man who wants to establish his own carpeting and tiling business when he can raise the necessary capital, expresses the views and values of the community that is doing all it can to cover most needs and problem areas of its people. The elderly and the young scholars get reductions in community-sponsored food stores and in tuition. As one of the school administrators pointed out when questioned about the length of the school day even for the young classes:

> You see, there is purpose behind it – not just a longer school day and more learning. All our students, poor and rich alike, from nursery age on, come here, eat a healthy and ample breakfast and good lunches. Many of our mothers have large households, and quite a few cannot afford as much as others. This way, having their children from 3½ years and up taken care of almost the whole day, except for the youngest classes, is a big help to them. Besides the health and nutritional aspects, our teachers are with the youngsters all the time. And the children learn much of proper conduct in the cafeteria and on the playground, or later on in the dormitory and in the summer camps, not only in the formal classes. In the informal give and take, in the washing of hands, in saying the *brachot*, the blessings, and *benshen*, saying grace, and all the other big and little experiences we make it more likely that they will grow up in the right spirit and the proper conduct. The camaraderie, the guidance of older, wiser fellow students, and under the watchful eyes of their *melamdim* – that is what we consider *hinuch*, effective education. It means as much, if not more than book learning in the classroom.

This school official's concern for the whole child, not just the student, is typical of the outlook of the whole community where there is no compartmentalization of care. The weekly *Der Yid* mirrors this total concern in the announcements that cover every area of life, from the hours of the Primary Health Center, even on the Sabbath and Jewish and secular holidays, to counseling centers, services, treatment facilities, and citywide services for the needy and ill. Yet, one must not overlook the fact that in these announcements there are also the indications of the financial, physical, and emotional or mental strains on the young couples who marry early, have children, and are not always able to cope with the consequences.

Though minute compared to the divorce and separation rates in contemporary society as a whole, separation and divorce do exist in the hasidic community, largely as a consequence of the strain and difficulties caused by early marriage and having large families. In *America's Jews in Transition* (1983) Chaim Waxman reports the rising divorce figures for the American Jewish community that have emerged in recent demographic studies. They point to a direct correlation with the degree of homogenization of the Jewish community into the surrounding suburban culture. Yet, as Waxman stresses, the Jewish separation and divorce rates remain far below the rates for American society in general, where one out of three marriages ends in divorce or separation. Figures for the American Jewish community remain around 5 percent in national and local demographic studies, as for example in the studies done by Gary Tobin in *The Jewish Communities of Washington, D.C., and Baltimore, Md.* in 1985/1986 (they are about 25% in 1994). As far as the Orthodox Jewish community is concerned, Waxman emphasizes that there are almost no exact data available. He mentions the statement of a guidance counselor in an Orthodox Jewish girls' school in Boro Park, quoted by this writer, who stated that at the end of the '70s there were twelve students out of one thousand whose parents were divorced.[2] Yet as recently as the '50s there was not a single case of divorce among the parents of the same school, which then had about two hundred girls in the elementary division.

The director of the Hasidic Rabbinical Organization and its court in Williamsburg indicated that while there was some increase in divorce and breakup of families in the late '70s and early '80s, the current divorce rate in the community lies below 1 percent. This figure, inaccurate as it may be, still indicates the extremely small proportion of divorces in a community in which close to 500 couples marry each year and remain in the neighborhood. He emphasized that the rabbinic court has a number of specialists who have much experience dealing with and guiding young couples whose married life is in trouble.

They, and a number of private groups, are actively involved in similar work of preventing problems before it is too late. The rabbinical court has been particularly effective in helping women who have serious problems to obtain a *get*, the divorce document, from their husbands, some of whom take advantage of the situation to extort large sums of money from their wives' families before they issue a *get*, so that the woman is free to marry again. People not only from Williamsburg, but from other Jewish communities occasionally turn to the hasidic courts because of their reputation for handling complicated cases effectively, as attested by a former Williamsburger, a rabbi who has a business in Williamsburg, though he has moved to Flatbush. He himself has acquired a reputation as a specialist in helping women in delicate situations in pending divorce cases. He praised the young and middle-aged rabbis on the hasidic court with whom he frequently collaborates in difficult divorce negotiations. He, too, confirms that the divorce rate in the Orthodox Jewish community is not higher than 1 percent.

Another young rabbi and businessman, a former Williamsburger, who volunteers his services to help cases of *agunot*, women who have difficulties obtaining the divorce document from husbands who have deserted them, assured this interviewer that the actual number of cases he has worked with is not higher than about one hundred. But, he stated, there are many more such cases of *agunot*, which unfortunately for the women and their children, are never resolved. When interviewed in 1989, a year after the initial conversation, he indicated that the number of divorces and separations is rising due to a growing me-attitude and a degree of bitterness he had not experienced before. But again, he, like the young rabbi/businessman and the head of the rabbinical court, asserts that the number of divorce cases in the hasidic community is much smaller than in the broader Jewish community because there is a more effective community spirit and more channels for official and unofficial help. They intervene and ease tensions and help resolve conflicts before they result in the breakup of the marriage.

One factor that warrants special mention and that contributes a great deal to the stability of the hasidic family, in contrast to other non-Jewish as well as Jewish communities, is the role played by grandparents and relatives in general. Elsewhere senior citizens have been relegated to nursing homes, senior citizens villages, and similar institutions, especially in the sunbelt states. In Miami, Florida alone over 100,000 elderly Jews from the New York area have settled over the past decade. Birthday cards, Mother's and Father's Day greetings, and occasional calls are all the contact these older people have with their children and grandchildren, who lack the warmth and benefits of a three-generational family.[3]

Such is not the case in Williamsburg's hasidic families, where grandparents remain living near or with their children, if at all possible. They are important because they strengthen the spirit and cohesiveness of the family by being with and giving and getting the love of children and grandchildren. This is what one *hasid* said when speaking of the newest addition to his already large family. "Our new baby has given my mother a new lease on life. She has taken her on as her own charge because she cries easily when not taken care of instantly, to the relief of my wife, who has her hands full attending to the needs of our two- and three-year-olds, especially when the older girls are away at school." Both grandfathers and grandmothers play a special role in the rearing and education of their grandchildren since most of the fathers are away from the home from morning until evening, studying and working, eking out a living for their large families. Except for Sabbath and holidays they have little time for intimate contact with their children, to attend to the daily needs of education and of the emotional and spiritual crises that require male authority and occasional intervention. Grandfathers, because of the special bond of love for their *einiklach*, can *farher*, listen to and review their grandchildren's homework and otherwise implement the teaching of the classroom in many subtle ways. *Bubbeh* and *Zeideh* are not distant figures, as in the Jewish and non-Jewish society in general. They are important links in the strong three-generational hasidic family and community. They do not only represent the ideal of present-day *hasidim*, but they can relate the past of the old-world *shtetl* life to their grandchildren who are native Americans and eager to learn more about it from this close personal source.

Another important characteristic of the hasidic family is the role of older siblings in the rearing of frequently much younger brothers and sisters. It is quite common to see older sisters attending to the needs of young children while their mothers and fathers are otherwise occupied. Girls as young as 8, 9, and 10 carry their baby brothers and sisters, pick them up when they cry and comfort them, feed them, and, wheel their baby carriages. This care weaves a bond of mutual trust and devotion among the children. This is particularly important when mothers have to divide their attention among several children getting them ready for school at a staggered schedule in the morning, and picking them up or awaiting the buses for their return. One young lady about to get married put it forcefully when she pointed out: "I am not afraid of having and caring for children. Since I was 5 I have helped my mother with the household chores and caring for the little ones from diapering and feeding them, to supervising and helping them in their studies. I give them the counsel of an older sister who has gone through the woes and worries of their daily life in school, at home, and in the street." Thus, playing big sister and little mother is a valuable part of the growing up experiences of girls in Williamsburg, more so than in other communities where teenagers are very much occupied by their own social life, hanging out with their school crowd and friends, both female and male. Many of these tensions are alien to hasidic girls who do not date. As one put it, "I don't know any boys, except my brothers, and they are away most of the time in the *yeshivah*." Brothers, too, play a role at home, but a much smaller one than the girls because of the brothers' long day in the *yeshivah*.

This is not to say that fathers do not play an important role in the personal guidance of their children, leaving it all to the mothers, siblings, and teachers. Perhaps one of the most striking scenes this writer witnessed was a conversation between a tall, middle-aged, heavy-set Williamsburger in full hasidic regalia and his preteenage daughter. As they stood close to each other in a corner of a large room, he looked straight into her eyes and talked to her earnestly, his body continuing the same shaking motion with which he studies and prays. Instead of chiding her after one of the usual tiffs that occur among teenage sisters, this father of ten girls and two boys took the time to speak with the tall, thin girl for what seemed like a long while. Finally, he kissed her on the head and returned to the *Gemara* he had been studying before he was roused by the argument between his daughters. Nowhere in his decades of experience as an educator has this writer seen a more intimate, effective tête-à-tête between a father and a young child.

Though this *hasid* has a limited secular education, and knows nothing of formal pedagogy and psychology, he displayed a great understanding of the needs of his children in a subsequent interview. He is one of the few who, as he explained it, for the well-being and education of his children left Williamsburg to live in a small suburban community established by one of the hasidic Rebbes. "Life is simpler, more genuine than in the city, even here in Williamsburg," he said. And he gladly travels every day an extra hour to and from work to afford his family this better atmosphere. The fact remains, though, that there is a closer bond between fathers and sons, as they share, on weekends at least, the special experiences of the hasidic setting, attending together the services and festive meals and celebrations in the synagogue and in the home of their Rebbe, and increasingly engaging in the intimacy of the study and discussion of Torah.

Thus, despite the established distance of authority and respect, and the pressures of large family life, the three-generational family dynamic is full of intimacy. It is emotionally as well as spiritually satisfying, fulfilling the needs of the old and of the young in the give and take of daily life and its challenges and crises.

Another major factor affecting the structure and dynamics of the hasidic family is the changing economic pattern and, related to it, the expanding role of hasidic women in business, as partially discussed earlier. As pointed out before, in spite of persistent poverty among at least 35 percent of the elderly, on the one hand, and, on the other, the young at the beginning of their careers, the general mood is optimistic in the hasidic community. Even during the recession that hit in the beginning of the '90s, there is evidence of growth in the formerly disintegrating local shopping area. The spirit of enterprise is revamping the Williamsburg scene. The younger generation of *hasidim* is entering and consolidating its place in the mainstream of American business. According to the head of the Satmar community, as many as 50 percent of the young prefer starting a career or a business venture than going into a trade. Their commercial and industrial enterprises have spread to major business and trade centers in Brooklyn, Long Island, Manhattan, and New Jersey. Their places of work may be found throughout Manhattan, not only on the Lower East Side, as was the case years ago. In their hasidic garb, they frequent concentrations of manufacturing and trade from Wall Street to the fur, textile, and garment districts and the diamond and jewelry center around 47th Street. They are as active in the real-estate markets of the Upper West Side and the Upper East Side of Manhattan, as in the industrial backlands of Long Island. This acceptance on the national and international scene has produced an attitude of optimism and self-reliance, despite their sociocultural isolation and patterns of conduct governed by their beliefs and strictly Orthodox laws and life-style. The crisis of the beginning '90s has put a damper on this expansion, as business in general has slowed down and funds gotten tighter. But with the end of the Gulf War *hasidim* in Williamsburg, like businessmen everywhere, hope for a gradual recovery and return of the general optimism in the American market.

This new spirit affects the attitude of the men and women, their mutual relationships, and their relationships to their children, who devote many years of their young lives to religious studies. They have little concern for their future outside of the *bet hamidrash*, the house of study, true to the ideals inculcated in them by their teachers and by the Rebbe. No longer does one find the self-deprecation and disparagement of the old-world garb and customs, or even the language of the parents and grandparents, most of whom were immigrants, that were rampant in the earlier phases of Jewish Williamsburg and in the other immigrant ghettos of New York, which had turned away many youngsters from the Orthodox beliefs and the traditional ways in which they had been reared.[4] The relative success and acceptance of *hasidim* in the world of commerce, trade, and industry has become a challenge to the young and a source of mutual respect in the family, a confirmation of their basic beliefs and values in the environment in which they are growing up. This spirit is expressed in the comment of a middle-aged hasidic businessman who, when he was challenged by some professionals with whom he was chatting in a synagogue outside of New York, stated with obvious pride: "Our *yunge Leit* have not gone to college, but many of them make out better than most of your academicians, professionals, and government employees here."

The point he was making was that though the younger *hasidim* have spent almost all of their school years on intensive religious studies, it has not impaired their ability to make their mark in business and earn a good living for their large families. His own daughter had just become engaged to a young scholar who was to spend additional years on advanced talmudic and rabbinic studies, supported by him and by his daughter, who had just accepted a job as a nursery teacher. "My daughter does not worry, and I am happy to support them as best as I can. For this I have been working so hard, to bring up my sons as Torah scholars, and to have my daughters marry young men who will spend years in the *kollel*, regardless of what they will do after they are leaving the *Bais Hamedrash*." This same confidence inspires his daughter and the other graduates of Beth Rachel high school and the other hasidic girls' schools. Their faith in the help of the kind Lord, as they keep stressing, is reinforced by the success of other young *hasidim* who are eventually able to support their families properly after they have learned a trade or some line of business, though it may mean years of struggle and doing with the bare minimum. One such young woman, who was working as secretary in a hasidic girls' school and was engaged to marry a promising young *yeshivah* student, put it squarely: "My grandmother in Hungary had to work all her life to support the family, so that her husband was able to devote his full time to his studies. Why shouldn't I be ready to struggle for a few years after I get married?"

This attitude of faith in the future acquired in the years of schooling and reinforced by the relative success of many of the middle-aged Williamsburg couples, remains as strong even years after marriage and struggle trying to make ends meet, as a number of young married women indicated when interviewed. Here is the comment of one of these young mothers still in her late twenties, who was walking with two of her children holding on to the baby carriage she was pushing up Lee Avenue, doing her shopping for the weekend. When questioned about the future she said: "No, I don't worry too much about the future. My sisters married scholars who are now in business. My husband is still learning in the *kollel*. He is as capable and bright as anyone else. As long as we and our children are healthy and we have what we need, we have *bitahon*, faith, in Divine Providence." When she saw me looking at her, as she was wiping her face and the sweat of her brow, breathing heavily from pushing the baby carriage made heavy by the bags of groceries and the hands of the toddlers, she continued, "No, I am not disillusioned, being bogged down trying to cope with my chores, here and at home. We young hasidic women are troupers. We are willing and able to do what it takes to work our way up by the sweat of our brows, as the Holy Bible says."

In the same basic spirit, if in an entirely different atmosphere, came the response of an elegantly dressed young woman, the daughter of a successful hasidic businessman who had worked up his trade from a small store owned by his father-in-law to a large one in the center of Boro Park's busiest shopping area. She had gotten married less than a year before to a young scholar and was obviously pregnant. When asked whether her husband was working, she replied:

> No, I wouldn't want him to work. He has a brilliant mind and is quite *geshickt*, handy. He can do anything around the house or here in the store when he comes occasionally during a few free hours, to help my father. Some day, when he is good and ready, he will enter my father's business, just like my father came into my grandfather's business; thank God, he has done quite well, even though he wears his hasidic clothes all the time. His beard and *peyot* have not held him back and he holds his own with the big businessmen and firms with whom he is dealing.

Unlike the other young married woman from Williamsburg, who dressed simply, this young woman wore fine jewelry and had a large, well-furnished apartment in a house owned by her grandfather. Obviously her married life is a happy and uncomplicated one, and she looks confidently into the future. "My father has twenty-four people working for him here in the store, in the warehouse, and in his office. My husband is as smart as any of them. So, why worry? We have *bitahon*, trust in the Lord's help, come what may."

Both the less and more financially secure young married women expressed the same spirit of faith in the future, although their husbands are currently pursuing their rabbinic studies in a *kollel*.

This optimistic outlook, backed by the opportunities in business and trade, has a beneficial impact not only on the husband and wife, but also on their parents and children. Parents no longer have an inferiority complex, as did many of the immigrant parents of pre-World-War-II generation Williamsburg. Their children attended college, spoke perfect English, and associated with nonreligious or non-Jewish fellow students and coworkers with negative consequences for their family life and for the maintenance of their religious beliefs and life-style. In contrast is the hasidic mother-in-law who expressed her satisfaction that her sons-in-law are Torah scholars who are now engaged in business: "They do very well in business. They read the *New York Times* and communicate well with their customers and their suppliers, though they have not spent more than a year on their secular high school studies." This explains the attitude of her youngest son, a 14-year-old boy, when he was asked whether it would be good for him to finish his secular high-school studies instead of spending all his time on intensive religious learning in a small *yeshivah* for gifted students. Indignantly, he rejected the very idea. "*Why?*" he asked. "My brother and brothers-in-law are doing fine without having gone to English after their *bar mitzvah*. Why should I waste time instead of learning Torah as much as I can. This is what I love doing and want to give my whole life to, just like my father." Obviously, the business success of his family reinforces his determination to follow in the footsteps of his father, who was always struggling to make a living for his family as a teacher and as a *dayan*, having eleven children and several *kollel* couples to support before they left to enter business.

Part of this positive outlook toward the future is the changing role of women and their participation in the world of business in Williamsburg, on the local, national, and even the international scene. As we have seen, hasidic women are not ashamed of their modest hasidic clothes, of keeping their hair covered all the time, and of the limitations imposed on their participation in some of the social activities that are part and parcel of the general world of business. Although the number of hasidic women going to work to help meet the heavy burden of their family budget is declining, according to the head of the Satmar community, more women are engaged in running local stores for their husbands, themselves, or other people. Of the small sample of hasidic women surveyed. 12 percent work with their husbands in business or have established a business of their own.

At least a quarter of the shops and stores that advertise regularly in *Der Yid* are run or owned by women. Most of these stores sell infants' or children's clothes, wigs, or jewelry, or are boutiques for women's garments and underwear. Quite a few of these are located in basements or in stoop apartments of brownstone houses. Two of these, which have already been mentioned, are typical of the spirit of enterprise among hasidic women. One runs a children's clothes shop in the basement of her house, which was mentioned in the *New York Times Children's Wear* spring section as the only place in the U.S. where one can find an exclusive line of expensive boys' suits from France and England. A second hasidic woman owns and runs a large wholesale and retail store that sells lamps, chandeliers, and imported crystal out of a factory loft on the outskirts of Williamsburg. She employs a number of relatives and her loft is a favorite with young engaged or newly married hasidic couples when they are about to furnish their new homes.

Other women have started stores that import linens from Ireland, England, or China. Several of them travel as far as Korea and other Far East or European countries. Obviously, the business acumen of these women contributes much to improve the level of their lives.

There are now different groups and institutions that help women take care of preschool children and working women have access to helpers whom they can hire to handle the household chores while they are away from home. It is a psychological as well as a financial boost to the family life and budget if they can supplement their husbands' often limited income. It gives them satisfaction and a measure of social recognition. At the same time it indicates that there is no particular stigma attached to women going to work, as long as they abide by the religious restrictions on their conduct and interaction with the outside world. Only one of the 175 hasidic women interviewed complained that an increasing number of younger women are leaving their children to the care of others, which has an unfortunate impact on their homes and the emotional well-being of the family. Most men and women, however, believe that working women do not carry the spirit of the outside world into their homes. It seems to be generally felt these women are not at all affected by the life-style of others because of the strength of their convictions, and because most of them are perfectly satisfied with their home and marital life. One of the hasidic women who works as a computer programmer expressed this positive outlook colorfully when she was questioned about the impact of her work on her personal life. She said:

> I work for a computer information programming company that is owned by Orthodox young men who allow me to dress and act the way a hasidic woman has been trained to conduct herself. I can arrange my hours of work to suit my household chores and responsibilities toward my children, all of whom are of school age and away most of the day in *heder*. Thus I have no guilt feelings about neglecting my kids or my husband, who is a *yeshivah* teacher, who handles the 6:00 to 2:00 P.M. shift of his class. He is at home early and does not mind preparing his lunch and taking care of the younger boys, who must be picked up from the bus, until I come home in plenty of time to prepare supper and handle all the other wifely duties.
>
> "Between us we give our children what I consider excellent role models as responsible and good hasidic parents who invest all their strength and love in raising them properly. My husband is a Torah scholar and devotes all his time to the study and spreading of the knowledge. I want our boys to grow up like him and our girls to seek out husbands who are *talmidei hachomim*, talmudic scholars, though it means doing with less of comforts and luxuries that others can afford. I never went to work while our children were still small. And, I assure you, we did not have an easy time making ends meet, until I was able to go back to my computer job that pays me decently and affords us a much-needed larger apartment equipped with the furnishings and appliances that make life easier for women, such as a good washer and dryer, a freezer, and similar up-to-date equipment. I find fulfillment and satisfaction in my home, not like some of the women I met when I trained for my work and others on the job who crave expensive luxuries, jewelry, and a career that will give them a feeling of equality and independence. No, that is not for me! *I am proud to be a hasidishe housewife and good mother!*

One other aspect of the changing role of the women in the new Williamsburg is their increasing involvement in the expanding network of community organizations and institutions. They are active in formal and informal welfare projects and similar activities discussed in detail in succeeding chapters of this study. They participate in the support groups and activities that make the problems of large families, and of the still rampant poverty, illness, and physical and emotional stress in the hasidic community more bearable.

Time and again the people of Williamsburg stress the charity work, the *tzedakah vehesed* projects, done in the neighborhood to a degree unmatched anywhere else. Many of these programs and projects have been copied in other Jewish communities and are of enormous benefit. Hasidic married women and single girls, from the widow of the Old Rebbe of Satmar, who since their settlement in Williamsburg in 1947 has carried on the extraordinary charity and support work of her illustrious husband and who continues her special projects actively, to the wife of the present Rebbe of Satmar, find a niche and assume a major role in sharing the burdens of local community life. In many cases, whole families are involved and work together, especially the financially secure. They choose some particular challenge and invest time, money, and personal efforts.

Such is the case of the two women who almost singlehandedly organized the much acclaimed *Bikkur Cholim* projects. One organized the daily visit program to hospitals all over New York, with fleets of buses, vans, and stationwagons donated by another woman and her family. The other converted the lower half of her large house into elaborate kitchen facilities where teams of volunteer women prepare fresh food daily for many hundreds of religious and also some less religious patients; the kosher food is delivered daily by a fleet of vans equipped to keep the food hot or refrigerated. There are a number of other such valuable welfare and social service programs, which have been copied in other communities, such as Boro Park, Flatbush, Monsey, and other urban and suburban neighborhoods. Some of the women who have established and continue to direct these projects have gained a measure of public recognition and appreciation, with beneficial impact on their families. They inspire others to follow suit, to the benefit of their own and the broader community. A major part of these activities is not new. They are the standard fund-raising programs of Jewish institutions, such as bazaars, luncheons, teas, auctions, and parlor meetings in private homes. One prominent school administrator put it bluntly:

> To my knowledge, there is just no Jewish neighborhood where more *tzedakah* and *hesed* work is done than here in Williamsburg. This is largely to the credit of capable women who throw themselves wholeheartedly into the work where and whenever it is necessary. They are, and I say this without reservation, a major factor of the success and growth of our own and other large and small institutions. They set an example for their whole family. Sometimes they are the initiators, and their husbands and children lend a helping hand, particularly in the running of the financial phases; or they give their full support to projects in which their husbands or friends are involved.

As this school official pointed out, the active role of the hasidic women in the community networks of institutions and organizational programs does not detract from their traditional role as homemakers. It serves to strengthen their own position and with it that of their entire family. It gives them status without the negative toll that the families of Jewish and non-Jewish women pay for their drive to play an equal role in public life. Whereas some look down upon the "old ladies' " luncheons and teas, the hasidic women don't care. They know that they are giving valuable help to the limited fund-raising efforts of the people in charge of the social welfare programs in the community. Thus, their activism is perpetuating, not deviating from, the traditional role of the Jewish matriarchs who have always played this supporting role in Jewish history.

One increasingly serious problem, which has been vexing the broader American Jewish community, but which has been successfully skirted by the hasidic community because of its sociocultural isolation, is that of intermarriage. Once a rare phenomenon, it has increasingly loomed on the horizon of the Jewish future in proportion to the degree of the entrance of Jewish people into the wide open circles of contemporary American society, without the restrictions that had held them to the limited and limiting setting of the Jewish ghetto.

The fear of socialization and intermarriage may have been one of the reasons why the hasidic community of Williamsburg has from the very outset chosen to focus on sociocultural isolation, which keeps the traditional family pure. *Yichus*, the family background of prospective spouses, is a major concern of hasidic parents of children of marriageable age. The college scene, where most young men and women of different faiths socialize without the usual barriers, is of little concern to the hasidic community because hardly anyone ever goes to college, except for a few individuals who for professional reasons must take courses on college campuses, like those for real-estate or financial management, and insurance license requirements. Wearing the hasidic garb is a further barrier that discourages socialization even for those who work with men and women of different faiths outside the hasidic community. This is also the effect of the strict adherence of *hasidim* to the religious laws and customs that prevent participation in the social phase of American business, such as shared lunches and dinners, and similar forms of entertainment that are part and parcel of commercial success.

Another more complex problem that has largely been avoided by the Hungarian-type hasidic communities such as Satmar is that of *baalei teshuvah*, the attraction of nonreligious men and women to the Orthodox life-style. Both in the U.S. and Israel the number of *baalei teshuvah* has increased dramatically, especially in the '70s and '80s, partially as an outgrowth of the '60s movements, such as interest in religious, national, and ethnic pride, especially after the Six Day War. Some major hasidic movements, such as Lubavitch, have put major efforts in attracting and educating nonreligious people. Even in the most Orthodox communities, the number of *baalei teshuvah* has been growing steadily, and special schools and whole communities of these newly, and often intensely, religious young men and women have become a major factor in the increase of religious life in Israel and America. Not so in the hasidic community of Williamsburg, which does not join in the outreach movement that has become so popular even in the most Orthodox circles, and in the *yeshivot*, the centers of Jewish education in the contemporary Orthodox Jewish world. It is only now in the beginning of the '90s, after the floodgates of Russian Jewish emigration have been opened releasing large numbers of Russian Jews who lack even the most basic knowledge of things Jewish, that special efforts have been made in Williamsburg as well as in Israel and in the other hasidic centers to establish special learning opportunities for the new Russian immigrants.

However, upon the request of the Old Rebbe of Satmar, major efforts were initiated by the Satmar community to aid the escape and resettlement of large numbers of Jews from countries of persecution such as Iran and the U.S.S.R. through *Rav Tov*, its international rescue and relief organization. It set up temporary and permanent centers, schools, and resettlement centers in such crucial places of transit as Vienna and in Italy, Israel, and the U.S., which have literally helped thousands of Iranian Jews, many of whom have spent considerable time in the newly organized *yeshivot* to learn more about their Jewish heritage, to acquire new skills to be able to settle in America or in Israel. Similarly, even greater efforts are invested in the spiritual, as well as the technical, rescue and training centers for the large masses of Russian Jews now pouring out of Russia daily.

But, in general, neither Satmar nor most other Hungarian hasidic movements engage in the efforts that focus on outreach to nonreligious Jews in this country and elsewhere. As pointed out before, the reason is fear that the close contact and association may impair the purity of the family, in view of the fact that there are frequently serious questions about the religious marriage of the parents, and similar problems of *yichus*, the family background, of the *baalei teshuvah*. Hence, the hasidic community rather prefers to lavish its most serious efforts and attention on the education of its young and on the creation of a small, controlled environment to safeguard the wholeness and wholesomeness of its future families.

It is small wonder, then, that most of the men and women interviewed expressed their loyalty and readiness to perpetuate the hasidic life-style, as well as their hasidic values and intellectual heritage in their own lives, preferably in Williamsburg. They also anticipate that their children will want to remain there, close to the Rebbe and to the schools and *yeshivot* that have educated them. One woman, questioned about her opinion of the future of Hasidic Williamsburg, spoke for most when she said: "I love Williamsburg, . . . and young women will continue to live here, just like their mothers, because this is the life we have been taught to love and perpetuate in our and our childrens' future." A second housewife, a member of the small sample of hasidic women surveyed, said:

> I would not want to live any place else. All my brothers and sisters, except one who works and lives in Kiryas Joel, reside here, not far from me. We love and help each other all the time. Our children go to the same *heder*, or girls' school, to which my husband and I went when we were young. What else do I want, my family, my children, the Holy Rebbe, and our schools and *shuls*. All I hope is that when our boys and girls grow up they will want to remain here, too, or wherever our Rebbe will choose to establish his community, until the Coming of the *Moshiah* when all will go up to Eretz Yisrael.

Another perceptive respondent wrote in answer to a question in the questionnaire: "My family and I enjoy living here where the stores cater to what we *hasidim* need." A woman who is a bit more critical, wrote:

> Every place has its pros and cons. Williamsburg is a beautiful *hasidishe* neighborhood. The *tzedakah* and *hesed*, the welfare and charity work, done here cannot be imagined. I doubt whether there is a second neighborhood that can even come close to what men, women, and youngsters do, how they spend money, time, and their best efforts to help others in need, or to support the community and its activities. But there is now too much emphasis on fashion, almost like in Boro Park. Everyone is trying to outshine the others with their clothes, their homes and cars, though it is a far cry from what is the standard of luxuries in Flatbush, in Monsey, and in other richer places.

On the other hand there are the opinions of women like the one who responded: "The trend is toward more and more *frumkeit*, piety. The young women, nowadays, have a much better education than in Hungary. And that is showing. It is all a matter of a good *hinuch*, education. We can look forward to a still better community, as the younger men and women are taking over." Similar optimistic viewpoints were expressed by the majority of the men and women who were interviewed, both in the oral and in the written responses to the questionnaires.

SUMMARY

The discussion of the changing family structure in Hasidic Williamsburg confirms the description of the last phase of the changes in my previous report (1961). There it had been pointed out that the massive influx of Hungarian *hasidim* meant a strong return to the traditional family, which had been seriously weakened by the acculturation of the immigrant parents of pre-World War II and the blending of their young into the mainstream of American life. As Louis Wirth predicted in *The Ghetto* (1928): "The extent to which the solidarity of the family has been affected by modern life has the community been weakened and the allegiance to old heritage been periled" (p. 37).

What started gradually in the '50s has become a strong trend, systematically developed and constantly reinforced by the effective sociocultural isolation and the intensive educational system for boys and girls established by the Rebbe of Satmar and the other heads of the hasidic community.

In spite of serious crises and obstacles, the new Williamsburg evolved because of the loyalty of its members to their Rebbe and to the sociocultural values that shape the vibrant community life. At the end of the '80s, it could take pride in the fact that there is *no generation gap* in its population. A major factor of this impressive achievement is the strength of the traditional family as the most effective bulwark against penetration by the negative forces that have weakened the American Jewish community and Jewish communities throughout the world.

Besides the loyalty to the Rebbe and to the hasidic life-style, the intense religious and cultural climate weaves a strong bond between husbands and wives, between parents and children, teachers and students, and between fellow scholars. As a result, young couples about to marry prefer to remain in the neighborhood, instead of moving to Orthodox Jewish communities with better facilities and services, like the young in other neighborhoods. This has led to the development and constant reinforcement of the unique three-generational hasidic community in Williamsburg.

Other effective factors of the changes in the family structure and dynamics are the large size of the average family, and the pattern of early marriage, in spite of occasional problems it causes in a relatively small percentage of the hasidic population. Equally crucial for the strength and cohesiveness of the family is the educational system for boys and girls that molds the emotional, spiritual, and intellectual growth of the young from childhood until marriage and beyond. Psychologically, the economic situation's improvement has meant more than bringing a measure of greater comfort and better living conditions to all but the most indigent families of Williamsburg. The commercial success and acceptance of hasidic entrepreneurs in American business life, in spite of their limited secular education and hasidic life-style, reinforces the ideals and values upon which the traditional family is structured. Nor has it hurt the strength of the intergenerational relations that a growing number of hasidic women have entered business and trade without yielding an iota of their strict adherence to the religious laws of the ultra-Orthodox life-style even though it limits their participation in the social life that is part and parcel of American business mores. Thus both fathers and mothers remain strong role models for their children and for their intense concentration on their religious education.

Last but not least, the discussion pointed to the important role of grandparents who continue to be part of the intimate family dynamics, fostering the intergenerational bonds of love and devotion to the hasidic ideals.

Though rejecting the popular outreach efforts of the broader Orthodox Jewish community, the hasidic community continues to grow and expand by concentrating on their young as the key to a strong family and to the future of Hasidism in this country and elsewhere.

The following portrayal of Rav, an American hasidic family whose younger members were born in the United States of America, serves to illustrate major aspects of this discussion on the structure and dynamics of the hasidic family life in the new Williamsburg and other hasidic communities.

RAV: THE CASE HISTORY OF AN AMERICAN HASIDIC FAMILY

The patriarch of the Rav family was a disciple and devoted *hasid* of Rabbi Yoel Teitelbaum, the late Rebbe of Satmar. He had received his talmudic and rabbinic training at the *yeshivah* of Satmar for more than 6 years, when he was chosen to head the congregation of a town in Hungary. A survivor of Auschwitz, where he lost his first wife and five children in the concentration camp, he remarried and arrived in the U.S. in 1950 with his second wife and three of his nine children. At the request of the Rebbe of Satmar, at whose table he spent the first Sabbath in Williamsburg, he settled in a city near New York, to form his own congregation around the nucleus of a few Hasidim. In the 40 years since then, he has become a major figure in the Orthodox Jewish life of the city. Yet, at all times he remained close to the *"Heiliger Rebbe,"* as he continues to call the Old Rebbe of Satmar, and after his death, to his successor, Rabbi Moshe Teitelbaum. His four sons received their major education at the Satmar *yeshivah* in Williamsburg, while his five girls remained at home and attended the local elementary and high school of Bais Yaakov. The four sons married girls from hasidic families in Williamsburg, and continued their intensive talmudic and rabbinic studies at the *kollel* for a period ranging from 3 to 8 years, supported by their father and partially by the families of their wives. They were doing with the bare minimum, living in cramped quarters, as their children were born. They were satisfied and happily blended into the setting and life-style of hasidic Williamsburg as loyal followers of the Rebbe of Satmar.

Similarly, the five daughters of Rav married young hasidic scholars from the advanced level of the Satmar *yeshivah*, all of them intent upon continuing their rabbinic studies at the *kollel*. Like their brothers, the daughters of the Rav were happy to set up their homes in Williamsburg under bare minimum standards, supported by their father, while the husbands spent all their time on talmudic and rabbinic research. All of the Rav's children married around the age of 18 or soon afterward. By the end of the '80s, they had presented their father with close to one hundred grandchildren, or 8.1 per family. The older ones, now in their forties, have between five and twelve children. The oldest of the granddaughters and the oldest of the grandsons presented their beloved *Zeideh* with eighteen great-grandchildren. The oldest grandsons, too, are young *kollel* scholars. They are married to women from hasidic families, and have already made a name for themselves as superior talmudic students, just like their fathers.

All the grandchildren of school age attend hasidic schools for boys and girls and are grooming themselves to be serious students, while enjoying the life of hasidic youngsters to the fullest. Thus they are giving their *Zeideh* much *nahas*, joy. They love and admire him more than anyone else, except for the *"Heiliger* Rebbe." They visit him whenever possible, and are very close to the stepmother of their father or mother, since the wife of the Rav died a few years ago, while her children were still in their teens, from an illness contracted during the years of suffering in the concentration camp. They call the stepmother *Bubbeh*, and she treats her husband's grandchildren as if they were her own. Whenever they spend a Sabbath with the Rav, they look forward to showing their knowledge and prowess as young Torah students, when he *farhers* them, gives them a test. The older granddaughters, even after they are married, correspond with their beloved *Zeideh*. Their letters are written in beautiful Yiddish and are the pride of the Rav. In fact, all the grandchildren speak Yiddish with the same unmistakable Hungarian accent as their grandfather and most of the residents of Williamsburg. Though they are quite proficient in English, they speak exclusively Yiddish at home and amongst themselves.

All nine children of the Rav lived in Williamsburg while the men studied in the *kollel* for years. Five are still residing there, and by their testimony, they have no intention of leaving it, their Rebbe, or the hasidic life of the neighborhood, which they have come to love. Four, two sons and two daughters, moved to other hasidic communities – Boro Park, Kiryas Joel, and Monsey, a relatively new hasidic center in upstate New York.

The second oldest daughter of the Rav was first to move to Boro Park, after she married one of the outstanding scholars of the Klausenburg *yeshivah*. Her husband spent years at the *kollel*, until he accepted a job teaching the highest class at *Chush*, the school for hasidic boys with learning disabilities. He takes particular pride in his record of having developed a number of his students to a point at which they were able to be mainstreamed to a regular *yeshivah*, and enter into classes with students about their age. Eventually, the son-in-law of the Rav was chosen to head the religious studies division of *Chush,* where his competent work with the staff and the students have earned him a reputation as a most devoted and gifted educator. His oldest sons have grown up to be superior Torah students themselves. The oldest son, gifted with a phenomenal memory as well as industriousness, spent years on advanced study in Israel at Kiryas Zantz, the Community of Zantz, built by the Klausenburger Rebbe. He returned to become the star pupil of another Hungarian *yeshivah.* At the age of 18 he married the daughter of a noted hasidic rabbi and scholar. Since then he is a member of one of the most prestigious *kollels* at which the most gifted of young hasidic scholars study, paid a considerably higher fellowship than the small stipend paid at most *kollels,* so that they can grow without worry to become future leaders of the hasidic world of scholarship. Recently, the second son, following in his brother's footsteps, married at the age of 18 the daughter of a prominent hasidic scholar from Montreal, Canada, who had been the Rav's study companion in Satmar. He is now pursuing his advanced talmudic studies at the Satmar *kollel* in Montreal.

Another daughter of the Rav married the son of a prominent nonhasidic rabbi and scholar, who has become a *hasid* and now directs a *Talmud Torah* of one of the major hasidic movements in Monsey. Like all her sisters, this daughter of the Rav attended Bais Yaakov high school in her home town, and is a gifted writer and speaker who is frequently called on to address women's groups. She contributes articles and stories to a hasidic women's magazine, while handling the office of her husband's school. Still in her thirties she has seven children, yet devotes much of her time to the administration and planning of a new school building for the hasidic *Talmud Torah.*

Equally gifted and known as an excellent speaker is her youngest brother, a superior talmudic scholar and educator. He was one of the outstanding students of the Satmar *yeshivah* when he was chosen by a prominent Williamsburg busi- nessman for his bright daughter, who had been his assistant in running his thriving business. The father-in-law bought the young couple a comfortable, large home in Kiryas Joel, where the young scholar eventually established his own *shtiebel,* a hasidic congregation, in the outskirts of Kiryas Joel. After years at the Satmar *kollel,* this son of the Rav was chosen to teach the highest class of the Beth Medrash division of Satmar in Kiryas Joel, which is growing by leaps and bounds. He now heads the entire division, which meanwhile has built its own building, after years of learning in a large study hall on the upper floor of the magnificent synagogue of Satmar on a high hill, in the very center of the hasidic new town. Frequently he is called on not only to deliver scholarly discourses, but also to address large meetings for a broader public as one of the renowned speakers of Kiryas Joel. Though still in their midthirties, his wife and he have eight children, who frequently visit their grandfather and give him much joy by their knowledge and industriousness. Recently he was chosen to head a new branch of the Satmar *yeshivah* in Monsey.

The most interesting case of the four children of the Rav, who left Williamsburg after years of study at a *yeshivah* and *kollel,* is that of his second son. Like his brothers he married the daughter of a prominent hasidic family from the Satmar community. He continued to live there in small, cramped quarters until the ninth of his eleven children was born. After years at the *kollel* he had taken a job working for a medical services company, managing its warehouse. When a group of his former fellow *kollel* scholars decided to establish a hasidic settlement adjoining a hasidic *yeshivah* center in upstate New York, the second son of the Rav joined them, though he and his family had become very much part of the life in Williamsburg. When interviewed, he said:

> Here I live in a large, spacious home for not much more than what I had to pay for an inadequate, cramped apartment, with little prospect of ever being able to afford a large one, if it became available. Here my children have a garden, fresh air, and a group of playmates their own ages of the same background. Most important of all, I am happy to move to a simpler life-style than that of Williamsburg. Though not quite like that of Boro Park, there was too much emphasis on clothes and other luxuries as people became more successful. I don't want my children to grow up in this competition.

The move to the suburb of New York meant a great deal of inconvenience for this son of the Rav and for his older children. Before going to work he had to deliver his oldest daughter to Beth Rachel high school in Williamsburg; and his second oldest daughter had to stay during the week at the home of her uncle, while going to school in Beth Rachel of Kiryas Joel, helping her aunt with the children. The other children were attending the *yeshivah* and girls' school of Nitra, a neighboring hasidic settlement, the earliest of the hasidic exurban townships; and the youngest are attending the new *heder* school of the settlement which he had helped establish.

Meanwhile, this son of the Rav took over a small crafts shop in the outskirts of Williamsburg, when the expenses for the upkeep of his large household required more income than the warehouse job could provide. Without having any technical training or knowledge, by sheer hard work and determination, as he stressed, he was able to successfully work up and expand the trade of his shop and to install state of the art machinery and technology that enabled him to move into new lines of production. Soon he was able to employ his two oldest daughters, when they graduated Beth Rachel, instead of having to send them out into the world for work where, as he put it, they would be exposed to all kinds of negative influences. It did not take long, however, before the two young women became engaged to promising scholars from the Satmar *yeshivah*. One settled in Kiryas Joel, where her husband attends the Satmar *kollel*. The second married a brilliant scholar from Israel, who now studies at a *kollel* in Jerusalem. Both daughters have given birth to children, though they are barely 20, and the third, who has proven herself to be an excellent teacher, has become engaged to another outstanding young *yeshivah* scholar who with the help of his father-in-law hopes to spend years in a *kollel*. The increased burden of having to help support the three households of his daughters induced the second son of the Rav to look for new sources of income. Eventually he sold his crafts shop, and he is now concentrating on expanding a new line of computer software.

The oldest son of the Rav, who had been the first to leave his parents' home and attend the Satmar *yeshivah* in Williamsburg, had set the pattern by marrying a young woman from a prominent hasidic Williamsburg family and spending long years on study at the Satmar *kollel*. Eventually he was chosen to teach a class in the middle division of Torah V'Yiroh, the Satmar *Talmud Torah* in Williamsburg. After a few years he was selected to head the entire division of twelve classes, and is considered one of the outstanding talmudic scholars and educators of the community. In the past few years he has married off three of his ten children to bright young *yeshivah* students who are now attending a *kollel*, while he and their wives are helping to supplement the small stipends that the *kollel* provides for their advanced scholars after a year of proving their competence.

A third son of the Rav, after years of intensive study at the Satmar *kollel*, taught a high class at *Chush*, the school for hasidic youngsters with serious learning disabilities. His enthusiasm and his skill in motivating his students and helping them overcome their handicaps were instrumental in building his reputation as a foremost educator. While still a relatively young man, with a family of sixteen children, he was chosen to head the high-school division of the oldest of the hasidic *yeshivot* of Williamsburg. Though it had lost some of its prominence and popularity after the arrival of the Rebbe of Satmar and the establishment of his educational systems for boys and girls, it is still a major institution, and is again attracting older students as a result of the reputation and strong efforts of the son of the Rav to reinvigorate the higher division of the *yeshivah*.

The oldest son-in-law of the Rav, after years of study at a *kollel*, was the first of the family to learn a trade and establish his own business in the industrial area north of the Jewish Triangle of Williamsburg. Until her recent untimely death, his wife, the oldest daughter of the Rav, had helped him in his growing business by taking care of the bookkeeping. He employs a number of *hasidim* in his business, which he shares with his brother. After graduation from Beth Rachel High School, his oldest daughter taught nursery in the second largest hasidic *yeshivah* system of the Rebbe of Pappa. Soon she married a serious young scholar and, as she put it, she is ready to work for years so that her husband can study to become a *talmid hachom*. Similarly, a son of the oldest son-in-law of the Rav married the sister of his aunt, and is now studying at the Satmar *kollel* in Kiryas Joel.

The second son-in-law of the Rav spent years at the *kollel* of the Klausenburger *yeshivah*. Eventually, while continuing to live in Williamsburg, he left the *kollel* to head a hasidic *Talmud Torah* in Boro Park. After a few years he took over a small business on the Lower East Side. By industry and hard work he was able to expand its trade and develop a wholesale business of children's clothes. He imports better clothes, and has begun to attend national trade shows and deal with large national store chains. Though he has not studied secular subjects since shortly after his bar mitzvah, he says he has no difficulty dealing with his suppliers and customers. Both he and his wife man their booths at the trade exhibitions in their customary traditional hasidic garb. When questioned about their ability to do business in their traditional outfits, he said: "If you have good merchandise, are fair, and competitive, people will overlook the accent and the hasidic clothes. We are doing much better at the exhibitions than we expected when we first started out. Our merchandise is now sold in some of the prominent department stores in the country." Though the recession has hit his business, like other companies in his field, he is optimistic that things "are beginning to look up."

The husband of the youngest daughter of the Rav is the scion of a family of hasidic scholars. After years in the *kollel*, he is now managing the warehouse of a large photo supplies company, and still makes time, after his return from work, to spend hours in the evening on his religious studies. He and his wife are in their midthirties and have five children and are expecting a sixth. They live simply, but are quite satisfied with their ability to cope. The woman and her children are always well dressed. Their children are students in the Satmar schools. The oldest boy is named Yoel, like almost half the students in his class who were born shortly after the death of the Old Rebbe of Satmar. They love Williamsburg and its life-style and feel privileged to carry on the tradition of the Rav, as loyal *hasidim* of the Rebbe of Satmar and the community he has built for them.

Thus, following the pattern outlined in the preceding discussion of the hasidic family, more than half of the Rav's children are devoting their life to the study and teaching of Torah and *Hasidut*. The others entered some trade or line of business. They have blended successfully into the mainstream of American business, in spite of their scholarly background and hasidic appearance and conduct.

All five daughters of the Rav married scholars, as did their daughters when they were of marriageable age. They are taking an active part in the community affairs of Williamsburg, or in those areas where they have moved, in spite of their large families. They are happy and satisfied with the hasidic education of their children in Williamsburg or in the exurban hasidic communities where they reside. They are bringing up their children the way they were reared. They remain loyal followers of the Rebbe of Satmar, or of the Klausenburger Rebbe, like their parents.

There is no question in the mind of the grandsons and granddaughters that they will continue to live according to the life-style and spirit that their beloved *Zeideh* has transmitted to their parents, and which they absorb in their daily studies in the hasidic schools. The girls marry young scholars who will continue their talmudic and rabbinic studies at a *kollel* after marriage, although it means years of sacrifice and doing with little of what the average bride in the Jewish and non-Jewish community expects. They want large families like their mothers and grandmothers, and hope to bring their children up to become Torah students and hasidic Jews. The boys reject any suggestion that they continue their secular studies after *bar mitzvah*. And the thought of perhaps attending college like the youngsters even of the nonhasidic Orthodox communities is alien to them. One 12-year-old grandson of the Rav, when asked whether he would want to study mathematics at a college since he likes arithmetic best of all his secular studies, said emphatically, shaking his head and long *peyot*: "Me going to college!?! I don't want to be among *apicursim* (nonbelievers). I have *bitahon*, faith, that the *Oibershter*, the Lord, will help me without my going to college, just like my father, my uncles, and my *Zeideh*!"

The Rav family is a close-knit hasidic family whose three generations share the same values and life-style, whether they live in Williamsburg itself, or in Kiryas Joel, or other hasidic communities. They have become integrated into the very fabric of the religious, social, and economic life, and educate their children so that they too will be. Each in his own way contributes to the community, as the Rebbe of Satmar told the Rav at a family *smihah* celebration. "Your children are a real *koah*, a source of strength, and contribute much to our *yeshivah* and to our *kehillah*."

When interviewed, the Rav said humbly, with joy and obvious satisfaction:

Some day, over 120, or when the *Moshiah* comes, I will be able to introduce my children and grandchildren to my parents and grandparents. Though they have grown up here in America, I won't have to be ashamed of any of them. Their *frumkeit*, their piety, their love and devotion to *Torah* and *Hasidut* can match those of the generation among whom I grew up – something I never thought possible when I came to this land. And for much of this I have to thank the *Heiliger* Rebbe and what he has built up in Williamsburg. With the help of the Lord, my children and grandchildren will continue to live and perpetuate what I have tried to implant in them since their earliest youth.

5

Social Structure and Community Leadership

> Social status is accorded in direct proportion to one's scrupulous conformity to Hasidic values.
>
> Solomon Poll, *The Hasidic Community of Williamsburg*

In my 1961 study I emphasized that the Jewish Community of Williamsburg was not functioning in a social vacuum. Its values and life-style were influenced by those of the urban environment of twentieth-century America. The emphasis on social success and on economic and social advancement resulted in a devaluation of the rabbinic authorities and of Torah scholarship, similar to the de facto devaluation of the church and the clergy in Middle America, though officially they were treated deferentially.[1] The cultural assimilation of Jewish immigrants and of their children and the acquisition of higher income and the tokens of higher social status continued to affect the social stratification of the Jewish community of Williamsburg even after World War II, as it did in most other Orthodox and non-Orthodox Jewish communities. But the steady arrival of Orthodox newcomers, the refugees from Nazi persecution, and the survivors from the concentration and DP camps, including some of the famous scholars, gradually produced a remarkable change. Aided by the growth of a new generation of Orthodox young men and women, the products of the spreading day-school and *yeshivah* movement, and the emergence of native American Torah scholars, they returned Torah scholarship and rabbinical authority to the top of the crucial values that determine the Jewish community structure. Yet the successful businessmen and professionals who had dominated social life in Jewish Williamsburg, as elsewhere, continued to wield the greatest influence in most institutions.

A major reason for this covalence of religious and nonreligious values in post-World-War-II Williamsburg was the emphasis on an equally good secular and religious education for the young, even in the Orthodox day schools and *yeshivot,* so that graduates could qualify for entrance to all levels of higher education just like their contemporaries from the public high schools. It enabled them to acquire the training and academic degrees that would open the doors to the professionalization that became the overwhelming trend in the American Jewish community as well as, if not more so, in Middle American society in general. Though completion of a *yeshivah* high school, for both boys and girls, and devotion of some time to intensive religious study in American or Israeli institutions had become the norm in the Orthodox communities, most young men and women chose a career in academia or in the professions that would afford them a better life-style and higher social status. Only the most idealistic chose to remain in advanced Jewish education and devote their lives to Torah scholarship, to the rabbinate, or to the still less appreciated careers of religious functionaries.

Thus, while Torah scholarship and the authority of the religious functionaries were gradually restored to their traditional places in the community, the dreams of Jewish parents and children remained fixed on the professional–the doctor, the lawyer, the scientist working in a prestigious university or a private laboratory, achieving prominence and social recognition. Some entered government services, others prepared themselves for the increasingly open channels of advancement in the financial and managerial world and their concomitant promises of economic and social rewards. Though not as crass as the proverbial disdain for the rabbinate as "a profession not suited for a Jewish child," the professional and social ambitions of the young caused them to leave the increasingly Orthodox Jewish Williamsburg and settle in other centers of religious Jewish life. They brought with them the intensely Jewish spirit and activism for Jewish education and Orthodox causes wherever they went. They became respected professionals and academicians who continued to devote time to further study of Torah and to the advancement of Jewish education.[2]

The transformation of the Jewish community of Williamsburg in the '50s and '60s, which led to the establishment of Hasidic Williamsburg after the rapid departure of the earlier Jewish population, including some of the very Orthodox, had a deep impact on the evolving new structure and community leadership. As stressed in the preceding chapters, the major goal of the Rebbe of Satmar and the other Hungarian hasidic leaders was the development of a maximum of social and cultural isolation in Williamsburg that would not preclude participating in the general economic and political life open to them at the time. This goal required control of the media and a thoroughly different educational system capable of displacing the powerful influences of the general value systems of the non-Jewish and Jewish environment and of replacing them with an ultra-Orthodox hasidic valuation in every phase of the community life.

Already in the '50s, some hasidic groups established their own new small exurban settlements for the express purpose of maximal social isolation, cultural independence, and concentration. New Square, outside of Spring Valley, New York, headed by the Rebbe of Skvira, is one of these; another is the *yeshivah* of Neutra in Mt. Kisko, New York; and another is the Yeshivah Center of Klausenburg in Union City, New Jersey. Settled considerably later are the upstate exurban centers of the Rebbes of Pappa and of Kaschau, among others. The largest and fastest growing of all is Kiryas Joel, in Monroe, New York, founded by the Old Rebbe of Satmar and named in his honor, to meet the urgent need for apartments and new institutions for his community's younger generations. By the end of the '80s it already had a thousand, mostly young, families, and its educational institutions had over three thousand students.

In contrast, the hasidic community of Williamsburg revamped or shaped anew the various phases of the religious, cultural, and social life right in the middle of the largest, most powerful concentration of twentieth-century culture. It set out consciously to defy the impact of the media that dominate the atmosphere of most American homes and influence the young even more than the adult population of society in general. Both Solomon Poll, in *The Hasidic Community of Williamsburg* (1961), and Israel Rubin, in *Satmar: An Island in the City* (1972), have pointed out some of the major valuational changes and essential features of the hasidic stratification system quite adequately, though one may question some of the details and their terminology as they attempted to portray this veritable revolution in contemporary American and Jewish social history.

Many of the basic features of the value structure and social dynamics of the new Williamsburg are identical with those described by Poll and Rubin, as well as my 1961 report on the early phases of the radical innovations set in motion by the genius and determination of Rabbi Yoel Teitelbaum, the Rebbe of Satmar, his community, and the other Hungarian hasidic Rebbes and their congregations. Yet, the subsequent consolidation, expansion, and transformation, which produced the new Williamsburg, require restatement and reformulation to do justice to the new physical, social, and intellectual dimensions of the modus vivendi created in this neighborhood of North Brooklyn. This will enable us to gauge the manner in which the hasidic community is coping with the realities of life in America while preserving the purity of its ideology and ultra-Orthodox life-style, as it had done in the Hungarian shtetl before the Holocaust.

Two major factors shaped the social structure and leadership patterns of the hasidic community since its inception. In the first place, it was the rise of the hasidic leaders, particularly the Rebbe of Satmar, to supremacy and dominance of every phase and facet of the Williamsburg life as its central force and focus. In addition to occupying the highest rank, the Rebbe's charisma and mystic qualities create a distance between his saintly being and his faithful followers, his *hasidim,* who believe in him and adhere to his guidance because of their belief in his deeper sources of knowledge and the power of his prayer and blessing. The relationship to him, as pointed out by Poll and Rubin, determines the status of individuals and institutions in his community. Directly or indirectly, officially or unofficially, his personal approval, concern, and blessing initiate, support, and sustain the vast majority of the programs, organizations, and institutions that constitute the full range of the interpersonal, interinstitutional, and interorganizational dynamics of all phases of community life. Though de facto in existence since the beginning in Satmar, in Hungary, since the '30s, and since its reestablishment in the U.S. in 1947, the full force and power of this extraordinary personal metastatus reached their zenith with the explosive growth of the new Williamsburg. After the death of the Old Rebbe in 1979, they have been perpetuated and further expanded by the less charismatic but equally dynamic new Satmar Rebbe, Rabbi Moshe Teitelbaum. In the decade since his assumption of the leadership of the local community and the international movement of Satmar *hasidim* and Hasidism, he has maintained the superstatus he inherited from his sainted uncle. He has further expanded the network programs, projects, and the organizational structure with the help of a staff of competent co-workers from the ranks of the older as well as the increasingly active middle-aged and younger generations of his followers. Though riding in on the strength of his predecessor's charisma, his scholarship and masterly perpetuation of his sainted uncle's views, policies, and conduct of the hasidic community's intense life-style, he has proven his qualification. Hence, he has been fully accepted, after some initial traumatic tensions and lingering problems of the painful transition caused by a group of the Old Rebbe's associates and followers who could not get used to seeing anybody else in their leader's place. As the present Rebbe of Satmar, Rabbi Moshe Teitelbaum, stresses all the time, no one can really take the place of Rabbi Yoel Teitelbaum as the *Heiliger* Rebbe, the holy Rebbe, nor reduplicate the mystique of his extraordinary stature. Thus, in spite of the loss of the source of the original charisma, the Rebbe of Satmar continues to dominate every aspect of the structure of the major community of Williamsburg as the ultimate leader. This holds true, although the Jewish and general press delight in blowing certain minor incidents such as the problems caused by the B'nai Yoel in Kiryas Joel, who have their own school and synagogue, all out of proportion as indicative of internal strife.

The second major factor is the dominant role of piety, ritual observance, and adherence to the values, dictates, and practices of the intense hasidic life-style traced throughout the discussion of the preceding chapters. It is as crucial in the new Williamsburg of the dawning '90s as it had been in the old country, since the very beginning of the hasidic movement more than 250 years ago, in the determination of the social status of the individuals, groups, and organizations. But here, too, the radical changes of the past three decades that have replaced the heterogeneity of the former Jewish community of Williamsburg with the near-total homogeneity of the Hungarian hasidic life-style, further intensified, articulated, and restructured the role of piety and adherence to ritual and hasidic practices in the social life of the new Williamsburg.

Before going into the details of the impact of these changes, it must be emphasized that this transformation was not a simple, gradual shift, but rather a multiphased process driven by a combination of factors. These include: 1) the population change; 2) the hasidic population explosion; 3) the battle of the hasidic community against the inroads made by other ethnic and racial minorities into Williamsburg in the '50s and '60s, as into other lower class neighborhoods of Brooklyn; and 4) the recognition of the hasidic community as a disadvantaged minority. Secondary factors included: 1) the impact of urban renewal programs on the neighborhood; 2) access to a number of other vital government programs for physical and economic growth; and 3) the trend toward entrepreneurship among the middle-aged and young *hasidim*. All of these factors are responsible for the processes that continue to transform the appearance, atmosphere, and spirit that sustain the social life of Hasidic Williamsburg.

In spite of new crises, such as the demise of the late Rebbe of Satmar and the need for new leadership to sustain and further expand the infinite number of local, national, and international organizations and the concomitant pressure to procure the millions of dollars needed to fund them in the face of skyrocketing costs, the processes of expansion continue unabated.

One major factor that enabled the new Rebbe and his co-workers to pull off this near-miraculous feat is the role of the new generation of *hasidim*, the so-called *avreichim*, who are products of the hasidic school system and of the other institutions built conscientiously by the Old Rebbe for this very purpose. As stressed in the preceding chapters, particularly in the development of the new economic patterns, the new Williamsburg is no longer a community run only by aging survivors of the Holocaust. Increasingly, the young, native American leaders are rising to the challenge, gaining prominence and carrying their share of the burdens and responsibilities in the same spirit of zealous Hasidism, devotion to Torah scholarship, and fealty to the Rebbe and his programs. This limited "Americanization" of the children of the original immigrant groups and their ability to make use of the economic opportunities to blend into the mainstream of the world of business without yielding anything of their hasidic life-style and strict adherence to the ritual requirements of their ultra-Orthodox beliefs is a major key to the successful transformation and survival of the Jewish community of Williamsburg. Instead of moving elsewhere, like the young of the less religious older populations, they remain and increasingly take their place in the administration and direction of the community life in Williamsburg, except for the limited group that has moved to Kiryas Joel and other exurban hasidic communities. Thus they gain prominence and status, and they represent more than 50 percent of the middle levels of the social structure, except for the young at the beginning of their careers, who are either still in the *kollel* or who are learning a trade. Some of the most gifted and active of the young leaders have advanced into the higher and inner circles of the community's administration. They head a number of the newer programs and organizations, which were initiated in the '80s. New power structures have evolved around some of these important projects that reflect the expanding needs of the population.

These new developments have in no way diminished the central role of the Rebbe himself, nor the status of his old guard, the men who have been at the Rebbe's side since before his arrival in this country, and who have helped build and maintain the broad sweep of this local, national, and international empire. Those who remain active are still in charge, and all are thriving. As one of the Rebbe's closest associates put it: "Those who have stood by the *Heilige* Rebbe and have helped him in his endeavours *hoben nisht zugeleigt*, they have prospered in their own personal enterprises." They, their families, and their associates still form the core of the Satmar community's leadership, though illness and death are thinning their ranks. Several have become prominent businessmen, still devoting the better part of their time and efforts to the affairs of the hasidic community. Their faith in the Rebbe and in the power of his blessing have been the major force that attracted the masses of Satmar *hasidim* in Eastern Europe and in the U.S. Even after the death of Rabbi Yoel Teitelbaum, his nephew and successor has successfully perpetuated this original charisma and power of blessing and guidance by virtue of his wisdom, scholarship, masterful direction, and personal supervision of the constantly broadening range of the activities and programs built by his predecessor. This close personal contact with the younger generations which have grown up in the schools of Satmar and have been imbued with the saintliness and wisdom of the Rebbe over the years of their study and in the constancy of the hasidic life-style has become the foundation of the new Rebbe's strength and popularity. As such it is not affected by the superimage of the late Rebbe that even more than a decade after his death remains fresh and real in the minds and hearts of Satmar *hasidim* women and men alike.

Thus, the expanded central role of the Rebbe of Satmar is the prime factor of the social structure of the new Williamsburg. His position is unlike that of any other hasidic or nonhasidic leader in any other Orthodox community, with the possible exception of Rabbi Menachem M. Schneerson, the Lubavitcher Rebbe. But his community and following is not as centralized as that of the Satmar Rebbe, and he concentrates more on reaching out to the broader masses of the worldwide Jewish community with his own network of organizations. There are also others of the top ranks of the famous hasidic Rebbes, scions of the dynasties of Belz, Ger, Vishnitz, and Bobov, who have large numbers of *hasidim* in the U.S. and in Israel. But none has the superconcentration of a Williamsburg, with the loyalty of about forty thousand hasidic men, women, and children who organize their entire life around the hallowed personage of the Rebbe of Satmar. Most have their centers of power in their congregations and schools in Boro Park, Flatbush, Monsey, Jerusalem, or other heavily Orthodox communities. This was the genius of the Old Rebbe of Satmar: to use the power of his charisma to establish such a broad base in the limited area of the Jewish Triangle of Williamsburg. By now, Satmar congregations and schools in Boro Park, Flatbush, and Monsey, as well as in Canada, London, Antwerp, and Israel can match those of other Rebbes in size and intensity of their *Hasidut* and life-style, regardless of the environment.

Probably second among the hasidic leaders of Williamsburg in status and following is Rabbi Yaakov Greenwald, the Rebbe of Pappa, who has inherited the leadership of his community from his late father, who built it from his small center on Bedford Avenue, at the lower edge of the old Jewish community. Like the Rebbe of Satmar he has put his greatest efforts into a large and thriving school system from nurseries to a *kollel* for advanced rabbinic study for boys and girls. Similarly, the Tzelemer Rebbe and the Klausenburger Rebbe, who started even before the arrival of the Rabbi of Satmar, or the Vishnitzer, Spinker, Kaschauer, and Krasner Rebbes have developed congregations and schools, and exurban centers outside of New York City. All of these and a number of other hasidic leaders have concentrated a great deal on and contributed to the community life of Williamsburg on a level and on a scale that can vie with the largest of the East European centers of pre-Holocaust fame.

What is essentially different in Hasidic Williamsburg is the American dimension. Though definitely still low income, there is strong evidence of the spirit of expansion, growth, and entrepreneurship that provides ever new chances of advancement for the young of the community without their having to move elsewhere, as did the young of earlier phases of Jewish Williamsburg.

In my 1961 report on the Jewish community of Williamsburg, I compared the social order of pre- and the post-World War II, seeing it as a result of the radical changes that took place between the midthirties and the midfifties. The synagogues, the schools, and other institutions that then served as the framework of comparison are no longer in existence or have faded to insignificance, their leaders and members having moved to Queens, Boro Park, and elsewhere, including some of the newer hasidic and nonhasidic groups. Yet, the basic value system that had been responsible for the social status of the various occupational groups is still valid enough to yield insight into the results of the significant shifts in the socioeconomic, cultural, and political realms. What is new in Hasidic Williamsburg, as in broader American society, is the increasing impact of technology, the knowledge and service economies that are dominated by science, by government, and management organizations that are developing new dimensions and coordinates in the social texture of society. In spite of the effective sociocultural isolation of the hasidic community of Williamsburg, the younger generation is moving consciously into new realms of business and trade that are directly or indirectly affected by the contingencies of the technotronic age, as pointed out in the discussion of the economic patterns.

The first three columns of Table 5.1 are taken from the 1961 report. The last column has been added to provide perspective on the impact of the most significant changes, which will be discussed below.

As pointed out in the introduction to this chapter, the most striking change in the transformation of the Jewish community of Williamsburg is the restructuring of the social stratification of the hasidic community from one that like other Jewish and non-Jewish communities was geared to economic and professional success to one that is almost totally geared to the religious and hasidic values of piety and Torah scholarship, as expressed in the hasidic life-style. Even in the transition period in the late '40s and '50s when the rabbinic leadership and the authority of Torah scholars were gradually returned to their traditional rank at the top of the social structure of Jewish Williamsburg, they had to share this position with successful businessmen and professionals, like lawyers. Until then they had been the dominant elite in almost every phase of the communal life because of their socioeconomic success and higher education, though some of them had a good Hebrew education as well.

Since the late '60s, the supreme status of the Rebbe of Satmar as the charismatic head of the dominant hasidic group ranks him far above any secular or religious leader or professional, wealthy or not. But unlike some other hasidic or nonhasidic leaders, though highly revered by his followers and invested with the mystique of

TABLE 5.1

Comparison of the Social Structure of the Jewish Community of Williamsburg since before
World War II

Phase I Pre-World War II	Phase II Post-World War II	Phase III 1950–1965	Phase IV The New Williamsburg
1. Successful businessmen, lawyers	Successful businessmen, lawyers	Religious leaders, rabbis, scholars	The Satmar Rebbe
2. Professionals	Professionals	Successful businessmen, professionals	Rebbes, Torah scholars, high religious functionaries
3. Rabbis, religious leaders, scholars	Rabbis, businessmen, religious functionaries	Religious functionaries	Successful businessmen, heads of major organizations (e.g., ODA), religious functionaries, educators
4. Government employees, religious functionaries	Government employees, religious functionaries, skilled tradesmen	Government employees	Skilled tradesmen, business executives, managers, insurance, sales personnel, financial service executives
5. Small businessmen	Government employees, business employees	Small tradesmen, business employees, skilled workers	Business employees, small tradesmen, organizational functionaries
6. Skilled workers, religious teachers	Semiskilled workers, religious teachers	Religious teachers, semiskilled workers, business clerks, sales personnel	Semiskilled workers, clerks, sales personnel
7. Semiskilled workers	Unskilled workers	Semiskilled workers, unskilled workers	Unskilled workers
8. Unskilled workers		Religious deviants	Religious ignorants, religious deviants

his calling, the Old Rebbe of Satmar did not stand on a high pedestal, far above and removed from his network of organizations in Williamsburg, and in other American and worldwide communities. On the contrary, his frail health notwithstanding, Rabbi Yoel Teitelbaum, the Old Rebbe, was and always remained until almost the very end of his long life the ultimate initiator, arbitrator, and guiding force behind the major and minor programs of his *kehillah* and the organization of his *hasidim* everywhere.

Similarly, his successor, Rabbi Moshe Teitelbaum, though in his seventies, remains equally close to the thousands of his followers who seek his guidance, advice, and blessing. With the help of a large council and staff of capable co-workers, he directs the constant and special activities of his institutions in Williamsburg and throughout the Orthodox Jewish world. It is for this reason that the continuously growing empire places him far above everyone else even among the major Rebbes. The magnitude, intensity, and spread of the community life in the new Williamsburg is unmatched. For no other contemporary hasidic Rebbe has ever controlled a single, concentrated community on such a large scale, in addition to many thousands of *hasidim* the world over, with the exception of the worldwide empire of the Lubavitcher Rebbe.

One factor that elevates the position of power of the Rebbe of Satmar above most other hasidic and nonhasidic leaders is the fact that from the very outset Rabbi Yoel Teitelbaum insisted on the absolute independence of his community, his organizations and institutions, and especially his educational system. He rejected any form of financial or organizational affiliation or support. He wanted no interference, dependency, or supervision in order to preserve the purity of the strict adherence of his community to the Torah and hasidic values and life-style. Obviously, this independence placed a heavy burden on him and on his co-workers and followers from the time in 1947 when he established his community and the first of his *Talmud Torahs*, as his yeshivah schools are called, to provide the necessary funds, not only to survive but to be maintained on the level of dignity and functionality.

This stance of the Rebbe meant raising increasingly large amounts of money, especially in view of the hasidic population explosion and the constant need to provide new and better facilities for the huge classes of students, which double every 7 years, according to the head of the Satmar school system. The founding, expansion, and maintenance of his favorite project, the exurban community in Monroe, New York, alone cost over $10 million per year, according to a statement by the present Rebbe (interview with author, January 1988). Only the *koah*, the extraordinary power of the *Heiliger* Rebbe, he stressed, could raise such funds and the millions required to support the large social, economic, and welfare organizations network of the Williamsburg community, and of the other branches in New York and beyond, and in the other countries, such as Canada, England, Belgium, Austria, Israel, and in Latin America.

This near-miracle of independent fund-raising is a major credit to the faith and readiness of thousands of his hasidim, from the well-to-do to the poor, who from the very beginning made sacrifices beyond their means to support the Rebbe's causes and share the prayers and festive celebrations with him.[3] This extraordinary feat of the Old Rebbe, one that was perpetuated and further expanded by his successor, is even more astounding in view of the fact that the vast majority of the American Jewish contributors to Jewish causes would not support the Rebbe of Satmar and his projects because of his unpopular stand against Zionism and the political State of Israel, which he condemned because of the secular nature of its constitution and form of government. On the other hand, not being beholden to any one person or any of the Jewish world's major or minor organizations and funding reservoirs gives him the freedom to structure his community and its institutions strictly in line with his own ideas and the ideals of the ultra-Orthodox values of the Torah and *hasidut*. In turn, it means his independence in establishing standards and policies that diverge radically from those that guide the vast majority of the organizations of Jewish life in America and elsewhere. On the strength of this unpopular stance and unorthodox policy that recognizes only the authority of the Torah and the supreme values of Torah scholarship and piety he has been able to reshape the social structure of the new Williamsburg, in contrast to the powerful influences brought to bear on the environment by the mass media of the secular Jewish and non-Jewish world.

One interesting phenomenon related to the superstatus of the Rebbe of Satmar is the status of the Old Rebbetzin, Alta Feige Teitelbaum, the widow of the sainted Old Rebbe who, after the death of his only daughter from his previous marriage, was left without children. From the very outset of the reestablishment of his community in Williamsburg, the Rebbetzin took an active part in a number of welfare projects. She personally initiated some and sustained them, working closely with and supported by the Old Rebbe until his death 30 years later. As pointed out before, the Old Rebbetzin has never given up this unique function and status as the moving force behind these charity and welfare programs. She still organizes, supervises, and directs a number of annual affairs, such as auctions and luncheons or teas, and raises large sums to sustain the old and initiate new projects, such as the *Yeled Shaashuim* Postnatal Recovery Home for women and infants in the magnificent mansion that had been built for the Old Rebbe in Kiryas Joel shortly before his death. More recently, she purchased a string of houses to be renovated for the benefit of newly married couples from the *kollel* who cannot afford the relatively moderate rentals in Williamsburg. She lives in Kiryas Joel but comes into town at least once a week to the home built for the Old Rebbe on Bedford Avenue, where she holds open house for all those who seek her help.[4] Naturally, her extraordinary position and her activities on behalf of the needy of Williamsburg, combined with the special support of the group of *hasidim* from the ranks of the Old Rebbe's followers who have never been able to come to terms with the demise of their *Heiliger* Rebbe, have given the Old Rebbetzin a special status above any normally accorded to the wife of a rabbi or Rebbe, even among the most prominent Orthodox leaders. But, as pointed out before, in spite of a period of stress or occasional tension, the vast majority of the Satmar community has fully accepted the leadership of the new Rebbe and his perpetuation of the style, policies, ideology, and teachings of his uncle. Similarly, his wife, although less of a public figure than the octogenarian Old Rebbetzin, has increasingly taken her place at the formal and informal affairs of the new Williamsburg. This includes not only running a number of projects and fund-raising affairs, but also representing her husband, the Rebbe, on journeys such as her 1987 visit to Jerusalem, where she was given the royal treatment due her as the Satmar Rebbetzin.

No less significant in the consolidation of the power and status of the present Rebbe is the fact that he has a large family. His sons have increasingly assumed major functions in the administration of his Szigeter community, and of phases of the Satmar empire. One son has become the head of the large center of Sziget *hasidim* in Boro Park, which the new Rebbe built years before, long before he had assumed his uncle's position. Another son is the head of the original Szigeter community in Williamsburg. A third son heads the community of Kiryas Joel, the exurban branch of Satmar in Monroe, New York, and directs its large, constantly expanding school system for boys and girls. He has gained wide recognition as a superior scholar and as an inspiring orator, though some members, especially the so-called B'nai Yoel, resent his strong, authoritative leadership style. He is constantly called on to represent his illustrious father, not only on major occasions and large gatherings of the Satmar networks of institutions and organizations. The weekly *Yid* pages frequently feature large ads of the branches of Satmar in England, Canada, and Israel, welcoming this son of the Rebbe and according him the highest respect and high honors as befits his lofty status. This active involvement of the Rebbe's sons augurs well for the future of Satmar and the survival of the family dynasty, a major characteristic of the history of Hasidism.

Next in the social structure of the new Williamsburg is the group of close associates and administrators, some of whom had been with the Old Rebbe since before his arrival in the U.S. Among them was the legendary late Rabbi Lippe (Leopold) Friedman, in whose memory one of the plazas next to the largest public high-rise project has been named. Then there is Rabbi Joseph Ashkenazi, the publisher of the Old Rebbe's works and that of other talmudic and hasidic works, who now resides in Kiryas Joel. He had been Rabbi Yoel Teitelbaum's right-hand man even during the period of transition from his liberation from concentration camp and temporary stays in Switzerland and Israel, until his arrival in Williamsburg.

The officials most powerful and closest to the new Rebbe, as they had been to the Old Rebbe of Satmar, are Rabbi Leibisch (Leopold) Lefkowitz, the official head of the Satmar Kehillah, Congregation Yetev Lev, and its major organizations, such as ODA, where he has been replaced by Rabbi Yitzchok Schlesinger since his recent illness. The second and most versatile of the Rebbe's men is Rabbi Alexander Sender Deutsch, the publisher of *Der Yid*, who was largely responsible for the selection and installation of Rabbi Moshe Teitelbaum as the new head of Satmar, and who is his ambassador-at-large on most internal and external diplomatic missions. He is an incisive thinker and popular Yiddish writer and historian. He has also for decades been and is still responsible for the growth and expansion of the educational systems of Satmar in Williamsburg and elsewhere, as well as for a number of other major projects and programs of the international organizational and institutional networks of Satmar in the U.S. and in Israel. His skill as popular orator and diplomatic moderator have enabled him to assist the Rebbe in weathering a number of crises that confronted him and his predecessor over the years. Foremost among them was the transition of the leadership of Satmar, which was crucial for the survival of Hasidic Williamsburg, and for the acceleration of its expansion in recent years. His editorials and regular weekly articles in *Der Yid* enable him to wield probably more influence on the thinking of the people than anyone, aside from the Rebbe himself. He heads the council of the Rebbe's advisers and directs the work of the administrations of the vast network of the community's organizations and institutions, and the disposition of its assets which, in his estimate, amount to one billion dollars.

Not unexpectedly and not in contradiction to the premise of this section of the report on Hasidic Williamsburg, namely the replacement of the once dominant successful businessmen and lawyers at the top of the social structure, is the fact that there are a number of prominent businessmen and entrepreneurs among the closest associates of the Rebbe of Satmar. Rabbi Leibish Lefkowitz, for example, is a major importer of crystal and lamps. His assembly plant in New Jersey employs hundreds of *hasidim* from Williamsburg and elsewhere. In contrast to the former presidents and officials of synagogues and officials of the earlier phases of the Jewish community of Williamsburg, these businessmen and hasidic entrepreneurs are first and foremost *hasidim* of the Rebbe. Not only do they put their resources, know-how, and experience at the disposal of the Rebbe, but they also fully support and guide themselves by his decisions and by those of his council of Torah sages who are his closest advisers and direct major policies. They also make the major and minor daily decisions in the life of the individuals and groups or institutions of the community. In no other Jewish community in the U.S. do the representatives of Torah scholarship wield greater power or receive more respect and deference than in the new Williamsburg. And this situation arises from a consciously fostered plan of the Old Rebbe of Satmar from the very beginning of his efforts to reform the life of the neighborhood.

Next in the social ranking are a number of major and minor hasidic leaders, especially the four or five Rebbes who head the major subcommunities of Hasidic Williamsburg, the Klausenburger, Papper, Tzelemer, and Spinker Rebbes. Before and with the Old Rebbe of Satmar, they were instrumental in the transformation of the old Jewish community. They all have their subcommunities, which are mostly centered about their synagogues and schools for boys and girls, or at least a *bet hamidrash*, a study hall and seminars for groups of older, advanced, single or married young scholars who study under the guidance of the Rebbe. Then there are a number of lesser hasidic rabbis whom Poll (1961) and Rubin (1972) have called *Rebbishe Einiklach* or *Shtikl Rebbes*. These are backed by the prestige or mystique of their more or less famous ancestors, who were the founders and heads of hasidic dynasties in Poland, Hungary, or Romania, some of whom developed their own ideologies and life-styles or authored famous hasidic classics. Some of the bearers of the famous historical hasidic names had already lived in Williamsburg in its earlier phases. But almost all of them have followed their main supporters to Boro Park, Flatbush, Monsey, and other Orthodox Jewish communities, where they reestablished their congregations and are attracting new followers and supporters from among their new neighbors and acquaintances. A few have remained in Williamsburg and are enjoying the benefits of its strong hasidic milieu by virtue of their piety, scholarship, or hasidic life-style. Some of them have become employees of the Satmar community as educators, rabbinic authorities, and other rabbinic functionaries. Several are working on new editions or additions to the hasidic works of their ancestors. In a lighter vein, they are also a source of *yichus*, marriages, for the children of successful rabbis and scholars who seek to enhance their social status by marital affiliation to the sons or daughters of the scions of renowned hasidic dynasties.

Foremost among the channels of social advancement are the multitude of institutions and social, welfare, and political organizations whose administrative offices have become nerve centers of the new Williamsburg. Best known, and perhaps the most productive of all, is the headquarters of the local ODA office of the U.S. Small Business Administration. Its energetic head, Rabbi Tzvi Kestenbaum, has transformed it from its small beginnings as an office with limited functions to the most important economic and political beachhead of the community. It has opened up opportunities for the needy and for young *hasidim* to train and enter the world of American business and trade. It has made contacts and cultivated relations with the city, state, and federal government agencies from the district councilmen to U.S. congressmen, senators, and the president and members of his cabinet. ODA's Rabbi Kestenbaum spearheaded the more than 10-year effort to get full disadvantaged minority status for the hasidic community, which has already benefited hasidic people everywhere. He has been able to provide sorely needed funds for the most important renovation and construction projects, which have transformed the very appearance of the Jewish Triangle. Two such projects are the Partnership with the City, which involves the construction of new housing, and the expansion of the local urban renewal program. Each of these took years of active political contact and political pressure. The late U.S. Secretary of Commerce, Malcolm S. Baldridge, had been a visitor to the headquarters of ODA, where he was honored for his efforts on behalf of the hasidic community of Williamsburg's bid for the same benefits as other minority groups. Similarly, his successor, Robert A. Mosbacher, has visited and was honored at the ODA office in recognition of his support of the needs of the neighborhood. As recently as May 1992, Congressman Stephen J. Solarz announced a $320,000 grant from the U.S. Department of Commerce to the Williamsburg ODA, in recognition of its outstanding record of service to hasidic and other business people who are often not served by other agencies. He was quoted in the Jewish Press: "ODA provides first-rate services to small business people in our community. With assistance from ODA, many businesses in this area will learn to run a profitable enterprise. In this way, our neighbors can become more productive, and bring jobs to Williamsburg."

Rabbi Tzvi Kestenbaum has also been the major force behind the establishment, maintenance, and constant expansion of the Primary Health Care Center in the heart of the hasidic community that provides a broad variety of medical and other health services to the men, women, and children who crowd into the large halls of its headquarters at all times. Many of them would otherwise not be able to avail themselves of the different types of vitally needed physical, psychological, and dental services, which this health facility of the ODA adjusts to their particular requirements. In the beginning of the '90s, the Primary Health Care Center was moved from its original location to a considerably larger building in order to accommodate the constantly expanding services and professional staffs. The ODA, under the direction of Rabbi Kestenbaum, also administers a large WIC program in its headquarters on Heyward Street, at the very edge of the hasidic neighborhood. According to Rabbi Kestenbaum, this program handled 50,000 cases in 1989, and cares for 250 infants daily. WIC provides help to new mothers and their infants. It provides home care to about 10,000 among the aged and infirm, and offers regular food and nutritional support to those in need. The ODA is also responsible for the local merchants' association and for its projects, and for the renovation and beautification of residential and business streets, homes, and storefronts. Needless to say, the man responsible for these major achievements, Rabbi Tzvi Kestenbaum, is one of the most respected and powerful men in the community; he has a national reputation and has earned nationwide recognition and honors.

Though in earlier phases Williamsburg had produced a number of prominent educators and rabbinic and social leaders,[5] there had never been anyone among the numerous successful businessmen, lawyers, and other professionals who had such a broad impact on the life of the community as the current head of the ODA, the publisher of *Der Yid*, and the other administrators and directors of the economic, social, political, and welfare organizations. The reason was the heterogeneity and the fragmentation of the earlier community and its subgroups. In contrast, the intrinsic homogeneity and size of the Hungarian hasidic community, foremost among them that of Satmar, have created a variety of channels for the growth of new social structures and power centers, each of which provides ample opportunities for the social advancement of its individual members, groups, and organizations.

Another equally important power base in hasidic Williamsburg is the large and constantly growing educational school system. As pointed out there, the schools of Satmar are under the direct supervision of the Rebbe himself, who personally guides the teaching, supervising, and administrating staffs. Twice a year, he visits all the local schools, assisted by a group of supervisors who test the progress of all classes and students. At the same time, the heads of the Satmar and other hasidic schools do have a large measure of autonomy in the running of the schools and are close to parents and students. Hence they have the level of constant exposure that gives them recognition and status among the masses of the middle-aged and young *hasidim* whose children they educate. While not on the level of the administrators of the major social, political, and welfare organizations, they are among the most respected members of the community in Williamsburg, Monsey, and Kiryas Joel, where the older boys from the various local lower divisions are concentrated. They, rather than the successful businessmen and professionals who used to head the boards of directors of the earlier Williamsburg day schools, set policies by virtue of their scholarship and educational experience, together with the supervisory scholars of the Rebbe's staff.

The most striking development in this realm of the social dynamics and leadership is, again, the emergence of the mostly American-born men in their thirties and forties, who are increasingly moving into the middle ranges of the local social structure, with some of the most successful penetrating into the highest ranks of the Rebbe's inner council and boards. They are the bulk of the parents whose children are crowding the schools that require constant expansion, renovation, and new construction of facilities for their boys and girls. They are the *yunge Leit*, the young men and women who are taking over the established old businesses or are establishing new ones in Williamsburg and elsewhere. They are the bulk of the activists who are initiating or running the routine activities of the major social welfare and security organizations, and are helping the needy because of their available resources and know-how.

At the same time, they are respected for their Torah scholarship since most of them have been educated in the local *yeshivot*. From their ranks come the masses who flock to the early morning and evening classes that fill all available halls and rooms in the *batei midrash* and school buildings, offering opportunities of intensive study on all levels of the talmudic, halachic, and hasidic scholarship. At the same time a number of these younger *hasidim* are taking courses and training for jobs in new fields of technology, which enable them to get jobs and avail themselves of the opportunities for enterprising young people with the help of government- or company-sponsored training programs for minority group members. The knowledge and experience gained, as they make their mark in new realms like insurance, real estate, and financial management, enable these *avreichim* to contribute substantially to organizations and institutions in the community. Thus, they are moving into the middle of the social structures that they are helping to develop and sustain. Some are gradually advancing into the higher levels and are replacing the increasingly aging members of the old elite who had been among the pioneers in the establishment of the new Williamsburg and its institutional networks.

A close second to these entrepreneurs is the growing number of skilled tradesmen, which constitute about 25 percent of the hasidic work force. They are unlike the young of the earlier phases who, if they did not enter the then lucrative diamond trade, became accountants, entered government service, or joined their family businesses. Those who had the intellectual capacity and the drive needed to cope with the obstacles, moved into the academic professions. They became physicians, lawyers, psychologists, or scientists on the basis of their good secular education in the day schools and *yeshivot*, as already discussed.

In contrast, the young of the new Williamsburg take pride in becoming skilled tradesmen. They are printers, bookbinders, electricians, electronics and computer technicians. The advertising pages of *Der Yid* are replete with announcements of *hasidim* offering their services and establishing their shops in the neighborhood or at the outskirts of Williamsburg, or in other more industrialized neighborhoods of Brooklyn, Manhattan, Long Island, or New Jersey. They are not embarrassed by their hasidic background. Whereas the young of the earlier pre-World-War-II and post-World-War-II periods were ashamed to be seen in their blue-collar work uniforms, *hasidim* are visible everywhere in their work outfits, as they handle light and heavy mechanized equipment as expertly as the outsiders who used to provide these services in the Jewish community of Williamsburg of old. Hasidic locksmiths, carpenters, refrigeration experts, and the increasing number of those who work in some phase of the jewelry trade generally seem to do well. Yet, as pointed out before, a good many seem intent on eventually establishing their own trades or shops.

Unlike the masses of Jewish immigrants of the needle and fur trades, who had become dominant in the proletarian and political scene of post-World-War-I America, they are motivated by typical middle-class attitudes. A furniture restorer and polisher expressed this orientation succinctly when he said:

> First and foremost I am a *baale-battisher* young man. I spend my spare time in continuing my advanced talmudic studies with my former *haverim* from the *bet hamidrash.* I have a decent income. My children will get the same excellent hasidic education as the boys and girls from the most prominent homes in Williamsburg, or for that matter in Boro Park or Flatbush, though we don't have the luxuries and cannot show off with the marble front and chandeliers of our home. I drive a truck and have a station wagon that gives my family all the transportation we require. We can do very well without a Cadillac or a fancy foreign car. No, I am not jealous. The people respect me. I sit at the Rebbe's table like everyone else. I wear a *bekeshe*, have beard and *peyot*, and a *shtreimel* like all *baale-battishe Yiden* of our *kehillah.*

This attitude of the furniture polisher is quite different from that of a member of an Orthodox youth organization, described in my 1961 report, who worked in a factory during the day so that he could afford to go to night school and prepare himself for a career as a teacher in public high school. In the eyes of his *haverim*, the members of his Orthodox organization, he was an intellectual who would have been ashamed to be seen in his blue-collar uniform.

The contrast of the two attitudes reflected here mirrors the crucial difference between the skilled and semiskilled tradesmen of the hasidic community and others, particularly that of the vast majority of the earlier immigrant waves from Eastern Europe since the end of the nineteenth century. They consciously reject the proletarian attitude and ideology that characterized the earlier immigrants from whose ranks had come some of the most prominent ideologues and leaders of the American working class and of the Socialist and Democratic Parties of the first half of the twentieth century. The *hasidim* are not ashamed of their physical labor. Their overwhelming values are those of the vast majority of the products of the hasidic *yeshivot* who reject secular education and take pride in their ability to perform their trades as well as anyone else. They do not have the social and cultural benefits of the earlier generations of professionals from Williamsburg who became prominent in their new Jewish as well as the general communities. But the middle-class mentality of Williamsburg's *baale-battishe Yiden* does not value those sociocultural tokens of the suburban society. They do look forward to improving their socioeconomic position like anyone else. As already stated, they do have the middle-class goals of independence, but more so for the religious benefits it offers them in the observance of their strict adherence to the ritual requirements of the hasidic life-style than for the tokens of affluence they frequently deride when speaking of the excesses of some of the Boro Park and Flatbush elements. Those among them who have become successful will buy bigger apartments or houses, and their life-style will improve in the kinds of house furnishings, in the display of silverware and jewelry for the women, and for the girls to be married, and in the apartments they set up for young couples after they are married.

Essentially, however, the hasidic community is still largely lower class in appearance, and the majority of the people are at best low-middle class in their life-style. But there is strong evidence that as the middle-aged generation is gradually finding its way into more lucrative lines of business and skilled trades, the standards of life and tokens of their social status are increasingly enhancing the atmosphere of the neighborhood.

Though still a considerably smaller percentage than that of the Jewish youth in other neighborhoods, young *hasidim* are also entering some levels of government service (about 10 percent of those analyzed in the occupational hierarchy of a typical synagogue). But their strict adherence to the requirements of the hasidic life-style and their rejection of higher secular education keeps them on lower levels, and only in the types of jobs or work in which they are rarely visible to the public. In contrast, Orthodox young and middle-aged men who wear skullcaps at their jobs are increasingly becoming accepted in universities, in research laboratories, and in government offices where they do not have contact with the broader public. This type of opportunity is not offered equally to the men who insist on wearing their hasidic garb all the time. There are a few exceptions, as some *hasidim* are moving up in the ranks of the post office or the social-welfare departments. A few of the more prominent *hasidim* work with higher city or state officials as representatives of the hasidic communities of New York and as advisers to state and federal departments. But they are the exceptions.

One large group of *hasidim* whose lives have improved considerably as a result of the changes in the socioeconomic values of the new Williamsburg is that of religious functionaries. Twenty-five percent of the alumni of the *yeshivot* and day schools are finding jobs as rabbis, teachers, or *dayanim*, judges, on the rabbinic courts. Others become *shohtim*, religious slaughterers, and supervisors in the proliferating kosher industries not only in New York's Orthodox communities, but throughout the U.S., as the Orthodox life-style spreads into older and newer communities, especially in the large cities of the east, and more recently in the south and west of the country. A growing number of *hasidim* as well as non-*hasidim* are becoming *sofrim*, religious scribes, and similar religious functionaries, most of whom, in former days, had to be imported from Eastern Europe or Israel. In contrast, the young of the earlier phases had avoided seeking employment as religious functionaries in view of the extremely low income and the still lower social status accorded them. As pointed out in the discussion of the educational patterns, teachers and administrators in the constantly expanding school systems of Hasidic Williamsburg are highly respected. Their year-round salaries, while still low, are commensurately higher with the general rise in income in the hasidic community as a result of the special efforts and arrangements initiated by the old and the present Rebbes of Satmar to secure for the *Talmud Torah*s, *yeshivot*, and girls' schools competent permanent staffs of satisfied teachers, supervisors, and administrators. This is also true for most of the other types of religious functionaries: they no longer have to consider their jobs temporary work until they can find better paying and more highly respected careers.

Even the young idealists who were responsible for the phenomenal growth of the day-school and *yeshivah* movement in the '40s and '50s eventually yielded to the needs of their growing families and left *hinuch*, Jewish education, with a *krechtz*, a sigh of regret, as one of them put it. After long years of study at the *kollel* in Lakewood, he had enthusiastically thrown himself into teaching at a *yeshivah*.

> After my fourth child, I realized I just couldn't make it and give my children the kind of education and life-style that my wife and I wanted for them. I took some courses and qualified for a decent job at Social Security, where I have a chance to help many Jews who need advice and counsel in dealing with the complications of government regulations. Every evening I spend hours on Torah study, but it is not what I had dreamt of. But my late mother, who always wanted me to go to college, would be proud of me now.

This type of disillusionment and dropout of the most idealistic and dedicated educators was what Rabbi Yoel Teitelbaum wanted to avoid, because, as he frequently repeated, "The future of our *kehillah* and of our youth depends on content *mechanchim*, educators." Hence, as discussed in detail in chapter 2, he made considerable demands of the teachers, but balanced them with proper and prompt payment and chances of advancement and security for the staffs of his schools. Similarly, he was not satisfied with the status of the other religious functionaries. Hence he advanced those jobs on which the religious and ritual quality and standards of his community depended and made them attractive to the alumni of his institutes of advanced talmudic and rabbinic studies. Instead of depending on the dwindling ranks of the survivors of the older immigrant generation, he developed new generations of native American hasidic rabbis, *dayanim*, religious judges, *shohtim*, *bodkim*, and *menakrim*, slaughterers and supervisors of the various phases of the processing operations of the constantly expanding kosher food and religious articles industries, responsible for their reliability and high standards. As a result, the careers of religious functionaries have gained recognition and provide socioeconomic security for the young scholars who dedicate their lives to them, instead of their being occupations of last resort for those who did not qualify for anything else, or for those who used them as stopgaps until they acquired the training and qualifications for "better" occupations.

This contrast between the material and social rewards for those who devoted themselves to jobs as religious or ritual functionaries in the earlier phases of Williamsburg and those who do so in the new hasidic community remains significant. Even in the limited groups of the more glamorous occupations, such as that of the cantors, only the handful of famous *chazzanim* received good pay and won admiration, fame, and popularity. Only some of them, however, possessed the knowledge and degree of piety and religious observance expected of the cantor, especially in Orthodox congregations. Even with the expansion of Jewish radio programs, and with the popularity of *chazzanim* records, there were just a handful who could devote their life profitably to this function. Some of the new stars, such as Rabbi Shlomo Carlebach, Mordechai ben David, and others are thriving, their tapes, concerts, and programs proliferating; yet neither the public respect nor the economic rewards makes this field more attractive in broader circles.

Though hasidic *niggunim* and music are a major ingredient of the hasidic life, the hasidic community prefers the amateur *baal menagen* or *baal tefillah* to lead the services rather than the star cantors. The Satmar Rebbe himself was always the major attraction. His piety, his introspective prayers and melodies were what brought the masses from all over the United States on the High Holidays and other special occasions to his large synagogue; his *farbrengen* or *tishen*, the shared meals and celebrations in his home, were what attracted them.

In contrast to this avoidance of stars conducting the services, recordings and tapes of hasidic performers are an important part of the very limited types of entertainment found in the hasidic home. Public recognition and status are also accorded the stars of hasidic community life: the highly respected rabbis or scholars who conduct the popular Torah classes every morning and night that attract hundreds of participants, and such unlikely celebrities as the noted *dayanim*, the judges of the rabbinic courts, especially the ones in the headquarters of the hasidic rabbinic organizations. They have made this organization a center of sociopolitical power, which has had considerable impact on the conduct of the individual and collective life of Williamsburg. It serves as the political arm of the Rebbe of Satmar, promulgating his policies and ideology in massive full-page advertisements and in posters plastered on walls and bulletin boards in the neighborhood.

One of its major functions, which reaches far beyond the immediate hasidic community, is its kosher certification division, which is staffed by a growing number of experts in various phases of the production and supervision of the food and religious articles industries. In cooperation with some of the other kosher certification agencies, it provides valuable information to the Jewish public about new food products, medicines, and health services, which in former days had not been available to the hasidic and Orthodox nonhasidic communities. Equally important is the function of the rabbinic court, whose judges deal with business and family affairs that are part and parcel of a total community life, and which in former days were not available. As pointed out, some of these *dayanim*, the judges on the rabbinic court, have gained respect and prestige by their sagacity and skill in handling specific cases, such as divorce proceedings. It is therefore not surprising that these unique fields for religious functionaries provide attractive new career opportunities for the young scholars who find in them the desirable combination of advanced scholarship, job security, and public recognition.

There are a number of other such centers of power and status in the communal life of Hasidic Williamsburg on a scale that would never have been possible at any time in the life of the American Jewish community, such as the weekly Yiddish newspaper, *Der Yid*. Even at the peak of their popularity, such Yiddish newspapers as the *Forward*, which had served the masses of the Jewish immigrant work force as their daily source of information, entertainment, and education and sociopolitical indoctrination in the socialist and liberal ideologies, never had the deep impact that *Der Yid* has on the hasidic community in Williamsburg and beyond. Unlike the other Jewish, Yiddish, or English newspapers, the weekly *Der Yid* has a position of power that is rooted in the particular nature of the hasidic community of Williamsburg.

There are other Anglo-Jewish or Yiddish newspapers and magazines that have more than the 40,000 regular readers of *Der Yid*. Yet none is in the position of being the almost exclusive vehicle of information and ideology that the Old Rebbe of Satmar consciously set out to create by thoroughly controling the milieu in Williamsburg by insisting on a maximum of sociocultural isolation from the powerful media that influence almost every home in the U.S., especially the young who spend hours daily watching TV. As pointed out before, the intensive education and value inculcation of the hasidic youngsters in their schools and the very atmosphere of the hasidic life-style at home and in the streets are therefore an effective force that molds the minds and emotions of the young and makes them receptive to the near-total impact of Hasidism. In this configuration, the Rebbe consciously forged *Der Yid* as the major tool for conveying his own type of hasidic ideology, policies, and perspective on how to look at and deal with the major and minor phenomena of the daily news in the Jewish and non-Jewish worlds. Since TV is banned and spurned as "the *Yetzer Hara* box," the tool of the evil instinct, and neither radio, nor English newspapers and magazines, except for those which are read for their trade information, play a major role in Williamsburg, *Der Yid* is the crucial source of information, entertainment, and sociopolitical views. As the managing editor put it: "We are probably the most powerful Jewish newspaper in the American Jewish community, if not in the Jewish world." This fact gives its publisher, editors, and writers a unique position in the social life of Williamsburg. As pointed out before, the publisher is perhaps the most important figure in the administration of the community next to the Rebbe of Satmar, who depends on him to head many of his most important projects, institutions, organizations, and programs in the U.S. and Israel. His editorials and leading articles, written under a pseudonym, are prominently placed in each issue of *Der Yid*. They set the tone and provide the sociopolitical orientation for the majority of the weekly's readers. The advertisements are arbiters of social significance for most social and political events in the neighborhood and in the personal lives of the leaders of the community and of its institutions and organizations. The size and number of ads or announcements and their placement mirror the social status they hold or are assigned by the editors.

Similarly, the articles and special announcements by or about some of the important people reflect their standing in relation to the Rebbe and to the projects for which they are responsible. Each issue features a number of congratulatory ads to

the major and minor religious, social, or political heads of institutions or congregations, on the occasion of minor or major events in their or their families' lives.
Similarly, pictures of the leaders, such as the head of the ODA taken with famous
Jewish or non-Jewish political figures or government officials, members of Congress
or even of the cabinet are indicative of their sociopolitical status and of the role they
play in the welfare of the hasidic community. They have taken the place of the
lawyers and successful businessmen who in the earlier phases of Williamsburg
represented or directed its social and political affairs. *Der Yid* thus reflects and
consciously organizes the patterns of the major and minor structures and the
leadership configurations that determine social status, prominence, and recognition
in the hasidic community.

As in the earlier phases, unskilled workers are on the lowest level of the social
structure of the hasidic Community of Williamsburg, though neither in their past in
Eastern Europe nor in contemporary America have *hasidim* shunned physical labor
per se. But, as pointed out in the discussion of the economic patterns, most of those
who are physically and mentally capable are oriented toward moving into higher
semiskilled or skilled trades, toward setting up their own shops and businesses. A
drive through the main thoroughfares of Williamsburg, or any of the other hasidic
communities, will provide ample evidence of hasidic truck and bus drivers, of *hasidim*
handling all kinds of light and heavy machinery and mechanized equipment for
their own shops and businesses. They do the heavy menial work in their bakeries,
butcher shops, garages, or metal and plastics factories. Though, as pointed out, there
had been a few glaziers, plumbers, or a barber or two in the pre-World-War-II phase
of the old Williamsburg, these types of workers disappeared gradually. Now one
finds again Jewish carpenters, plumbers, electricians, and locksmiths, so that the
hasidic community has little reason to turn to outsiders, as during the post-
World-War-II era. But by the end of the '80s and the beginning of the '90s, one finds
again a growing number of minority members doing the heavy physical labor for
Jewish shopkeepers, such as the above cited former *kollel* scholars who run a thriving
computer business and employ strong minority workers to do the loading and
unloading of the heavy trucks of merchandise in their two stores. But these are still
the exceptions. There are committees of *yeshivah* scholars who constantly make the
rounds of local storekeepers and manufacturers to solicit work for their young men
who are ready to leave their institutions and are in need of jobs to support their
families. As one of them put it, when interviewed:

> We have a number of fine, capable young men in the Puper Yeshivah who are
> willing to accept any type of work. Why should they not have preference over any
> other non*yeshivah* men or outsiders. They are not afraid of doing strenuous physical
> work, and are as smart and capable, and usually more reliable, than others who may be
> into drugs, alcohol, and other addictions.

While being interviewed on Bedford Avenue, they stopped a local storekeeper who
promised them right then and there to hire two of their *yunge Leit* as soon as he
opened a new branch of his grocery products chain in the very near future.

Quite a few *hasidim*, young and old, handle various physical maintenance jobs at the *yeshivot* and other institutions. A still larger number do the physical and technical jobs in the offices of these institutions and organizations. Others are in charge of the food services of the boys' and girls' schools, and of shipping the breakfasts and lunches prepared centrally and distributed to the individual schools. They are the young people who man the fleets of buses and food-distribution vehicles, or vans of *Bikkur Cholim* and other welfare services and organizations who daily transport patients or visitors to hospitals and medical offices all over New York City. They provide and distribute the food that is freshly cooked every day by groups of volunteers and shipped to patients who request it. But, as indicated before, these types of jobs are mostly temporary and serve as stopgaps until these young men and women can qualify for regular jobs or careers open to them as *hasidim* who scrupulously abide by the hasidic life-style.

One interesting footnote is provided by the fact that, as indicated in Table 5.1, there is a category of residents in the new Williamsburg that did not exist in the more heterogeneous, more tolerant social structure of the earlier phases of Jewish Williamsburg, namely the class of Religious Ignorants, and beneath them, that of Religious Deviants. Most of them are probably people who for some personal reasons were not able to join the trek to Boro Park or the other relocation centers of groups of former Williamsburgers. Regardless of their occupation or their socioeconomic level, they are not made to feel welcome in Hasidic Williamsburg, as several of them complained when interviewed. "They think they are better just because they wear a *shtreimel* or *bekeshe*, or their *tzitzit* dangle from underneath their clothes," commented one elderly man who with his sick wife still lives in the apartment house that had been one of the best residences of the neighborhood more than half a century ago. "They do me a favor if they talk to me. And when they take my money in the stores, they do not accord me the respect I deserve by age alone. To me *menshlichkeit*, human decency, is more important than all their piety and *Hasidut*." But when questioned about the intensive welfare work done in the community by the hasidic institutions and organizations, he wholeheartedly stressed that never in his life had he seen so much *hesed* and *tzedakah*, lovingkindness and charity programs.

> I will never get used to living among these "primitives," but nowhere else will the needy, sick, and helpless be cared for better. They also have done wonders to make the neighborhood safer than ever before. We were afraid to deal with the hordes of youngsters from other ethnic and racial groups who began to roam the streets of the neighborhood all hours of the day and the night in the '50s and later. The *hasidim* take care of them. The cry of *"Haptzeh"* and their whistles swept the hoodlums away effectively.

A second respondent stressed that "unfortunately" he never had the chance to study Torah in his youth, in contrast to the people who now live in Williamsburg.

> We had to go to work as soon as we were able to. Our parents were poor immigrants and they depended on what we earned. We could not spend years in

Jewish or even in public school. At best we had Hebrew School lessons that stopped after *bar mitzvah* for most of us. But that does not make us second- or third-class Jews, the way they treat us around here. I was a respected member of the Hewes Street Shul, where I *davent* regularly, paid my membership, and contributed as much as any other working man. Our children preferred *davening* with their friends in Young Israel until they moved away to Long Island, where they are bigshots in their communities. Now there is really no place where I feel comfortable. We have a small *minyan* of leftovers from the earlier days who are too old, too poor, or too sick to move where they would be treated as equals.

This feeling of being treated as second-class citizens is one of the by-products of the Hungarian hasidic concentration on their own and on preserving the purity of their life-style. There are hardly any efforts made to reach out to other, less religious Jews, like the Lubavitch do, for instance, although there is the exception of recent efforts to work with Russian newcomers. Still, the nonhasidic Jews are made to feel out of place in Hasidic Williamsburg, where adherence to the strict standards of ritual observance and Torah study are the keys to acceptance and recognition.

It must, however, be stressed that a good many of the older residents left from the earlier phases of Jewish Williamsburg are now regular attendants of the Senior Citizens Center organized and directed by the hasidic community. There they benefit greatly from the various types of social, educational, and cultural programs, including regular classes of Torah study conducted by volunteers, in addition to good, nutritional meals and companionship.

STATUS SYMBOLS

One of the more fascinating aspects of the social dynamics of the hasidic community life and its underlying values is the presence of endemic status symbols. This does not mean that the typical status symbols, such as the size and type or location of the house, the kind of car and home furnishings, which characterize other Orthodox, as well as non-Orthodox and non-Jewish communities in the United States are not relevant gauges of social status and affluence in the new Williamsburg. Jewelry and good clothes that conform to the proper hasidic strict rules of *tzni'ut*, modesty, are an important factor considered by parents who, with the help of professional *shadhanim*, matchmakers, are surveying the *shidduch*-market for prospective grooms and brides for their children. In recent years, as incomes have risen and young girls have begun to graduate from Beth Rachel and other hasidic high schools with a decent earning capacity, the external tokens of social status and desirability are assuming greater importance than in the earlier years when most of the hasidic were lower-income people. The silver and jewelry stores in Williamsburg attest to the importance of their merchandise and to the role it plays in hasidic households, especially when their children reach young adulthood and the quest for *"passige,"* proper mates, becomes relevant. Though far from the luxury-oriented life-style of Boro Park, Flatbush, and Monsey, the new housefronts, porches, and quality of clothes, including the *bekeshes* and *shtreimels* of the men, attest to consciously sought upgrading of the life-style of the Williamsburg community.

Yet here, too, even if the status symbols are the same, and superficially they seem to indicate a growing emphasis on the tokens of greater affluence, they do not always have the same meaning. In the context of the hasidic community's social and economic situation a car or van may mean more than an expensive sports car import in front of the typical suburban community home. As in other upwardly mobile lower-income neighborhoods, a truck or a van is a significant symbol of the entrance of the owner into the world of business. However, a van or a stationwagon may connote that the drivers are either embarked on some new venture or have accommodated the needs of transportation for their large and growing families.

But there are other status symbols whose values and meaning are directly related to the hasidic life-style. Some of these are equally valued by nonhasidic members of the younger, Orthodox communities, the products of the day schools and *yeshivot* who have moved to the "right" and have adopted some of the outer and inner tokens of the hasidic life-style. In many of the broader American Jewish communities these hasidic status symbols are viewed negatively as curious or even anachronistic, unless they are heirlooms or items for Jewish antiques collections. The appreciation of a *mitzvah* of a divine commandment, such as a *sukkah*, a *lulav*, or ritual objects such as a *kiddush* cup, an *etrog* box, a *besamim* spicebox, the Hanukkah *menorah*, or a Sabbath candelabra for the table have become tokens of hasidic aesthetics, and more recently their values have become status symbols. They are part of the dowry of a hasidic bride and groom when they establish their home. The groom expects the gift of a deluxe edition of the multivolumed Talmud and other rabbinic and hasidic classics, the tools of the young Torah scholar and *kollelnik*. In fact, according to the favorite legend of the professional and amateur *shadhanim*, the matchmakers, there is a hierarchy of the hasidic and nonhasidic *yeshivot* based on the size of the dowry. One father, when interviewed, complained: "When I proposed a *shidduch* for my daughter to the family of a young scholar from one of the elite *yeshivot*, I was told that their *kollel* scholars get between $50,000 and $75,000 minimum, in addition to the pledge of support for additional years of advanced *kollel* study, after marriage."

Deservedly or not, the renown of the elite nonhasidic *yeshivot* plays a major role in the marriage prospects of their young scholars. In a sense, the future groom has himself become a status symbol in the hasidic as well as the nonhasidic social structure. As pointed out before, hasidic *yichus*, family background, tracing the lineage of the prospective groom or bride to a more or less famous *Rebbishe* dynasty, also plays a major role in the judgment of marriage chances as it reflected in the number and size of the congratulatory ads and announcements in the weekly *Der Yid*. The lesser tokens of this status are the gifts given to the groom by the family of the bride, such as a precious *etrog* box, *menorah,* a silver *atarah*, a silver decoration for the festive *tallit*, prayer shawl, of the groom, an expensive fur *shtreimel*, some of which cost as much as $1,500. The bride's diamond ring and jewelry are tokens of appreciation by the groom's family, in addition to the standard silver candlesticks. Though these exchanges of precious gifts are not exclusively part of the hasidic life-style, symbols such as the hasidic *yichus*, once derided in the egalitarian American approach of the Jewish as well as non-Jewish community, they have gained prominence in a community like Hasidic Williamsburg, as in other contemporary centers of hasidic life, large or small.

The joinings in marriage of the scions of famous hasidic Rebbes have become festive occasions celebrated on a large scale. The most prominent of these are featured not only in Jewish publications, but in the public press, such as a huge wedding that took place in a large sports arena in Long Island and was attended by more than 50,000 *hasidim* and curious spectators. The family affairs of such top hasidic leaders as the Rebbe of Satmar, or the Bobover, Muncaczer, Gerer, and Belzer dynasties are massive social affairs attended by many thousands and fill large armories and public halls. They not only reflect the affluence and generosity of the followers of these famous Rebbes and their popularity, but the vitality of the contemporary hasidic life decades after the experts had declared Hasidism and hasidic community life in America doomed. The very size of the gatherings, the prominence of the younger generations of native American or Israeli *hasidim*, and their communities thriving as never before, in some instances even more than in the small East-European towns, belie these gloomy predictions. Though these large spectacles attract a large number of the curious in addition to the masses of the genuinely concerned hasidic followers of the famous Rebbes, they provide evidence of the appreciation of *yichus*, the hasidic background, throughout the contemporary Orthodox Jewish world.

Though not quite as spectacular, the marriages of the children of the new aristocracy, the leaders of the hasidic institutions, and of the successful businessmen and entrepreneurs reflect the essential values and gauge the recognition of the parents in Williamsburg, Boro Park, Monsey, and Kiryas Joel of their services and roles in community life. Of course, all hasidic marriages are arranged, and what counts more than anything else are the piety, religious observance, and Torah scholarship, not the usual love or convenience factors. There is no dating or formal or informal meetings of young adolescents at the social events that are part of the high-school and college life of the boys and girls of the broader Jewish and non-Jewish society, where as many as 40 percent of the religious intermarriages originate. One of the functions of the exclusive use of *shadhanim*, the traditional matchmakers, is to maintain the purity of the hasidic life-style.

There are other significant hasidic gauges of social status, most of which derive from the central role of the Rebbe and the individual *hasid*'s place at his services, at the routine and special activities and festivities, such as the seat assigned at the tables at the regular Friday-night *tishen*, the *seudah shlishit*, the third meal of Sabbath, or at the *melaveh malkehs*, the gatherings on Sabbath night in the home of the Rebbe, or at special celebrations, such as the anniversaries of the liberation of the Old Rebbe from concentration camp. These are hallmarks of a *hasid*'s social ranking. Similarly, one may view the seating order in the synagogue or in the *bet hamidrash*, in the study halls, relative to the individual's closeness to the Rebbe. Likewise, the honors distributed during the regular and special services on Sabbaths and holidays are indicators of the *hashivut*, the prominence of the individual members of the community. Much of this, of course, depends on the money, the time, and the effort that the individual *hasidim* invest in the various phases of synagogue life, and in community projects and causes, as a means of achieving a certain rank among their peers.

But more important than this social component is the fact that the *hasidim* want to be close to their Rebbe and will pay often beyond their means to spend the holidays with the Rebbe, to take part in the services he conducts on the High Holiday, for example, and to receive the blessings of this association with his hallowed personality.

SOCIAL MOBILITY

As pointed out in my 1961 report, the social structure of the hasidic community is open and fluid, determined by the strong religious values of community life rather than the socioeconomic values that determine the stratification of the broader Jewish and non-Jewish society in the U.S. Piety, observance of the ritual laws and Torah scholarship are the factors that propel the individual to higher or lower status, except for the top ranks, which are held by the people of *yichus*, of important family background. But in a value-oriented community like new Williamsburg even this *yichus* status is only as strong and relevant as the conduct of the individual. Any serious decline in the rigid observance of the highest standards of the hasidic life-style or laxness in the scrupulous adherence to the letter and spirit of the *halachah*, the religious laws, seriously undermines the benefits of a person's *yichus*, or that of his family.

In my 1961 study, I pointed out that there were five major factors that determined social mobility during the third phase, which marked the change from a moderately Orthodox to a Hasidic community. Though the situation has changed radically since the '50s when the research for that study was concluded, the same forces are still at work and still determine the social dynamics and the channels of advancement in the institutional and organizational life of this community a generation later.

The Basic Orthodoxy of the Individual's Beliefs and Religious Practices

As pointed out in the preceding discussion of the relative strength of *yichus*, and as emphasized by Poll and Rubin in their analyses of Williamsburg prior to its major expansion and transformation, abiding by the essential hasidic values and life-style is the crucial factor of social status. Its significance has increased proportionately with the growing intensity and multiphased expansion of hasidic community life to a level that has never before existed on the American Jewish scene. In the earlier phases of the Jewish community of Williamsburg those whose values and life-style did not conform or who did not want to accommodate to the tightening of the level of his religious observances and beliefs moved to less ultra-Orthodox neighborhoods. The increasing crises of the '50s and '60s further intensified this outmigration of the less than ultra-Orthodox and of some of the more moderate hasidic elements. As pointed out, they sought not only the greater comforts and advantages of the better neighborhoods, but the flexibility and variety that allowed them more individual freedom than the essentially homogeneous Hungarian hasidic community of Williamsburg dominated by Satmar. Consequently, the central role of piety and scrupulous adherence to the dictates of the hasidic life-style became even more significant for social advancement. Most of those who remained were committed to their loyalty to the Rebbe of Satmar and other Rebbes, such as the Klausenburger, Puper, Vishnitzer, Kaschauer, Spinker, and Krasner Rebbes, and their educational institutions, and thus to the channels of social mobility they provided.

Rise in the Occupational Hierarchy

My earlier report had already emphasized that advancement in the occupational hierarchy is essential for social mobility in any social system. It gives the individual access to higher income and allows him to associate with others who possess the tokens of a higher standard of living, such as better clothes, residence, and care.[6] The association with and the adoption of the life-style of those of higher social status result in appropriate rise in the social structure commensurate with the higher valuation of the new occupation. As pointed out there, the symbols of social status, such as the type of residence, car, and the money spent on communal causes routinely and at special occasions are important in Williamsburg.

Yet they do play a lesser role in the patterns of social mobility. In the first place, the spread of occupations available to *hasidim* with a limited secular education is limited compared to the choices of professions that opened to the young of the earlier phases because they were able to acquire higher academic training and the degrees that are the prerequisites of advancement in the social structure of contemporary American society. In the second place, the life-style of the hasidic community does not allow the individual to display that higher income and cultural background even in such Orthodox neighborhoods as Boro Park. One young woman complained: "In Williamsburg, it's difficult to tell the differences between the poor, the middle class, and the rich because everyone must dress alike, have the same jewelry, and so forth. And it puts a financial burden on most people."

As she and another single girl in the small sample survey point out, the constantly rising prices of the hasidic garb do strain the resources of the poor and young at the beginning of their careers. On the other hand, compared to the cost of life in Boro Park, Flatbush, or Monsey, where there is more emphasis on the outer tokens of social class, the relatively simple hasidic "uniforms" of the new Williamsburg are a much smaller burden on the budgets of the majority of its lower-class population. But the number of the young and middle-aged successful businessmen is growing, and despite some setbacks in the late '80s and early '90s, as a result of the general recession, there is ample evidence of upward mobility within the parameters of the hasidic life-style.

The Relational Configuration

The 1961 report pointed out that the relational configuration is as important as the rise in the occupational hierarchy for advancement into a higher social class, which is frequently closed to outsiders even if their financial resources are more than adequate. This was true for the Jewish community of Williamsburg as much as for most other Jewish and non-Jewish communities.

It is even more important in the hasidic community than it had been in the earlier phases where there had been crass class differences between the older, mostly lower- and lower-middle-class American elements who looked down upon the greens. They held themselves above and apart from the members of the various waves of newcomers before, during, and after World War II, though many of these spoke better English and had a better professional and cultural background than the old elite. This situation changed only when the young men and women began to associate and intermarry, often to the chagrin of some of their more stubborn elders. Many of the newcomers, however, preferred to move to new religious communities where they were accepted as equals, rather than be treated as refugees by the old-timers. The large Russian-Polish synagogues were prime centers of these old prejudices, which set up barriers to the social advancement of the newcomers, until they disintegrated. Only in the more intimate setting of small *shtieblach,* the informal storefront, or basement synagogues, or the *shuls* of the Jewish political organizations of the Orthodox young native products of the day schools and *yeshivot,* did these barriers vanish with the strengthening bonds of common religious, ideological, and scholarly values, which changed the character of the Jewish Community of Williamsburg in the post-World-War-II phase.

The massive influx of survivors from the Holocaust and DP camps enabled them to set up their own synagogues, organizations, congregations, and institutions. They established their own social structures around some of the famous Talmud scholars, rabbis, or hasidic Rebbes who settled in Williamsburg because of its Orthodox milieu.

The relational configuration became a powerful factor in the evolving networks of personal and group hierarchies of the Hungarian hasidic community. The social, economic, and educational institutions became centers, each of which evolved its own leadership and activists as the expanding needs of the rapidly growing population required organization. While the old associates of the Rebbe of Satmar and other heads of the major and minor subcommunities are largely still in charge, they have gradually been replaced by the upward surge of the *avreichim,* the massive new generation of middle-aged and young *hasidim* whose socioeconomic advancement has been a major factor in the consolidation and further expansion of the new Williamsburg. They, in particular, have found their niches and are creating new ones in the networks of institutions they develop as their families, study cohorts, and hasidic associations provide channels of advancement.

Organization like *Hatzoloh,* the *Shomrim, Tomche Shabbos, Bikkur Cholim,* to mention just the most famous, depend almost totally on the *avreichim* to carry the heavy burden of their routine and special functions. Those who display organizational talents and leadership qualities are co-opted by the established *kehillah* top ranks to join them, as one of them put it. At least half of the boards and executive committees come from the increasingly important ranks of these young activists, giving them the chance to advance quickly in the wide open channels of the hasidic community's social structures. The massive social life of *melaveh malkehs*, banquets, luncheons auctions, and other routine and special celebrations for the benefit of schools, shuls, and institutions, which fill the pages of the weekly *Der Yid* ads and announcements, reflect the evolving new structures.

It is also here that the hasidic women of the new Williamsburg have their best chance to gain recognition and status by sponsoring the teas, luncheons, and other social meetings of the numerous ladies auxiliaries for the local, national, and international hasidic welfare organizations. Most of the women interviewed, even the few who were critical of the hasidic life of Williamsburg, expressed admiration for the *hesed* and *tzedakah*, the charity activities that are their major social outlets. These give them a chance to contribute to the survival and maintenance of the institutions in Williamsburg, as well as in other hasidic communities in the U.S., Israel, and elsewhere. At the same time they are provided opportunities for social mobility and public recognition.

Though socioeconomic success and the ability to make financial contributions are factors of advancement, they are much less so than in other Jewish and non-Jewish communities. Family relations, the age cohorts, the *yeshivah* and *havrutas*, study groups, are more important in the expanding, hence wide open, social structures of the hasidic subcommunities of Williamsburg.

Acquisition of the Patterns of Superior Class Behavior

For the same reasons as mentioned in the opening of the preceding discussion, this factor of social advancement has little if any significance for social mobility in new Williamsburg. In the first place, the old class differences have almost totally disappeared with the departure of the population of the earlier periods. Secondly, the hasidic life-style of the vast majority of the current population has little room for variation in class behavior, except for the display of affluence in the type and size of homes, cars, and jewelry, and the money spent on the important community causes. As the young woman quoted indicated, there is a high degree of uniformity that, in fact, puts some strain on the budget of the poor, within the relatively rigid framework of the ultra-Orthodox ideology and adherence to the letter and spirit of the law. Perhaps the type of marriage to members of higher social ranking, such as the weddings of prominent Williamsburg hasidic community leaders to equally successful hasidic businessmen or outstanding scholars in London, Antwerp, and Jerusalem, which are featured prominently in the pages of *Der Yid* and celebrated in high style, are the exceptions.

Increasingly, the attempt is made in the hasidic communities in New York and in Israel to fight the bane of costly wedding celebrations, which have become part of the Orthodox as well as the general Jewish life. Some groups are limiting the number of guests to be invited and the amount of money to be spent on the standard forms of entertainment. What varies considerably is the size of the *nadden*, the dowry, given to the girls and the type of household established for the young couple by the parents. And here, too, it is the intensity of the scrupulous adherence to the religious life-style and scholarship of the groom's or the girl's family that matter rather than the usual class differences. Thus, it is almost impossible to pinpoint traces of superior or inferior class behavior among all levels and types of the hasidim in Williamsburg.

Torah Scholarship

In contrast to the preceding criterion of social mobility, this factor is perhaps the most significant in indicating the transformation of the social life in the hasidic community of Williamsburg. The impact of the day schools and *yeshivot*, and the massive influx of famous scholars from the highest Eastern European talmudic academies and hasidic leaders with their masses of followers had already raised the social recognition and status of Torah scholarship during the decades of the transformation. Yet, as already pointed out, the emphasis on a good secular education and on preparation for professional careers, even for those who spent additional years after graduation from high school in the U.S. or in Israel on advanced talmudic and rabbinic studies, was still the standard for the young in the Orthodox Jewish communities.

There is no question that the products of these post-World-War-II *yeshivah* and day-school education systems established their own, thoroughly religious life-style, quite different from that of their parents, with an accent on continuous study for themselves and for their children. They generally also have large families and lavish much more attention on the observance of *mitzvot* than the older generation, even in their appearance and in their cultural pursuits. But their broader background and their professional choices require standards of conduct and life-style that are radically different from those of the hasidic communities, such as Williamsburg. Except for the minority of those who have remained in Jewish education with its limited rewards, most have established themselves in business. Some have entered their parents' or in-laws' businesses or have pursued careers in government service, financial management, insurance, or computer work. Quite a few have become scientists, researchers, or academicians. Their Torah scholarship is still a major factor in their personal and social life, but not the exclusive factor, as is the case in the hasidic communities, whose young have limited their secular education to devote most of their adolescent and young adult years to intensive training in the talmudic, rabbinic, and hasidic literature.

This basic orientation is the crucial background for the differences of the role of Torah scholarship in Williamsburg and elsewhere. In former years the reputation of Hungarian *hasidim* was mostly based on piety and scrupulous adherence to the ritual laws rather than on talmudic scholarship per se, as in the Lithuanian type of *yeshivot* and in the American academies founded by the handful of survivors from among the outstanding scholars and their superior students. As discussed in detail in Chapter 3, this crass difference is no longer valid. Ever since the Old Rebbe of Satmar, himself one of the foremost scholars of the Jewish world, established his intensive Torah educational system more than 40 years ago, the emphasis in his *yeshivot* has been on the creation of new generations of young hasidic men steeped in Torah, in rabbinic and hasidic literature, whose level of learning compares favorably with that of the elders among the survivors. Though their basic orientation is less theoretical than that of the Lithuanian type of *yeshivot* in the U.S. and in Israel, the addition of *kollels* has produced hundreds of young *hasidim* whose talmudic scholarship matches that of their contemporaries in the *kollels* of the Lithuanian *yeshivot*. This has been attested to by visiting teams of prominent scholars who were invited on an exchange of knowledge and to evaluate the schools so that they can qualify for governmental or private foundation grants for advanced Hebrew scholarship. It is also attested to by the high quality of Torah journals published periodically by the young scholars of the advanced hasidic institutes.

This almost exclusive emphasis on continued devotion to Torah study among the masses of students of hasidic schools had a deep impact on the role of rabbinics and of Torah scholars in the social structure of the hasidic community. Consequently, Torah scholarship has become a prime factor of social mobility, and of social recognition, second only to the role of scrupulous adherence to the requirements of the hasidic life-style. The outstanding scholars of Satmar and those of the other hasidic *yeshivot* are a prime source of the most desirable *shidduchim*, marriage partners, for the girls of the hasidic communities not only in Williamsburg but elsewhere in the U.S. and throughout the Orthodox Jewish centers of the contemporary world. Though a good family background and economic considerations play a significant role, they are secondary to the value of Torah scholarship. The select among these young men of the *kollels* are chosen to head the new schools of the proliferating educational systems of Satmar and other hasidic groups. As discussed before, they have become stars of the lecture halls, which are crowded in the *batei midrashim* of Williamsburg and elsewhere. Others have become renowned *dayanim*, judges, of the *batei Horo'oh*, the courts that handle most of the ritual as well as the family and business affairs of hasidic and other Orthodox communities. The broader ranks are filling the growing need for religious functionaries on all levels. And even those who are pursuing careers in the trades and in business are further cultivating their scholarship before and after going to work.

Consequently, every phase of the social as well as the religious life of the new Williamsburg is largely dominated by scholars. They are the de facto elite of the community. The rabbinate is no longer ridiculed as a job "not suitable for a Jewish young man," as in the earlier phases of Williamsburg and elsewhere in the country. Similarly, the fields of teaching and of other religious functionaries are no longer the last resort for those who do not qualify for other careers, as they still are in many nonhasidic communities. Though the successful businessmen and entrepreneurs among the middle-aged and young are playing an increasing role in the organizations and in the management of the affairs of the hasidic communities, they are not treated as "impractical" Torah scholars. Their own years of advanced Torah study and their hasidic orientation create the type of atmosphere that was the prime aim of the Rebbe of Satmar and the other hasidic leaders when they established Williamsburg as an "island in the city." Nor is this a return to the *shtetl* as suggested by some observers. It is rather an American version of the classic synthesis of Torah scholarship and participation in the mainstream of the host country when and wherever it was permitted, in order to preserve the purity of the traditional Jewish life in exile, until the coming of the Messiah. This is the ideology of the Satmar community, as it had been that of the faithful over the past 2,000 years, since the destruction of Jerusalem and the Jewish state.

SUMMARY

In retrospect, the social stratification and leadership patterns of Hasidic Williamsburg express the central values and ethos of the hasidic community as much as any other phase of its individual and collective life. Due to the metastatus of the charismatic Rebbe of Satmar, piety, Torah scholarship, and an intensely religious life-style have become the prime factors in social advancement, unlike in most other Jewish communities in the U.S. and elsewhere. This value shift produced the crucial difference between the old and the new Williamsburg. Headed by the Rebbe of Satmar himself, Torah scholars are the social elite, not merely properly respected and treated with deference, like the clergy in other Jewish and non-Jewish communities. They are the ones who are actually setting policies; who actively engage in, direct, and determine the course of development of the major phases of community life. They are aided by the know-how and experience of professionals. But at all times it is Torah scholarship, piety, and the intense hasidic life-style that are the criteria for leadership and status throughout the structures of Hasidic Williamsburg.

Most important, it is the generation of young native American *hasidim* who are increasingly assuming responsibility for the affairs of the community. As they move into the centers of the structure and the leadership, they provide the stability with which to perpetuate this unique hasidic society in the waning years of the twentieth century.

➽➽ 6 ⋘⋘

New Patterns of the Synagogue

T he introduction to the discussion of the synagogue in my 1961 report emphasized its centrality not only as the house of prayer but as the hub of Orthodox Jewish life. Directly or indirectly, all phases of an individual's personal and social life are connected with the synagogue through ceremonies and customs, formal and informal group functions. Hence any changes in the spirit and patterns of the community express themselves in the basic structure and dynamics of the synagogue.

Contrary to the findings of Louis Wirth's classic study *The Ghetto* (1928) and Marshall Sklare's *Conservative Judaism* (1953), which associate the Orthodox synagogue with the lower-class population of the first settlement, the Jewish community, and with it the Orthodox synagogue of Williamsburg, did not disintegrate with the social advancement of its members and the secularization of community life. Though the ecological and economic conditions that might have doomed the community were present, as in most similar older Jewish neighborhoods in Brooklyn and New York City, the Orthodox synagogue went through a remarkable process of revitalization. This renaissance was due primarily to the influx of new elements, the growth of a generation educated in the local day schools and *yeshivot*, and to the influx of large groups of refugees from the countries of Nazi occupation and the Holocaust. They took the place of the rapidly declining membership of the older, dominant Ashkenazic Russian-Polish synagogues, whose congregations left the neighborhood after World War II. Focusing on these developments, and rejecting the predictions of doom for the Orthodox community, my 1961 study made this statement about the renaissance of the Orthodox synagogue: "Instead of becoming monuments of a bygone era and of 'institutional decay,' they have become the very center of the social, cultural, and political, as well as the spiritual life of the community" (p. 155).

This intensification of the religious life of the Jewish community of Williamsburg in the '40s and '50s, in which the hasidic synagogues, the smaller ones as well as the larger *shtieblach*, the *shuls* of the nonhasidic *yeshivot* and of the Jewish political organizations replaced the large Ashkenazic Russian-Polish synagogues as centers of community life, was not to last. As pointed out throughout the preceding chapters, the mounting crises of the '50s and '60s, the rapid outmigration of the former residents and many of the more recent immigrant groups, including some hasidic newcomers, and the transplant of their institutions threatened the survival of Jewish Williamsburg. The turning point came with the decision of the largest Hungarian hasidic community, headed by Rabbi Yoel Teitelbaum, the Rebbe of Satmar, to take a stand against the threatened collapse and reverse the processes of disintegration everywhere in evidence.

Already in the '50s the large hasidic centers had become the foci of the colorful religious life that attracted busloads of Jewish and non-Jewish visitors to Williamsburg, especially on such festive occasions as Simhat Torah, when synagogue life spilled out into the streets. In the face of these crises, the hasidic leaders threw themselves into intensive campaigns, developing programs and projects to effect the physical, economic, social, and political renewal and reconstruction of the Jewish Triangle described in the preceding chapters. Consequently, the hasidic congregations and their dynamic leaders became the prime factors of the inner and outer reorganization that led to the development of the new Williamsburg.

Rarely in the 2,000 years of exile has the synagogue served its function as the "movable sanctuary," the central institution of the entire Jewish community life, more than in the hasidic community of Williamsburg. Already in my 1961 report it was shown that even among the most religious Jewish neighborhoods of New York and elsewhere in the U.S., including the Orthodox pre- and post-World-War-II communities, there had been no intentional patterns of displaying any aspect of religious and ritual life outside of the synagogue. The ideal of the period of enlightenment of being a Jew in the house and a human being like others in the street affected the Orthodox Jews in Western Europe and in the U.S. no less than the nonreligious communities of secular Jews. Perhaps the memories of centuries of persecution and oppression and the shadows of the ghettos in the back of their minds caused them to avoid rousing *rishut*, anti-Semitic reactions in the broader environment. Beyond this, they perceived little intrinsic value in displaying their different life-style in public. Thus, they refrained from letting their individual or communal observances, festivities, and celebrations, even of such happy holidays as Purim or Simhat Torah, spill out of the synagogue into the street. Even the so-called Jewish alternative, the display of the *menorah* instead of the Christmas tree, was and still continues to be done in an unobtrusive manner, except for the recent display of large *menorahs* by the Lubavitcher Outreach Organization in central public places on Chanukah.

The hasidic community had little respect for this attitude. As one famous Rebbe, cited in my 1961 report put it: "They will respect us more if they realize that we take our religion seriously."

The new Williamsburg is concerned neither with potentially provoking hostile reactions from their non-Jewish neighbors nor with earning their respect. From the very outset the Rebbe of Satmar and the other hasidic leaders were intent on creating their community in maximal isolation from the sociocultural environment and in an atmosphere permeated by the spirit and life-style of Hasidism. They aimed for a setting in which to bring up their young the same way they had done in the East European *shtetl*, while at the same time participating in the economic life of society at large. In line with this attitude, they built the synagogue into the very center of the neighborhood, around which most facets of community life are structured. This structure has been visually represented in the construction of the hasidic utopia in Kiryas Joel, the exurban branch of Satmar built by and and named in honor of Rabbi Yoel Teitelbaum, their Rebbe, 90 minutes north of Manhattan. This community, which 15 years after its founding has 1200 families, is dominated by the large, impressive synagogue and house of study built high on a hill in the center of the new township, which is growing by leaps and bounds.

In the Jewish Triangle of Williamsburg, the old *shul* of Yetev Lev of Satmar was somewhat off center, in one of the mansions left over from pre-World-War-I non-Jewish life on upper Bedford Avenue. After more than two decades of explosive growth, the Satmar *kehillah* built a new synagogue in the very center of the neighborhood. Though cutting through two blocks it is only noticeable from the outside because of a new front entrance added at the end of the '80s. This is in strong contrast to the impressive fronts of the old, large Ashkenazic synagogues, which had been located in former majestic church buildings. The main hall of the Satmar *shul* accommodates more than 2,000 people, and has a number of other prayer and study halls, plus additional facilities to serve the religious and ritual functions of the congregation. An adjoining building houses the administration offices and a large community meat market. The Russian-Polish synagogues, which had dominated pre-World-War-II Williamsburg, where rarely able to fill their large *shuls*, with open galleries for women, except on the High Holidays and on special occasions when famous cantors gave concerts, or when they were used for public meetings.

The equally large main synagogue of Satmar is packed to capacity on regular Sabbaths, with services going on simultaneously in some of the side halls and in the increasing number of branch synagogues established in the past decade to meet the needs of the young and middle-aged families residing in the marginal areas of the expanding hasidic neighborhood. Plans have been drawn up to build an even larger synagogue on the large area cleared behind the mansion of the present Rebbe and purchased legally from the government for this purpose and for the now newly constructed fifty-four classroom *yeshivah* building and housing for the faculty.[1]

The new school buildings and the plans for a new synagogue confirm the confidence of Hasidic Williamsburg in its ability to survive and to accommodate the future generations of its large population. It also confirms the loyalty of the *hasidim* of Satmar and other hasidic subcommunities to their Rebbes and their desire to remain close to them and their religious services and inspiration.

Though the large synagogues of Satmar, Pappa, and the Spinker congregations lack the magnificence of the facade of the old converted churches of the Ashkenazic synagogue buildings, they are far from the small, Spartan *shtieblach* in which they had started and which have proliferated on practically every block. Through the generosity of some of the local *hasidim*, whose business ventures have prospered, and of admirers from afar, large chandeliers and similar splendid appointments indicate a measure of affluence and the gratitude of the *hasidim* who attribute their success to the blessing of their Rebbe.

Significantly, the loyalty of the Williamsburg *hasidim* to their leaders persists, although three of the major Rebbes of the first generation of immigrants who settled in Williamsburg after World War II have passed away in the past decade. They were Rabbi Yoel Teitelbaum, the Old Rebbe of Satmar, the most revered and powerful, Rabbi Levi Yitzchok Grunwald, the Tzelemer Rav, who in many ways initiated much that became characteristic of the new Williamsburg, especially in the areas of *kashrut* and education, and Rabbi Joseph Grunwald, the Rebbe of Pappa, whose community is the second largest after Satmar. Neither the Rebbe of Satmar nor the Tzelemer Rav left children behind. But the son of the Pappa Rebbe and the stepson of the Tzelemer Rav are continuing to lead the congregations and to coordinate the programs and activities developed by their predecessors. The inner discipline of their communities enables them to carry the burden thrust upon them at a relatively young age.

Most impressive is the success of the new Rebbe of Satmar, Rabbi Moshe Teitelbaum, the nephew of the Old Rebbe, who had always been close to his uncle, and who had built his own hasidic community first in Williamsburg, then in Boro Park. As pointed out throughout the previous discussion, no one can really take the place of the Old Rebbe in the love and veneration of his huge following. But once the leadership of the Satmar congregation decided on their choice, the nephew was able to take over and successfully carry on and further expand the empire of his sainted predecessor. He earned the respect and reverence of the vast Satmar community by his wise yet restrained conduct, by his scholarship, eloquence, and his extraordinary organizational talent. (This is true notwithstanding the occasional outbreaks of friction caused by a group of *hasidim* who were not able to accept anyone else after their *Heiliger* Rebbe, especially the group of B'nai Yoel in Kiryas Joel. They cling to the widow and several formerly close associates of Rabbi Yoel Teitelbaum. Thus they give the impression of an active opposition and splinter groups.) As Rabbi Moshe Teitelbaum carries on and further expands the policies, worldwide projects, and community programs, he is assisted by a staff of close advisers who successfully initiated and masterminded the smooth transition after the new Rebbe's ascendance to the position of his sainted uncle. Equally important, he has been able to select some of the most capable of the younger generation of leaders who have assumed responsibility and displayed leadership qualities on all levels of the spiritual, social, political, educational, and welfare branches of his administration. As a result, a decade later, the Rebbe of Satmar is solidly in control of the huge congregation and worldwide following he inherited from his predecessor, Rabbi Yoel Teitelbaum, the larger than life Old Rebbe.

Having successfully weathered this most serious of the internal crises threatening the continuity of the new Williamsburg, the hasidic community is largely guided by a combination of older survivors and the new, American-born hasidic leaders and activists. They continue to plan and further expand the role and functions of synagogue life in keeping with the spirit of Hasidism transplanted to American soil by the Rebbes and leaders of the Hungarian survivors who came to Williamsburg after the Holocaust.

There are two interesting innovations in the synagogue life of the new Williamsburg Satmar *kehillah*. One is the establishment of a separate congregation of older, retired *hasidim* numbering over one hundred members, who share classes through most of the day as well as the services. The second is a growing congregation of Sephardim, mostly Iranian Jews, who were saved and brought to Williamsburg by *Rav Tov*, the rescue and relief organization established by the Old Rebbe of Satmar to aid Russian and Iranian refugees and provide them with religious training as well as with economic, social, and welfare assistance.

My 1961 report focused on the following four aspects of change that transformed the synagogues and synagogue life in the Jewish community of Williamsburg from before World War II through the end of the '50s: 1) The role of the rabbi, 2) the types of services, 3) customs and mores; and 4) the role of women in the synagogue. More than three decades later, the same strategy of analysis provides valuable insight into the dynamics of the changes that produced what is probably the most important pillar of the central structure that has evolved since the middle of the century in the community life of Williamsburg. For, as indicated in the opening, the synagogue has moved ever more into the very center of the institutional and organizational structure, focused on the hallowed person of the Rebbe, on the services he conducts, and the ritual celebrations he orchestrates in and around the synagogue. For, true to its traditional ideology, Hasidism has since its beginning concentrated on providing the masses of the ignorant or less scholarly with the religious experiences of praying with the Rebbe in order that they will be inspired and elevated by his saintly conduct and guidance, for sharing his activities that transform even the most mundane act, such as partaking of food, singing, and dancing, and endows it with deeper meaning and function as a service to the Lord. The great hasidic Rebbes who survived and came to this country, such as the Rebbes of Satmar and of Lubavitch, were able to engender this same spirit and attitude among the immigrant and native followers on American soil as they had in Eastern Europe.

THE ROLE OF THE RABBI

As indicated in the discussion of the changes in my 1961 report, the most dramatic reversal produced during the post-World-War-II period in the Jewish community of Williamsburg was the restoration of the rabbi to his proper place as the highest spiritual authority and head of the traditional Jewish community, a position that he had held throughout the history of Jewish exile. Not only was he by religious law to function as the supreme authority in matters of ritual and religious life, but by virtue of his training and scholarship, he was to be the authority in all matters of concern in the synagogue, and in the educational, social, and political life of the community itself.

No other aspect of the acculturation and assimilation of the Jewish community in the U.S. had a more significant impact on its structure than the gradual seculariza-tion of synagogue life when the emerging Reform and Conservative movements imported from Central European countries, such as Germany and Austria, tried to make the synagogue "contemporary," as they put it. Their central aim was to replace the traditional, centuries old patterns with new ones that would "liberate" the individual Jew and the collective life from what they considered "outdated," old-fashioned restraints based on obsolete values. Above all they intended to bring Judaism and Jewish life up to modern standards, in line with broader American values, which were largely determined by socioeconomic considerations, centered on success and social advancement.

In this reevaluation of all Jewish religious and communal values, the image of the rabbis, many of whom had to be imported from Eastern Europe even in the Orthodox synagogue, had largely been devaluated. His domain was to be the synagogue and the basic religious functions and ceremonies still maintained by most first-generation immigrants, and decreasingly by the members of the second and third generations. We find evidence for this in most historical and sociological studies of the American Jewish community, such as Louis Wirth's *The Ghetto* (1928) and Marshall Sklare's *Conservative Judaism* (1955) and *The Lakeville Studies* (1979). Beyond the life-cycle functions from marriage and birth to bar mitzvahs and burials, the community paid increasingly less attention to the rabbi as an authority figure outside the synagogue. Gradually, the Reform synagogue transformed him into the Jewish clergyman, somewhat on the order of a Protestant pastor as pictured in the classic *Middletown* studies by the Lynds (1929 and 1937), a respected public figure with little de facto influence on the daily lives of his flock.

As pointed out in my earlier study and in this update, in the discussion of the socioeconomic structure, the assimilation to the general socioeconomic values affected the Orthodox synagogue as much as the Reform and Conservative com-munities in such neighborhoods as pre-World-War-II Jewish Williamsburg. The rabbi was relegated to synagogue life. He was paid a minimal salary, and the renewal of his annual salary contract was at the mercy of the successful businessmen and lawyers who had increasingly become dominant in the religious, as well as in the sociopolitical life of the community. Frequently, this led to lessening of the proper respect and valuation of the status of the rabbi, as indicated facetiously in the popular stereotype of the position of a rabbi as not fit for a Jewish young man.

At the same time, the Jewish professional became the vocational ideal of the vast majority of young Jews who increasingly turned to academic, scientific, or techno-logical careers. This was and still is equally true for the young of the Orthodox Jewish community, including the graduates of the day schools and *yeshivot*. All but those on the extreme right of the spectrum take pride in the number of their alumni who have achieved prominence in some realm of the world of academia, of science, or of technology. And those who are honored at public functions are not the scholars, as one father recently told his son who is still pursuing his postgraduate talmudic studies while trying to subsist on the meager support from the kollel and parents to maintain his family of five children. "Look who is sitting at the head table and receiving the honors and accolades? Not you who knows a 1000 *Blatt* of *Gemara*, but the fellows who dropped out of the *yeshivah* high schools, who became successful businessmen. They can afford to live a lavish life and are in the position to contribute large sums of money to their favorite institutions." Though there is an increasing recognition of the scholars in the more intensely Orthodox communities, this somewhat bitter comment of a father, who is himself a *hasid* and successful businessman, is still valid. While he generously supports his two sons, who are spending more years on intensive rabbinic studies, he chose a young dental student graduate of a *yeshivah* as his son-in-law and supported him until he was ready to set up his own dental practice. When asked whether his sons would eventually join his flourishing business, he remarked with resignation: "They wouldn't even step into my shop. A few more years and I will have to sell my factory, and they will have to eke out a meager living for their already large families." This moderate Boro Park *hasid* does not for a minute regret the intensive *yeshivah* education he gave his brilliant sons. But he would have preferred it had they eventually turned to some profitable profession, like insurance, financial management, or computer programming, which have become mainstays of the Orthodox young, including the Hungarian hasidic *yeshivah* alumni.

The general attitude of the masses of the hasidic community of Williamsburg toward the role and position of the rabbi and scholars is radically different even from the moderately Orthodox post-World-War-II population's attitude, most of whom have since moved to Boro Park, Flatbush, Monsey, and similar religious communities. The impact of the day schools and *yeshivot*, especially since the arrival of the famous *roshei yeshivah*, such as Rabbi Aaron Kotler, had already produced a positive view of Torah scholarship and of continued Torah study after graduation from high school. It had prompted the gradual acceptance of advanced study in the *kollel* in the U.S. or in Israel, even after marriage. With the outmigration of the older elements, the synagogues and synagogue leadership became more intensely Orthodox; small and larger hasidic *shtieblach* and *shuls* were headed by scholars or Rebbes who commanded greater respect from their congregants than the rabbis of the earlier period. But the most powerful factor that radically changed the spiritual climate and social structure of Williamsburg was the arrival of the famous Hungarian hasidic leaders, foremost among them Rabbi Yoel Teitelbaum, the Rebbe of Satmar. Though preceded by such hasidic luminaries as the Tzelemer Rav and the Klausenburger Rebbe, who attracted new elements to their following and changed the standards of the religious life, it was the Rebbe of Satmar whose superior scholarship, saintly life-style, and fame brought hundreds of his former and new *hasidim* to Williamsburg.

More important yet was the fact that he was not satisfied with a passive role atop a pedestal of reverence and admiration. Rabbi Teitelbaum was determined to systematically create the kind of intensely hasidic community life that would inhibit the ongoing process of assimilation that had affected even the synagogue and with it the position of the rabbi and the scholar. From the very outset he realized and stressed that this was a matter of education and control of the basic realms of community life. At the end of the '40s and into the early '50s, such an ambitious, far-reaching approach seemed rather unrealistic. The rampant crises and increasing threats to the survival of the Jewish neighborhood seemed to doom his early efforts and those of the other hasidic leaders, as ever larger numbers of even the most Orthodox and some hasidic groups chose to relocate to other Orthodox neighborhoods in New York or to suburban communities that offered greater security and a more promising setting for survival and future growth. There was little reason to assume that the efforts of the Rebbe of Satmar and the other hasidic leaders could stem the process of disintegration that beset Williamsburg in the '50s. Like many other older Jewish neighborhoods, Williamsburg was affected by the massive influx of ethnic and racial minorities, which further aggravated the already difficult housing and living conditions.

As discussed in the preceding chapters, it took superhuman efforts on the part of the hasidic community and its leaders to stem the increasing friction and destruction, once they made the decision to remain and fight for survival. Progressive blight decimated the still available usable areas of the Jewish Triangle, which was already beset by severe housing shortages, especially in view of the large size of the hasidic families. Thus, the first line of attack was to hold and reclaim the still usable territory of the Jewish Triangle, to renovate and recondition or reconstruct the aging stock of brownstone houses and pre-World-War-II apartment houses, and from there to set about reclaiming the Jewish neighborhood and restructuring the community life. One of the primary goals of the Rebbe of Satmar and the other hasidic leaders was to reverse the diminishment of the role of the rabbi and the scholar, and return them to the role of active, decisive functionary in all realms of the community.

This phase of change was relatively easy, in view of the focal role of the Rebbe in every aspect of community life. Unlike some of the great scholars, who concentrated exclusively on their intellectual and spiritual life and did not actively deal with practical day-to-day questions and problems of ritual life, leaving these to local rabbis or *dayanim*, the Rebbe of Satmar and some of the other Hungarian Rebbes made the study of practical *halachah* the cornerstone of the curriculum of their *yeshivot*. Their main purpose was to produce hasidic rabbis who, unlike many of the contemporary Orthodox rabbis, would not have to depend on outstanding *poskim*, expert halachic authorities, such as the famous late Rabbi Moshe Feinstein, to guide them in all but the most common *sha'lot*, questions of ritual law, in the direction of the congregational life.[2]

This was one of the main strategies of the Rebbe of Satmar, to systematically change the environment of his community through systematic education. He focused on the need for competent rabbinic authorities who could meet the demand for spiritual and ritual leadership of the hasidic masses. Unlike the rabbis of the large Ashkenazic pre-World-War-II congregations in Williamsburg and elsewhere, they would be molded to play a significant role in every phase of the community's individual and collective life. His advanced *yeshivah* and *kollels* trained cadres of *dayanim*, judges and ritual experts, to supervise and direct his demanding higher standards of *kashrut*, food processing, and the distribution of new food lines, which the members of his community produced.

Similarly, he consciously developed teams of rabbis who specialized in becoming competent educators to staff the rapidly expanding network of his *Talmud Torahs*, *yeshivot*, and schools for boys and girls in his own and in other hasidic communities. He conscientiously cultivated other teams of rabbis who specialized in various areas of the religious, ritual, and business life, and who would be able to man his *bet din*, his court, and his *Beth Horo'oh*. These are available to the hasidic community on regular schedules even during the summer when they convene in centers of the Catskill Mountains where Satmar and other hasidic communities have established their bungalow colonies.

Thus, together with the parallel efforts of the great *roshei yeshivah*, the deans of the famous advanced talmudic academies, such as the legendary Rabbi Aaron Kotler, a new climate evolved in the Orthodox Jewish communities in general. In Hasidic Williamsburg, the authority of the scholars and rabbis rose to the highest level in the social structure, which had traditionally been assigned to them as the spiritual guides in all realms of individual and collective life. Unlike the rabbis of pre-World-War-II synagogues, they are not restricted to the religious functions of the synagogue. They are the highest arbiters when it comes to policies and decision making in all realms of social and business life, not only in ritual matters, as is the case in most nonhasidic congregations. Thus it is to the credit of the efforts of the advanced *yeshivot gedolot* and the hasidic leaders that a veritable revolution has taken place in the U.S. and in other countries so that in main street stores, and not only in the Jewish ghetto communities, a broad range of kosher products that meet the highest standards of the most observant Jews can be found. Individual rabbis, such as the Tzelemer Rav, Rabbi Levi I. Grunwald, Rabbi Joseph Breuer of Congregation Jeshurun of Washington Heights, and the massive efforts of the Union of Orthodox Congregations combined to create and popularize the channels of availability and of public awareness of the availability of these tokens of higher standards of observance, not only in the food lines that have proliferated in the past decades. Hotels, institutions, and organizations that decades before would never have acceded to it now advertise that they are *Glatt Kosher*, they have the kosher certification of the Union of Orthodox Jewish Congregations (the UO), and other reliable organizations. Thus they are attracting tourists even in places far off the beaten path of the Jewish trade. Obviously, the hasidic revolution has been a major factor in this breakthrough of ritual and religious life in this country.

More important, however, than these ancillary effects, the most radical change was the social reevaluation of the role and status of rabbis, scholars, and religious functionaries in the eyes of the broader intensely Orthodox Jewish masses in Williamsburg and far beyond.

TYPES OF SERVICES

As indicated in my 1961 report and throughout this discussion of the major changes in the Jewish community of Williamsburg, the era of the large Ashkenazic Russian-Polish congregations had already declined during and after World War II due to natural attrition and the rapid outmigration of their middle-aged and older membership. Even earlier, the younger elements had chosen to leave the neighborhood and move to other, more convenient communities. Gone with them was the glory of the old formal services that featured star cantors, choirs, and rabbis who were pulpit artists. Such rabbis perceived their function as much to attract and to entertain as to inspire the large crowds that gathered on holidays and on other festive occasions by their eloquence and the timeliness of their sermons.

The nonhasidic *yeshivah* services and the moderately hasidic *shuls* that emerged in the decade after World War II as a result of the changes in the population, and, after them, the *shtieblach* of new hasidic congregations were mostly conducted by *baalei tefillah*, lay readers, who had pleasant voices, proper religious conduct, and mastery of the proper *nusah*, the ritual order of prayers and the traditional recitative style. These they spiked with popular *niggunim*, hasidic and nonhasidic melodies created by such contemporary masters as Rabbi Shaul Taub, the late Modzitzer Rebbe, and native young American Orthodox singers. But the increasing pressure of the crises that caused the massive outmigration of the bulk of the Orthodox residents of Williamsburg to Boro Park and other Orthodox communities resulted in the closing of most of these older nonhasidic and hasidic smaller congregations, *shuls*, and *shtieblach*, some of which reopened in the new locations of their members.

Consequently, the services that became dominant were the informal hasidic types of smaller and larger congregations, whether headed by their own hasidic Rebbe, by descendents of famous hasidic lines, *einiklach*, by noted scholars, or by lay committees. All of these rejected the kind of synagogue service that had dominated Williamsburg before, during, and after World War II, which frequently featured music written by nonobservant composers or performers in classic or contemporary vernacular. But since singing is endemic to the ideology and the life-style of Hasidism, all the Hungarian and other hasidic congregations structure their services to include the intermittent use of *niggunim*, melodies, some of which trace their origin to the founders of the various schools of Hasidism. Or more likely, they use the popular songs of the ever broadening stream of hasidic melodies that proliferate in the world of the synagogues, the *botei midroshim*, the study halls, and *shtieblach*. For, contrary to all expectations, the fires and ashes of the Holocaust have not been able to destroy the glorious sources of music and prayer that rise again phoenixlike. It comes from the Jewish heart and soul in this country and in Israel, wherever *hasidim* have rebuilt their centers.

Old established creators of hasidic music, like Rabbi Yaakov Talmid of Ger in Israel, the Modzitzer Rebbes, and the new generations of native American and Israeli hasidic and nonhasidic composers have broadened this flow of *niggunim*, hasidic music, especially with the help of the records, tapes, and cassettes, which have proliferated in the past decade. These melodies run the full gamut of emotions from pensive and introspective to happy, joyous, and lively dance melodies, and from majestic *tish niggunim* to *marshen*, marchlike, compositions.

The dignity of the services in hasidic synagogues does not derive from formal procedures and rituals. It is the huge crowds of loyal *hasidim* who pack every inch of space, who hang on every word of prayer the Rebbe recites, and the moods he creates, and who participate in the full-throated communal singing. They provide the spirit and inspiration, and a strong inner discipline. Even in the most serious and somber services of the High Holidays, the tears and sobs of contrition blend with *niggunim*, majestic or even lighter melodies sung a cappella, and are very much in place, though in a formal service they might have been considered vulgar or unbecoming. Yet, they do express and highlight the mood, the type of text of the prayers they convey.

Hasidism, in general, emphasizes the joy of prayer, the close relationship between God and man in the experience of the sacred. In the kabbalistic sources of the hasidic ideology, the *Heichal Haneginah*, the Temple of Song, is next to the supreme *Heichal Hakedushah*, the Temple of Holiness. Thus it is not at all out of place for the community to join the Rebbe in fervent songs of contrition, or pleadings for forgiveness. Or, at the other end of the spectrum, the huge crowds always gathered in the large synagogues of the Rebbes of Klausenburg and of Satmar sing, clap, and stamp their feet for hours on Simhat Torah. The Rebbe himself might dance for hours round and round the huge crowd in the narrow corridor they opened for him, clasping a small silver Torah to his chest. He literally carries the inspiration of the individuals and their prayers and pleas on the wings of song to the higher spheres to which he has access by virtue of his saintly life and deeper knowledge and thoughts. Even the youngest or the most ignorant *hasid* can thus reach out to the heights to which he could never aspire on his own. Thus, the *niggun* is a powerful medium of transcending the vast gaps and differences, blending the masses of the praying into a genuine community serving the Lord with heart and soul.

The fervor of this type of formal or informal prayer is the hallmark of Hasidism in the synagogue or in the festive communal regular or special celebrations of the holidays – especially if they are conducted by such masters as the Rebbe of Satmar. For this unique experience *hasidim* gather to partake in the holiday services, from as far as hundreds of miles away. It is the spirit that spills out into the streets that attracts hundreds of outsiders who flock to Williamsburg by the bus and carloads on such occasions as Simhat Torah, or celebrations of weddings in the families of the famous Rebbes, such as have recently filled huge armories and even a sports stadium where thousands of participants gladly paid for this experience. They have no need for cantors or choirs or sermons to provide the emotional and spiritual stimulation. It is the core of their life, and for this the young want to remain close to the Rebbe and to the services and celebrations that he conducts. It is the strength of the three-generational Williamsburg community and the assurance of its survival.

This same spirit is also the very essence of the *farbrengen*, the informal get-togethers in the halls of the synagogue or in the residence of the Rebbe, where the faithful spend Friday evenings after they have finished their private meals, and Sabbath evening, the *seudah shlishit*, or later after the conclusion of the Sabbath, the *melaveh malkehs*, a festive communal celebration to "accompany the Queen of Sabbath." At these occasions the Rebbe addresses the crowds, inspires them, admonishes them, and exhorts them to ever greater efforts and devotion.

Of course, not all the services of the hasidic congregations are conducted by the Rebbes themselves. But here is one of the major differences in the lay conduct of the informal hasidic services. The *baal tefillah*, the reader, is chosen not so much for his mastery of the melodies and of the *nusach*, the order and text of the prayers, as for his *yir'at shomayim*, his fear of Heaven and his scholarship. Equally basic is his scrupulous observance of the commandments and his personal conduct, in contrast to some of the famous cantors whose personal life was often a travesty of the basic ritual and religious laws of observant Judaism.

In contrast to these performers, some of whom still command high salaries and fill temples and concert halls, those who conduct the hasidic service, whether such masters as the Rebbe of Satmar or the routine *baalei tefillah*, lay readers, do not entertain. Those praying are participants and their prayers are punctured by such characteristics of the hasidic style as a *krechtz*, a sob, a hiatus of silence, a scream of despair or abject contrition, or of the ecstasy of devotion and inspiration. Most of the schools of Hasidism and their famous Rebbes created their own style, their type of recitative, or melodies that vary widely, like those of the Hungarian, Polish, or Russian *niggunim*. Yet all emphasize this very personal, individual link, the ladder up which the individual has to ascend. The accent is not on intellectual penetration; rather it is on the emotional shaking up and shaping up as one transcends from his own lowliness to the height of communication with the Divine, to whom he entrusts himself, and on whose forgiveness he depends. This goal is what the *hasid* seeks and finds in the service in the presence of the Rebbe who is his guide. Alone he could not hope to find the right path or expression of his feelings.

There is also an element of flexibility in the schedule of the services of the hasidic congregations, such as Yetev Lev of Satmar, which deviates somewhat from the rigorous requirements of the code of law of ritual observances maintained by the nonhasidic services, which are guided by the exact time of sunrise or sunset. Thus, for example, the services of the Rebbe of Satmar start much later in the morning, in the late afternoon, or in the evening. These deviations are not arbitrary, but are based on hasidic traditions, most of which have kabbalistic roots.

There are also a number of crucial differences in the text of the prayers of the hasidic and nonhasidic congregations. In fact, there are a number of variations in the different hasidic traditions, as some of the famous founders of hasidic schools have changed the standard texts, added or taken away certain prayers, or introduced variations in the wording. Most of these variations are based on authentic historical sources, particularly on the innovations introduced by Rabbi Isaac Luriah, one of the most famous kabbalists of the fifteenth century. The same applies to a number of differences in the format of the services. There are a number of different prayerbooks published by various hasidic schools, which are structured around differences in the texts of the prayers and the order of the prayers. But each is consistent with the teachings and traditions of a founder or a famous Rebbe and go back two hundred and more years.

This type of flexibility and variability is characteristic of the services that are standard for the new Williamsburg and other intensely hasidic congregations. They are in contrast to the formal, more rigorously structured services of the nonhasidic Ashkenazic services, although here, too, there are variations, which originated in the historical backgrounds of the Polish, Russian, or Lithuanian Orthodox communities.

CUSTOMS AND MORES

The differences between the customs and mores of the hasidic congregations of Williamsburg and those of the formerly dominant Ashkenazic Russian-Polish synagogues are even more significant than the variations in the services. These differences are largely due to the fact that the synagogue plays an all-encompassing role in the ideology and life-style of the hasidic community.

The reasons for these differences, like those of the services, are rooted in the history as well as in the web of ritual and social interactions that take place in and around the synagogue and in the general dynamics of the hasidic life. Furthermore, as highlighted in the preceding discussion, the hasidic movement was essentially a "folk renaissance." Folklore, as well as strict adherence to the ritual precepts, produces a rich texture of customs and mores, which affect every phase of the individual and collective life of the hasidic community. Unlike the nonhasidic community, which does not seek distinctiveness in the life-style of its people, the intensive hasidic ideology, as suggested before, takes pride in its external as well as its internal distinctiveness. Most Eastern European immigrants discarded their old world garb, appearance, and behavior as tokens of their acculturation.

In contrast, the waves of Hungarian *hasidim* who flocked into Williamsburg after World War II, such as those led by the Rebbe of Satmar, dedicated themselves conscientiously to the preservation of the outer tokens of their distinctive life-style in their pursuit of maximal sociocultural isolation. Thus, they retained the traditional hasidic garb, the black *bekeshes*, the *shtreimel*, the fur hat, especially on Sabbath and holidays and on festive occasions, exactly as they had done in the East European shtetl. This became the hallmark of their battle to preserve their life-style, in Williamsburg and eventually in the other hasidic communities. Even in the more moderate hasidic communities, this insistence on distinctiveness in clothes was maintained, though it was mainly reserved for Sabbath and holidays. Not so in Williamsburg, where the garb of the synagogue came to be worn every day, and not only in the neighborhood itself. As pointed out in an earlier discussion, one may find *hasidim* in their dark hasidic garb not only in Williamsburg but also in New York, in the business centers of the wholesale and retail trades both downtown and uptown, in international trade shows and in manufacturing centers.

In a sense, this represents a major breakthrough in American history: except for a few small islands of such groups as the Amish, the life of the synagogue has spilled over into the streets, and into the workshops of daily life. No longer is it a characteristic of economic advancement to become externally as well as internally assimilated. Quite a few hasidic entrepreneurs, women as well as men, have made their mark in various lines of wholesale or retail business, or in manufacturing, while adhering to the sociocultural restrictions required by the hasidic life-style. As stressed throughout this report, this is all the more remarkable because members of the second and third generations of native American *hasidim*, even more so than their parents or grandparents, insist on continuing in the Eastern European life-style. Paradoxically, this is a result of their having *Americanized*: they feel it is their right as Americans to choose and display the tokens of their religious upbringing in daily life on the outside – in the world of business and in other professions. It is this scrupulous adherence to the hasidic customs and mores on the outside that is characteristic of the attitude of the population of the new Williamsburg.

Obviously, wearing the traditional hasidic garb, even for youngsters past the toddler stage, is a virtual must for participation in the synagogue services, every single day, not only on Sabbaths, in all seasons, regardless of weather, fashions, or other conditions. Similarly, attendance of the *mikvah*, the ritual bath, not only for women as in most strictly Orthodox communities, is expected. Thus, while in the earlier phases of Jewish Williamsburg it was an insurmountable job to raise the funds for a new, proper ritualarium for the entire neighborhood, even in the '50s, most of the hasidic congregations built their own *mikvot*, if possible, separate ones for men and women. Ever since the Tzelemer Rav, Rabbi Levi I. Grunwald, came to Williamsburg and pioneered a number of such innovations, even before the arrival of the Klausenburger and the Satmar Rebbes, the construction of a *mikvah* became a sine qua non. The size and comfortable style of his large *mikvah*, compared to the old, single *mikvah* of the so-called Polish *shtiebel*, which had served the Orthodox community for decades, set the pattern. Daily attendance, not only on Sabbaths and holidays, is a requisite for full participation in hasidic synagogue life. Even in the world of the *yeshivot*, attendance of a *mikvah* for most was and still is required only before the High Holidays and other special occasions, such as for the groom before his wedding.

Similarly, while most of the strictly Orthodox require their women to attend a *mikvah* at the conclusion of the postmenstrual period purification, many do not insist on their wearing a *sheitel*, a wig, or hats to cover their entire hair after marriage. In recent years, though, this has changed a great deal for those who live in intensely Orthodox neighborhoods, like Boro Park, Flatbush, and Monsey, perhaps under the impact of the hasidic revolution. This is equally true for the wearing of beards, even among the outstanding scholars of the famous advanced institutions of talmudic research, the *yeshivot gedolot*, in Eastern Europe as well as in the U.S. Only when the wearing of beards became accepted in the outside world in the '60s did the strictly Orthodox of the nonhasidic world make wearing beards, though not long *peyot*, part of the proper appearance of *Bnai Torah*, those devoting their lives to the study of

Torah, even after they have left the "four walls of the Torah," so that it is now the standard for the most Orthodox in this country as well as in the rest of the Jewish world.

In contrast, it would be inconceivable for a *hasid* in the synagogue and in all other realms of religious life not to wear beard and *peyot*, as it would be for his wife not to wear a *sheitel* or a hat to cover all her hair. Nor may she wear any clothes but those that cover almost all of her body. Thus she will be seen in long sleeves and skirts even in the heat of a stifling summer in New York, just as in Israel's ultra-Orthodox neighborhoods.

There are a number of other customs and mores characteristic of hasidic life connected with the synagogue in Williamsburg. They can be observed as well in the other intensely Orthodox communities. For example, the *yahrtzeit*, the anniversary of the death of the founders of the hasidic dynasties and other famous leaders, is scrupulously observed in the synagogue with the lighting of candles and the serving of refreshments upon the conclusion of the service. Very unusual, and positively unacceptable in the nonhasidic Orthodox circles, is the omission of saying the prayer of *Tahanun*, which is a plea for help and forgiveness of one's iniquities, which is part of the daily morning and afternoon services, on the days of the *yahrtzeit* of the famous hasidic Rebbes. Many of the major hasidic communities, in addition to serving refreshments and not saying the *Tachanun* prayers on the *yahrtzeit*, organize festive meals in the synagogue, in the social halls of the synagogues, or in the residences of the current Rebbes to observe the anniversary of the death of the famous leader. In the hasidic ideology, based on the kabbalistic tradition, the great merits of the saintly departed take the place of the prayers of supplication. Hence these are omitted, just as they are not said on Sabbaths and holidays. To the nonhasidic, this skipping of prayers and partaking of liquor and refreshments, wishing each other *L'Haim*, to life, and expressing the hope that the merits of the departed may "protect us," is not condoned. Similarly, the individual *hasid* observes the *yahrtzeit* of the anniversary of the death of a close relative not only by saying *kaddish*, the prayer of the bereaved, but by offering liquor and refreshments in the synagogue upon the conclusion of the services. All those who partake express their wish that the soul of the departed may rise to greater height in the realms of the sacred souls, on the merit of the blessings said over the refreshments. This is in stark contrast to the somber fasting of the nonhasidic on the *yahrtzeit* of their departed. Obviously, this custom, which is almost sacreligious in the eyes of the non-*hasid*, is directly related to the hasidic ideology and ritual life-style, which emphasizes *simhah*, joy and happiness, in place of sadness as the proper path to godliness. This perception transforms the partaking of refreshments into a sacred service to the Lord.

This is also, as pointed out earlier, the central idea of the celebration of the *tishen* or *farbrengen*, the shared communal meals with the Rebbe, because they represent the transformation of the most physical function, that of eating, into an *Avodah*, a service to the Lord in a form that angels, as spiritual beings, cannot offer to the Divine. In other words, these customs become mere extensions of the synagogue service as focal occasions of inspiration and ascendence to higher levels of spiritual experience.

In the same vein, the constant use of *niggunim*, melodies sung with or without text, as part of the regular synagogue services as well as of the communal meals and the regular Sabbath meals in hasidic homes, serves to inspire and elevate or deepen the religious experiences. They impart to the Sabbath and holiday prayers an element of flexibility, and provide meaning and, above all, joy and happiness, which break through the routine and somber spirit of the praying.

Most hasidic schools have developed their own style and types of *niggunim*, which vary greatly and are often regionally differentiated. Some of the great hasidic Rebbes have become famous as composers of this quintessential mode of inspiring the masses of their followers. Among Hungarian hasidic leaders, the founder of the Kahlever dynasty, which has a *shul* in Williamsburg, was known to have taken his disciples out to the fields and woods to teach them how to listen and to perceive the music that fills nature as each creature contributes to the strains of the heavenly music in praise of the Creator. This type of approach is central to the hasidic ideology and permeates the very atmosphere of the hasidic service, from the most serious to the happy celebration of such holidays as *Simhat Torah*. It provides the aura of seeming informality, in contrast to the formal, rigorously structured type of service, which was characteristic of the large Ashkenazic synagogues of pre-World-War-II Williamsburg as well as elsewhere. As one of the famous hasidic thinkers put it: "A *niggun* can express what words cannot convey. A *niggun* can carry prayers to the heights of inspiration and contemplation where rational human thought cannot ascend."

This emphasis on singing and dancing and festive celebration is endemic to the milieu of Hasidic Williamsburg. Far from the connotation of levity, it expresses itself in the spirit of emotional openness that extends beyond the walls of the synagogue into the life in the streets. It is behind *hasidism* not being embarrassed to display sadness and mourning as well as joy and enjoyment of living, all equally part of a God-given, God-pleasing life. One of the founders of Hasidism expressed this idea poignantly (*Anthology of Hasidic Thought*):

> When I get up in the morning I dance with happiness for the opportunity to serve the Lord with another day of joy. And I go to sleep with the same spirit of introspection and joy because I return my soul to its Heavenly source. And I look forward with excitement to the grace of having it returned the next morning, if I am deservant of it. As long as I have the strength to get up, to walk around, to go to Shul and serve the Lord I break out into joyful singing and dancing, overwhelmed by the experience of being close to Him all the time that I am awake or asleep.

This spillover from the synagogue into every phase and realm of life is the very essence of the folk renaissance of Hasidism. From its inception, its purpose was to give even the simple man living in difficult and often depressing circumstances a chance to rise above it as he shares the communal spirit of joyful service. It is a tribute to the effectiveness of the hasidic education that it has been able to engender this spirit and feelings among the young native Americans who pack its crowded schools. This is true, notwithstanding the fact that nearly 50 percent of the Williamsburg population in the '90s lives in poverty or at least in less than comfortable circumstances. Large families crowd into small apartments. The head of the household earns a low income, or they have to live on public or communal assistance. Yet, most are far from the spirit of defeatism that fills the poverty-ridden ghetto areas around Williamsburg. They display few of the common indicators of crime and filth, of the drug-ridden dwellings so prevalent in New York's slums.

Much of this spirit is produced by the not infrequent celebrations of synagogue life – the *tishen*, the communal meals, the *yahrtzeit*, circumcisions, *bar mitzvahs*, wedding festivities. A visitor to the central synagogue of Satmar reported twenty-four circumcisions taking place that day in the various study halls and siderooms, each of which was crowded with large numbers of guests. And, as pointed out to him, this represented only a small part of the programs and activities carried on in or around the synagogue centers constantly. Small wonder that the spirit of *simhah*, religious happiness and joy, permeates the life of the neighborhood side by side with the hustle and bustle of the busy economic activities that energize the once quiet, even sleepy atmosphere.

Thus, directly or indirectly, every phase of the individual and collective life of the hasidic population is connected to the synagogue, which has become more than the mere house of prayer or religious study it remains in other communities.

THE ROLE OF WOMEN IN THE SYNAGOGUE

My 1961 report indicated that both officially and unofficially women played a considerably more active role in the nonhasidic synagogues that dominated the pre-World-War-II era than in the moderately Orthodox hasidic and nonhasidic shuls and *shtieblach* of the post-World-War-II phase.

By contrast, the women of Hasidic Williamsburg are little involved in the conduct of the official affairs of the synagogue; they do not have a say in ritual matters, policies, or the administrative decisions related to synagogue life. The once considerable influence of the wife of the *shul* president, whose favor or disfavor of the rabbi or the outfits of his wife was said to determine his future in the synagogue, the renewal of his annual contract, or the raise of his meager salary, is something unthinkable in the type of setting created by the Rebbe of Satmar and the heads of the other subcommunities in the past three decades. In the large Ashkenazic congregations headed mostly by successful businessmen and lawyers, it was vital to involve their wives in the conduct of the *shul* affairs, commensurate with the decline of the respect for the rabbis and *Torah* scholars and their authority in all matters of the religious and ritual life. This remains the case in most Orthodox congregations in New York and its suburbs. There were no strict *mechitzot*, dividing walls or heavy curtains, separating the men's sections from the women's. In most synagogues women sat in open balconies. All formal and informal synagogue affairs, from banquets and meetings to weddings, featured mixed seating, allowing the women to take an equal share of the responsibilities, though a large percentage had at best a very limited Hebrew school education.

In contrast, the younger generation, which grew out of the day schools and *yeshivot* since the '40s, had a good religious background and knowledge, and their attitudes toward the synagogue and toward the authority of the rabbis and the ritual laws were much more in line with the strictly Orthodox standards than the values of the women of the preceding generations. Together with their *yeshivah*-educated husbands they changed the climate of synagogue life radically in the decade before they left the neighborhood.

As suggested in the conclusion of my earlier report (1961), the role and influence of women in the new Williamsburg, as in other intensely hasidic communities, is relatively minor, if gauged by the general standards and values of the women's liberation movements, which are striving for full equality and which are rampant in the Jewish suburbs of contemporary America as everywhere else. In the first place, even in moderately Orthodox synagogues women are not seated beside their husbands. They sit in separate sections that are set apart by a *mechitzah*, a dividing wall or heavy curtain, of the height required by ritual law. But in almost all communal social affairs inside and outside the synagogue, husbands and wives sit together. However, under the impact of the *yeshivah* education, an increasing number of Orthodox communities are introducing strict separation of the sexes. Some synagogues have one-way glass dividers, which allow the women to see, but not to be seen. In fact, when one of the intensely Orthodox synagogues of a large community outside of New York introduced separate tables in the social hall of the *shul*, where refreshments are served upon the conclusion of services on Sabbaths and holidays, one former Williamsburger, an Orthodox, middle-aged woman, was upset and complained bitterly:

> We never had separate seating of men and women in our Williamsburg *shul* affairs. Only during the services were we separated by a proper *mechitzah*. Now they are imitating the Hungarian hasidic style here, as synagogues and groups are vying to outdo each other in introducing ever more *humrot*, stringent restrictions in every phase of social life.

Yet, she is a firm believer in the importance of abiding by the Orthodox standards required by the religious laws, has a good day-school education, and has given her children a thorough yeshivah training. Her attitude is typical of the post-World-War-II moderately hasidic climate of Jewish Williamsburg, when her family moved to another strictly Orthodox community. It is, however, far from what she perceives as the extremism of the new Williamsburg.

In contrast, the women of the hasidic community of Williamsburg, just like their mothers and grandmothers before them, accept the strict separation of males and females in the synagogue as something that is beyond question or debate. None of those questioned or interviewed in the small sample survey of hasidic women expressed even a doubt about the correctness and wisdom of the stringent separation of men and women at all times in the synagogue. Nor did they feel that there was anything wrong with strictly abiding by the separation of men and women, husbands and wives, at the social affairs of the *shul* or of their family celebrations, like weddings or *bar mitzvahs*. From their earliest youth they have been imbued with the propriety of this religious arrangement, which is in accordance with the *halachah*, the religious code of law. On the contrary, they seriously question the values and orthodoxy of the women who in their search for equality object to the rigid separation of men and women. As one of them put it:

> These are the pitfalls that lead to the moral decline and ultimate corruption of the Jewish community in this country, unfortunately. Just as it happened in the non-Jewish world, the women want to be equal. They want to have the same rights and status as the men. Thus they tear down the vital barriers that the Torah has set up to maintain the purity of the Jewish family and of the spiritual *oisgehaltenkeit*, consistency of our homes. We have been educated to perceive our growth and fulfillment as women true to the ideals of the Torah, and as interpreted by our rabbis. Our Holy Rebbe has worked hard to create the kind of community life that would produce the spirit and life-style that make it easy for us to live up to these ideals. We hasidic women have our rights, duties, and obligations. We don't feel the need to be and act like the men. We have been created differently, and we feel proud of having chosen to maintain the heritage of our forefathers in this country, just like our mothers and Rebbes did in the *Alter Heim* in Europe.

This is the viewpoint the hasidic women of Williamsburg have been taught in Beth Rachel and in the other hasidic girls' schools and they accept and perpetuate it without question. They ridicule the drive for women's liberation and they glory in their duties as housewives and mothers, the *akeret habayit*, the classic term for the foundation of the home on whom the future of the Jewish people depends. Thus, they do not aspire to share the functions of the men in the services and in the administration of the synagogue and all the attendant affairs and activities.

On the other hand, the women of Hasidic Williamsburg have been taught to be an active support group for the broad range of functions and the functionality of the congregation as for the other community institutions and organizations.

Obviously, this attitude highlights the success of the hasidic girls' schools. As one of the principals pointed out:

> Make no mistake, our education is not just a matter of restrictiveness and limitations imposed on the minds of our girls. They are not ignorant. They are no dummies. They see what is going on around them in the world, even if they go only as far as Boro Park or Flatbush or Queens. They confront the reality of life when they go to work uptown or downtown in Manhattan, as well as in Brooklyn in the stores and shops they frequent. They are dressed well, albeit strictly within the bounds set for them by the hasidic life-style, and their children are dressed as well as youngsters

anywhere until they go to the *yeshivah* and put on the hasidic clothes. But they have genuine values that mean more to them than those they observe among the people they meet on the outside.

Women who have this general value attitude will not complain or consider their role in synagogue life unjust or unequal. They would never go so far as did the young wives of a strictly Orthodox new congregation in a popular New Jersey suburb of New York who recently organized specifically to lend support to their rabbi in the small, but rapidly growing synagogue. They were instrumental in seeing to it that his salary was increased despite the fact that he refuses to play the generally expected role of social director who spends much of his time on the welfare of his congregants. He is, and primarily wants to be, a scholar who teaches classes to the women as well as to the men, to an extent not acceptable to hasidic congregations. All of these women are products of advanced day-school education in the U.S. and in Israel. They make it their business to play an active role in *shul* affairs, although all of them have growing families and their budgets are limited.

The hasidic women of Williamsburg who have a good Jewish education, although they are taught mostly in Yiddish without the use of the Hebrew texts, would never consider meddling in synagogue affairs, especially those that concern the position and status of the rabbi, like the women of the pre-World-War-II Ashkenazic synagogues or the young wives of the New Jersey congregation. The hasidic women, many of whom work with their husbands or by themselves in business, do not lack the experience or managerial skills to run the *shul* affairs; they simply reject this type of a role. As one put it:

> My sisters, daughters, and daughters-in-law are all very active in the ladies auxiliary of our *shul*. One of my daughters runs the computerized bookkeeping system of her husband's business. My oldest daughter-in-law has her own children's clothes business, and knows how to get along with other people in the world. But they stick to the activities of our women's organization. They help organize the annual *melaveh malkeh*, the luncheons, teas, and auctions, which bring in a sizable portion of the annual budget of our *kehillah*. But, at no point would it occur to them to want to interfere or have a say in the synagogue policies or the administrative decisions. This is not how they have been brought up. Just like us, the older women, they consider it *nisht passig*, unbecoming. They themselves would call any young woman who dares to want to meddle in matters concerning the Rav or other ritual concerns *chutzpedik*, stepping way out of line.

Of course, it must be stressed that neither men nor women would dare to question or discuss the status and role of the Rebbe, whose position is too lofty, far beyond the level on which the *hasidim*, the members of his congregation, function. One must display utter reverence, the highest form of *derech eretz*, respect, even to address him; none talks about him in any but the most restrained manner. As in the case of the demise of the Rebbe of Satmar—or of Pappa, or of Tzelem, in the past decade—once the elders of the community have decided on the successor, there is no further discussion of his position or future in his congregation and the broader movement he now heads, especially if he is the son or a close relative of the late Rebbe. Hasidic women would not want to partake in the deliberations prior to the selection of the successor, as do the women of the Reform and Conservative and many of the moderately Orthodox congregations. Perhaps the only exception was the widow of the Old Rebbe of Satmar who, by virtue of her special position as the close co-worker of the Rebbe for decades in the administration of many of his welfare projects, continues to pursue her own projects. Although an octogenerian, she still maintains an active role and has a following of her own, which until recently caused occasional dissent or friction.

The very constitution of Yetev Lev, the congregation of Satmar, excludes the right to vote and the participation of women in all but the auxiliary functions for financial support and welfare projects. It would therefore be sheer lèse-majesté for women even more than for men to attempt to have any form of input concerning the role and status of the Rebbe, whose conduct and expansion of the policies and projects of his saintly uncle, Rabbi Yoel Teitelbaum, have made him unquestionably one of the most powerful leaders in the contemporary Jewish world. In the eyes of the hundreds and thousands of his male and female followers he is far above even the top level of any normal social structure that might be accessible to human judgment.

This love and reverence for the Rebbe is therefore the strongest positive force in the individual and community life of the hasidic men and women of Williamsburg. To them he personifies the supreme authority as a scholar and as a divinely blessed personality to whom they entrust their spiritual and physical welfare. Hence, they turn to him with their requests for blessing and for prayers for their personal welfare and solutions of their problems and difficulties. He is held up to the children as the model of saintliness and a life dedicated to scholarship. In turn, they look at their husbands in similar vein, carrying over the respect for faith and Torah scholarship into their personal lives. One woman described her life and her role as a housewife and mother of seven children, the oldest being fifteen, in the following terms:

> We are not like the nonreligious women who feel slighted by the separation and rules of conduct of the synagogue. On the contrary, this is exactly what we want. We marry husbands who are Torah scholars, and are happy to take care of our homes and children. They are the ideal models for our children. Hence, it would be unbecoming for us to assume and act as if we know better what are the proper ways and laws of the Torah that must guide everything we do.
>
> Even more important, we have something else that nonreligious women do not have, we have a Rebbe whom we trust. He leads us on the right path, for he is tuned to the sources of higher knowledge. His insight and understanding guide us. Outsiders may call this the blind faith of ignorant people. We know better. We are as intelligent as anyone else. But we realize our limits, and feel that it is a blessing to be able to look up and turn to someone who has deeper knowledge, wisdom, and vision. He is closer to heaven and has the *koah*, the ability to carry our prayers and pleas to the higher realms of divine blessing. Hence, we entrust our and our children's welfare to him as our spokesman.

Her response is typical of the basic attitude of most young as well as the middle-aged and old women who reject the popular trends of women's liberation, and the concomitant drive for equality and fulfillment outside of the home. Hence, they do not feel that it is their place to question the rules of synagogue life, though on the surface it may seem to reflect discrimination.

For the same reason the women of Hasidic Williamsburg find fulfillment in putting all their spare time, efforts, and even funds into the work for the various institutions and organizations that cover the broad range of the constantly expanding needs of the people crowded into the limited number of blocks of the Jewish Triangle. In fact, they are often the initiators and assume responsibility for ever new efforts to meet new problems, working with the indigent, the ill and aged, and women and their large families before, during, and after they give birth. They have broadened the scope of their work, such as that of *Bikkur Cholim*, to other areas outside of Williamsburg. Thus, this focus on *tzedakah* and *hesed*, charity and help to the needy, which they call *"our mitzvah,"* makes them feel fully equal and even more fulfilled, as one put it, "than as if we try to run the synagogue and the affairs of our *kehillah.*"

ASHKENAZIC SYNAGOGUES IN THE NEW WILLIAMSBURG

The vast majority of the synagogues in Williamsburg are the hasidic *shtieblach*, and the large synagogues of the congregations of well-known Hungarian hasidic Rebbes. Yet there are still several of the synagogues left that have retained the Ashkenazic ritual throughout the decades of rapid change. But they are mere shadows of their glorious past. Most of their members are the old or indigent, or those who for personal reasons have not been able to take the trek to the other neighborhoods and suburbs that have attracted most of their more fortunate fellow congregants. One of these old-timers, who was not able to move to Boro Park like his brother, happily uses the special bus line that connects Williamsburg and Boro Park every day to visit his brother, who is too ill to take care of himself. Interviewed on the bus crowded with hasidic men and women, the latter sitting in the back section, he commented, somewhat irritated: "These people have left me and my wife almost no place where we can go to daven." Yet, like most of the remaining members of the old Ashkenazic synagogues, he admitted freely that the *hasidim* have achieved a great deal for their people that he admires, like the bus he makes daily use of.

The surviving Ashkenazic synagogues are mostly located at the outskirts of the Jewish Triangle. They feature small *minyanim*, services, but have larger ones on Shabbaths and holidays, especially on the High Holidays. With the exception of Congregation Adas Yereim, the branch of Agudath Israel that had been started by a group of Viennese and German newcomers in the old Zeirei Agudath Israel building at 616 Bedford Avenue, the Ashkenazic synagogues no longer play a significant role in the community life. Even those that have retained their rabbis or have affiliated institutions or organizations are merely biding their time until the "last *minyan*" of their congregants has left the neighborhood.

Young Israel of Williamsburg

The changes in the status and role of Young Israel of Williamsburg, which is still located in the very center of the neighborhood, highlights the transformation of the community through the major phases better than those of most other institutions and organizations. It is the local branch of a national organization of young and middle-aged Jewish men and women, which still flourishes in many communities, especially outside of New York. Significantly, the national organization that always took pride in its politically neutral, centrist Orthodox position has moved to the right, in line with the general trend in the religious Jewish world in the U.S. as well in other countries. As such it is no longer a catchall for mostly single young adults who find it a natural setting for the traditional social life they require.

Early in its history, the Young Israel movement developed its own youth-oriented and youth-directed type of services, with a maximum of communal singing in which both men and women participate – something unthinkable in most Orthodox synagogues of the '80s. Generally, men and women had equal status and shared responsibilities in the conduct and policy decisions of Young Israel's congregational and organizational affairs. The High Holiday services were conducted by one of the prominent older members for decades. Eventually they hired rabbis to take charge of the ritual and spiritual aspects of the *shul*. Major emphasis shifted to elaborate programs in which the young men and women mixed freely, including even dances, something outright shocking to the generation of those educated in day schools and *yeshivot* as a serious infraction of the Jewish law. But these social programs were attracting and holding on to Jewish youth who might otherwise have found their place in less religious circles and organizations. The popular saying of the post-World-War-II era was that Young Israel was like the Red Heifer: It purified the impure and defiled the pure. Indeed, it is one of the proud achievements of Young Israel, both the national movement and the local branches, that they helped keep many religious Jewish youngsters close to the Orthodox tradition and reached out to others who came from nonreligious backgrounds. Yet, since the late '40s and '50s, when Williamsburg's Jews moved significantly to the right, toward more intensely Orthodox standards of life, and when religious political movements grew stronger and built effective youth groups, the position of Young Israel in Williamsburg has been declining. It was already in decline even before the general outmigration of the elements whose young adults had joined its ranks. For students of the day schools and *yeshivot*, being associated with Young Israel was tantamount to a declaration of their intention of leaving the ranks of the strictly Orthodox.

Young Israel still functions in its once proud and beautiful building, which had been the location of a social organization of the old pre-World-War-I Brooklyn elite. But characteristically, the building has been sold to Congregation Adas Yereim, the largest of the still functional Ashkenazic communities, for their own independent branch of Bais Yaakov School for Girls. It is now the only one of this girls'-school movement that had flourished in Williamsburg, both on the elementary and high-school levels, until the mass exodus of the strictly Orthodox caused their transfer to Boro Park and other Orthodox neighborhoods. The facilities of Young Israel have been transformed into classrooms. But Young Israel still has the right to maintain its services, especially on Sabbaths and holidays. Its rabbi, one of the dynamic leaders of the post-World-War-II phase, has his office in one of the basement rooms. He is not too sanguine about the future of his congregation, almost all of whose members are older men and women who grew up in the movement and were among the prominent residents of the neighborhood before the mass exodus of the moderately Orthodox. At this time it seems only a matter years if not months until Young Israel will have to close its doors on more than half a century of valuable service to the youth and to the centrist Orthodox adult community who dominated Orthodox Williamsburg before and after World War II.

Congregation Adas Yereim

The largest and most important of the Ashkenazic congregations is Adas Yereim. It was founded by a group of Viennese and German Jewish members of Zeirei Agudath Israel who had already been active in the movement in Europe. They joined the flourishing young adults organization and services of Zeirei Agudath Israel at 616 Bedford Avenue, which played a major role in the rescue and immigration aid work during and after World War II. Used to the Ashkenazic *nusach* type of services, the Viennese and German members established their own small services on the second floor of the building, and soon proved to be one of the most dynamic and rapidly growing congregations in the neighborhood during the crucial years of the post-World-War-II era when many other survivors from Central Europe who had grown up in the Ashkenazic tradition, found a home in the *shul* of Adas Yereim. Soon after their establishment, Congregation Adas Yereim leaders purchased a building on the southeast side of Williamsburg, beyond Brooklyn Broadway, which had housed the synagogue of a congregation whose members had long before moved away in the face of the rapidly disintegrating area. Meanwhile, the dynamic congregation had hired Rabbi Jonathan Steif, one of the prominent scholars and rabbis of Hungary, who had been the head of the *bet din* of Budapest, to be the rabbi of Adas Yereim, soon after his arrival in this country. His extraordinary scholarship and competence in matters of ritual law soon made him one of the highly recognized spiritual and religious leaders of Williamsburg, whose decisions were accepted equally by the hasidic and the nonhasidic communities of Williamsburg and beyond. Both Rabbi Moshe Feinstein and the Old Rebbe of Satmar, at whose side he sat at festive celebrations, acknowledged his superior knowledge and consulted him in matters of ritual difficulties they confronted.

Thus, from the very outset, Adas Yereim tended to build a more formal structure than most of the other smaller congregations in Williamsburg. In 1952 it purchased the large building of a former movie theater in the very center of the Jewish Triangle.

It attracted large numbers of the most intensely Orthodox nonhasidic lay and rabbinic newcomers and blended them into a forceful community, which was effectively organized and had a broad program of educational activities. While the large Ashkenazic Russian-Polish congregations were rapidly dwindling as their members moved away, Adas Yereim held on to its congregants long after the community around them had become the center of Hungarian hasidic congregations. As their president for over 40 years put it:

> From the very beginning we wanted a real *kehillah*, the way we had it in Vienna and in the other large centers of the *oiberland*, congregations that followed the *nusach* and customs established by the *Chasam Sofer* [Rabbi Moses Sofer, the famous nineteenth-century scholar and spiritual leader of the Central European Ashkenazic communities]. We had 150 members when we hired Rabbi Jonathan Steif to be our rabbi. In a short time we more than doubled our membership. We had no rich people among us. But we borrowed and worked hard, as we organized each phase of the growth of our *kehillah* life, foremost among them our own schools and *Talmud Torah*, Yesodei Hatorah, and a few years later our own Bais Yaakov school for girls, when the other girls' schools closed their doors and moved to Boro Park and elsewhere. Similarly, we borrowed large sums of money when we purchased buildings for our *shul* and for our schools for boys and girls in Boro Park, years later, after the majority of our members had moved there. We did the same thing again, when a number of our active leaders and members, especially among the younger generation, moved to Monsey, New York, and established there a flourishing synagogue and a yeshivah for boys and a school for our girls for our type of parents who prefer our more moderate, modified approach to *hinuch*, education.

The large synagogue of Congregation Adas Yereim is still relatively full, though nothing like the crowds that packed it decades ago, mostly with more recent residents who prefer the Ashkenazic services. One major factor of this continuity and growth was the dynamic rabbi chosen to follow Rabbi Jonathan Steif, after the demise of this great scholar. The congregation built a new *mesifta* building and a private house for its rabbi in the yard behind their synagogue. They also built a brand-new large facility, the first of its kind, to serve as an old-age and nursing home for its own and other Orthodox residents of the community, *Aishel Avrohom*. It became a model of care and activities that are particularly geared to the needs of the elderly inmates, such as the educational programs, which they would not get anywhere else. It is also a center of community volunteer participation for the young and old of the entire Williamsburg hasidic community, whose youngsters and women give of their free time to make the elderly men and women of *Aishel Avrohom* comfortable and provide services that the institution itself would never be able to maintain on this level in view of their limited funds.

The earlier establishment of their own cemetery and funeral parlor is typical of the spirit and activism of the leadership and members of Adas Yereim, who are maintaining all their programs and projects in exemplary fashion, although most of the original members have long since moved to Boro Park or Monsey or elsewhere.

Radically different from the old, large Russian-Polish Ashkenazic congregations, Adas Yereim became a major factor in the thriving Jewish life that made Williamsburg one of the most important centers of Orthodox Jewish life in the contemporary Jewish world. Its members carried this spirit with them to Boro Park, and subsequently to Monsey. Their young have successfully blended into most hasidic as well as nonhasidic Orthodox circles and they served as a convenient bridge between the post-World-War-II era and the the evolving Hungarian hasidic community of the new Williamsburg. Already in the '50s and '60s, a growing number of the members of Adas Yereim began to wear *kapottes* and *shtreimels,* and the students of their *yeshivah,* under the guidance of the dynamic rabbi and *rosh yeshivah,* are practically indistinguishable from the students of the other hasidic *yeshivot.* Yet the congregation of Adas Yereim has maintained much of its more moderate spirit and life-style, which characterized it since its beginning and which is still perpetuated by the members of their second and third generations who are now increasingly carrying the responsibility for its large and growing community in Boro Park and Monsey.

Clymer Street and Hewes Street Shuls

The fate of the Brisker, or Clymer Street, *Shul* at the upper end of Bedford Avenue, on the corner of Clymer Street, is in stark contrast to the thriving life of Adas Yereim. It had been one of the largest and politically most active Ashkenazic congregations before, during, and after World War II. The *shul* was packed on Sabbath and holidays, and on the many occasions when it served as the location of mass meetings and celebrations or protests on behalf of the larger Jewish community. Its rabbis were prominent scholars and orators, and its members were active in the local Democratic Club. Like most of the large Ashkenazic synagogues it had few youth-oriented programs, except for gatherings of the Mizrachi, or National Religious Party activities. Most of its elderly and middle-aged members left the neighborhood in the '50s and '60s. A disastrous fire destroyed the huge building with its elegant architecture. In its place there is a small building, which is still too large for its small congregation. Officially it has about 150 members, but the regular attendance rarely gets up beyond thirty, even on Sabbath. On the High Holidays it attracts between fifty and a hundred men and women to its services – a far cry from the more than eight hundred who would pack the synagogue on these and similar festive occasions. The volunteer caretaker pointed out that the congregation still owns two large cemetery plots, a token of its old glory but a major source of income.

Similarly, the still larger and even more formal Ashkenaz congregation of the once prestigious Hewes Street *Shul,* at the other end of the densely Jewish segment of Bedford Avenue, lost its members even before the crises that decimated the Jewish population of the neighborhood. These two largest, formerly massive upper-middle-class synagogues, which featured famous cantors and choirs, had been the strongholds of what is now known as centrist orthodoxy. By World War II they had already lost most of the younger and the less Orthodox elements. Even without the radical changes in the composition of the local population, they were doomed by attrition. The facilities of Hewes Street Shul are used by the classes of Beth Chanah, the girls' school of the Klausenburger hasidic community. Clymer Street Shul, in its small present format, is only open for the morning and evening services for a mixture of old-timers and newcomers who have not found a place for themselves in the numerous small and large hasidic synagogues. The huge gray facade of Hewes Street Shul, still most impressive in its stark massive architecture–it was a former church building–is a symbol of the radical changes that have reshaped the essential spirit and life-style of the Jewish community of Williamsburg in the past half century.

Congregation Beth Jacob-Ohave Sholom

This relatively new synagogue is tucked into a corner at the outskirts of the Jewish Triangle, off Brooklyn Broadway. It was built by the remnants of two of the large Ashkenazic congregations of the older part of Jewish Williamsburg east of Broadway, the area hit hardest by the impact of the construction of the Brooklyn-Queens Expressway and the influx of large numbers of ethnic minority groups. It is headed by a dynamic rabbi, a renowned scholar and orator, who is the director of the national movement of Jewish day schools. Though by nature rather ebullient, he is quite skeptical when he speaks of the survival of the last of the proud old Ashkenazic *shuls*, which are still open and have regular services. On High Holidays his synagogue attracts between three hundred and four hundred mostly older men and women from the Ashkenazic population, the majority of whom reside in the public high-rise projects. It has about seventy-five members, but draws only about half to the regular services. The hope of the founders of this congregation was that it would draw many new members from the Lindsay Project, once the nicest and most lavish of the public-housing projects constructed in this area. It had been designed to attract residents from the local, middle-class, white population. For this purpose, the management offered prime apartments to local rabbis and community leaders and promised to reserve the apartments on the lower floors for Sabbath-observant Jews, who would not use an elevator on Sabbath and holidays. This hope faded because the Lindsay project was located too far–"on the other side of the tracks"–for the older residents of Jewish Williamsburg. *Hasidim,* who otherwise are trying to push into new directions in their urgent search for adequate housing, shunned the Lindsay because of one of its most prized features, its large swimming pool, which is visible from almost every apartment. The *hasidim* do not want their young exposed to poolside social life. Hence the vast majority of the Lindsay residents are Puerto Ricans, blacks, and other ethnic or racial minority group members. Consequently, the hope of the leaders of Congregation Beth Jacob-Ohave Sholom to draw members from this project is practically nil, and the prospects for survival are bleak.

There are a few smaller congregations, which are maintained by the handful of survivors of the old pre- and post-World-War-II Ashkenazic population; but in each case the situation is the same as that of the larger synagogues. They, like a few of the small, old Sephardic congregations that survived from the days before the mass immigration of the Hungarian hasidic newcomers, are merely biding their time until they have to close their doors.

Thus, the numerous small and large Hungarian hasidic congregations, like those of Satmar, Pappa, Klausenburg, Vishnitz, or Spinka, and the *shtieblach* of some of the Polish or Russian *hasidim* whose main locations are elsewhere in New York or in Israel, dominate the religious and spiritual life of Hasidic Williamsburg. They will continue to thrive, unless unforeseeable circumstances radically change the present situation.

SUMMARY

No other realm of the community life of Hasidic Williamsburg bears stronger evidence of the processes of change that have transformed the external and internal structure and dynamics of the neighborhood since before World War II than the patterns of the synagogue and the affiliated religious and ritual life.

The large, once dominant Russian-Polish Ashkenazic congregations disintegrated as a result of natural attrition and the rapid outmigration of their members during the decade following World War II. Similarly, most of the various hasidic and nonhasidic congregations that had flourished during the '40s and '50s closed their doors as crises in the community played havoc with the institutional and organizational structure and the living conditions of the neighborhood. Their place was taken by the increasingly large Hungarian hasidic communities, preeminent among them Congregation Yetev Lev of Satmar, and others led by prominent hasidic Rebbes who established their congregations in Williamsburg and attracted hundreds of followers. They built *shuls*, schools, and other institutions and organizations to meet the needs of their *hasidim*. Unlike the Ashkenazic congregations, they were able to retain their young and build up three-generational memberships because their young wanted to remain close to their Rebbe and to the institutions that had shaped their lives. This cohesiveness and the effectiveness of the educational systems made the survival and renaissance of the new Williamsburg possible.

The most important change in the structure and dynamics of the synagogue was the restoration of the high status and role of the rabbi, closing the chapter on the days when businessmen and professionals dominated most synagogues and institutions in Williamsburg as well as elsewhere in the American Jewish community. They had looked down upon rabbis, scholars, teachers, and other religious functionaries, most of them immigrants from Eastern Europe, as ignorant of the ways and needs of American life. Hence, these were at their mercy and they treated them as lower-class employees who had little actual input and influence on synagogue policies, although many of them were competent scholars. In contrast, the high status and role of the heads of the famous *yeshivot Gedolot*, the institutes of advanced talmudic studies, and the equally famous hasidic Rebbes who had survived the Holocaust and had come to this country, such as Rabbi Yoel Teitelbaum, the Rebbe of Satmar, and others, changed the general climate and attitude toward the authority of rabbis and scholars. Not only the prominent leaders, but the professional authorities and functionaries regained higher ranking commensurate with their competence. Thus, the intensely Orthodox community turned to them for guidance, judgment, and halachic decisions and direction. The most prominent Rebbes achieved superstatus by virtue of their saintly life-style, their *yichus* as heirs and bearers of historic charismas, and their superior leadership. This loyalty of the hasidic community and their discipline had a powerful impact on the whole of synagogue life and all of the religious and ritual phases of life directly or indirectly related to it.

Another major consequence of this radical change was the emergence of the hasidic types of services, including the informal, mostly lay structure and dynamics: the use of *niggunim*, folk tunes, throughout the emotionally charged services; and the emphasis on communal singing led by *menagnim*, amateur hasidic singers, rather than cantors. This informality carried over into the numerous informal synagogue-related celebrations and festivities – the *kiddush*, the *tishen*, and other *farbrengen* at religious and ritual occasions, which are the heart of the hasidic ideology and life-style.

Still more significant is the change in the role of the women in the official and unofficial dynamics and structure of the synagogue. In contrast to the status and power of women in the conduct of the pre-World-War-II Ashkenazic synagogues and in the strictly Orthodox *shuls,* as well as in the Conservative and Reform congregations in the U.S. and elsewhere, hasidic women do not play an official role in any part of the synagogue, in the conduct of its services, or in the determination of its policies. But they are most active in the informal, social functions, which are vital in the synagogue-centered hasidic community. By virtue of their education and the general spirit of the hasidic life-style, they do not aspire to the tokens of women's liberation and equality in the conduct and administration of synagogue affairs. They approve of the strict separation of men and women not only during the services, but in all communal and personal affairs, such as celebrations of weddings, all of which feature a *mechitzah*, a partition between the participating men and women. They have been imbued with the values that consider this separation not a mark of discrimination and inequality, but a clear indication of the distinction of the roles assigned to men and women by the Creator.

As we have seen in the preceding chapters, the most positive factor of the strength of hasidic synagogue life is the fact that the younger generations play an increasingly active part in it, thus assuming the perpetuation of the underlying ideology and life-style into the future.

⫸ 7 ⫷

The Women of Hasidic Williamsburg

My report (1961) did not deal with the women of Jewish Williamsburg in a separate chapter. Yet throughout the discussion of the processes that changed the structure and dynamics of the old Jewish neighborhood before, during, and after World War II, significant comments from women highlighted their role in each phase of the transformation that replaced the earlier Jewish religious population with groups of more intensely Orthodox residents.

The radical developments, which evolved from the impact of the crises that threatened to destroy the Jewish community and the turnabout resulting from the decision of the Rebbe of Satmar and other Hungarian hasidic leaders to make a stand and fight the forces of blight and disintegration, require separate treatment of the role and status of the women. Their values and attitudes are a major factor in the successful rebirth of the neighborhood.

Hence this chapter focuses on the essential Weltanschauung and life-style of the women of the hasidic community of Williamsburg, for these set them apart from the vast majority of the women in other American Jewish urban and suburban communities, whose values and attitudes are largely identical with those of the non-Jewish society among which they dwell. They are also different from the values and attitudes of the women of the more intensely Orthodox communities, although their intensive Hebrew day-school, high-school, and post-high-school education have considerably narrowed the gap between them and and the learning and life-style of the ultra-Orthodox hasidic women.

METHODOLOGICAL NOTE

Like the other sections of this study of the hasidic community of Williamsburg, this chapter on its women draws on participant observation, on formal and informal interviews with men, women, adolscents, and leaders of institutions and organizations, in addition to statistical and archival sources. But unlike the preceding chapters, this section uses facts and figures garnered from the findings of a small random sample survey of 175 single, married, widowed, and divorced women of the neighborhood. Seventeen, or about 10 percent, are single young women between the ages of 15 and 22; 141 are mostly young married women between 19 and 44 years old; and 13 are women 45 years old and older. Almost all of the respondents of the sample are first-, second-, or third-generation immigrants, survivors of the Holocaust of Hungarian hasidic background. The average age of the total sample population is 32.6. This indicates that the emphasis of the survey is on the values, attitudes, and life-style of what is now the most important element of the hasidic population of Williamsburg, the young and middle-aged so-called *avreichim* and their mostly second- or third-generation American hasidic wives.

It must be emphasized that the hasidic women of Williamsburg are not essentially different from hasidic women of other Orthodox neighborhoods. But the large size of the more or less homogeneous population of 40,000 and the intensity of the living conditions provide significant information not easily yielded in other, mixed, more varied, and less concentrated Orthodox communities in New York or elsewhere in the U.S., Israel, and the rest of the Jewish world.

About 80 percent of the young and middle-aged women, and about 60 percent of all 175 women surveyed were born in the U.S. About one-third have come from Israel or from the countries where their parents took temporary refuge before they were able to immigrate to the U.S. The majority are loyal followers of the Rebbe of Satmar and other Hungarian hasidic leaders, such as the Rebbes of Pappa (Puper), Tzelem, Klausenburg, Vishnitz, Spinka, Krasna, and others living in the neighborhood or in new suburban or Israeli communities. The young women are not remnants of an old world immigrant enclave, which, according to many experts, is on the brink of disintegration. As repeated again and again throughout the preceding chapters, the heads of the Hungarian hasidic groups were able to rebuild their communities in this neighborhood on a sound foundation.

Thus, the information on the values, attitudes, and life-style of the women of Williamsburg is significant as an aspect of ultra-Orthodox Jewish life in pluralistic America that is unique. They stress that they enjoy the freedom of their new homeland, particularly the freedom of religion it affords all immigrants and ethnic and racial minorities. Although the hasidic community prefers to live in sociocultural isolation, some of their important values are consonant with the very essence of the American spirit of enterprise and with its vital concern for the welfare of its needy and suffering.

Most of the young and middle-aged women of the survey population are products of the intensive Hungarian hasidic educational system, which was developed by the Rebbe of Satmar and the other leaders. They have been reared in a significantly different manner from even the students of other Orthodox Jewish girls' schools, such as Bais Yaakov, which dominated post-World-War-II Williamsburg. The combination of the hasidic home atmosphere, the hasidic school education, and the milieu of the very streets of the new Williamsburg is largely responsible for the strength of the values, views, and life-style of the women interviewed.

Hence the findings have broader significance and explain some of the responses and convictions of the women as they emphasize their wholehearted acceptance of the ultra-Orthodox strictures, which to outsiders might seem out of step with the requirements of life in twentieth-century America.

The survey was designed to elicit the characteristic values and attitudes of young American-born hasidic women. It focused on their views of marriage, on their choice of husbands, on the size of their family, and on the education of their children. Specific questions dealt with their personal interests, their attitudes toward staying in the neighborhood, toward going out to work or staying at home, and toward trying to find a job in the neighborhood. They were asked about the milieu they encounter when they do venture out into the radically different climate of the world of business in Manhattan or elsewhere. They were asked about their views on women's liberation and self-fulfillment outside of the home, and about their all-consuming duties as housewives, mothers, and members of the hasidic community. Finally, they were asked to speak about their participation in the religious, social, and political life of the community, and about their cultural interests and activities.

Obviously, the survey had to respect the particular sensivities of the respondents and their families; certain questions could not be asked. It was thanks to the cooperation of several women from the three major hasidic subcommunities that we were able to procure the valuable information that emerges directly or indirectly from the responses of the sample of women interviewed. Though limited in size and scope, the survey serves to complement the analysis and discussion of the other chapters in this study of the ultra-Orthodox hasidic community of Williamsburg and its underlying values and attitudes, which are essential to its survival and functionality in the final decade of this century.

FAMILY PATTERNS

Chapter 4 dealt with the hasidic family and spelled out in detail the major factors behind the strength and cohesiveness of the three-generational family and, by extension, the entire community, foremost among them the effectiveness of the hasidic education and the hasidic ideology. We saw the primary role of the demographic changes, the large size of the typical hasidic household, and the resulting population explosion as second-generation *hasidim* are reaching middle-age and are gradually assuming a larger share of the responsibility for the maintenance and expansion of community life. It also emphasized the important role of older siblings, especially the girls who help carry much of the burden of the large household and thus are gaining valuable experience and skill handling babies and children of various ages.

Throughout the discussion of the family, characteristic quotes from women highlight their position and attitude toward their life and role under the restraints and pressures of the ultra-Orthodox Hungarian hasidic customs and mores.

This section of the chapter on the women of Williamsburg focuses on the information gathered in the sample survey as it relates to these matters. Some of the facts and figures highlight and reinforce the most intriguing aspects of the values of the hasidic women, which distinguish them from the majority of the women in other religious and nonreligious Jewish communities of contemporary Jewish and non-Jewish society.

Demographics

As already discussed, one of the most significant aspects of the new Williamsburg is the large size of the average household. Students fill a school building as soon as it is opened and, as the head of the administration of the school system of Satmar stresses, new classes have to be added every two months. At a single Sabbath in the spring of 1989, there were thirty-two circumcisions in the main synagogue and its branch services. Reflecting on this fact, the top administrator commented that in three and a half years two new beginners classes will have to be added, one for the boys and another one for the girls, because usually there are as many girls born as boys, just from the children of this single weekend. This projection, plus the fact that every school year new buildings have to be added, is borne out by the findings of the small sample survey. Of the 158 households surveyed, that is, after deducting the seventeen girls from the total of women surveyed, the average number of children in the 40- to 49-year-old groups is 7.8. The 25 percent of respondents between the ages of 35 and 40 have 7.09 children on the average. Those between 45 and 59 have an average of 6.18 children. And those 55 and over, the older immigrant women who lost years of their life during and after the Holocaust, have on average 4.7 children. Those in their early twenties have 1.5 children on average, and those between 25 and 34 have 4.1 children. Among those between 35 and 44, one has fourteen children and six have 9 children. Altogether, one-third of the women in this age group have 6 children or more. In a study of the Amish and Hutterites, two American groups to whom *hasidim* are frequently compared because of their large families, the author (Kephart 1976) reports that the largest households among the old style Amish have 7 children. There is a total of 15,000 Amish in their major center at Lancaster, Pennsylvania, compared to the approximately 40,000 *hasidim* in Jewish Williamsburg.

Obviously, the largest households are in the middle-aged group of the respondents. Yet, not one of the women questioned expressed the intention or desire to stop having children at this stage in their lives. In contrast, the majority of women in American society at large have two or three children and are determined to limit their birth career at this stage.

Only six of the married women in the survey population do not have any children. Two of these have only recently been married, two are pregnant, and one of the remaining two has not yet given up and expresses the hope that, "with the help of the Lord," she will yet have and raise children. Regarding this attitude one of the community leaders commented: "You can see that our women consider having children a divine blessing and the realization of their destiny. To them birth control and abortion are sins. Only in cases of a serious threat to their health and life will they and their husbands consent to an abortion." The same official emphasized the blessing of children in the hasidic community, in contrast to society in general, where 10 percent of married couples cannot have any children. "Thank God," he said, "this is not a problem in our community, except in rare cases."

This positive attitude toward the blessing of having children emerges clearly from the responses of both the single and the married women in the survey. One of the divorcées only, who was an outsider and never accommodated to the life-style and attitudes of Hasidic Williamsburg, voiced disapproval of this attitude toward having so many children. Yet even she admired the willingness of most hasidic women to have and handle large families without grumbling and regret. All other respondents expressed the view that their having children was a blessing and the greatest source of happiness and joy for a woman. As one put it: "Having children is a source of pride. It makes life worth living. It is a woman's destiny and makes staying at home and caring for the children and raising them as *ehrliche Yiddishe Kinder* worthwhile. Unlike other women, we hasidic women, just like our mothers and grandmothers, consider having children the greatest blessing." One intelligent woman who runs a small business of her own to help support her husband, who is a scholar and earns some money as a teacher while continuing his advanced talmudic study, states that she cannot understand the attitude of women who feel the need for satisfaction and self-realization outside of their home.

> I am grateful for every hour I can spend with my children and do not need a baby-sitter. No one, not even a close relative, not even my aunt or cousin, can take my place with the children. And what is sweeter and more rewarding than a smile from my children, and the happy cooing of satisfaction from my baby. Make no mistake, I enjoy running my own business, but it cannot compare to the satisfaction I derive from being a good wife, mother, and housekeeper. Our family are Satmar *hasidim* from way back in Europe. We are all thrilled to live near the Holy Rebbe, to take part in his *tishen*, to listen to his *drashot*, and to be able to *daven* with him, especially on the High Holidays. We look forward to send our children to the Satmar Yeshivah and Beth Ruchel.
>
> To me there is no greater source of happiness and satisfaction. I am not a bit jealous of the women with whom I have contact in business. Thank God, our life and values are different from theirs.

The same woman also made a point of stressing something that concerned a number of the women interviewed, "Make no mistake, we are not uneducated, ignorant women from the dark ages, or from the hinterlands of civilization who are happy because they do not know better."

Almost all of the women in the small survey population have the usual 8 years of elementary and 3 years of high school education at Beth Ruchel or the other hasidic girls' schools. Over 80 percent worked before marriage on jobs that took them out of Williamsburg and brought them together with women and men of different values, attitudes, and life-styles. Hence, they feel they are not blind, brought up behind Chinese walls or shutters. Still, with just a few exceptions, they approve of the sociocultural isolation of their neighborhood. One young woman stated: "We don't want the kind of fashion-consciousness and competition that prevail on the outside. We have been imbued with the values and beauty of our life, with the standards of *tzni'ut*, modesty. We happily abide by these standards in the way we dream and think and conduct ourselves, regardless of what is in on the outside."

Dating, Marriage, and Choice of Husbands

Of course, dating and courting in the usual fashion of American society do not exist for the young of Williamsburg, though much of it is common in less-religious Jewish communities. Marriages in hasidic and recently also in nonhasidic Orthodox communities are arranged by the parents, frequently with the help of amateur or professional matchmakers, *shadchanim*. Boys and girls move in separate circles, and one never sees boys and girls walking together in the streets in pairs, unless they are engaged or young married couples. They may meet several times before a match is approved and the official process of engagement and nuptial arrangements are made. The wedding takes place usually within a few months after the engagement, thus avoiding long, dragged-out engagements, which are considered unbecoming and improper from the perspective of *tzni'ut*.

As discussed elsewhere, most of the girls of marriage age have worked 1 to 3 years in order to help defray the high cost of the wedding and of establishing a home. Furthermore, this fact is important because the vast majority of these girls are intent on marrying young Torah scholars who will continue their advanced talmudic and rabbinic studies at least 1 to 3 years after marriage. This means that they will have to subsist on a minimal income – the small *kollel* stipend and whatever the parents can afford to give them. As a result, almost half of the young married women continue to work after marriage and between having children, at least until their husbands are ready to leave the institute of advanced rabbinic study and start a career in education, in the rabbinate, or in communal professions such as administrators or executives of institutes or organizations. For those who plan to train for a trade or start their own business, if possible, the financial help of their wives is a major factor of their coping with the heavy pressures of meeting their growing financial needs.

In the survey, all but three of the 157 married women got married between the ages of 18 and 24. Ninety-five percent of the young and middle-aged married men had spent at least 1 or 2 years on advanced religious study in a *kollel*. The implications of this fact are that these young women have to be satisfied deferring the realization of most of the dreams of young brides everywhere until years later. The only exceptions are those brides whose parents are in a position to establish them in a comfortable home with more than the bare minimum that is the lot of the average *kollel* couple. It is a tribute to the strength of the education and of the values that motivate these young women that they are willing to make sacrifices in order to preserve their ideals of marriage, of a husband, and of the role of Torah study and religion in their life.

As the responses of most of the women interviewed indicate, many would like to be able to wear elegant, expensive clothes and fine jewelry like young women everywhere. They also know what style, elegance, and a well-appointed home mean. But almost all stressed that their priorities are different even from those Orthodox women who enjoy the comforts and luxuries in a better neighborhood like Boro Park or Flatbush.

An interesting by-product of this attitude of the women of Hasidic Williamsburg, in contrast to those of other neighborhoods, is the fact that one hardly sees any women driving cars in Williamsburg, although the car is an important status symbol in Boro Park, Flatbush, and Monsey. Large advertisements in *Der Yid* and posters in the streets militate against hasidic women driving as improper and potentially conducive to immoral behavior. The women of Williamsburg, as indicated by those interviewed, are perfectly happy letting their husbands do the driving. It is another expression of their willingness to make sacrifices for their ideals, and of their rejection of the kind of conspicuous consumption rampant in other, higher-income Orthodox neighborhoods.

The situation is somewhat different when it comes to wearing jewelry and purchasing fine silver religious articles or decorative articles, such as bowls for the beautification of the Sabbath and holidays in the home. It is common practice for parents of young ladies approaching the marriageable age to see to it that they are properly dressed and have jewelry befitting a future *kallah*, a bride. One father went so far as to leave Williamsburg because, in his opinion, there was still too much emphasis on clothes and jewelry even there. Yet when the two oldest of his nine daughters were about to become engaged to bright young Torah scholars, they wore gold chains, bracelets, and exquisite clothes. For, as he explained, this is what future in-laws even more than the prospective grooms are expecting. The women of Williamsburg give two major reasons for this appreciation of jewelry. One said:

"When we were in the camps, we dreamed of having what other women have. The Nazis took away everything we possessed before they tortured and killed us by the thousand. It took years of privation and hard work until we could again think about buying what makes women feel good and desirable. We are not ashamed of it. When we escaped from the hell of the camps, we earned the right to a bit of peace, light, and beauty, like other human beings."

Another old woman who had spent years in concentration and DP camps before reaching the safety of the U.S. put it this way:

I think this is still a holdover from the terrible experiences we had when we could only take with us what we were able to hide, something light and valuable. Often a jewel was the last resort that enabled us to buy a piece of bread, or life, or a forged paper allowing us to gain freedom. We are still shocked by these traumas, and don't mind admitting that we still treasure rings, chains, or trinkets that so often had enabled us to escape the terrible fate of so many around us. It is not easy to shake off these horrible memories.

In a somewhat similar vein, the parents of prospective brides or grooms speak about the custom of exchanging precious silver gifts, such as Sabbath candlesticks or candelabras, a *menorah, mezuzzot, etrog* boxes or *seder* plates, in preparation of establishing a home for their children that is properly furnished and equipped with the things of beauty and value to them as Jews. One father said:

> We don't want to show off with our riches like the people in the fancier neighborhoods. But we also don't mind showing that we are no longer the poor, pitied refugees or the ragtag camp inmates that we were when we were liberated. We came to this country with little more than what we carried on our backs and what the relief organizations gave us to sustain us for the first few months of frustration and searching for means of survival and getting a new start in life. Our hearts still hurt when we think of our children and wives having to do with so little when most people around us were well dressed and comfortable. We worked by the sweat of our brows. We were not jealous or begrudging of what others had, but we yearned to give our families some of the *menuhah*, the inner peace and happiness to be *menshen*, respected people like others. And having a home with beautiful furnishings is part of this yearning which drove us during the early years of our struggle to make it.

Another woman emphasized this idea in a less dramatic way:

> We are proud of our husbands. Once they leave the yeshivah or the *kollel*, they work hard to be good providers. We are not wasteful or show-offs. But when *Shabbat* or the holidays come around, or when we celebrate family *simchot*, like *bar mitzvot* or weddings, we want to show that we have dignity, a sense of style and beauty like other people.

One of the hasidic scholars stated, "*Tiferet*, beauty, is part of the hasidic spirit and ideology, which is discussed in most of the classic literature of Hasidism based on kabbalistic sources. It obligates us to fulfill a *mitzvah*, a divine commandment, in the most beautiful way of which one is capable. This sense of esthetic perception of the perfection in the divine creation is reflected in a precious *etrog* box, in a sparkling *menorah*, in beautiful candlesticks, *mezzuzot*, or *tefillin*. They create not only a milieu of harmony, beauty, and appreciation of the kindness of the Creator. They also convey our gratitude to Him who is enabling us to serve Him in beauty, to the best of our means, as do all the other creations."

Then this scholar added a thought that is not often verbalized in public by hasidic men:

> We also want our women to enjoy the holidays in a happy, festive spirit. The appreciation of the joy of life, which is basic to *hasidut*, comes with our being dressed in

our best, with beautiful, clean clothes, with jewelry for our women, if the kind Lord helps us, and we can afford them. They are only a small token of our appreciation of their constant hard work of keeping the house clean and in proper shape; of bearing and raising our children, and all the other tasks of maintaining a hasidic home. They are entitled to their *Yomtov* of *Shabbos* for which they have prepared by the sweat of their brow.

Let's be honest, they bear the brunt of the burden of maintaining the home (italics mine). It doesn't leave them much time for leisure and enjoyment. They do not have the privilege of sitting by the Rebbe's *tishen* and of celebrating the festive holiday ceremonies in the *Bais Hamedrash*. It is their *zechus*, their merit or credit, that they let us sit and learn when other husbands spend time with their families or socialize with friends after work and on holidays. The nice furniture, the silverware, and the jewelry are at best mere tokens to show how much we owe and appreciate them.

In a similar vein a hasidic woman, showing the interviewer her bracelet, commented:

Every *Yomtov* my two sons and sons-in-law buy me something to show their love and appreciation. They make it their business to visit us with their children, so that they give *nahas*, joy, to their *Zeideh* and *Bubbeh*. And every time they come they bring *seforim*, important books, for my husband and a trinket or something else valuable for the house. This is one of their ways of showing *kibbud Av va-Eim*, honoring their father and mother.

This is perhaps one of the most characteristic expressions of the value and valuation of beauty in the life-style of the *hasidim*, in their homes, in their clothes, in the ritual objects, and in the jewelry of their women. They perceive it as an expression of their fulfilling a divine command in the right spirit; it is similar to their focus on eating and drinking not merely as an act of fulfilling their physical needs, but as a form of service to the Lord. To them it is a transformation of the animalic or mundane into an act of spiritual significance.

One woman, with a smile in her eyes as she looked with pride upon her daughters in their new holiday outfits, wearing chains and bracelets, said unabashedly:

They are now of the age when we have to think of doing *shidduchim*, proper marriages. And, you know, people judge you by these tokens of *baale-battishkeit*, a good home and family. What is going on in the privacy of your home is one thing. But when it comes to making a good *shidduch*, you must not save on these things. To attract good *hosson*, prospective grooms, who have *yichus*, a good family background, and are promising *talmidei hachomim*, talmudic scholars, one has to go out of one's way even if it means stinting on other less vital things.

Seeing a look of quizzical doubt in the eyes of the questioner, she added:

Of course, everybody knows that there are more important values and character qualities, but knowing how to dress and make herself attractive is quite appropriate for a young girl, and not at all a sign of superficiality or spendthriftiness. It serves not only to attract a good *shidduch*, but it is a major ingredient of a happy married life, as you know quite well. As long as our daughters know that there is more to life than being *farputzt*, all dolled up, like what you call a JAP in other Jewish communities. I think our *chinuch*, our education at home and at school, is doing a good job of imparting to our girls what are genuine values and what is the veneer of makeup.

In a world where there is almost no dating at all, no formal courtship and none of the usual features of the dating game, there is no stigma attached to this honest attitude of a mother who is anxious to display the beauty and attractiveness of her daughters of marriageable age. In a similar vein, some of the *hasidim* emphasize the importance of having a well-appointed home, a large bookcase whose shelves are packed with the classics of the Torah literature, and of *Hasidut*, the masterworks of the founders and thinkers of the hasidic ideology. They also look with pride at their silver chest, which is filled with the usual valuable ritual objects, with silver bowls and vessels, and with sparkling crystal. It is part of *baale-battishkeit*, having the proper home atmosphere. It indicates that the home is filled with the right spirit, order, sense of beauty, and appreciation of the joy and enjoyment of life that is endemic to the hasidic life-style. One middle-aged *hasid* who has built up his own business by the sweat of his brow added somewhat ironically but proudly: "In your world there are other indicators of what is desirable. In our world, a *baale-battishe*, a proper home, says much about your values and the appreciation of what the kind Lord enables you to afford."

Education

The preceding discussion of the other phases of the hasidic community emphasized the central role of education for the realization and perpetuation of the hasidic ideology and life-style. It stressed the importance of its effectiveness in view of the tremendous pressures of metropolitan life, the media blitz, and the radically different, if not outright hostile, trends and values that dominate the broader sociocultural scene beyond the invisible walls of the voluntary ghetto of Williamsburg.

In chapter 3 the essential features of the boys' and girls' educational systems established by the Rebbe of Satmar and the heads of the other Hungarian hasidic subcommunities were discussed. It highlighted the differences between these schools and other strictly Orthodox Jewish day schools and *yeshivot*, differences of underlying ideology, of curricular and the extracurricular offerings, and of the shaping of the personality and the ideas and ideals and ambitions of the male and female students. As pointed out, there are several crucial differences in the approaches of the Hungarian hasidic schools. The *yeshivah* education of the boys concentrates from early youth on the study of Torah, the Bible, and on the classic talmudic literature. Particular emphasis is on the study of practical *halachah*, the codes guiding the daily religious life of the individual and the community, plus an admixture of the classics of hasidic literature and contemporary writings, such as the works of the Rebbe of Satmar. The study of secular subjects is held to the legal minimum of required courses and in most cases ends soon after the age of *bar mitzvah*.

In contrast, the girls' education of Satmar and similar Hungarian schools does not center on the study of Torah in the Hebrew language, and avoids the standard texts, which are paramount in the other, even the most Orthodox, girls' schools, such as Bais Yaakov. Hasidic girls' schools, such as Beth Ruchel of Satmar, abide as much as possible by the classic talmudic prohibition of teaching Torah to girls because it might lead to improper views and behavior. Instead, after teaching girls to read Hebrew in order to understand the language of the prayers, most instruction is done orally in Yiddish. In the past decades, however, there has been a massive growth of various types of texts and workbooks in Yiddish initiated by the Rebbe of Satmar, written by some of the best educators of his school systems and published by the publication organization he specifically created for this purpose.

Not only is the text study of Torah avoided conscientiously but also any use of *Ivrit*, the modern Hebrew language, which elsewhere has become one of the most important aspects of the Jewish day-school curricula and which has fostered the almost mandatory practice of Jewish high-school graduates to spend a year or more of study at Israeli institutions. As pointed out previously, the ideology propounded by the Old Rebbe of Satmar considers modern Hebrew a profanization of the sacred language of the Bible. Equally he was staunchly opposed to the modern State of Israel as a secular polity that violates the spirit and the law of the Torah. This attitude eliminates a major segment of the daily program of the usual Jewish day-school curriculum. In its place, there is much emphasis on the study of the customs and laws, and of the mores that apply to *kashrut*, Sabbath, and the holidays. Other major topics, especially for the older classes, are the study of the regulations of purity, of physical as well as spiritual health, of the stringent requirements of marital relations between husband and wife, and the proper conduct of women outside of the home.

The impact of these foci of the hasidic girls' education is clearly evident in the thinking and conduct of the girls and women in Hasidic Williamsburg, as expressed in their responses to questions concerning the supreme importance of the study of Torah for the men, the scrupulous observance of the law and of the hasidic life-style, and the stringent constraints on their appearance and conduct. Without exception, the girls in the sample survey emphasized that they wanted to marry Torah students who would continue to spend a good part of their time on the advanced study of the talmudic and halachic literature after marriage and after they have left the *kollel* to earn a livelihood.

The focus of the responses of the young and middle-aged married women was on their firm intention to bear and educate sons who would become Torah scholars, *talmidei hachomim*, instead of the caricature of the Jewish mother's dream of "my son the doctor" or "my son the lawyer" or "my son the rocket scientist." De facto, 90 percent of the young and middle-aged women in the survey population had married husbands who did spend between 1 and 3 years in a *kollel* after marriage. Conse-quently, the majority of the women had been forced to continue working after marriage and in between having children, while their husbands devoted all their time to intensive talmudic and rabbinic studies. Not one of the women, regardless of age and marital status, not even the divorcée who was somewhat critical of life in Hasidic Williamsburg, objected to this attitude and burden of newly married hasidic women.

Obviously, this shows the impact of the girls' education, as does their attitude toward having children and spending most of their time on raising them and on the routine chores of keeping a proper hasidic home. Not one objected to the fact discussed before in connection with the demographics that a third of the women in the survey, age 32.6 on the average, have six children or more. Nor did a single one of them indicate that she desired to stop having more children or voice anything but strong objection to all forms of birth control and abortion, except in cases of serious threat to the life of the mother. Most made a point of stressing that living in Williamsburg affords them the opportunity to give their children the same educa-tion and to raise them in the same spirit of love for Torah and Hasidut and loyalty to the Rebbe that they had acquired. In the same vein, not one of the married, not even the divorced, women was critical of the high level and quality of the educational systems for the boys and girls, though a few had some reservations and even outright criticism of the pressure of the community on the individual to conform.

Thus, we understand that the women of Hasidic Williamsburg reject the general trends of society, popular even among Jewish women in the less Orthodox com-munities, to achieve equality in all realms of community and personal life and self-realization outside of the home. Five of the women who did or are still going to work stated that they enjoyed getting out. Yet, not one of these admitted any further implications of this enjoyment for their life or that of their children. Similarly, the fifteen women who work with their husbands in their businesses, and the growing number of those who have established their own businesses in Williamsburg and elsewhere, deny any impact of this association with members of the outside world on their own attitudes and values. Despite hardships and obvious difficulties, they persist in wearing their hair covered all the time and long-sleeved clothes even during the hottest, most humid months of the summer. Yet, generally their garments are fashionable while being modest by the most stringent standards. They maintain the required restraint in social dealings, which are so vital in the world of business where so much business is conducted informally, over lunch and dinner, in restaurants and night clubs.

Obviously, the hasidic education has a strong enough influence to counteract the temptations inherent in being involved in business or in jobs that constantly test the strength of the values of these young and middle-aged women. For, in their vocational training in the high school of Beth Rachel they have prepared themselves for careers that require contact with a world that practices and glorifies conduct radically different from the strict standards of their hasidic upbringing. The mere fact that many of the middle-aged and young women have a number of children shows their relative immunity to the fashionable trends in the society in which they have to function if they venture outside of their community.

Social Structure

The same underlying values that produced the strength of the traditional family and the demographic facts cited are also responsible for the attitude of the women of Williamsburg toward their role and status in the community life. As pointed out, to outsiders the position of hasidic women strongly suggests discrimination in public life and a measure of inequality that would have been intolerable even to the women of pre-World-War-II Williamsburg. They achieved considerable power in major realms, especially in the central institution of the synagogue. They exerted influence on the choice of a rabbi, on his authority and obligations, on his salary, tenure, and dismissal. They had considerable input into the religious policies, as well as the ritual and educational life of the community, as do the women of the suburban Orthodox communities, though many are products of religious Jewish girls' day schools.

There is no question that the hasidic ideology, in line with its halachic substructure, has little room for this type of equality in a realm that that does not recognize any authority other than the one vested in the official rabbinic authorities based on their scholarship. This attitude applies to all realms of the administration and policy decisions concerning ritual and general religious matters, whether in the synagogue, in the realm of *kashrut*, or in the policies that guide the educational system.

The strict separation of men and women which in the Reform and Conservative synagogues, or even in the left of center Orthodox branches, continues to be a matter of controversy in the drive of women for equality and the objection to any form of real or imagined discrimination, is beyond discussion in the hasidic community. The halachic requirement of separate seating and of a *mechitzah*, a dividing wall or curtain, in the synagogue is considered an insult to the intelligence and self-control of women and men and disregard for the value of the family praying together. There is no room for democracy, the will of the members, which reigns supreme in the American synagogue, in the hasidic as well as the other strictly Orthodox nonhasidic congregations when it comes to clearly defined halachic matters.

By their upbringing and values hasidic women reject the very idea of their seeking a voice in the administration of the synagogues, in the selection of a rabbi, the determination of his salary, functions, or dismissal. To hasidic women such matters are not open to discussion and surely not within the jurisdiction of the broader membership. The most significant evidence of the acceptance of the separation between the male and female realms of the synagogue is the ubiquitous *mechitzah*, a dividing wall or opaque curtain, between the sections reserved for men and for women. At a time when even Orthodox synagogues feature balconies or elevated platforms reserved for women or a chest-high wall across which they may communicate or at least have eye contact with relatives or friends, the *mechitzah* of the hasidic *shul* excludes any form of contact. "When I pray for my and my family's welfare," said one of the women questioned, "I want to be totally alone with my thoughts and innermost feelings, and far from any form of distraction that might infringe on my *kavvanah*, my devotion, seriousness, and sincerity, in my pleas for forgiveness and blessing."

Another woman, when questioned about her reaction to the total separation and exclusion of women in matters of ritual and religious concern, put her position even more strongly when she said:

> How can a woman have the right *kavvanah*, the proper concentration and spirit of reverence and contrition, if she is all decked out in her finery to see and be seen. It's beyond me how an *ehrliche*, a pious woman, would consider this strict separation of men and women an affront to her dignity and equality. When I stand before the Lord all alone I don't want anything to interfere or distract my attention, so that I can really pray from the depth of my heart that He will forgive me and my beloved ones' iniquities and shortcomings and hear my prayers for their health and welfare. When I was young I saw my mother and grandmother shed bitter tears when they stood immersed in humble prayer. Would that I could grow worthy of the same level of sincerity and humbleness and self-abrogation at these moments of trying to break through to the heavens in my prayers.

Most of the women stress that they are perfectly satisfied with their auxiliary role in the affairs of the synagogue and of the *yeshivot* in which their children are getting their education. They are members of the parents' organizations and the ladies' auxiliaries of these institutions. They attend the meetings and sponsor or help organize their luncheons, teas, auctions, bazaars, or banquets. They try to attend some of the classes for women advertised weekly in *Der Yid*, especially those that help prepare them for the holidays. The wife of one of the younger leaders of the Puper Yeshivah said emphatically: "I am happy and satisfied if I have the time and the opportunity to attend the regular and special functions, the celebrations, and the affairs arranged by our Rebbe and by his Rebbetzin for the many worthy causes that they support on behalf of our congregation, the hasidic community, and for the poor and needy here, and in Israel."

Not a single member of the survey panel or those interviewed in depth expressed regret or indignation at the thought of having to play a secondary role in the official matters of the synagogue, and in the setting of policies concerning any phase of the religious or ritual life. They have been taught and willingly accept that only those with the knowledge and the authority, based on Torah scholarship, are competent to make decisions in matters of *halachah* and *hashkafah*, the basic weltanschauung, beliefs, and ideology that guide the life of the hasidic as well as the strictly Orthodox nonhasidic communities.

Economic Patterns

The earlier discussion of the economic revitalization pointed to several crucial factors in the gradual turnabout of the economic situation in the hasidic community of Williamsburg. One of the two major factors is the demographic change, as about five hundred young couples annually choose to remain in Williamsburg, near their families and their Rebbe, inspite of the acute housing shortage and the rising cost of rentals and real estate. The rejection of birth control and abortion resulted in a virtual population explosion in the neighborhood. In addition, the middle-aged second- and third-generation residents, the *avreichim*, gradually assumed responsibilities and moved into the ranks of the leadership of the community. As stressed throughout this report, this inner transformation has had a deep impact on the very essence of the communal life in general, but particularly in the realm of the economic revitalization and the development of the entrepreneurial spirit of the younger elements who led the progress into new realms of business and trade.

As suggested in that discussion, perhaps the most significant factor of this turnabout was the official recognition of the hasidic community as a Disadvantaged Minority by the U.S. Department of Commerce in 1984 after years of limited recognition and protracted negotiations. This new status enabled members of the hasidic community to claim a share of the opportunities in the training programs and in the open competition for government contracts and for other federal, state, and local programs of assistance in various realms of manufacturing, industry, and business, which had previously been closed to them. In turn, this significant development led to the increasing involvement and readiness of the mostly native American young and middle-aged *hasidim* to venture into various new types of enterprises in spite of their lack of experience and of handicaps inherent in their life-style. Furthermore, it enabled large numbers of *hasidim* to enter and blend into the mainstream of American business. Lacking the higher level of secular education that directed most of the young of the American Jewish community into the higher professions, young *hasidim* turned to careers in business and trade, manufacturing, retail and wholesale, export and import. Since the early '80s, growing numbers moved into such managerial services as real estate, financial management, insurance, and the expanding sectors of investment brokerage. Eventually, quite a few turned to the technical trades, such as those offered in electronics and computer technology, which do not require higher levels of education.

This broadening of the economic opportunities for the men and women of Hasidic Williamsburg and in other neighborhoods resulted in a gradual improvement of the economic situation. By most estimates close to 50 percent of the hasidic population is still living in poverty or depends heavily on governmental and community relief programs, especially since the onset of the serious economic crisis in the early '90s. Yet the general spirit is sanguine. The people in the street and the leaders of the hasidic community of Williamsburg remain optimistic in their belief in the chances of its young to blend into the mainstream of the American economy, while maintaining their concentration on Torah study and adherence to the hasidic ideology and life-style.

Against this economic background, we have to look at the situation of the women who benefit equally from the gradual opening of formerly closed doors in business. Of the 175 women in the survey, 60 percent indicated that their husbands are engaged in some realm of business and trade. Of these about one-third are working as bookkeepers, sales personnel, in management or as clerks. Fifteen, or about 10 percent, of the married women work with their husbands in business. Others indicated that they help their husbands in their free time, at night or after they have completed their household chores. Several take care of the books full-time or part-time. Others handle the correspondence or scan magazines and catalogs to advise their husbands in the selection of their merchandise. In the '50s a large number of the women traveled to Manhattan and elsewhere to work in the standard immigrant trades and industries as operators, seamstresses, pressers, and secretaries, to do their share to ease the burden of the family budget. Now not more than a third of the women still do so, according to the estimate of the leaders of the community.

But they are not part of the erstwhile type of Jewish proletariat that worked in the garment industry and needle trades. Those who do work after marriage are engaged in some phase of education, are qualified bookkeepers, secretaries, computer programmers, or sales personnel. A growing number are moving into some level of management, especially in the local trades. They work with their husbands, or have established their own shops or stores in the basements of their homes or on the stoops of the sidestreets of Williamsburg or in the thoroughfares.

Some of the hasidic women have achieved a measure of prominence among Jewish women because they provide services not easily available elsewhere. Most of these work in the *sheitel*, wig, industry, in lingerie, undergarments, and imported goods needed in the home. They run children's and women's clothes boutiques, jewelry and house furnishings stores, with their husbands or by themselves. A number of hasidic women have become part of the approximately 10 percent of Williamsburg's entrepreneurs. A few of the outstanding ones established their trades in some phase of the imported clothes lines, in wholesale and retail jewelry, lamps, crystal, and related lines.

Naturally, Orthodox women prefer to be served by women with the same or similar backgrounds. Hence Orthodox women from other neighborhoods and even from out of town travel to Williamsburg for certain lines of clothes, underwear, or lingerie. Two of such women entrepreneurs, cited several times in this report, have acquired widespread renown.

A number of hasidic women have established specialty shops in the neighborhood. Some carry fine linen imported from China, Korea, Ireland, and England. Some specialize in particular lines of elegant clothes, so that several of the respondents in a shopper's survey commissioned by the local merchants association stressed that they no longer have to travel uptown. They can get all they need right at the shops in the neighborhood at comparable, if not at more reasonable, prices, and are served by people who speak their own language and understand their particular needs. Other respondents in this shopper's survey indicated that they find certain items here they cannot get elsewhere. One woman, a wealthy Long Island matron, commented that she regularly meets her two sisters in Williamsburg, one from Queens and the other from out of town, for periodic shopping trips, especially before the holidays. All three come from prominent upper-middle-class families and do not have to search out the stores with the cheapest prices.

This preference for shopping in Hasidic Williamsburg is also expressed by young and middle-aged women from the Orthodox suburban New York communities who do all the shopping for their children's clothes here. One of the popular stores frequented by them had been established soon after World War II by one of the so-called refugees on a corner stoop, together with his sister. Now he has a large store in the same, most unattractive, poor neighborhood adjacent to the center of Williamsburg, east of Brooklyn Broadway. Shoppers from the entire New York region seek out his shop because of the high quality and exclusivity of his clothes, and his still reasonable prices. In the beginning of the '90s he established a second store in Flatbush, which is also attracting customers from near and far.

A woman who got her start in Williamsburg and has now developed her own famous lines of *sheitels*, wigs, has stores in several locations, and her line is carried by stores nationwide. More recently she has established a school for training young hasidic women in the production and servicing of her exclusive wigs. Her designs are known for their elegance, yet they meet at the same time the highest standards of modesty required by the ultra-Orthodox women. A few of her select designs cost as much as $2,000, and her studio has lines of women waiting for their appointment made weeks in advance to be fitted by her personnel, especially before the holidays. A famous hasidic family, members of one of the most prominent Rebbes' dynasties, imported one of these exclusive *sheitel*-makers to Israel for the wedding of one of their girls to the scion of a Rebbe from New York. Since they expected guests from among the most aristocratic families of America, Europe, and Israel to participate, they made sure that they had a renowned sheitel specialist on hand to service and outfit the women for this special occasion in contemporary hasidic society. Her trip was paid for by a wealthy *hasid* of the Rebbe who volunteered to cover all wedding expenses as a token of his appreciation and reverence for the Rebbe on whom he calls constantly for his blessing and counsel.

A growing number of women work in the jewelry and diamond line, uptown, though not quite as many as had engaged in this trade during the early years of the post-World-War-II era when the diamond industry brought a measure of wealth to the Orthodox community of Williamsburg and elsewhere. On the other hand, women are prominent among those who in recent years have opened jewelry, silverware, and bric-a-brac stores, as evidenced in every issue of the weekly *Yid* ad sections. Obviously, girls of marriageable age and their families are among the prime customers, as pointed out before. One of these young women said:

> We have so few opportunities to express our individuality and appreciation of esthetics. There is no denying that we want to be attractive to our prospective husbands. They are not blind. We do not have elaborate dating like the girls elsewhere, even those who graduate from the Orthodox day schools. And yeshivah *bachurim* have different values by which they judge the women whom they wish to marry and be the mothers of their children. But they can spot unattractive girls and the opposite, as well as anyone else. Given the choice, after considering all other factors that the families of good young men are looking for, good appearance, the ability to dress and to look proper may be crucial in making the kind of ideal *shidduch* we hasidic young women are dreaming of.

Of course, as stressed several times in this report, some of the girls disapprove of luring future husbands by "attractive appearance and jewelry with which they *behang* themselves," as one of the serious Beth Ruchel students put it. Contemptuously, she added: "Inner beauty, which is the pride of the Jewish woman, is what counts, not the makeup, the fancy clothes, and the price of precious designer jewelry." Similarly, posters in the streets and large ads in *Der Yid* call on hasidic women not to wear provocative clothes and to avoid trying to look like women elsewhere who display their vanity and superficiality in their appearance. Yet, parents who want to do good *shidduchim* will go out of their way to have their daughters look attractive and well dressed. Hence, they do not mind that good jewelry is one of the factors prospective in-laws expect when they go shopping for brides for their sons. Thus, jewelry stores in Williamsburg do quite well thanks to the fact that every year large numbers of girls reach the age when parents are concerned about giving them a fair chance. They do not consider it a threat to their moral standards that they give their girls good clothes and fine jewelry. They believe that they have given them a good education and sound moral values at home, at school, and in the community. One woman teacher said: "As long as it is not overdone, our girls are entitled to enjoy this vital stage in their life. And there is no need to begrudge them this opportunity to display their individuality."

One of the significant considerations in the choice of trades or vocations for which girls prepare themselves during their years at the vocational high school of Beth Ruchel is not merely the eventual earning power it gives them, though this is no small matter. They have to be able to help their husbands, especially during the early years. But as important as the money they will be able to earn is the fact that they must find a field, like computer programming, for example, that allows them the flexibility of setting up a schedule that will not force them to neglect their jobs as mothers and housewives. As one young mother put it:

> I cannot leave the house until the youngest of my children is picked up by the *yeshivah* bus. And I want to be home when the first one is returned. I don't want to be one of those career-oriented absentee mothers whose children are taken care of by neighbors. Therefore, I chose and am happy that I got the training and a job as a programmer. It allows me to give my family what they need and the earning power of a halfway decent, much-appreciated income.

Incidentally, as pointed out in the discussion of the educational system, these working women are aided by the central food program that provides hot breakfasts and lunches to all the boys' *yeshivot* and girls' schools. Thus all students, regardless of the situation at home, get the same nutritious food in the morning before classes start and during the noon break. This aspect of the food program is vital in view of the long hours they spend at school. At the same time, as one of the administrators pointed out, these meals allow the mothers who have to go to work to leave without having to worry about making breakfast and preparing lunches for the children of school age. They can thus devote their full attention to their infants and toddlers if they do not go out to work.

Typical of the women who used to leave their children and homes to work in the factories during the early years of the developing hasidic community is the owner of a small, modest, thriving stoop shop in her own house on a side street off Lee Avenue. She was a victim of maltreatment and serious malnutrition during the Holocaust, which cost her one eye. After her arrival in this country she learned to sew, repair, and adjust female undergarments, such as corsets and bras, in order to help her husband meet the growing needs of her family. Eventually she developed such skill and expertise that her reputation spread. From small beginnings in a small room of her apartment, she built up a large clientele of women all over New York and from out of town, not only from among her hasidic neighbors. She is constantly adding rooms in her house to accommodate her customers who often wait for weeks for her merchandise. They line up to be served by the owner because they appreciate her skill, as observed by this writer during the half hour he waited for a relative who was on line to try on some garments she had ordered weeks before, on a frosty winter morning. The street was covered with snow, or what had been snow before the busy traffic cruised through. One woman from a suburb of New York waited patiently as the owner adjusted three new corsets she had ordered weeks in advance because she could not get them anywhere else in New York. She gladly paid the rather steep price. It was all worth it, she said, knowing that here was a place where she can get what she wants and have it adjusted to her needs. Meanwhile an elegant young woman in an expensive fur coat from one of the affluent neighborhoods purchased undergarments for a sizable sum and drove off in her luxury car.

Then a group of several hasidic women arrived, one of them a bride. They were shopping for lingerie for her and her relatives to go with their wedding outfits. One of the older women was a regular customer here and took pride in introducing the members of her family, each of whom left a sizable order. Meanwhile an elderly hasidic woman appeared with a baby carriage, which she had pushed through the snow on the sidewalk. The baby was the newest of her grandchildren. She was watching it for her daughter. She brought a large bag full of used undergarments that showed wear and tear and needed adjustment. A young woman was assisting the owner, taking care of the customers in the new merchandise room, while the owner was taking care of the fitting and adjusting in a converted former bedroom. The young saleswoman indicated she had recently lost her still-young scholar husband, and was left to care for her two small children. As she explained, she could only take this limited job for a few hours a day, when her mother, the widow of a renowned rabbi, was available to take care of her babies.

The owner and her assistant are typical of the hasidic women who in recent years have set up their own small, intimate enterprises in their homes, in basements, on stoops, or in expanded or converted apartments. From their homes they can attend to the business without depriving their families of their care, and without having to compromise their stringent standards in dealing with the nonhasidic or even the non-Jewish world and its mores.

As pointed out, this mushrooming neighborhood trade has radically transformed

Williamsburg from what had primarily been a residential area, with a few shopping streets, into one that features light industry established by *hasidim* at the outskirts, and an increasingly thickening network of smaller and larger commercial retail or wholesale shops in the brownstone houses in the side streets that cross the Jewish Triangle from side to side, and are now expanding into areas that had been largely lost to the Jewish population.

Interestingly enough, quite in line with the ideology of the hasidic community, neither men nor women are entering the professional fields that have been attracting the young of the broader American Jewish community. While *hasidim* are increasingly moving into various managerial and service fields, the neighborhood depends entirely on outsiders to provide medical, legal, psychological, and related care because their young shun higher secular education. Consequently, the constantly growing local primary health center, organized and directed by the local ODA office, although it is staffed by men and women almost all of whom are Jewish, most of them Orthodox, has no *hasidim*. Similarly, the weekly *Yid* carries advertisements of physicians, lawyers, and other professionals who indicate that they speak Yiddish or that they are Sabbath observant, who are opening offices in Williamsburg. Obviously, hasidic men and women are more comfortable with professionals of this type who speak their language and who can handle their physical and other problems in a manner that does not require violation of their moral and religious scruples.

Of the 175 women who responded to the survey questionnaires, only one indicated that her husband was a professional. Since she did not elaborate, it seems likely that he is the principal of one of the hasidic *yeshivot*, like the 25 percent of the husbands who engage in some level of Jewish education as teachers, administrators, executives, or supervisors.

One of the incidental indicators of the somewhat higher economic level of the Williamsburg *hasidim* in the '80s and early '90s, of particular benefit to the women and children, is the fact that a large percent are spending the summer months in bungalow colonies in the Catskills. They are giving a sorely needed boost to this once popular Jewish resort for New Yorkers which fell on hard times once cars, planes, and higher incomes created new resort areas in domestic and foreign vacation centers. Just like the formerly more affluent members of the Jewish community of Williamsburg, *hasidim* are now flocking to the mountains for the hot and humid July and August months. They rent bungalows in the mushrooming colonies established by hasidic and nonhasidic communities, as well as by private entrepreneurs. A good many *hasidim* rent bungalows, if possible, not far from the large summer camps that hasidic *yeshivot* and schools for boys and girls have set up in the Catskills for their students to spend the summer in regular study programs. Even the younger children who do not attend summer camps as yet have special teachers hired by the bungalow colonies so that they too can study and have at least part of the long summer days structured.

To accommodate the large number of hasidic families in their summer residences, many stores that serve them in the city have branches in central locations of the bungalow colonies to provide them with all they need, unlike in the earlier era, when Orthodox summer residents had to take all they required with them when they moved to their bungalows. Still more impressive is the fact that the hasidic community of Williamsburg has brought some of its vital services to the mountains, such as *Hatzoloh*, the medical volunteer corps, and others. Thus, the hasidic residents by and large feel quite comfortable, although a recent incident in the summer of '91, when a hasidic retired man was slain by a robber in his bungalow, has served to remind them, as one of the rabbis commented, that even up here in the isolated Catskills they are still subject to the dangers of living in exile. Annually, at the beginning and at the end of the bungalow season, the hasidic community arranges large mass meetings in the public-school auditorium, which are addressed by Rabbi Edgar Glueck, the Jewish special assistant to the state police, and by police officers, to counsel them on the requirements and risks of safe travel and security.

One pleasant by-product of the concern for their members of the hasidic communities in Williamsburg is the establishment of a special summer cafeteria in the center of the neighborhood, which serves ample and nourishing food to husbands and others who cannot make the trek to the Catskills and would otherwise have been forced to subsist all week long on their own makeshift provisions or the rather expensive restaurant meals, instead of the nominal fee charged by the communal cafeteria. A constant flow of vans, car services, and the regular buses provide the transportation to allow for the regular weekend and midweek trips of the heads of the families who have to remain in the city.

Social Welfare

As mentioned several times, no phase of the formal and informal community life of Williamsburg is more important or of greater concern to its women than the welfare of the people in the neighborhood, and beyond. While some aspects of this work were mentioned in my 1961 report, it was not part of the characteristic structure and dynamics of the community any more than in any other Jewish or non-Jewish neighborhood.

In fact, this is one of the most significant of the changes that have evolved since the '60s, with the growth and expansion of the hasidic community of Williamsburg. The relatively high degree of poverty and the pressing needs of the population, most of whom had been survivors of the concentration and DP camps until they immigrated to this country, required a maximum of official and unofficial attention. Hence, as mentioned throughout, major efforts on the part of the Rebbe of Satmar soon after the reestablishment of his community in Williamsburg were devoted to alleviating the distress and meeting the constantly growing needs of his *hasidim*, such as the creation of his Million Dollar Charity Rotation Fund and other projects directed partially by his wife. Ever since, social welfare organizations, institutions, and communal and private projects have taken up a major portion of the efforts to cope with the constantly growing needs of its exploding population, especially the women. Unquestionably, social welfare programs have become part of the most important substructure that has created a solid foundation for the functionality and vibrancy of community life, in spite of the fact that at least one-third of the Williamsburg population still lives below the national poverty line, which in the beginning of the '90s was $13,360 for a household of four in the U.S. The significance of this fact emerges boldly when compared with the considerably higher needs of the typical hasidic household, which has seven to eight children and much higher costs of education, in addition to the usual cost of food, clothes, and shelter.

It is particularly this realm of social welfare that the women of Williamsburg have chosen as the predominant domain of their interest, activism, and official and unofficial involvement. This fact is borne out by the responses of the women in the survey sample and by the majority of women, young and old, who were interviewed in depth. They are involved almost without exception, unless, as one pointed out, "I am much too bogged down with my chores as a homemaker, wife, and mother to have any time or strength left for any work for the *klal*. My husband and seven children have first call on my time right now. Perhaps a little later when my children are older, I'll be able to devote myself to some *hesed* work." Both the single girls and the married women expressed their enthusiastic participation in some phase of the *tzedakah vehesed*, the charity and kindness projects of the community. They belong to various charity and service organizations, which have been set up by the various hasidic communities separately or jointly. Favorites among them are visiting patients in the hospitals and inmates of hospices and other institutions. Some do volunteer work at the local *Aishel Avrohom* nursing home. Others join teams that daily prepare fresh food for patients in the New York hospitals who request it. Many are members of the *Bikkur Cholim* teams, which visit hospitals on a fleet of vans and buses leaving Williamsburg in the morning and in the afternoon. Others concentrate on visiting hospitals and hospices where hasidic patients have difficulties communicating with non-Yiddish-speaking staffs. They help feed them or just keep them company. Many, including the young girls, indicated that they are involved in some fund-raising projects for the needs of the Williamsburg population, or for the many institutions in Israel, which constantly clamor for help.

The pattern for this involvement of the Williamsburg women had been established by the Old Rebbetzin of Satmar since her and her husband's arrival in this country. Though in her eighties, she is still continuing some of her old, and constantly adding new, projects, even now, more than a decade after her husband's death. With the help of her team of women, who have assisted her for more than four decades, she runs auctions, bazaars, luncheons, and other programs that, are a major source of income for local and national institutions of Satmar. Similarly, the wife of the present Rebbe of Satmar, Rabbi Moshe Teitelbaum, has assumed a large share of the ever growing efforts to meet the needs of the exploding hasidic population.

Chapter 9 deals with the magnificent efforts made by both men and women in this realm for which Hasidic Williamsburg has become famous as the initiator of service and relief organizations and projects that have spread to other hasidic and nonhasidic Orthodox communities in New York, and in such suburbs as Monsey, and Monroe. In fact, one of the prominent leaders of the hasidic community has even criticized the tremendous pressure that this concentration on charity and welfare work imposes on the lower-middle-class and working-class members. To the rich, he says, it does not matter that practically every Sabbath features a major appeal for contributions in the local synagogues. They can afford it. But for the rest it may mean doing without some things their own families require because one cannot stand aside as everyone is called on to participate and give to the innumerable causes championed by the hasidic community. The vast majority of those interviewed, however, feel proud to be involved in working with and for the *klal*, the communal welfare.

In the view of the women, two major areas of the hasidic values and ideology are of special concern to them. First and foremost is their God-given role as wives and mothers of the future generation. Second, they engage in some realm of official or unofficial, communal or private *hesed*, such as help to neighbors in need, to the elderly or sick, or to women who because of their large families are bogged down in their household chores. While the study of Torah is the first and foremost challenge of the men, the women have been educated to think of themselves as *Eishes Hayil*, women of valor, who dedicate their lives to the duties of the home, the family, and the needy. "This is our *mitzvah*," many of the women responded when questioned about their keen interest in welfare activities.

As pointed out in the discussion of the social structure, charity work is also one of the major avenues for women to gain a measure of prominence and public recognition. While they do not compete with the men in the direction of the policies and activities of the other realms of the community life, especially the synagogue, the ritual, and educational institutions, they do take the initiative in a number of prominent welfare programs and carry the responsibility for financing and maintaining these projects. The woman who was responsible for initiating *Bikkur Cholim*, teams and buses that visit New York's hospitals, hospices, and other institutions, is also one of those responsible for renting apartments near the hospitals where hasidic patients are treated. These enable relatives and friends to remain nearby on Sabbaths and holidays to provide the much needed psychological support.

It was another such woman who converted the basement of her house into a large facility where teams of women are busy every morning before dawn preparing huge amounts of fresh food to be delivered in specially equipped vehicles to patients who request this service, even if they are not Orthodox. The same woman also runs various financial projects to maintain these activities. The pages of *Der Yid* are filled with announcements of social affairs, lunches, teas, auctions, bazaars, and so forth being held by the women's groups and hosted by prominent hasidic women in their own homes or in communal halls. Other activities of these leading women emerge from the numerous advertisements in the *Yid* that express the gratitude of the institutions and organizations to the women who enable them to carry on their welfare and service work. But time and again the women interviewed stressed that they were not seeking this type of publicity or prominence, that their only concern was to help those in need. One of the women teachers voiced this sentiment when she said:

> We have been taught that each creature in the Divine Creation of the world has a function to fulfill. As strictly observant Torah Jews we know that nothing is as important as helping others in need, whether with a kind word, with money, or with physical or emotional support. We women feel that here is where we can best fulfill our *mitzvah* by extending this *hesed*, this act of kindness, to others.

The impact of this attitude clearly emerges from the responses of the single girls in the survey, all of whom stress that they had been trained to devote some time to charitable work for those in need. They are given time off from classes to visit sick or old people who have no one to talk to them or to help them. Other girls stress that at least one morning they spend an hour or two before school to volunteer their services in *Aishel Avrohom*, the local old age home, or help women who have given birth and require help after they have returned home. One stressed: "This is my favorite leisure activity, when I can give of myself to help others feel better, to ease their suffering or loneliness." A married woman with a large family emphasized:

> There is just never a time when things aren't piling up. My home, my family always require attention and work, work that never seems to end. But I make certain that at least once or twice a week I put everything aside to help others who are less fortunate than I. This is just as important for my own state of mind as it helps others.

An elderly woman who has no family left and lives all alone said:

> The girl from Beth Ruchel who comes to see me on Sundays is like an angel to me. I have no one else left in the world. I don't know anything about her, only that her name is Miriam. She is better to me than my own grandchildren were, before they moved far away. Miriam sits with me, tells me stories, and what she has learned the past week in her classes. All week long I am waiting for her, like we are waiting for the *Moshiah*.

Leisure Activities

This attitude of having higher values, different priorities that motivate the strong concern and involvement of the women of Williamsburg emerges also from the responses of the women to the questions about their cultural interests and leisure activities. Though they have been educated in sociocultural isolation in their enclave in the very midst of metropolitan New York, they are not ignorant or oblivious to what is going on all around them. All but a few of the older women have a 3- or 4-year high-school education, which gives them little more than a passing acquaintance with the value, life-style, and perspective of the world in which they function. Yet all, even those who are critical of one or another aspect of the life-style in Williamsburg, distance themselves from the values that dominate society and from the impact of the media, which shapes the thinking of their contemporaries outside of their self-imposed ghetto. The responses of the young as well as of the older women clearly back up the relative immunity and claims of independence made throughout the discussion of the preceding chapters of this report on the hasidic community of Williamsburg.

Most of the married women stress that they have little time for social and leisure activities beyond those organized by their congregations and by the schools of their children. Those of the 153 married women who can afford it and are not totally absorbed by their household chores, attend some of the *melaveh malkehs*, teas, lunches, or banquets, as part of their obligations and their loyalty to their Rebbe and to the institutions he established for them and their families.

Generally, the respondents indicated three groups of such activities in which they participate whenever possible. About 27 percent invest time, money, and personal efforts in institutions and organizations for the needy, poor, and sick. Fifty-six percent, or about one-third of the women in the survey population, state that they visit patients or the elderly in hospitals or nursing homes. One woman, for example, who has six children of her own, volunteers an hour almost every morning to *Aishel Avrohom*, the local nursing home, after all of her children have been picked up by their school buses. The administrator of this facility stresses that he is largely dependent on the assistance of the volunteers to implement the work of his chronically overworked staff, especially in the program of activities on behalf of the old men and women who otherwise would sit in their wheelchairs, staring into the air, after they have been washed and fed breakfast or lunch.

The local girls' schools give their students some free time to engage in some of the *hesed* projects, which are central to the education of hasidic youngsters. As the directors of *Aishel Avrohom* and of similar projects stress over and over again, this service is vital for the spirit and welfare of their patients. Equally, if not more important, are the men and women who come to the old-age home in the morning before they go to work, or come in the evening after they have returned, at a time when much of the paid staff is no longer there or not yet available. Their services cannot be paid, nor be replaced by the professionals, because of their enthusiasm, spirit, devotion, and personal care.

A number of the single girls who do not take part in the regular *Bikkur Cholim* team visits to the local hospitals indicated that they on their own visit elderly women or men who are bed- or homebound and have no one to visit them regularly, to talk to them, and to keep them informed of what is going on in their community and in the world, in general. Some write letters or even do the bookkeeping for their charges, and perform other services. One group states that they assist women who have many children and cannot afford help. Other girls seek out women who are about to give birth and help take care of the household while the women are away or even after they have returned home. A large number of the women join teams of *Bikkur Cholim*, already described. Other women give up time in the early every morning to help prepare the kosher fresh food that *Bikkur Cholim* provides.

Interestingly enough, some of the nonobservant Jewish residents of Williamsburg, who are generally not too fond of the *hasidim* and their life-style, expressed their admiration for the work of *Bikkur Cholim*, especially those who know people who have benefited from the gracious assistance of the volunteers, or who have themselves so benefited. The fame of *Bikkur Cholim* has spread far beyond the neighborhood and similar organizations have been set up in other Jewish communities in New York, Monsey, Monroe, and even in Canada.

One-third of the women in the survey sample indicated that they are actively involved in one or more of the fund-raising projects for the local needs, the schools, *shuls*, and social welfare organizations and institutions. Other women help to raise funds for institutions and organizations in Israel, in Austria, and in Latin American hasidic communities. Some of the women concentrate on particular fund-raising projects, such as auctions and bazaars. Some of the more affluent women offer their homes to serve teas to invited guests on behalf of institutions. Others sponsor luncheons and similar social events to benefit the local and national or international hasidic schools and other institutions.

One woman, who, like so many others, is too busy with her large family, nevertheless contributes regularly to the numerous relief organizations, especially those that assist women before, during, and after they give birth. "That is the least I can do," she asserts, "as long as I am tied down by caring for my children." The woman who donated half of her house to the teams of women who cook and prepare the huge amounts of fresh food delivered to patients in the hospitals by *Bikkur Cholim* proudly displayed a large batch of checks from a small loan organization she heads, and which also provides funds to the poor who are too embarrassed to turn to the official relief organizations.

> All of these checks have been distributed to poor people this year already. They are too "bashful" to approach the other *gemilut hesed* funds that make them sign papers and check their financial situation. Or they are among the many who do not qualify for the communal or governmental financial-aid organizations.
>
> Somehow quite a few find their way to us. We help them without the usual formalities and rigors that are part of getting help from the big organizations. Not a single one has ever defaulted on us, unless we ourselves gave them the money as outright gifts, if the situation warranted it. My husband and I are very happy that we are privileged to serve this function of *matnas aniyim beseter*, helping the poor without anyone knowing about it.

A third woman proudly pointed to a row of *pushkes*, charity boxes for worthy causes, that line the windowsill in her kitchen. "All members of our family, even the young ones, put a few coins into these boxes on Friday before *Licht Benshen*, the lighting of the Sabbath candles, or on other special occasions. My 5-year-old girl insists that all the money she receives from her uncles on her birthday be put into her favorite *pushkes*. 'Mommy,' she says emphatically, 'you give me everything I need, but these poor people depend on what we put into the boxes for them. What better birthday present is there than helping them.' This," the woman stressed, "is what our children learn at the yeshivah and at home. It is more important to us than another bit of knowledge they may forget soon after they have learned it."

One harried woman, absorbed in her household chores, stated unequivocally:

> I am sorry that I do not have the strength, after I am done with my housework and with taking care of my small children, to go out and help some worthy cause. We are also not able to give to the constant appeals for one thing or another. But we have promised ourselves that someday when our business takes off and our children are older, we will make up for what we cannot afford to do now. Until then we have trouble to help our children's schools and our *shul*. But from the depth of our hearts we look forward to when, with the help of the Lord, we shall be able to do our share of *hesed*.

Cultural Activities

As pointed out in the methodological note and elsewhere, the majority of the women in the survey sample are American-born second- and third-generation *hasidim*. It is therefore all the more impressive to observe the success of the efforts of the Rebbe of Satmar and the other community leaders to re-create the kind of milieu in Williamsburg of the small Hungarian or Czechoslovak towns or villages from which they hail. The responses of the young, as well as those of the older women, indicated a moral level and inner strength that speak of the effectiveness of the educational system in a society that is beset with problems and the moral break-down of the family and of the religious institutions among the young even more than among the adults. Compared to the rising rates of alcoholism, premature sexual activity, teenage pregnancies, abortion, and addiction in middle-class neighborhoods as well as in the poorer areas, the cultural level and moral orientation of the single girls in Hasidic Williamsburg seem like a throwback to earlier, simpler, morally sounder times. It is quite obvious that the strength of the family life and of the religious institutions and teachings are the primary factors responsible for the positive attitudes reflected in the responses to the questions about the cultural values and interests that motivate their thinking and leisure activities.

One major fact that emerges clearly from the brief responses is that these women are not, as some observers suggest, caught in ignorance and lack of understanding of the world about them. They are not blindly following the line fed to them by their leaders because they do not know any better and are unwilling to leave the shelter of the East European shtetl, which their parents and grandparents had brought with them from deepest Hungary. Nor is there any sense in comparing these hasidic women with the women of the Amish or Hutterites, apart from the fact that they, too, reject birth control and abortion and have large numbers of children. They do share a sincere faith, which guides their conduct and affects their status in the concentration of their ethnic groups in the American or Canadian Bruderhofs or townships, which make a virtue of being out of step with the technology and level of civilization all around them. Though Williamsburg chooses a maximum of cultural and social isolation, its people are very much part of and engage in trade, business, and enterprises, which bring them in close contact with all kinds and types of people who live a radically different life-style. Yet they are so strong in their values, views, and conduct that they, the women as well as the men, take pride in and maintain the high standards required by their scrupulous observance of the ultra-Orthodox mores and laws of conduct.[1]

As pointed out throughout this discussion of the hasidic women of Williamsburg, they are attuned to what is going on in the world about them. Hence, they have consciously chosen to set limits to their dealing with society at large, including their interaction with those with whom they work or do business, regardless of the consequences. In fact, a good many stress that their unwillingness to make compromises earns respect and confidence rather than mockery or ridicule, which is common in some circles of society fraught with religious, ethnic, and racial prejudice. This is the conviction of one young woman who mans her husband's booth at trade fairs dressed in her modest hasidic clothes, her husband wearing the dark hasidic garb. At first the customers or suppliers may be reluctant or outright hostile. But eventually a good many overcome their initial reaction and begin to deal actively with their company because they have confidence in her and her husband's sincerity. A similar reaction was reported by the woman who runs a successful lingerie business in her house. "At first," she said, "I could not get any merchandise from the better manufacturers. Now they are only too happy to deal with me, after they have seen my reliability and the volume of business I am doing, thank God." Like these two, a number of other women indicated that they have credit and credibility, although they have to limit their business contacts in line with the strict restraints on some of the crucial areas of American business life.

Thus, while quite successful in their contacts with the outside world, the women of Williamsburg adhere to the central values and life-style of the hasidic community.

TV and Newspapers

It was not at all surprising to find that all but one of the single girls and married women in the sample population deny watching or owning a TV set. Quite a few express their rejection of "this instrument of the *yetzer hara*," the evil drive, or of the "filthy instrument," by adding the phrase "*has vehalilah*," God forbid, in their response to the question. The only one who admits having and watching TV is an outsider who rejects the views of Satmar, and does not read the *Yid*. This rejection of TV seems to play into the hands of those who call the attitudes of the hasidic women an anachronistic relapse into the Dark Ages. Yet, some of these women ridiculed as primitive and ignorant read the *New York Times* and other newspapers for business and for information of interest to them in their professional and private lives. One of them voiced keen interest in the rich offerings of the Sunday *New York Times*, and others pointed out magazines and various publications they peruse regularly or periodically to stay up on issues and problems or national and international affairs.

It may be easy to ridicule this contrast as an indication of their uncritical or inconsistent behavior. Yet, in their responses to a number of related questions these same hasidic women of Williamsburg demonstrated that their stance is carefully chosen and based on critical reasoning, which compares favorably with that of the broader reading public in American society. Almost one-third of the young married women in the survey population read *Baby Care* and other health magazines in order to stay well informed and to avail themselves of the advanced knowledge and products that have made life for the average American family healthier, more comfortable, and more productive. Although these women constantly stress that they want to live up to the religious standards of their mothers and grandmothers, they do not think it inconsistent to keep abreast of any progress made in health care and in scientific and technological achievements that may benefit their families. Twenty-two of the married women indicated that for this reason they read *Good Housekeeping*. Visits to lower- and higher-middle-income homes, not only the more luxuriously appointed rebuilt or newly constructed houses of the successful entrepreneurs, show that the women know how to furnish their homes tastefully, and that they have the appliances and appurtenances of which the average American housewife is proud. Yet, the same women wear sheitels, wigs, and are generally dressed in the modest, though good, clothes that meet the highest standards of the religious laws.

Of course, although read by quite a few (eighteen) of the respondents, the *New York Times* is not the favorite of the hasidic community. One hundred and twenty-two of the 175 hasidic women indicated that they regularly read the weekly *Der Yid*, the official publication established by the Rebbe of Satmar, which is published by the head of the Satmar hasidic community. For the vast majority of the *hasidim* it is the major source of information and means of influencing and shaping the views of their families. Of the 30,000 plus published weekly, 25,000 are sold in Williamsburg and are part of the typical household in the neighborhood. One of the girls interviewed expressed its wholehearted acceptance by all when she said: "The *Yid* has all the information I need and want to know." No doubt, this points to some degree of the insularity of the residents. Yet, it is their conscious and conscientious choice to draw knowledge and inspiration from their Rebbe's publication. They find in it his views and guidance in all matters of local, national, and international concern. "It gives us the Torah view," said one of the women. "We prefer it to the morally and politically corrupt perspectives of the general newspapers, and the filth, crime, and sensationalism that are smeared across the front pages." Another young woman put it this way: "Let others make fun of us, call us biased or intolerant, or even ignorant. We choose carefully what picture of the world we want to present to our youngsters in order to guide them on the proper way that will preserve the purity of their impressionable young minds."

This is what the Old Rebbe of Satmar had in mind when he bought and reshaped *Der Yid* to be the official publication for his community. It is the vehicle of transmitting his views on the events of the week, on the significance of the dates, and as a powerful tool of teaching and inspiration for the entire family of his followers. In this he succeeded, as in most of his plans and projects to create a total milieu in Williamsburg, as evidenced by the responses of the women in the survey. Only about 40 percent indicated that they did not read *Der Yid* or any other newspaper regularly. Eighteen stated that they read the *New York Times* regularly; and one, as pointed out before, reads and enjoys the Sunday *New York Times* and enjoys its rich contents. Ten women indicated that they read the *Yid* and the *New York Times*, which their husbands bring home from business when they think that it contains information of interest and value to them.

One respondent, who professed a particular interest in history and politics, expressed her need to read several newspapers and magazines. Most of the women, however, including the ten who read the *New York Post* and *Daily News*, and those who read the *Wall Street Journal* because they work with their husbands in business, also read *Der Yid*. They emphasize that they are resolved to abide by the sociocultural isolation that their hasidic life-style and the teachings of *der "Heiliger* Rebbe" require of them. Yet, there is no denying that a good many of the women have broader interests, if only for the purpose of being properly informed on matters concerning their business. They are not blind or ignorant, fitting themselves completely into the mold preshaped for them by their educators and their role models at home and in the community.

Books

This fact emerges equally from the responses to the question about the reading habits of the women in the survey population. Eighty-two of the total of 175 women indicated that they read books, while almost an equal number profess that they do not have any time or interest in reading books. Of the almost 50 percent of the women who do read books, sixty-one, or three-quarters, stress that they read only Yiddish books, which in this case, as in the general hasidic lingo, means books written by authors who are Orthodox and whose work expresses the proper hasidic or Orthodox spirit. Twenty, or one-quarter, among them several teachers, stated that their reading had a broader scope, that they read some of the classics, or books of historical or intellectual significance. But without exception, even these groups stressed that their reading was carefully chosen so as not to conflict with their thoroughly Orthodox values. Six of the twenty indicated that they do read books for relaxation or interest, such as the *Condensed Reader's Digest* books. Seven stated that they are reading good books of English literature, while five others claimed that they read books of educational or historical content in their leisure time.

Magazines

Of the 175 women surveyed, roughly 68 percent (112) indicated that they do not read any magazines at all. Forty-five, or close to thirty percent, read magazines of interest to them. Twenty-two read *Good Housekeeping*, ten read *Baby Care* or other health magazines, fourteen read *Newsweek* or *Time* magazine. Quite a few read the

Orthodox monthly, The *Jewish Observer*, and others. Thus, at least one-third of the women pursue broader interests. When questioned about articles in such magazines as the *Readers Digest* or *Newsweek* that contradict or conflict with the Orthodox Jewish perspective they have acquired in their upbringing, they expressed indignation. One single girl put it this way:

> I think I am intelligent enough to choose the content of what I read. And I feel I am mature enough to cope with articles or pictures I come across in my reading that may violate my sensibility. I am confronting much more serious challenges at my place of work, in the subways, or in the streets I walk to and from my job. It would be sad and a poor testimony to the strength of my education at school and at home, which has imbued me with good values and the power of good judgment and genuine piety so that I can discriminate and remain firmly within the realm of our convictions.
>
> We hasidic women do not have to walk around with blinders. We have, *baruch Hashem*, thank God, inner resources that safeguard and protect us from falling for the millions of temptations that trap the weak and unaware. Of course, I agree with our school counselors who are trying to place the girls in strictly Orthodox jobs after graduation, if possible. Thus they won't have to confront the constant *nisayonoth*, challenges, that will test their inner strength and convictions.

This intelligent young woman expressed what most of the hasidic respondents' felt when similarly questioned about confrontations and temptations they confront when working outside of the walls of Williamsburg.

Radio

Again, as in the case of reading books, eighty-five, or about half of the 175 women, indicated that they listen to radio programs, whereas eighty-seven said that they do not listen to any type of radio presentation. Quite a few of them lump radio together with TV and the other public media. The picture becomes more significant when we consider that two-thirds of those who confirmed listening to radio indicated that they turn only to stations like WEVD, which carry programs with reliable Orthodox performers. They enjoy listening to English or Yiddish speakers who provide food for serious thought, such as presentations on the weekly portions of the Torah or *Mussar*, the wisdom of the Sages in the Talmud or the other classic Torah literature. Five of the respondents indicated that they listen to programs on health to keep abreast of what is going on in the world of science and medicine in order to better be able to protect the health of their families. The majority of those who listen to radio turn to news programs primarily. Others enjoy programs that star Orthodox Jewish cantors or musicians, popular stars like Mordechai ben David, a hasidic folksinger, or the popular Orthodox boys choirs, like the Miami Boys or Pirchim choirs, and their tapes and records.

Stereo and Audio Tape Cassettes

It is quite significant that a large number of the Williamsburg women indicated that they have stereos and enjoy listening to classical music or the records of the popular Orthodox and hasidic cantors. Practically all stated that they most enjoy listening to the various collections of hasidic *niggunim*, records or tapes produced by the various hasidic groups, or by choirs from the *yeshivot*.

But most significant is the almost unanimous use by most of the women of the growing number of various tapes for their cassette decks. In the past decade or so a veritable flood of musical, educational, and entertainment tapes has been produced by Orthodox artists and bands, and by scholars for all levels of audiences. The women in the survey group stress particularly three types of tapes they use in their homes. First, there are the tapes now produced by hasidic groups, and advertised weekly in *Der Yid*, for children of all ages. A second group are the types of tapes that provide learning, inspiration, and knowledge for all ages. There are numerous tapes of *mussar*, lecture series presented by prominent Orthodox and hasidic scholars, which discuss ethical values and principles of faith, and Jewish history. There are also numerous series of tapes from the classics of the vast Torah literature, and from the classics of the hasidic ideology.

Most popular are, of course, the tapes that provide entertainment as well as inspiration, like those of Orthodox singers or boys choirs mentioned before. There are now popular tape libraries, which make the new offerings available to the hasidic households, for the inspiration and entertainment of their families. Since singing of *niggunim*, melodies, is an intrinsic part of the hasidic ideology and life-style, the availability of these tapes is a valuable breakthrough, which enriches the religious and cultural experiences of *hasidim* of all ages. One of the older hasidic women stressed what this introduction of tapes means to her and to her family.

> We did not have anything of this sort to provide us with educational material or with reliable kinds of entertainment that we can play whenever we have the time or the need for learning and inspiration. Our children and grandchildren are indeed fortunate. Whenever my daughters and daughters-in-law go shopping they bring home new tapes of Torah *shiurim*, Torah lectures, or *niggunim*, melodies produced by hasidic or yeshivah groups and choirs. Some of the tapes tell hasidic stories. They teach the young children in a way that is fun and which they enjoy. Practically all of our friends have tape collections and enjoy exchanging them and making their own copies. Our men have cassettes in their cars and vans, so that they can listen to the Torah tapes or the hasidic *niggunim* while they travel. I, myself, listen to the hasidic and some classical music, or to the Torah and *mussar* or Jewish history tapes in the evenings when I have time to relax. What a blessing these tapes are for us who don't have the variety of entertainment others have.

This is, of course, true for all Orthodox Jewish homes, not only for the *hasidim*. But it is of particular importance to the hasidic men and women who do not even attend the frequent concerts of Orthodox Jewish singers, cantors, and choirs like the rest of the religious communities who flock to the mass performances of the popular Orthodox musical groups that fill large halls, like the Brooklyn College auditorium or even Lincoln Center on *Hol Hamoed*, the semiholidays, or on Hanukkah.

This is further evidence of the cultural interests of the hasidic women and of their educational motivation. It is particularly significant and valuable for the hasidic women, who do not have the constant stimulation their men draw from spending their free time on study in the *bet hamidrash* before or after work, and on Shabbath and holidays. Characteristically, a spokesman for the Satmar community stressed that "we are not culturally deprived. We are culturally and intellectually different," echoing the slogan that has been used frequently by minorities, such as the American Indians. But the increasing availability and quality of records and tapes is a boon to the hasidic home and to the hasidic milieu even more than elsewhere because of the important role of hasidic music and stories in the ideology and life-style of the contemporary hasidic community in America, as it had been in the famous centers of Eastern Europe.

Political Attitudes of the Hasidic Women of Williamsburg

Generally, as confirmed by the responses of the women in the survey and in personal interviews, hasidic women make a point of stressing that they follow the position and views of their husbands, as spelled out by their Rebbes and by their spokesmen, and as publicized in *Der Yid*. Yet, they do take a keen interest and, as they assert, have much discussion at home and amongst themselves on what is going on in the community, and in the Jewish and the non-Jewish world around them. They take part in public actions of the hasidic community, like the demonstrations on behalf of their and their families' welfare, as in the case of the planned building of a huge garbage disposal plant in the navy yard, adjoining the Jewish Triangle. They also participate in demonstrations against the State of Israel, when policies threaten the religious concerns and welfare of the ultra-Orthodox non-Zionist community in Jerusalem or Bnei Brak, for example.

Along these lines, some of the women have stressed that they were among the thousands of hasidic women who pushed their baby carriages across Brooklyn Bridge in the mass demonstration before city hall against the construction of the recycling and garbage-disposal facility, which would have spewed poisonous emissions into the air they and their children breathe in Williamsburg. They also take an active part in such important political actions such as the election of hasidic representatives to the local community school board. With the help of their women the hasidic community succeeded in getting three of their own people on the District 14 Community School Board, one more than the Puerto Ricans. They consider this not only a vital gain in terms of protecting their own interests, but a demonstration to the broader public of their concern with the welfare and interests of the broader community. Even more important is the fact that their strong showing indicates to the political establishment that they have political clout and can deliver solid blocks of votes in the local and national elections.

Equally important was the participation of the women in bringing out the vote for President Bush in the 1988 presidential election. According to a report in the *New York Times* (May 2, 1989), Bush won the highest number of votes in New York in the hasidic communities, except for one solidly Republican district in Staten Island.

The article stressed the favorable attitude of the *hasidim* toward the Republican candidate because they felt that they had more to gain from a Reagan-type administration than from one headed by a liberal Democrat. This is true for their attitude on the election for the highest office, although they generally follow the traditional Jewish vote pattern when it comes to lower level elections. Characteristically, however, one official of the New York educational establishment called the hasidic community of Williamsburg "a solid, traditional conservative element," whose input on the local community boards he called a welcome, valuable contribution for this very reason. The importance of the hasidic women in the local and national elections emerges from the articles and advertisements of *Der Yid*, which appeal to them and to their help in achieving the political goals of the hasidic community. Otherwise, the hasidic women of Williamsburg do not have any specific, feminist causes they espouse and for which they would work independently of the stance of their husbands and the hasidic community in general. To them, there is only one authority that is qualified to speak for them, that of the Torah as pronounced by the rabbinic authorities. In the case of Williamsburg, it is the Rebbe whose authority is supreme and beyond question.

This faith in and loyalty to the authority of their Rebbe and his views also guide the political stance of the hasidic women. Most prominent is the anti-Zionist stance forcefully promulgated by the Old Rebbe of Satmar, by his successor, and by other famous Hungarian hasidic leaders, past and present. The women interviewed expressed their full agreement with this generally unpopular stand, which guides the educational policy at Beth Ruchel as well as in the *yeshivot* for the boys. As pointed out in chapter 3, this results in the rejection of the use of modern Hebrew in their studies. It also results in the rejection of the State of Israel, and in the wholehearted support of the institutions and organizations of the *Aidah Charedit*, the ultra-Orthodox non-Zionist community of Jerusalem, whose members do not consider themselves part of the State of Israel and do not participate in the elections or accept financial support and other benefits, which the broader Orthodox Jewish community and religious parties share with the rest of the Israeli population. But here, too, the hasidic women do not play a role in the Jewish political debate by themselves, as do the majority of the Jewish women in other religious communities. Their stand is fully consonant with that of their husbands and with the policies espoused by their Rebbe.

At the same time it is a matter of their values and their choice, not an expression of their lack of interest or ignorance. They are *hasidim* of their Rebbe, not women with vested feminist concerns, as one of them put it when questioned about her political views.

THE DIVORCED AND WIDOWED

The Divorced

As discussed in detail in chapter 4, there is a very low rate of divorce and separation in the hasidic community, not only compared to broader society, where one out of three marriages ends in divorce or separation. It is also lower than that of most other Jewish communities, particularly in the suburbs, whose social and cultural patterns are very much affected by those of their environment. The number of breakups of marriages of hasidic couples has risen somewhat, especially during the '70s, but has stabilized since, according to the administrator of the local rabbinic court and other officials. In many cases this is due to the fact that some of the men and women, who generally marry at a very young age, are neither psychologically, nor emotionally, nor financially ready to shoulder the burden thrust upon them, especially if they have children in rapid succession and do not have the resources to cope with the ensuing complications.

A number of the hasidic rabbis and women have organized groups to prevent problems and crises before they evolve to the breaking point. Their major function is to serve as support groups for the troubled families. Indications are that divorces and separations are more frequent in the higher-income communities, such as Boro Park or Flatbush, according to the testimony of some of the volunteers and professional counselors. One of the latter pointed to the attitude of these neighborhoods: "they have put too much emphasis on *me*," as he found in the cases with which he has dealt in recent months. On the other hand, poverty and inadequate income are major factors in a neighborhood like Hasidic Williamsburg, where a large proportion of the heads of the young families are still full-time students in a *kollel*, as the head of one of the support groups stressed, or are at the very beginning of their training for a career. In spite of their strong faith and intensive religious studies, the early years after marriage is a period bound to result in tensions among those who lack adequate inner and outer resources.

In the small survey population there were two relatively young women, both in their early thirties, who were divorced. Their cases may be not typical in every respect, yet their responses and the attitudes underlying their responses are helpful for an understanding of the tensions and problems young married couples experience before and after the breakup of their marriages in a close-knit community, which allows little room for privacy. Both divorced women have two children 5 years old and younger. One of them describes herself as a "real Williamsburger," although she was not born there. The second divorcée stated openly that she married and moved to Williamsburg *"because I had to get out of Boro Park."* Clearly, however, she never really adjusted to the intense life-style Hasidic Williamsburg imposes on its members. Although her parents have the same Hungarian hasidic background as most of Williamsburg's residents, she attended a regular Orthodox Jewish day school for girls for the required eight elementary and four high-school years, from which she received an excellent religious and secular education. Obviously, she does not read the *Yid*. Instead she subscribes to the *New York Post*. It stands to reason that her marriage did not have the strong ideological bonds of a hasidic couple in which husband and wife both had come from the same type of Hungarian hasidic school system as a basis on which to build their shared life. In retrospect, she has no regrets about her divorce and wants to get out of Williamsburg as soon as possible. But like all the hasidic women in the survey population, she is quite sanguine about the future of Hasidic Williamsburg and about the readiness of its women to abide by the stringent demands of their life-style. Unequivocally she stated: "The young women here are more *machmir*, more stringent, in their scrupulous observance of all the requirements of even the less important than their mothers and grandmothers had been. Hence, *Yiddishkeit* is strong here, and it will continue to thrive."

The second divorcée has the usual Hungarian-Czech background found throughout the community, although her family moved to Williamsburg from Canada because they were loyal *hasidim* of the Rebbe of Satmar and wanted to live near him. She, too, true to her upbringing, is a wholehearted admirer of the Rebbe and, like the other women, fully subscribes to the stringent demands of the hasidic life-style. Regardless of the unfortunate circumstances that caused the breakup of her marriage, she intends to remain in Williamsburg to be close to the *Heiliger* Rebbe and to his "blessings and personal guidance." She studiously avoids mentioning the circumstances that led to her divorce. She is happy to be able to take care of her two children, whom she loves dearly and wants to raise as good hasidic youngsters, in spite of the hardships of life as a divorcée. Enthusiastically she states: "I want to stay here because I think it is a good place in which to raise my children properly. *It's a beautiful way to live*, the way the Rebbe planned it and set it up for us." She is convinced that Williamsburg will continue to grow and thrive in the future, "until the coming of the Moshiah."

The Widowed

Two women in the survey sample were widowed. One of them is only 28 years old and has four children. Her husband, who died a few months prior to the interview, was a native *hasid* just like she herself. Fortunately, she had worked 3 years before her marriage and was able to return to her old job part-time, and her mother is able to take care of the children. In spite of the pressure of having to care for her youngsters all by herself, she makes time to help others who are less fortunate than she. She attends a few social affairs, such as luncheons sponsored by the ladies' auxiliary of her children's schools. And if and whenever possible, she visits sick people in her immediate vicinity. For her and her children's entertainment she has a tape cassette deck and is thrilled by the growing variety of tapes that are available to make life more enjoyable and inspirational. But being a rather introspective person, she regrets that there are not more tapes of *mussar*, which guide and exhort the listeners to improve their moral and ethical thinking and conduct. She finds that some of the women are too fashion minded. She reads books in Yiddish or English written by Orthodox authors. She is optimistic about the future of Williamsburg and blesses herself that she lives in this neighborhood close to the Rebbe and can send her children to schools he has built for the young. In her opinion, the younger generation of the *hasidim* is better educated and even more serious about their hasidic beliefs and life-style than their elders, and will perpetuate this faith and inner freedom in their own families.

The second widow is a first generation immigrant from Hungary who was educated in her native country and who spent years in concentration camp and in several DP camps before coming to the U.S. She never had an easy life. She worked quite a few years prior to her marriage, and to her regret she never had any children. She had worked with her husband in his business until his sudden death. She is a member of the Tzelemer *Arugas Habosem* congregation. She is active in and attends the meetings and social affairs of its organizations and institutions. She is very active in its *Bikkur Cholim* volunteer corps and supports the educational institutions of Tzelem to the best of her ability and limited resources. She reads the *Jewish Press*, as well as the *Yid* and the *New York Post*, which she gets when she travels to her job on the subway. For entertainment and enlightenment she listens to various kinds of tapes. She calls the cassettes her best means of relaxing in the evenings when she is not out doing her share for the social welfare of the community. She has relatives and friends in other hasidic communities but prefers remaining in Williamsburg because she likes its spirit of togetherness and mutual help, as she puts it, which help her not to feel too lonely or abandoned. She is convinced of its future and growth because of the strength of faith and activism of its younger generations.

The case histories of the divorced and widowed women display the same sanguine attitude about the future of Hasidic Williamsburg. Though personal circumstances induced one of the divorcées to reject its intensive life-style for herself and for her children, she does not deny the strength of its values and spirit. The other three appreciate the closeness of the members of the community, which is particularly beneficial to them in their difficult personal circumstances and helps them cope with the severe traumas of their individual tragedies. They are loyal followers of their Rebbe and believe in his guidance and his impact on the future of their community.

THE SINGLE WOMEN

Seventeen, or about 10 percent of the survey sample of the hasidic women, are single and between the ages of 15 and 23. All but one are second- or third-generation American Hungarian *hasidim*. All have the standard girls' education of 8 years elementary and 3 years vocational schooling; just like one-third of their parents who were born and raised in Williamsburg. One of the single girls had the regular 4 years high-school education of an Orthodox girls' day school in another community until her family moved into the neighborhood. Without exception, the girls stressed that they would like to marry a young Torah scholar who will continue his advanced religious studies at one of the *kollels*, regardless of the sacrifices this will entail, which they know well enough. They stressed that they are willing, if necessary, to continue working until and in between having children, while their future husbands devote all their time to advanced rabbinic studies until they are ready to leave the *kollel* and pursue a career in education, as teachers or administrators, or enter the rabbinate, or, if given a chance, enter business. Equally, without exception, all emphasized that they wanted to have children, "as many as the kind Lord will give us," one of them wrote. They also made a point of stressing that they intended to raise their children in the *Yiddish* way, to become Torah students and good hasidic Torah-observant Jews. Quite a few of the single girls reiterated that they wanted to live and raise their children in the same spirit and manner of their own mothers and grandmothers.

They consider the ideas of women's liberation and self-fulfillment outside of the home, with which they are quite familiar, "alien" and improper for a Jewish woman. One nursery teacher called these ideas "a rather selfish and negative approach to life as we have been taught to perceive it." Another referred to this attitude as "a sacrilege to *kedushat habayit*, the sanctity of the proper Jewish home."

In contrast, these young women think of themselves and their future as the *akeret habayit*, the very foundation of the Jewish family, with all the characteristics, duties, and challenges that their husbands sing about in the paean to their wives on Friday evening, after returning from the synagogue. Yet, the single girls emphasize that their attitude is not the result of ignorance. Most of them are graduates of the hasidic high school, where they have received as fair a vocational education as the students of secular schools. Four of the seventeen girls in the survey read English newspapers and magazines as well as the weekly *Der Yid*. About half listen to Jewish news programs and other valuable radio presentations. Twelve of the seventeen girls read books by "reliable" authors. And one, a teacher in the secular department of a hasidic school, states that she reads English classics to improve her command of the language. Several of the single respondents expressed a more serious attitude than others and deplored the fact that many girls are too fashion-oriented. They prefer to listen to *mussar* tapes, which provide them with inspiration, knowledge, and the inner resources "to become more immune to the many temptations one faces when one travels downtown or uptown for a job, and to enable them to deal with people who have different values and attitudes than we," as one particularly serious young lady put it. Another of the girls voiced what most feel when they speak of their love of and their preference for living in Williamsburg: "I love Williamsburg because I have not seen another place that has half of its spirit, its *Yiddishkeit* and concern for the welfare of everybody else."

All the single girls stressed that they have engaged in some form of *hesed* work since their high-school days. They visit the sick or the elderly and help the poor and needy to the best of their abilities and resources. Quite a few of the young women belong to organizations like Bnos, Bnos Torah, and others, which are sponsored by their own subcommunities. Only one girl, who was born and had lived elsewhere prior to coming to Williamsburg, indicated that she would like to live somewhere else where there is less community pressure. Three said that they would like to see more green where they reside, and would prefer to move to a place like Kiryas Joel, which has the spirit of Williamsburg and the advantages of living in the country, fresh air and a peaceful setting. Some may have complaints or criticism of the not always clean, crowded living conditions. As one wrote: "I have seen some poor families whose children sleep in triple bunkbeds or on mattresses that are put away into closets in the morning." But none of the single girls is critical of the hasidic life-style. They firmly believe in the future of Hasidic Williamsburg and the perpetuation of its milieu and way of life. As the youngest of the girls, who is still in high school, put it: "This is how we have been educated at home and at school. We believe in it and want it continued until the coming of the *moshiah*." They do not deny that occasionally they like to go uptown or to Boro Park for some shopping, to see what is in and what would fit in with their modest way of dressing. Most stress that they have cassette players and tapes to which they love to listen for inspiration, knowledge, and for entertainment. They also listen to some radio programs in English or Yiddish, which are produced by Orthodox performers.

The overwhelming impression one gets is that these seventeen young ladies are intelligent and fully aware of what is going on in the world beyond the invisible walls of their voluntary ghetto. But their education has done a good job convincing them of the great value and meaning of the life-style of the ultra-Orthodox community into which they have been born or brought at a very early age. They believe in the way of life of their mothers and grandmothers, and want to be like them not by simply imitating their life-style, but by displaying their piety and spirit. They reject the values of the world about which they read and which they meet when they travel to work outside of their community. Their ideals center on the home, on a life that is dominated by Torah and Torah study, and they recognize Torah scholarship as the ideal for their future husbands and sons. All want to get married, and want their spouses to devote years after marriage to continued intensive talmudic and rabbinic study at a *kollel*. For this they are ready to make sacrifices. Like the married women in the survey population, they perceive them-selves as future housewives, mothers, and loyal *hasidim* of the Rebbe, ready to live by his teachings and guidance.

Nothing in their responses suggests any form of rebellion or the hidden desire of getting out of this highly structured life. They are trained to work, to become competent in their chosen trade or profession, while remaining faithful to their heritage as Jewish women who know and are able to draw the line when it comes to interacting with people with different backgrounds and mores. They love Williamsburg, and in spite of some minor complaints are convinced of its hasidic future. Thus, they confirm the effectiveness of their education and upbringing. They do not feel restricted or handicapped. On the contrary, they are proud and convinced of the propriety and rightness of their life for themselves, for their community, and for the Jewish people.

SUMMARY

The findings of the interviews and the responses to the questions of a relatively small sample survey of women of the hasidic community of Williamsburg highlight the strength of their convictions and their central role in the transformation and growth of their community. Their willingness to make considerable personal sacrifices in order to live up to the letter and spirit of the law are crucial to the viability and growth of this primarily Hungarian hasidic neighborhood, contrary to the expectations of failure and the predictions of doom by the experts.

The prime factor of this extraordinary social phenomenon is the strength of the hasidic upbringing and educational system. It enables the women to maintain their ultra-Orthodox attitudes and to cope with the challenges they encounter at work, in business, and in the intellectual realms to which they are exposed, in spite of the sociocultural isolation of their community. Their religious faith rejects birth control and abortion, leading to a near population explosion. It further negates the popular notions of women's liberation and self-fulfillment outside of the home, which dominate most women in contemporary Jewish as well as non-Jewish society. They emphasize their roles as homemakers, wives, and mothers of future Torah scholars and hasidic men and women, "just like our mothers and grandmothers," though a majority are second- and third-generation Americans.

The women of Williamsburg play an increasingly significant role in the economic life of the community. They successfully cope with the requirements of business conduct, while strictly adhering to the norms and mores of the hasidic life-style. The women are loyal followers of their Rebbe and comply with his directions and guidance in all matters of their personal and communal life. They accept the authority of Torah scholarship and the halachic decisions of the rabbinic authorities unquestioningly. Hence they do not aspire to a separate role in the religious and political policies of the community. But they take a keen interest in and play a major role in the constantly expanding network of social welfare institutions and organizations, which deal with the vital needs of the population, particularly those of the indigent, sick, and aged. Their leisure activities and cultural interests are largely determined by the spirit and norms of the hasidic life-style, though they are familiar with the popular trends of society outside of their enclave.

This attitude of the young, as well as of the middle-aged and older, women of the hasidic community of Williamsburg is largely responsible for the survival and continued growth of this neighborhood that is unique in American pluralist society.

➤➤ 8 ◀◀

Patterns of Political Activism: The Dynamics of a New Spirit

We will fight for our rights, any place any time. We will not hesitate at any time in the future to resort to the courts if the need should arise.

Rabbi Leopold Lefkowitz

Despite its 19th-century air, this enclave [Williamsburg] of hasidic Jews, an Orthodox sect rooted in Eastern Europe, is a *Model of Modern Machine Politics*. U.S. senators, cabinet members, mayors, and Washington bureaucrats pay regular homage to its bloc vote [italics mine].

Margot Hornblower
The *Washington Post*, 9 November 1986

INTRODUCTION

My earlier report (1961) on Hasidic Williamsburg did not contain a separate section on the political behavior of the community. The reason was that there were no significant differences between the political behavior of its residents and that of other heterogeneous religious and nonreligious Jewish communities in New York and elsewhere in the U.S. for the period I was treating. Their organizations and institutions, like those of most other Jewish and non-Jewish neighborhoods, called on elected or appointed city, state, and federal officials when they wanted help for the causes or needs of their people in this country or abroad. Quite a few of the leading lay and religious leaders of Jewish Williamsburg were active in the Seneca Club, then as now the local district headquarters of the Democratic Party. They cultivated their relations with the city council members, the state delegates, and U.S. congressmen and senators like any other typical, liberal, reliably Democratic district in New York with a mixed constituency of mostly low-income and low-middle-income people.

The shocking news of the persecution of Jews in Nazi Germany and the subsequent brutalization of the Jewish communities of the European countries that Hitler's armies invaded during World War II cried out for massive American Jewish action. It did not come forth on the scale needed to fight the intransigence, if not outright negative attitude of the political stance, of the American government, as amply documented by such studies as David Wyman's *Abandonment of the Jews* (1984), his *Paper Walls* (1968), and others. Serious efforts were made by small Orthodox Jewish organizations, such as the *Vaad Hatzalah* and the Williamsburg branch of Agudath Israel, who with their inexperienced but enthusiastic members mounted increasing efforts to provide papers and other aid to the refugees from Nazi persecution, war, and the Holocaust, who began to arrive in the U.S. and settle in Williamsburg and elsewhere. As the terrifying news of the brutal treatment of the Jews poured into their offices from personal contacts in Europe, they turned to the major political figures known to have influence on the government in Washington for help. Through them they requested immediate rescue and relief efforts, in addition to officially and unofficially conveyed displeasure and objections to the German government.

The minimum they hoped for was to initiate the opening of the doors for the immigration of thousands of victims, beyond the trickle admitted through the quota system. But even such powerful, prominent political figures as Senator Javitz and Congressmen Emanuel Celler and Sol Bloom were not able to achieve a significant breakthrough in the face of the inertia of the major Jewish organizations and their leaders, such as Rabbi Stephen S. Wise and Judge Rosenman who had a great deal of influence on President Roosevelt. Even such efforts as the march of four hundred prominent rabbis on Washington, in October 1943, fell on deaf ears, as documented by David Kranzler's *Thy Brother's Blood* (1987) and Rafael Medoff's *The Deafening Silence* (1987). They were not even received by the president. One wonders what a march like the one organized by N. Shcharansky on behalf of Soviet Jews, decades later, might have achieved if combined with determined efforts by the Jewish establishment and a massive outpouring of demonstrations and giant rallies in the big cities.

It is against this background of the tragic consequences of lacking political clout and activism that one must regard the massive efforts of the hasidic community of Williamsburg over the past decades to cope with the needs of its people and the problems of its precarious situation in the face of mounting external and internal crises. After years of trial and error, its leadership developed new strategies to assure its survival, including political activism and effective channels of close contacts with the crucial levels of the local and national power structures.

THE SPIRIT OF POLITICAL ACTIVISM

For the past 28 years (political candidates are taking into account) the growing political power of New York City's Hasidic and Orthodox Jewish communities and their ability to deliver tens of thousands of votes in a solid bloc . . . The hasidic community listens to its leadership.

New York Times, 2 May 1989

The terrible consequences of the inadequate efforts of the American Jewish establishment before, during, and after World War II must have been in the subconscious of the leaders of the hasidic community of Williamsburg, almost all of whom were survivors of the Holocaust, when they searched for new channels and vitally needed resources for their members, more than half of whom were forced to live below the national poverty level. Disregarding traditional patterns of political behavior and the disapproval of the Jewish establishment, they systematically set about to develop the contacts that might be instrumental in providing access to the various levels of the government that control and decide the distribution of aid extended to the poor and low-income populations. In retrospect, their success in the face of improbable odds to create the foundation for their socioeconomic survival and eventual progress in the past decades attests to the wisdom of this decision.

From the very outset, however, it must be stated that this new spirit of political activism that evolved in the hasidic community of Williamsburg, and which was adopted by other hasidic and nonhasidic Orthodox communities in and around New York, is largely rooted in the background of its people. One source is their basic attitude, which was already mentioned in the 1961 report by way of an anecdote reported by a trained social scientist dating back to his youth in Poland, and which left a lasting impression on him. As he related it, he observed, to his surprise, a group of Hungarian hasidic workers in a crew employed for a road construction job in his hometown, not too far from the Hungarian border. As he was watching the husky hasidic workers with beards and *peyot*, their large *tallit katans* with long, heavy *tzitzit* dangling outside their work uniforms, several young local hooligans approached the *hasidim* to have some fun at their expense. When they came close and started pulling beards and the long *tzitzit* they were shocked to find themselves lifted up by the hasidic workers and given a thorough whacking, so that they ran for their lives. This, he pointed out, would never have happened anywhere else in Poland and other communities where fear of pogroms and provocation of violence imposed powerful restraints. My 1961 report pointed out similar incidents that displayed the less timid attitude of the new Hungarian immigrants, which changed the atmosphere in Williamsburg. This readiness to fight for their survival was particularly helpful during the late '50s, '60s and '70s, when large numbers of Puerto Ricans and other minority groups flocked to Williamsburg, as into other old, low-income neighborhoods of Brooklyn and New York, which disintegrated as a result of friction and incidents of violence and crime they brought with them. As one of the active leaders of the Puerto Rican community expressed it when interviewed by a reporter for the *Washington Post* (9 November 1986): "Hasidim play hard and fight hard. You cannot stop the Hasidim. This used to be our community. Now we are a minority in an area totally controlled by them." A similar report on the readiness of the *hasidim* to fight for their rights and survival in what had become a hostile atmosphere in the struggle of the tenants of the public high-rise projects was reported by *Time* magazine (7 August 1989) in a brief article titled "Dealing With Demography." It cited a hasidic tenant who said: "When we got into (the housing project) there was a struggle to survive. It was the late Seventies. At that time *we decided we were just going to stand up and fight.* (If someone tries a mugging) and we get him, you don't know what will happen." This same attitude was expressed by numerous officials and by the people in the street. It was the only way to cope with the constant threats, muggings, and other criminal conduct that plagued the residents of the neighborhood then, and still does occasionally. Yet, the readiness to resist and fight back has made Williamsburg one of the safest areas of New York, according to the statements of Jewish and non-Jewish officials and residents, who are cited throughout this report. The cry of "chaptze" (grab 'em) or whistles sounded by would-be victims bring out crowds of hasidim from their houses. Many attackers who had expected the usual reluctance of the people in the neighborhood to fight back have learned a bitter lesson. The local police have learned to take this determined self-defense of the hasidim seriously, in view of numerous reports of action taken by the hasidim when no official measures were taken to ensure their security.

In September of 1989, the Yid reported a meeting at the local district headquarters between representatives of the hasidic community and the commanding officers, after a number of elderly hasidim were attacked and mugged early in the morning as they were walking to early services or study classes. The hasidic leaders warned the police that "they would take matters into their own hands, unless serious efforts were made to stop the attacker." A few days later the attacker was arrested after one of the hasidim fought back and to his shock wounded him. The blood trail led to his hideout. In another highly publicized incident, a few years back, the Washington Post reported that thousands of hasidim had stormed a police precinct headquarters when no action was taken after the brutal murder of a Jew. A number of policemen were wounded in the hand-to-hand fighting.

Although there are still break-ins and thefts, especially on Friday nights or holidays, the local civilian self-help organization, the Shomrim, patrols the streets effectively and is frequently reported in the Yid as having been instrumental in the arrest of criminals and attackers. The New York City Housing Authority reports that the five public high-rise projects in Williamsburg have lower crime rates than all others in the city. This admiration for the relatively effective control of the neighborhood was also expressed by a high public school official in an interview: "After I leave here in the evenings when we have board meetings, I see hasidic women walking about unafraid. Obviously they have good reason to feel safe, something I would not say about other neighborhoods in the city of this type." Or as one of the Afro-American members of the janitorial staff of the oldest high-rise project commented when interviewed: "I prefer living right here. I don't have to worry about my wife and children being mugged or hustled by drug pushers around here." Consequently, hasidim are not worried about placing their Sukkot booths right on the sidewalks or in open yards next to their houses, and similar indications of confidence in the relative security of the neighborhood. This readiness of the Hungarian-type hasidim to stand up for their rights and "fight for their turf," as the Washington Post reporter called it, has been vital in the struggle to survive and to prevent the disintegration of the Jewish community of Williamsburg in the fore of the influx of ethnic and racial minorities since the late '50s, coupled with other crises discussed earlier.

This effective psychological factor has been attributed by some observers to the fact that a large number of the older hasidic residents of Williamsburg are survivors of the Holocaust. The thought "never again" is very much in their minds. It is even more evident in the reaction of the second- and third-generation *hasidim* who are native Americans and who have successfully fused their hasidic spirit with some of the characteristic American beliefs about equality and standing up for their rights.

The second, equally important, factor of the political stance of aggressive activism in Hasidic Williamsburg is derived from the ideological position of the Old Rebbe of Satmar before and since his arrival in the U.S. It manifested itself in his refusal to be affiliated with or supported or supervised by any of the major Jewish organizations that control much of Jewish community life in this country and in the Jewish world. As pointed out, his main motivation was the preservation of the purity of his community and the single-mindedness of its pursuit of its central goals, foremost among them its educational system. This insistence on total independence was achieved at the sacrifice of having to bear sole responsibility for meeting the huge and constantly growing budget for every phase of his multifaceted networks of community organizations and institutions without the support and resources that help maintain the vast majority of America's Jewish organizations and institutions, including most of the Orthodox here and in Israel. For example, the annual budget of the Satmar educational system, which is growing by leaps and bounds and is the largest in the Jewish world, amounted to $15 million in 1987. Similarly, the suburban branch of Satmar, Kiryas Joel, founded by the Old Rebbe of Satmar, has cost $10 million per year for each of the 12 years of its existence, and its budget is rising with the rapid expansion of its population to more than a thousand families at the end of the '80s.

This uncompromising insistence on independence has made it possible for the Rebbe of Satmar and the community of his followers in the U.S. and Israel to publicly and officially oppose the secular Zionist State of Israel and its policies. This anti-Zionist stand of Satmar is very much resented by most of the contemporary Jewish world. They condemn the public demonstrations and full-page ads in the *New York Times* that express their protests against antireligious policies or conduct in the Holy Land. One has only to think of the tragic consequences of the "Who Is A Jew?" controversy in connection with the 1988 election in Israel, which resulted in penalizing withdrawal of financial support for religious institutions in Israel and in the U.S. Yet, most still depend on the goodwill and handouts of the large philanthropic organizations that control the flow of funds contributed by the vast majority of nonreligious American Jews who resent the implications of their rejection by the Orthodox in the definition of who is a Jew.

This independence has forced the Rebbe of Satmar and the other Rebbes of the hasidic community of Williamsburg to search for other, nontraditional sources for the financial support of their constantly growing community and its expanding networks of institutions and organizations that evolved from the manifold needs of their mostly indigent members. Shortage of adequate housing, of opportunities, and of training for their young in trades and business were the primary concerns that caused the community leaders to develop effective structures and channels for political action that would enable them to link their efforts to the massive national war on poverty and urban renewal programs, which swept up the American people in the '60s. Treading on ground hitherto spurned by the major Jewish organizations, the hasidic communities of Williamsburg and other neighborhoods used the leverage of their demographics and their ability to muster large numbers of votes to enlist the help of city, state, and national officials to get themselves included among the ethnic and racial minorities that were the main beneficiaries of the programs designed to eliminate poverty and urban blight in affluent America during the Kennedy and Johnson era. The strongest factor in their favor was, of course, the fact that, according to the estimate of the *New York Times*, based on census figures, the average income of a Williamsburg family was $9,000, far below the official poverty level of $12,400 per household of four. And the average hasidic family has between seven and eight children.

The situation of the hasidic community was further aggravated by a lack of effective communication and the myriad complications arising out of the hasidic life-style that at the time made it nearly impossible for them to blend into the mainstream of American economic life. It took more than a decade of determined effort to make the necessary contacts and develop channels on all levels of the local and national government. It required legal battles to fight disadvantageous court decisions in 1979 and 1980, which refused recognition of the hasidic community because it was in conflict with the separation of church and state, until their major goal was achieved. As already pointed out, it was only in 1984, after 10 years of partial benefits, that the federal government fully recognized the hasidic community as a disadvantaged minority, entitled to the benefits accorded the American Indians, Hispanics, blacks, and other groups. Only since 1974, when the local ODA office of the Small Business Administration of the U.S. Department of Commerce was established, have resources been available to help the poor on a limited basis. But after the summer of 1984, the long, intensive struggle, which enlisted an impressive array of senators, congressmen, and government officials up to the level of cabinet members, opened the doors to a broad spectrum of programs made available to the poor and discriminated of the country, on behalf of thousands of *hasidim*. Opportunities for training, and for technical and financial help, resulted in enabling many of the young and middle-aged to enter various realms of trade, business, and industry. Eventually they were able to participate in the competition of submitting bids for government contracts and to engage in export and import in various lines of the international trade. Thus political activism became the key to the entrance of *hasidim* from Williamsburg and other Orthodox communities into the world of American business.

The turning point came with the granting of the Presidential Charter in an official ceremony in the federal building in Manhattan in June 1984. Before a large crowd of officials from all levels of the local, state, and national bureaucracies along with representatives of the major hasidic and nonhasidic Orthodox communities, a representative of President Reagan handed over the charter that designated *hasidim* a disadvantaged minority. It was a historical event, which demonstrated the new status of the hasidic community and its recognition in the world of American politics and official policies concerning the social welfare of its less fortunate citizens. What had started as a trickle in 1974 grew into a broad flow of programs, such as WIC for women before and after birth and care, food, and funds for their infants, which became one of the largest in the state of New York. A number of other vital programs were made available and are handled by the offices of ODA and the United Jewish Organizations. There is a large home care division, which supplies help for homebound elderly and disabled. And there is the constantly expanding Primary Health Care Center that is directed by the ODA. It is always adding new departments, vital services for children and adults, new sophisticated equipment, and staffs of medical, dental, psychological, and other health professionals. In 1989 this health facility serviced about 50,000 men, women, and children. Earlier chapters have spelled out some of the dimensions of this growing network of programs and projects that enabled many of the younger and more enterprising *hasidim* to reach out beyond the confines and constraints of the limited local trades. In turn, this produced a new spirit and a solid foundation for the socioeconomic advancement of the second- and third-generation members of the hasidic community that would not have been possible without the determined efforts of its officials.

The same political activism enabled the hasidic leadership to gain ground in their desperate efforts to cope with the increasingly serious problem of the housing shortage because of the large size of the average household and the loyalty of the young who want to remain close to their Rebbe, to their families, and the life-style of Williamsburg. Being forced to compete with the Puerto Rican and other minority groups for their turf, the hasidic community did not hesitate to use mass demonstrations and other means of protest and political pressure to protect their rights. When the Puerto Rican residents were promised 70 percent of the units in the newest and largest public high-rise project, the Clemente, 8,000 *hasidim* demonstrated before the Supreme Court building. Eventually they succeeded in being allotted at least 45 percent of the units, as against 55 percent for the Puerto Rican residents, because *hasidim* had a larger proportion of the apartments in the older public housing projects.

Similar evidence of their effective use of their political clout came some years later with the signing of a charter by the New York State legislature, which was endorsed by Governor Cuomo in 1989. It granted the schools of Kiryas Joel in Monroe the status of an independent school district. This enabled the residents of the exurban branch of Satmar to get government support for establishing their own facilities for the instruction of the learning disabled among their over three thousand boys and girls, and a number of other services, which the Orange County school board had tried to deny them in a number of long, drawn-out court battles. Although this charter was recently revoked by the New York Supreme Court, the hasidic community of Kiryas Joel has not yet given up the fight to reverse this decision. The case is now before the U.S. Supreme Court in 1994 and is rousing much interest and discussion in the media as a challenge to the separation-of-church-and-state issue.[3] Significantly, this struggle induced the head of the Orange County school board district to comment that Satmar *hasidim* seem quite inclined and adept at using political power and the political stage to achieve their goals. Characteristically, it is not only the district school board and its constituents who are continuing to carry on the battle against the granting of this charter. They are joined by several large Jewish organizations which consider it a violation of the separation of state and church.

At the same time the wise handling of the case of public school aid in providing instruction for severely handicapped and learning disabled children in Williamsburg itself enabled the hasidic community to be granted the use of a section of a public school building at the outskirts of the neighborhood for this purpose. This is in stark contrast to the open hostility and strife caused by the Latino residents when an unused section of P.S. 16, in the very center of Williamsburg, was given to the Satmar school administration for the instruction of several classes of girls with handicaps and learning disabilities in September 1986. The problem arose when the *hasidim* put up a wall, which they felt would help avoid friction. Soon the media was blowing the case of "the wall" all out of proportion when a group of Puerto Rican parents occupied the school offices and a 4-week strike ensued until the wall was taken down. The hasidic leadership decided not to make a case of this controversy and moved the classes of handicapped children back into one of their own buildings, bringing in a public school specialists. As one of their spokesmen put it: "The Puerto Rican community felt that this was the last bastion and the final battle for control of at least part of Williamsburg." This impression was confirmed by the statement of the Puerto Rican mother who was one of the leaders of the strike to a *Washington Post* reporter investigating the struggle for the removal of the wall (9 November 1986): "For years Hispanics and Hasidim have fought over playgrounds and racial quotas. Equal but separate can't exist . . . If we left that wall up our kids would understand that all their life there would be a wall. If we didn't take a stand now, we would teach our kids never to take a stand." In contrast, the head of the high school of Satmar made the following statement (*Washington Post,* 9 November 1986): "These classrooms in the public school were empty and collected dust. . . . [Hispanics] did not want our children in their school system. They made threats to our children in the streets: If you come to our school we will cut off your heads. . . ." Ultimately, this spokesman of Satmar pointed out, the inevitable result of the demographics of the population explosion of the Satmar community of Williamsburg will be the decisive factor, while the public schools empty out.

A similar determined struggle is now being waged by the hasidic community of Williamsburg against the erection of a fifteen-story-high garbage incinerator and recycling facility in the old Brooklyn Navy Yard, though the New York City Council had already set the date for the beginning of construction in November 1989. Using every possible avenue of political and other means to avert this imminent threat to the health of their young and future generations, the leaders threatened to block the construction "with our bodies." Ten thousand *hasidim*, men and women with infants in their carriages and toddlers by their side, marched across Brooklyn Bridge to stage a mass protest in front of city hall. Congressman Stephen J. Solarz submitted a bill in Congress and is holding public forums in New York to stop this city project and deflect the use of the empty navy yard to "what teams of experts and scientists have declared less harmful and more constructive purposes."

It was one of the smartest moves of David Dinkins as a candidate for the office of mayor of New York to promise a 5-year moratorium on the construction of the incinerator in the navy yard adjoining the hasidic enclave. Consequently, the *Yid* officially supported his candidacy and Councilman Noah Dear, spokesman for large numbers of Orthodox Jewish New Yorkers, appealed for the election of Dinkins as a friend of Israel and of other projects of concern to the Jewish people. In contrast, the *Jewish Press*, a large English language weekly of Orthodox Jews, came out in favor of Giuliani, like the masses of New York's Jews, because of the fear of racial bias of Dinkins (incidentally, a bias that was quite apparent during the traumatic riots in Crown Heights in the summer of 1991, after a car accident caused the death of a black child).

The vote of the hasidic community and other strictly Orthodox Jews may have been an important factor in the relatively narrow victory of Dinkins over his Republican opponent. Post-election analysis of Dinkins victory emphasized that his triumph was largely due to his endorsement by the Jewish leaders of Williamsburg's hasidic community and other Orthodox communities in Brooklyn and elsewhere. In fact, the 50th Assembly District, which includes Williamsburg and adjoining Greenpoint, was *the only white district* in New York won by Dinkins. Obviously, the hasidic community was counting on the help of the first black mayor of New York to stand by his promise in their struggle against the erection of the incinerator in their backyard. De facto, Mayor Dinkins, however, lead the faction that won the approval of the incinerator after an all-night battle in the New York City Council in September 1992.

Similarly, it took years of relentless struggle and costly court battles before the hasidic community won approval of their right to construct a vitally needed new school building on the large area behind the mansion of the Rebbe of Satmar, which had been cleared for urban renewal and had been legally acquired by Satmar, as confirmed by the state supreme court. This successful fight against the leadership of the Puerto Rican groups who were blocking the construction, and the active participation in the mayoral election are characteristic of the spirit and effective use of its legal and political power by the hasidic community to achieve its goals and protect the rights of its members.

Ultimately, however, the hasidic leaders have come to effect a measure of constructive cooperation with the Puerto Rican's and other minority groups on behalf of shared problems and concerns, such as the need for adequate housing, to gain access to urgently needed resources with the help of the political establishment.

THE POLITICAL STRUCTURE

As in the other realms of the hasidic community life of Williamsburg, the Rebbe of Satmar is the head of the political structure and the wellspring of its ideological orientation and dynamics. But, unlike the leaders of other communities, he is not just a figurehead. Directly or indirectly, he functions as the dynamo, as one of his associates called him, whose thinking and will make everything that takes place in Williamsburg among the thousands of his followers become a reality. He provides the underlying motivation, makes the decisions in crucial issues, and takes an active hand in the organization of the projects that he considers important. And he remains on top of the campaigns that he initiates, and which he wants undertaken on the local, national, or worldwide levels of his empire.

Therefore, the Rebbe requires an elaborate staff of advisers, co-workers, and proven leaders who have the vision, the know-how, and the power to translate his ideas and will into workable realities. They produce the framework and the dynamics necessary for him to achieve the major and minor goals for his community. With their help he is able to establish the vital basis of its continuity and future.

A quintessential example of such an outstanding leader who was the right-hand man of the Old Rebbe of Satmar: Rabbi Lippe (Leopold) Friedman had the vision, knowledge, and the public recognition to direct and control the vast network of organizations he helped build. His name is inscribed on the plaza of the largest public high-rise project and his impact still inspires rhapsodic praise from the members of the older generation who witnessed the community life of Williamsburg develop under his skillful guidance. In their eyes no one ever wielded such influence and control over every phase of the institutional structure he established at the behest of the *Heiliger Rebbe*. Rabbi Friedman was a key to the success of the Satmar Rebbe. In the words of one of the Rebbe's most astute associates:

> Beyond any doubt, the Old Rebbe of Satmar, next to Rabbi Aaron Kotler, had the greatest impact on the renaissance of Orthodox life in this country. But he was fortunate, or rather he had the ability to select and groom such superior assistants as Rabbi Lippe Friedman, who was able to carry out his directions. He translated his decisions into reality with the help of an effective framework of organizations and institutions that flourished and remained close to him as the conduit of the Rebbe's will and intentions.

Of course there were a number of other outstanding leaders who worked with the Rebbe and with Rabbi Lippe Friedman. Together they wrought the miracle of the new hasidic community of Williamsburg and brought to it the same standards of orthodoxy, of *Kashrut*, of *Hasidut*, and of a life-style like the old Satmar community in Eastern Europe, but on an incomparably larger scale.

The two most important men whom the Rebbe groomed to translate his ideas into a functional reality were Rabbi Alexander "Sender" Deutsch and Rabbi Leopold "Leibish" Lefkowitz. Over the course of the past critical decades, they have been in charge of almost all aspects of the large networks of organizations and institutions of Hasidic Williamsburg, of Kehillat Yetev Lev of Satmar, and of its branches in Boro Park, Monsey, Monroe, and of the affiliated international communities in Israel, Canada, England, Belgium, and in Latin America. Rabbi Sender Deutsch is the popular, much admired publisher of *Der Yid* who writes its lead articles and has a tremendous impact on the thinking of the entire community. He is the active head of the vast educational systems of Satmar for boys and girls, from nursery to the *kollels*. He is responsible for raising the funds to meet its $15 million budget, and for providing the facilities, the staffs, and the organization that molded it into such an effective operation that it is the largest of its kind in the world of Jewish education. He was largely responsible for the selection of the New Rebbe, Rabbi Moshe Teitelbaum, and for the relatively smooth transition of the leadership to this nephew of the Old Rebbe of Satmar. Rabbi Moshe Teitelbaum is a superior scholar and innovative thinker who had been working closely with his much revered uncle as he built his own hasidic community of Sziget in Williamsburg, and subsequently in Boro Park.

More than a decade after he was chosen to succeed his illustrious predecessor, the new Rebbe of Satmar has gained the confidence and reverence of the hundreds of thousands of his *hasidim* everywhere. But it took all the skill of Rabbi Sender Deutsch, an accomplished speaker, strategist, and organizer, to achieve this transition fraught with crises initially and then during the years of adjustment as the older *hasidim* come to terms with their grief at the death of their beloved, saintly *"Heiliger Rebbe."* For them, it was nearly impossible to think of anyone else taking his place. It was also Rabbi Sender Deutsch who, with the other leaders, successfully managed to cope with the challenges of the incredible growth of Satmar and its repercussions.

The other equally revered and effective leader is Rabbi Leopold "Leibish" Lefkowitz, the president of the hasidic community of Williamsburg and of Kiryas Joel. He is the head of the most important organizations, such as the ODA, and until his recent illness he actively directed the growth of Williamsburg and of Satmar in general, as it grew to become the unique three-generational community it is today. An aristocratic personality, he built a large crystal and lamp business on an international scale and is as highly respected by the heads of governments in the countries with whom he deals, as in the world of the *hasidim*. Rabbi Lefkowitz employs several hundred *hasidim* and other Orthodox Jews, and has been one of the most trusted associates of the old and the new Rebbe of Satmar. He has been the official head of the hasidic community in most political dealings with the local, state, and federal governments. Together with Rabbi Sender Deutsch he has carried the mind-boggling job of handling the official affairs of Hasidic Williamsburg, carrying the responsibility for the huge budgets and the direction of the various organizations and institutions. Although slowed down by illness in the last few years, he continues to be the recognized front man who is also the mayor of Kiryas Joel and has been since its inception in 1979.

Thus, these three outstanding leaders, Rabbi Lippe Friedman, Rabbi Alexander Sender Deutsch, and Rabbi Leopold Leibish Lefkowitz have steered the hasidic community through its struggles for survival, through the phases of its gradual growth and expansion, making it possible for the new generations of Williamsburg *hasidim* to move into the front ranks and take over the responsibilities of the community. From among these younger elements, Rabbi Lefkowitz, Rabbi

Deutsch, and their associates have assembled effective staffs, directors, and managers to handle the organizational networks they helped set up.

As pointed out in chapter 5, the social structures of the hasidic community of Williamsburg have evolved considerably, particularly in the realms of the political, socioeconomic, and educational aspects of the community. Foremost among the new leaders who have emerged in the past decades to head the administrations of these networks is Rabbi Tzvi Hershel Kestenbaum. He is the current director of the ODA and has almost singlehandedly developed this originally limited government agency office into the center of the sociopolitical, social welfare, and economic programs and projects that have radically changed the social conditions, and the physical as well as the commercial bases of Hasidic Williamsburg. Already in the more than 10 years between the limited and full recognition of the *hasidim* as a disadvantaged minority, this former head of the United Jewish Organizations Council had brought various programs to the neighborhood to benefit the indigent and sick. Foremost among these is the Primary Health Care Center already mentioned, which became a major boon to the physical and psychological welfare of the community. Under his forceful leadership the ODA has innovated ever more services to meet the growing needs of the people. His skill of cultivating the contacts of the urban, state, and federal bureaucracies resulted in making new resources available that improved the physical appearance and the range of services for the social welfare of the *hasidim*. Even more important was the expansion of the role of the ODA as the conveyor of resources, training programs, and counseling to the enterprising younger elements who after the full recognition of the *hasidim* as a disadvantaged minority were able to enter all levels of trade, business, and industry.

Consequently, it was largely thanks to Rabbi Kestenbaum's efforts that hasidic businessmen were able to blend successfully into the mainstream of American business. This ability to search out and make available new opportunities and resources was stressed by a number of administrators of community agencies in other Orthodox Jewish neighborhoods, such as Boro Park. This quality made him a model for other administrators and purveyors of services on behalf of their communities, and thus enabled him to have an impact on other neighborhoods as well.

The official ceremony granting the presidential charter that recognized the hasidic community as a disadvantaged minority in June 1984 paid full tribute to the extraordinary efforts and capability of Rabbi Tzvi Kestenbaum. Most speakers who addressed the large gathering of Jewish and non-Jewish officials stressed his pioneering efforts and effectiveness as a spokesman for the hasidic and nonhasidic community. He won a number of awards, and recognition by Washington. His office in Williamsburg was visited not only by local senators and congressmen, but by such high officials as the Former U.S. Secretary of Commerce, Malcolm S. Baldridge, and later on by his successor, Robert A. Mosbacher, in whose honor the ODA printed special editions of newspapers, in which the local business and religious institutions paid tribute to them and to Rabbi Kestenbaum. Similarly, the publications of the U.S. Small Business Administration for Minorities interviewed Rabbi Tzvi Kestenbaum and cited him in great detail as to the broader functions of his office as a center that benefits not only the hasidic residents, but the members of the other minority groups as well.

More recently Rabbi Kestenbaum was the major representative of Hasidic Williamsburg in the negotiations for the establishment of the Partnership of the City of New York with the two major minorities in making city-owned land available and facilitating the reconstruction and new construction of much-needed new public and private housing. His office is handling the applications and drawing of lots for the first phase of the program, which was initiated by Mayor Edward Koch. Rabbi Kestenbaum has also been named to the Presidential Commission for the Preservation of the Ethnic Heritage for his special efforts on behalf of sacred places, such as cemeteries and communal buildings still in existence in Hungary and elsewhere. Thus, Rabbi Tzvi Kestenbaum is one of the most visible and recognized leaders of the hasidic community of Williamsburg for his efforts and achievements of securing government resources for the essential programs that have changed every aspect of the neighborhood life.

There are a number of other key figures who at different times have played major roles in the transformation of Jewish Williamsburg and in the organization of its hasidic community. One of the important men who in the early years worked closely with the Old Rebbe of Satmar and since with his successor, serving as a spokesman and a political adviser at all official and unofficial functions, is Rabbi Hertz Frankel. His major contribution is the organization and direction of the Satmar girls' schools, particularly of Beth Rachel High School, which he has headed and guided since its inception into the largest of all girls' high schools anywhere in the Jewish day-school movement. He has also organized a number of branches of Beth Rachel and affiliated schools, including nurseries and special schools for children with learning problems. He has excellent relations with the public-school officials. And over the decades of Williamsburg's growth he has been the official and unofficial spokesman for the hasidic community on all levels of government, including meetings with the president and with various members of the cabinet. His expertise and political counsel are sought by officials and laymen far beyond the range of his official duties as a school administrator.

Another of the men who have been responsible for the development of various phases of the Williamsburg community life is Rabbi Chaim Moshe Stauber. He headed the United Jewish Organizations Council. Now he devotes himself to the administration of *Pesach Tikvah*, the institution for the mentally handicapped, which he started and which has two overnight facilities for women, a day-care facility for men, and a summer camp with programs for youngsters and adults. Among the many projects and campaigns he has originated or directed, probably the most important is his powerful drive to stop the construction of the fifteen-floor-high garbage disposal and incinerator facility in the old navy yard, next to the very heart of the hasidic community of Williamsburg. Rabbi Stauber was instrumental in forging the vital Community Alliance for the Environment Against the City Garbage Incinerator in the Navy Yard with the leaders of the Latino groups. This campaign and most other internal and external official affairs of the hasidic community of Williamsburg are now headed by Rabbi David D. Niederman, who has emerged as one of the most dynamic younger members of the administration as the head of the United Jewish Organizations Bureau. Rabbi Stauber also organized the *Vaad Hakehillot,* the council of hasidic communities, which is responsible for the legal battles and hires batteries of experts from lawyers to environmental scientists to fight the project, which was approved by Mayor Ed Koch. Rabbi Stauber is an effective spokesman for Hasidic Williamsburg and has helped to guide its growth through decades of constant crises and threats to its survival.

A discussion of the top level of the political structure of Hasidic Williamsburg would be incomplete if it failed to mention the extraordinary role of the Old Rebbetzin Alta Feige Teitelbaum, the widow of Rabbi Yoel Teitelbaum. From the moment of their arrival in the neighborhood she had a major share in the initiation and direction of a number of projects, particularly in the realm of social welfare. She has remained a powerful figure more than a decade after her husband's death. Although now in her eighties, she retains a special place in the hearts of the close associates and admirers of the *Heiliger Rebbe.*

In this connection one must also mention the wife of the present Rebbe of Satmar, who is increasingly assuming more responsibilities and who initiates her own projects. She recently represented the Rebbe on a visit to the Holy Land, where she was received like royalty wherever she went, especially in the Old City of Jerusalem, the location of a number of institutions founded and supported by the old and the new Rebbe and their followers.

One of the wisest policies of Rabbi Yoel Teitelbaum, the Old Rebbe of Satmar, was the systematic development of new leaders among the younger generation. Giving each school administration a great deal of independence, while personally supervising the programs and progress of each institution, the Rebbe and his successor, Rabbi Moshe Teitelbaum, along with Rabbi Sender Deutsch, the official head of both the boys' and girls' schools systems, have been particularly successful in producing a large cadre of competent directors, managers, and organizers among the middle-aged and younger generation of hasidim. This policy was not only vital to the direction and control of the explosive growth of the needs of the population. It is even more important for the future of the community to avoid the usual specter of stagnation and gradual disintegration of communities whose once vibrant leadership is growing old. As new challenges rise to threaten the communal welfare they are increasingly met by members of the younger generation, native Americans who fortunately combine their intense hasidic spirit and scholarship with the knowledge of the requirements of dealing with sophisticated bureaucratic, political bodies and organizations.

An example of the new leaders who represent the hasidic community in the struggle to protect and promote its interests and needs are the four men who are members of the antipoverty community board, and the three elected hasidic members of the local school district board. Two of these have for years served with such distinction that the head of the school district has commended them highly for their competency and contributions. "They are thoroughly familiar with the proper procedures, are ready to assume responsibility, direct board sessions, and contribute ideas and innovative approaches. They display political know-how and familiarity with the legal requirements. For the past 15 years they have contributed much to the successful conduct of our board on behalf of our schools and students." This praise by a high-ranking school official is typical of the respect and recognition that the hasidic leadership has been earning in the conduct of the political and other affairs of the community. Similarly, hasidic members of the council of the tenants in the public high-rise housing projects, such as Joseph Garber, and on the committees that work with the local police, health, and sanitation officials, are well regarded.

Among those particularly singled out for their contributions are the *hasidim* who originated and head *Hatzoloh*, the emergency medical volunteer corps that is called on in all types of crises and emergencies, not only in Williamsburg, but in other communities, such as Boro Park, Flatbush, Monsey, and Monroe. Perhaps the most prominent of these leaders is Rabbi Edgar Gluck. His office at the state police headquarters has become a major resource for the Jewish community of New York. He is constantly called on by hasidic as well as nonhasidic communities in cases of serious problems or potential trouble, because of his excellent relations with the broader levels of the officials in charge of security and intergroup affairs.

Rabbi Gluck is the national head of *Hatzoloh*, and he is the effective liaison between the state and city police of New York who are in charge of large public affairs. Among other affairs he works closely with them during the annual mass exodus of the Jewish population of New York, including the *hasidim* of Williamsburg, at the outset of the summer, when thousands of cars, vans, buses, and other vehicles travel to and from the Catskill Mountains from July through Labor Day. Rabbi Gluck arranges presummer mass meetings in Williamsburg, at which high-ranking police officers discuss proper travel security, regulations, and problems. As head of *Hatzoloh*, it was also his duty to arrange for the emergency use of a police helicopter to deal with a serious road accident one recent summer. In these and in other types of crises he is the major contact to all levels of the police force. In turn, they respect his effectiveness and thorough knowledge of the needs of the broader Jewish community. Rabbi Gluck is also responsible for arranging the huge mass meetings, mass demonstrations, and mass celebrations of the hasidic community, such as the weddings of members of the families of the famous hasidic Rebbes. Similarly, he prepares and directs the annual pilgrimage of as many as twenty thousand *hasidim* who travel to Kiryas Joel, in Monroe, on the *Yahrtzeit*, the anniversary of the death of the Old Rebbe of Satmar, who is buried in this exurban branch of Satmar.

Most recently, in May 1994 Rabbi Gluck coordinated the efforts of more than 1000 volunteers who searched and helped find a hasidic 14-year-old girl who had been lost in the woods on a school outing in Connecticut. Rabbi Gluck is a prime example of the leaders whose impact has spread far beyond the confines of the hasidic community.

There are a number of other members of the middle-aged and younger genera-tions of Williamsburg *hasidim* who, like Rabbi Gluck, are specialists in specific areas and have risen to prominence by dint of their intelligent approach in dealing with the authorities and the various levels of the city, state, and federal bureaucracies to meet the constantly changing and expanding needs of the community. Typical of the respect of the officials for these representatives of the hasidic population is this comment by one of the heads of the local school district: "In contrast to others who want everything, justifiable or not, the hasidic representatives know what they can get, how far they can go, and where to leave off."

One special realm of the official structure of the hasidic community of Williamsburg affiliated with Satmar is the administration of the *Hithachduth Horabonim*, the Central Rabbinic Congress (CRC), the rabbinic organization that supervises the majority of the ritual, religious, and political functions of the local and wider hasidic community. As Rabbi Yitzchok Gluck, the dynamic administrator of this organization, to which most of the hasidic rabbis belong, has said, his office represents *the political arm* of the Rebbe of Satmar. His office is responsible for the large posters and full-page advertisements in the *Yid* and in other publications that are signed by the Rebbe of Satmar and the heads of the other hasidic movements in this country and in Israel, who follow his line of thinking. Most of these announcements relate to important principles of the moral, ritual, or political conduct of the community as a whole and of the individual members. They refer to such topics as the interdiction against watching TV or videos as conducive to moral corruption; to improper women's wear, such as long *sheitels* or provocative fashions, especially summer wear; the attendance of popular concerts that are sponsored by the Orthodox community such as the performances of famous Orthodox cantors or star singers and choirs; plays that fill large public halls on such special occasions as Hanukkah. The Central Rabbinic Congress of the U.S. and Canada, or the *Hithachduth Horabonim*, also publicizes the political stance espoused by the Rabbi of Satmar and other hasidic leaders concerning the State of Israel and its policies, which in their view conflict with the Torah perspective and the interests of the ultra-Orthodox or the broader Orthodox community in the U.S. and Israel. It spells out the position of Satmar and other hasidic groups concerning problems of *kashrut*, which recently have become issues that go beyond the purely technical aspects of what is kosher or not, and which indicate underlying friction among the leaders of major hasidic movements, especially in Israel, such as Belz, Ger, and Lubavitch.

Like the head of the Central Rabbinic Congress, the *Hithachduth Horabonim*, there are numerous other middle-aged and young members of the hasidic community who in the past few decades have emerged to play key roles in the political and community networks. They are administrators, spokesmen,and organizers within the Williamsburg community itself, or in the official committees and boards through which the political affairs and interests are pursued that are of immediate concern to the residents of Williamsburg or to the broader hasidic or the wider Orthodox Jewish community.

JEWISH POLITICAL AND INTERHASIDIC ACTIVISM

The spirit of activism that enabled the hasidic community of Williamsburg to successfully overcome crisis after crisis in its struggle to survive and reverse the seemingly inevitable disintegration of the neighborhood is equally in evidence in its relations with the broader Jewish, Orthodox, and ultra-Orthodox communities in the U.S. and Israel.

Unfortunately, some of the more extreme expressions of this zeal, which is largely rooted in the reverence for the *Heiliger Rebbe*, the late Rabbi Yoel Teitelbaum, and for his views and teachings, have provoked the intense resentment and ire of the Jewish establishment and masses, as well as some of the non-Jewish bodies and organizations. The hasidic community as a whole is being judged by the excesses of some exuberant elements, as one of the officials called it, which is symptomatic of certain negative attitudes and aggressiveness that "harm the Jewish image and affect the dignity of the Jewish people and its religion."

The most significant and most resented of the central political views and conduct of Satmar and other Hungarian hasidic communities of Williamsburg and their branches in the Jewish world is the rejection of the secular State of Israel. This position was originally promulgated by Rabbi Yoel Teitelbaum, the Old Rebbe of Satmar, ever since his rise to prominence in his native homeland because he considered Zionism and the Zionist state contrary to the spirit and letter of Jewish law and tradition. To him a secular Jewish state was the very antithesis of the divine purpose of the *galut*, the exile of the Jewish people from the Holy Land. As the prophets proclaimed, it will only be terminated by the coming of the Messiah, and the reestablishment of the Kingdom of the House of David, the rebuilding of the Holy Temple, and, above all, by the reinstitution of the Torah as the authentic constitution for the benefit of the Jewish people and all the nations of the earth. A secular state, regardless of the technological and cultural circumstances, is an outright sacrilege, which is bound to lead to a new national catastrophe. This firm conviction has a number of corollaries and concomitants, not the least of which is its impact on the educational system. It excludes the teaching of modern Hebrew, which is central in the curriculum of most other contemporary Jewish school systems, including the Orthodox day schools. Equally important, it excludes dealing with the realities of contemporary Israel as a state and it precludes any form of participation in its political processes, such as elections. In contrast, other ultra-Orthodox movements, such as Agudath Israel, have been actively involved in it since the beginning and one of its former leaders, a member of the family of the Rebbe of Ger, was a member of the early cabinets of the State of Israel.

Yet, the followers of the Rebbe of Satmar feel called upon to function as the most vocal of the anti-Zionists, true to the ideology formulated by their leader, as a religious duty rather than as the expression of a political viewpoint. In spite of the hostile reaction of the broader masses of the Jewish people, they persist in publishing full-page ads in the *New York Times*, in which they attack policies of the State of Israel, particularly those that in their opinion violate the rights of the Orthodox or the sanctity of holy places, for example, practices such as the drafting of women into the Israeli army, or the attempt to abolish the exemption of *yeshivah* students from military service. They call for huge demonstrations and rallies, not in Williamsburg, but in the most conspicuous places, such as Madison Square Garden. With their strong discipline, they are able to pack the large halls with their men and women, attesting to the powerful charisma of their Rebbe. Obviously, this policy, which violates the very sensibilities of the American Jewish community, to whom, especially since the Six Day War, Israel has become inviolate, and for whom any attack from within or without was deeply resented until the recent negative reactions to Premier Shamir and the expressions of sympathy for the Peace Now movement. To them, the ads and huge protest rallies mean washing one's dirty linen in public or worse. Their conduct is denounced as a *hillul Hashem*, a desecration of the most Holy One's sacred name, and a defilement of the very essence of religion. To say the least, this stance of Satmar is considered a breach in the unity of the Jewish people before the eyes of the world. Undaunted by such hostile reactions, the Hungarian hasidic Rebbes feel that it is their duty to make certain that the voice of Torah be raised for the sake of the survival of Orthodox Jewish life and the institutions of the *Aidah Charedit*, the community of the ultra-Orthodox in Jerusalem.

"Let the world not think that the State of Israel and its antireligious officials speak for the entire Jewish people," commented one spokesman of Satmar when questioned about the harm caused by the flagrant impropriety and negative image of the public protests that fuel anti-Jewish sentiments and justify the already powerful anti-Israel attitude among many of the world's nations.

> How can we stand by idle when the holiest of our values are openly and officially violated! We have suffered enough in our history that we are not afraid that our silence and accommodation may not, God forbid, cause another Holocaust we can ill afford, after we have lost so much in our very time. This is the warning and the challenge of our saintly Rebbe, regardless of the cost and consequences. His eyes saw deeper and further than ours, and we must follow his lead.

Obviously, this stand of the community of Satmar does alienate potential outside help. It requires tremendous funds to sustain the unabating campaign of protests on a large public scale, such as the full-page ads and mass rallies. But, as the Old Rebbe of Satmar always emphasized when it comes to a *mitzvah*, the fulfillment of a divine commandment, money must never be a consideration, and the cost not an obstacle to its fulfillment. To him the secular state was and remained a serious temptation, a *nisayon*, a test from above to find out whether the Jewish people are worthy of redemption. Yet, interestingly enough, when Rabbi Yoel Teitelbaum came to the Holy Land, he was treated like visiting royalty, and many thousands of all kinds and types of Jews came to greet him and pay their respects because of his worldwide reputation as a supreme Torah scholar and because of his saintly conduct.

Obviously, this struggle to have the voice of Torah and of Orthodox Judaism represented in public was not meant to take the violent forms it occasionally has, as when a few students burned an Israeli flag in front of the Israeli consulate. The Rebbe himself saw to it that they were promptly dismissed from the *yeshivah*, for he forcefully condemns violence and improper behavior of this kind as harmful to the spiritual cause it is meant to represent. This does not, however, mean any softening in the political struggle, and every issue of *Der Yid* carries essays, small articles, or full-page ads conveying the indignation and protest of the Satmar community against some policy of the State of Israel or some unofficial abrogations of the rights of the ultra-Orthodox, such as the rough treatment of protesters by the Israeli police at the not infrequent digs of archeologists on sites which the ultra-Orthodox consider sacred, for instance, newly discovered cemeteries. Similarly, the lead articles in the *Yid* spell out the anti-Zionist ideology of Satmar and forceful criticism of current policies in the political or civil life in the Holy Land. These articles mold the thinking of the readers and have an impact on their conduct, though, as pointed out several times, there are hasidic Rebbes with huge followings, such as the Lubavitcher, Gerer, and the Klausenburger Rebbes, who hold radically different views of the propriety of living and participating in the full range of the political processes of the State of Israel. Their *hasidim* play a significant role in the life of contemporary Israel.

There are also, of course, the Orthodox mass movements, such as Agudath Israel, which have been part of the political scene since the founding of the State of Israel, and whose elected representatives serve in the Knesseth, or have been cabinets members, though its highest authority, the Council of the Sages, rejects some of the crucial policies of the state, such as the military service of rabbinic students and of women. And then there is the more moderately Orthodox world movement of the *Mizrachi*, the Religious Zionists, who since the founding of the movement in Eastern Europe more than a hundred years ago have taught the masses of the religious that it was proper and vital to the interests of Orthodox Judaism to be full partners in the Zionist movement, in spite of its proclaimed secular nature. Its young men and women serve in the Israeli army while observing a maximum of the religious laws and duties. They reject exemptions of *yeshivah* students from military service. They subscribe to the Zionist ideology, in contrast to the members of Agudath Israel, who remain outside of the Zionist movement while participating in the daily life of the state as a necessary requisite of realizing the basic goals and providing for the needs of Orthodox Jews in Israel.

It is also typical of the go-it-alone attitude of Satmar and similar Hungarian hasidic communities that until the last decade of international crises they have not concentrated on reaching out to nonreligious Jews on a scale like that of the Lubavitcher and other hasidic and nonhasidic communities. The threats to Jewish survival and the needs for emergency help, as in the case of the rescue campaigns for the Jews of Iran, of Ethiopia, and numerous other endangered large centers of Jews in the countries of the former Soviet Union and elsewhere, have prompted massive efforts of the worldwide movement of Satmar and other *hasidim* to provide both physical and spiritual help wherever needed and possible.

But, generally, Satmar and other Hungarian hasidic movements have not been too receptive to the large numbers of *Ba'alei Teshuvah*, returnees to their inherited faith, who in search of their roots and genuine values in the past three decades have flocked to institutions that introduce them to the spirit, the substance, and knowledge of the Jewish faith. Many of these "returnees" to Judaism have since become fully integrated into the body of observant Jews in Israel and in the U.S. Special organizations, movements of religious scientists, as well as the established *yeshivot* have increasingly concerned themselves with providing the intellectual and spiritual channels to attract and hold on to ever more of the masses of the young who were disillusioned by the failure of their fallen idols and seriously responded to the outreach efforts that have wrought a new chapter in the contemporary history of Judaism and Jewry by the remarkable success of their personal efforts.

It has been in the past few years, since the increase of the Iranian and particularly Russian emigrés to Israel and the U.S., that Satmar and other Hungarian hasidic groups have joined the special efforts of spiritual and physical rescue. The Old Rebbe of Satmar had already initiated *Rav Tov*, a special organization that devoted massive efforts to help Jews from Iran and other countries of persecution to emigrate and settle in Israel and the U.S. It set up centers for their training and absorption in such countries as Italy and Austria to help facilitate their temporary and eventually permanent adjustment. But only in the late '80s did Satmar and similar hasidic groups actively devote major efforts to work with the new immigrants, especially with their children in their *Kiruv* centers. Before this, the leaders of Satmar had made a strong point of emphasizing their primary concern with their own and with developing an effective education system that would safeguard their ideology and life-style in the same spirit in which they themselves had grown up in Europe. Said one of their leaders, in response to the question about this lack of outreached:

> We'd rather concentrate on our own youth, on education and inspiring our boys and girls with the proper *Hashkafah*, the spirit of *hasidut* and *Torah* and *mitzvot*, to develop the strength of our communities from within. We welcome anyone who genuinely wants to join our ranks and is ready to shoulder the full burden of our life-style. But we are afraid of watering down the intensity of out total, traditional adherence to the *halachah*, as we have inherited it and seen it in action. We also don't want to break down the walls of sociocultural isolation we have erected as a protective shelter and insurance of our survival and future.

Yet, interestingly enough, one of the spokesmen of Satmar pointed out that in spite of their sociocultural isolation from the non-Orthodox and non-Jewish society, few leaders have had such a deep impact on American Jewish religious life as the Old Rebbe of Satmar, perhaps with the exception of Rabbi Aaron Kotler and the Lubavitcher Rebbe. His insistence on consistency and on brooking no compromises in the life-style of his community created trends that affected many more than the thousands of his followers in Williamsburg and elsewhere. His demand for Glatt Kosher standards in the food lines. his setting the style of wearing dark clothes, the black hat, beards, *kapottes*, and *peyot*, would never have gone over in religious communities like the old, pre-World-II Williamsburg or Flatbush. Yet they have become almost the standard in the nonhasidic *yeshivah* world, as well as in the hasidic community. One cannot point to a single major influence as being responsible for the so-called renaissance of Orthodox Jewish life in this country. It is rather the result of the combined impact of the more extreme hasidic, and the powerful nonhasidic, *yeshivah* life-styles, plus a number of other contingent factors. As a result, professionals and academicians as well as successful businessmen do not hesitate to wear beards and *peyot*, black hats, and *kapottes*, or *shtreimels* on Sabbath and holidays in such middle-class neighborhoods as Flatbush in the '90s. Similarly, the trend of *yeshivot* limiting the time allotted to secular studies and the avoidance of sending children to college point strongly to the powerful influence of the Old Rebbe of Satmar and the famous Roshei Yeshivah, the heads of the outstanding rabbinic academies. Their influence was indisputable even though neither Rabbi Aaron Kotler nor Rabbi Yoel Teitelbaum ever directly engaged in reaching out to the broader masses of the American Jewish people.

INTERHASIDIC RELATIONS

It is not at all surprising that the religious and political zeal of Satmar and other Hungarian hasidic communities of Williamsburg have had a significant impact on the relations among the various major hasidic movements and among their leaders.[1] Not only does the anti-Zionist stand of Satmar provoke other hasidic as well as nonhasidic people, which occasionally erupt in friction or even open conflict, to the glee of the media which are keen to exploit such incidents. There are also the well-known rivalries between some of the famous hasidic movements and their leaders over their ideologies and their life-styles, though all claim to adhere scrupulously to the same set of religious, ritual, and moral codes of Jewish law.

Best known among such rivalries is the one between Satmar and Lubavitch, both of which have hundreds of thousands of followers in America and the rest of the Orthodox Jewish world. There is no open personal antagonism between the two heads, both of whom have their headquarters in Brooklyn and respect each other's superstatus as superior scholars and leaders. But the masses of *hasidim* of the two dynasties are occasionally drawn into open clashes, as when a group of Lubavitch *hasidim* visited Williamsburg on the Sukkot holidays to spread the message of their Rebbe to the people, which they do in synagogues everywhere every year. The people in Williamsburg resented their appearing on their "turf," especially when they had been warned to stay away. The open conflict that erupted when a group of defiant young Lubavitcher *hasidim* followed the clash with a march of protest is said to have included the firing of warning shots by some outsiders who had attached themselves to Lubavitch; and this incident was fully exploited by the media.

Similarly, too much attention was paid to the open clash that occurred when one Lubavitch *hasid* was found teaching *Tanya* (1797), the major work of the founder of the Chabad Lubavitcher movement (*Likutei Hamaamorim* by Rabbi Shneur Zalman of Liady) to several interested Satmar yeshivah students. He was seized by five Satmar students, who treated him roughly and cut off his beard and *peyot*. Despite their ideological and political disagreements, a spokesman for Satmar immediately condemned the students and expressed outrage on behalf of his community. Satmar also offered the Lubavitchers their help during the three days of rioting that erupted in the wake of the car accident that killed a black child in August 1991, while other major American Jewish organizations and their leaders kept silent.

The reports of the friction between the heads of the Belz hasidic movement and the Satmar hasidim, following an incident in March 1981 when graffiti and caricatures of the Rebbe of Belz appeared in the streets of Williamsburg and some overzealous youngsters raided the Beth Hamedrash of Belz, were also exaggerated.[2] The perpetrators were severely punished and warnings against such outbreaks were announced in all classes of the Satmar and other hasidic schools. Obviously such isolated incidents, which indicate the underlying loyalty and love for their Rebbe, are part of the traditional feuds between the famous hasidic courts of long standing, going back to Poland, Russia, and Hungary. It is, however, remarkable that American-born young or middle-aged *hasidim* feel so strongly and perpetuate the negative as well as the positive effects of their partisanship. De facto there is a great deal of cooperation among the various major groups and communities of *hasidim* in this country, in spite of the occasional symptoms of tension and volatility that pit hotheaded followers against each other. Obviously their common interests and concerns create new alliances and strong bonds, which the leaders of the various hasidic movements emphasize. As one of them said:

> Every community has some people who like to get in a huff and, given the chance, will not shy away from *derlangen a few petsh*, slapping someone who disagrees with them. Most of our *hasidim* are balanced, intelligent people whose sole aggressiveness manifests itself in the battle of wits in the discussion of the Talmud, not in physical violence, especially against other Jews. They know that our *Heiliger* Rebbe was against any form of violence and strictly condemned aggressive behavior among the students of his *yeshivah*.

Occasionally, as pointed out before, the aggressive behavior or spirit of the *hasidim* will be used in a positive way, as in combatting hooliganism, and thievery, by thugs. The cry of *"Chaptzeh"* brings out crowds from their houses to fend off the attacks of criminals. Would-be attackers from the adjoining areas have been frightened off by this policy of active self-defense in the hasidic community, especially after the effective control of the streets by the *Shomrim*, the civil patrol. Occasionally this aggressiveness may also manifest itself as a form of indignation or protest against what may be interpreted as unfair behavior on the part of the police. It was this same spirit of indignation that showed itself when a large crowd of *hasidim* stormed a police district headquarters in Boro Park after an elderly *hasid* was murdered and no action was forthcoming from the police. It was also very much in evidence when a contingent of police officers got involved in a melee with yeshivah students outside the headquarters of Lubavitch in Crown Heights. Yet in all three major hasidic neighborhoods there has evolved a great deal of cooperation between the local police and the hasidic residents to ensure the security of the neighborhood.

Another minor incident, blown out of all proportion by the media who, as one spokesman for the *hasidim* said, enjoy "Satmar bashing," was an altercation between a few Satmar *yeshivah* students. Upon the death of the former Rebbe, some of his close followers, in the throes of grief, attacked some students as they were about to replace the tablet bearing the name of the Old Rebbe on his seat in the *bet hamidrash* of Kiryas Joel with one inscribed with the name of the new Rebbe. Similarly, the media exploited the torching of the cars of close followers of the Old Rebbe in front of the villa of Rabbi Yoel Teitelbaum in response to rumors that they had come to sell the residence of the Old Rebbe to another group of *hasidim* who would establish their own *kollel* in it.

More serious were attacks on two former members of the Satmar *yeshivah* staff who were said to be gathering groups of their close students about them to form their own movements. The more prominent of these, the head of the so-called *Mechalisten*, moved to Monsey, after someone broke into his home and allegedly removed a large box containing his manuscripts. He established his own congregation, *bet midrash*, and *kollel* in the name of his ancestor, Reb Schmelke of Nikolsburg, one of the early thinkers and leaders of the hasidic movement. He himself is an original thinker, scholar, and author, and claims to be a faithful follower of the Old Rebbe of Satmar, but disagrees with some of the more militant policies of the current administration.

Such incidents and squabbles are natural and bound to occur in any large movement that is held together by personal charisma so that any deviance is considered a personal attack and a threat to the movement as a whole.

SUMMARY

There can be little doubt that the involvement of the hasidic community of Williamsburg in the processes of American political life and its aggressive activism have been major factors in the successful fight for its survival, progress, and growth. Unlike the earlier Jewish community of Williamsburg, which had neither the homogeneity nor the intrinsic unity required to develop more than perfunctory political clout, the hasidic leaders, foremost among them the Rebbe of Satmar, defied the image cultivated by the broader American Jewish community of public restraint and benign invisibility. Driven by the urgent needs of their population, the majority of whose members were living below the national poverty level, they set out consciously to develop vital contacts on all levels of the city, state, and federal bureaucracies, and among the elected and appointed officials whose aid was essential to achieving their goals.

Three decades later, even detractors grudgingly admit their success in establishing what a reporter from the *Washington Post* (Nov. 9, 1986) called a "model of modern machine politics." Setting their sights on the broad range of opportunities created by the War on Poverty of the '60s, the hasidic leadership fought the opposition of government officials up to the New York State Supreme Court, as well as the Jewish and non-Jewish establishment, to be granted the status of a disadvantage minority, which entitled them to the same rights and benefits enjoyed by the other racial or ethnic minorities. It opened the doors to socioeconomic programs and training opportunities for their population.

Thus, the political activities enabled the hasidic community of Williamsburg to provide its members with the type of opportunities that had been closed to them because they lacked education and experience. Although the demographics, the lack of adequate housing, and the blighted environment maintain constant pressure for more intensive efforts, the socioeconomic level has risen to a point where the percent of those living below the official poverty line of $12,400 per year for households of four has been brought down to approximately 30 percent, according to some estimates (although at the time of this writing, in 1992, the estimates of people living below the poverty level place the figure closer to 50 percent). Even this figure loses some of its significance in view of the fact that it includes members of the older generation of immigrants, or young couples at the beginning of their training and professional careers. Of course, the serious downward trend since the end of the '80s has changed this situation radically. There is no telling what long-range effects this negative change will have on the economic situation of Hasidic Williamsburg.

Generally, however, the availability of new resources for the improvement of the neighborhood has contributed much to the spirit and appearance of the Jewish Triangle. It has also brought new respect and recognition of the hasidic community of Williamsburg from the outside, especially in political circles. As one of the older spokesmen put it:

> Politicians have something to show for their efforts. They come away from Williamsburg seeing some of the improvements and achievements largely due to their help. It is not accidental that the political climate of the hasidic community has turned to the more conservative candidates, especially when it comes to the candidates for the presidency. It provided strong support for former President Reagan and continues to do the same for President Bush. At the same time they remain loyal to the Democratic officials who have been and continue to be the mainstay of their political clout in Washington, as well as in Albany, and in the New York City Council.

The same spokesman also pointed out that more recently there has evolved a working level of collaboration between the hasidic leadership and the heads of the Puerto Rican and other ethnic and racial communities in the immediate and adjoining areas, with whom they had been engaged in constant battles over "turf." Political realities moved them closer to each other for their own mutual benefit, as in the case of the campaign for new housing and reconstruction efforts from the city and federal government agencies.

In Jewish political matters, the hasidic community of Williamsburg continues to keep mostly to itself. It maintains its independence when it comes to the direction and management of its educational and religious affairs, true to the mandate of the Old Rebbe of Satmar and maintained by his successor. Most significantly, it maintains sociocultural isolation from the Jewish as well as the non-Jewish environment. Its anti-Zionist stand holds undiminished, and it continues its policy of protests and demonstrations against what it considers antireligious policies of the secular State of Israel. At the same time, it has become active in the international efforts to preserve whatever is left of the Jewish heritage in the Eastern European countries from which most of them hail.

In retrospect, the political activities of the hasidic community of Williamsburg have accomplished a great deal for its population. Directly or indirectly, the community has raised the standards of life and the recognition of the hasidic community in the non-Jewish as well as the Jewish community. Because of its loyalty, inner discipline, and strong leadership, its political power is something to be reckoned with. In turn, this enables it to face the constant intrinsic and extrinsic crises with confidence for its future. In a number of important aspects it has become a model for other hasidic and nonhasidic Orthodox Jewish communities who now emulate its spirit of political activism and collaborate with it in areas of common interests and concerns.

From a historic perspective, the unconventional approach of Satmar and other Hungarian hasidic communities has been a crucial factor in forging the new spirit and role of Hasidic Williamsburg in the Jewish world, in spite of its sociocultural isolation, ultra-Orthodox ideology, and life-style.

⇛ 9 ⇚

Patterns of Social Welfare: The Spirit of a Community

My original report (1961) did not devote a separate section to the discussion of social welfare programs, organizations, and institutions in the then still heterogeneous Jewish community of Williamsburg. Not that there were not extraordinary efforts made by groups and individuals, particularly since before World War II, when hundreds of newcomers, refugees from persecution, war, and the Holocaust began to settle in this neighborhood because of its religious institutions and Orthodox climate.

There were prominent leaders, such as Rabbi Shrage Faivel Mendelowitz, head of *Mesifta Torah Vodaath,* who not only inspired generations of outstanding young men to become Torah scholars, educators, and active community leaders, but also absorbed a growing number of young newcomers and personally helped to integrate and settle them. He assisted some of the outstanding heads of the famous talmudic academies of Eastern Europe to immigrate and rebuild their schools in this country. He was also instrumental in bringing some of the illustrious hasidic Rebbes to establish new centers in Williamsburg and elsewhere for their followers. There were inspired laymen, like Reb Binyomin Wilhelm, who with his co-workers established day schools for boys and girls when the broader religious public was not yet ready for such a drastic step. There was Reb Chaim Gelb and other warm-hearted men and women who devoted their limited time and resources to helping the indigent and the sick.

And then there were outstanding lay leaders, foremost among them the legendary Michael G. (Elimelech) Tress, who almost single-handedly transformed the local branch of Zeirei Agudath Israel into the national headquarters of the movement and the center of international rescue efforts, which saved thousands of individuals and families. He organized national and worldwide operations and campaigns on behalf of the innocent victims of terror and genocide when other, larger organizations with the power and resources required for large-scale efforts sat idly by. He transformed the members of his youth organization into cadres of responsible rescue and relief workers. He established a refugee home in the headquarters of the movement, and provided its inmates and numerous others with whatever they needed for their immediate and long-range adjustment. He set up international communications networks to provide means of escape, food, and immigration documents from his small Williamsburg office, and subsequently in his constantly expanding headquarters in mid-Manhattan.[1] There were also then, as before, the standard projects of Jewish welfare in Williamsburg, such as a Free Loan Society, which were organized and maintained by the men's clubs and ladies' auxiliaries of the local synagogues and organizations typical of most Jewish neighborhoods in New York and elsewhere.

But there never evolved the kind of community spirit that is characteristic of the hasidic community of Williamsburg, which might have prevented some of the crises that precipitated the flight of the older and some of the new groups of recent residents who settled in other communities and took their renowned institutions with them. Thus Williamsburg suffered the mass exodus and the breakup of the institutions that had made it a center of the emerging renaissance of Orthodox Judaism in this country, causing the predictions of doom by students of contemporary Jewry.

They did not anticipate the massive influx of Hungarian *hasidim* and the impact of their Rebbes, foremost among them Rabbi Yoel Teitelbaum, the Old Rebbe of Satmar, after he decided to remain in Williamsburg, stop its rapid disintegration, and effect a radical turnabout in the conditions of life in the neighborhood.

One of the most important factors of this amazing reversal was the *Mobilization for Chesed*, for the care and concern of the well-being of one's neighbors, which the Old Rebbe set in motion soon after he settled in Williamsburg in 1947. Perhaps no other hasidic leader was faced with such a mind-boggling challenge as Rabbi Teitelbaum when he began to rebuild an American version of his center for his followers with the same ideology, life-style, and spirit that had made him so successful in pre-Holocaust Carpatho-Russia. Anyone else might have become discouraged by the tremendous odds and obstacles that threatened to vitiate any attempt to re-create the kind of community he envisioned, under such radically different circumstances.

In the first place, the very foundations of what had made Williamsburg so attractive to the newcomers were coming apart in the face of the physical and economic disintegration of the neighborhood. In the second place, the vast majority of the *hasidim* who had flocked about him were victims of the Holocaust and of the war and of postwar suffering. They were too old or too ill or otherwise lacked the experience and the means that were vital for success in the new American setting. Most did not master English adequately. Nor did they have the occupational skills or the technical know-how that would enable them to blend into the American mainstream easily, especially in view of their adherence to their ultra-Orthodox hasidic life-style and appearance. Nor were there other factors and forces that could be counted on to help the new hasidic community stem the influx of various ethnic and racial minority groups and their negative impact on the neighborhood. Thus, the prospects of creating the kind of community the Rebbe of Satmar envisioned seemed rather slim, especially since it hinged on a maximum of sociocultural isolation in a milieu that historically was geared to acculturation and assimilation of new immigrants since its inception.

Obviously, it needed a powerful force to counteract this combination of negative factors to generate the resources necessary to sustain the largely dependent population and to raise its standards of living without making the kind of compromises that had ravished most immigrant ghettos and undermined their structure. Furthermore, it required extraordinary efforts to allow the members of the hasidic community to venture forth and be able to interact with the outside world while remaining loyal to their own values and life-style, without yielding to the powerful pull of the environment and the lures of its promise of rewards.

This extraordinary force was provided by the utter devotion of the *hasidim* to their charismatic leaders, and by their discipline and readiness to make sacrifices to a degree hardly matched by other communities, even those like post-World-War-II Jewish Williamsburg, which shared their strong faith and Orthodox values. An example of this, cited in my original report (1961), told of the inability of the major organizations and institutions of the neighborhood to raise the funds for an urgently needed *mikvah,* even after they had purchased an adequate building. Yet, only a few years later, a number of hasidic Rebbes and their congregations managed to build *mikvot* of their own. The Old Rebbe of Satmar and his colleagues, the other prominent Rebbes, exuded the kind of faith and confidence that left no room for doubt; once they determined to see a project through that they considered vital, it was as good as a reality. His superior scholarship as well as his mastery of hasidic thought gained him worldwide recognition and were the major source of the loyalty and confidence of his *hasidim* and admirers from the outside who responded to his requests and actively supported his projects. Thus, counter to all expectations, he was able to achieve the miracle of the reversal of the disintegration of the neighborhood and the generation of adequate resources to transform the gloom and doom into a strong resolve and confidence in the future of his community to a degree that even the most optimistic could not have foreseen.

This extraordinary success story was produced by the impact of two phases of the community life on which the Rebbe of Satmar and his colleagues put their greatest emphasis in order to engender the strength and power required to achieve his goals. First and foremost, he pulled out all stops to create a total education system that would shape the basic values of the young, as well as of the older members of his community, and which would enable them to resist the temptations that face all new immigrants as they wrestle with the difficulties of adjustment and acculturation.

This focus on education of the Rebbes of Satmar, Klausenburg, Tzelem, and others was aided by the increasing homogeneity of the population of Williamsburg as the residents of the older Jewish community and some of the hasidic and nonhasidic subcommunities left the neighborhood. The Rebbes were further aided by the loyalty of the younger generation of their *hasidim* who insisted on remaining and staying close to their families and to the institutions that had nourished them even after they had married and had children of their own. This is in stark contrast to the general pattern of the younger generations in other Jewish communities in

New York and elsewhere who, as pointed out, prefer to strike out on their own and move to other, for them more attractive, neighborhoods.

The second and most crucial phase of the campaign of the Old Rebbe of Satmar to stop the decline and eventual disintegration of the community was the *Mobilization for Chesed*, which had already started before the decision to remain in Williamsburg. Almost from the very outset of rebuilding his community, Rabbi Yoel Teitelbaum was confronted with the urgent need for economic and other help for the large number of the needy, ill, and indigent among his own followers and among the rest of the residents, especially the old and poor of the Jewish community of Williamsburg. What began as a temporary stopgap operation with the help of some of his more affluent admirers inside and outside of his community, as well as from among his own *hasidim*, developed into a full-fledged major campaign to make *hesed* and *tzedakah*, loving care, concern, and charity, the central challenge on a scale that has dwarfed everything done in most other hasidic as well as nonhasidic communities in the U.S. Unfolding in proportion with the explosive growth of his *kehillah*, Rabbi Yoel Teitelbaum, his wife, and his associates developed programs, projects, organizations, and institutions to answer the economic, social, and spiritual needs of their people, and which are still proliferating three decades later.

Of course *hesed* and *rahamim*, care and charity, had always been characteristic of the Jewish people, known as *Rahamonim bnai Rahamonim*, a society motivated by loving-kindness and charity toward others, in the 2,000 years of *Galut*, exile, during the best as well as the worst periods, as it moved across cultures and continents throughout the centuries. It is surely a major force in Jewish life in the present as well as in the past, frequently replacing other functions of the Jewish religion in the process of acculturation and social advancement. It had also been a major factor of the survival of the large Jewish communities in Eastern Europe, which had been poverty-ridden and subject to other forces of inner and outer erosion in spite of their magnificent achievements in the spiritual and intellectual realms before the destruction brought by the Holocaust.

Thus it was natural for the leaders of the evolving hasidic community of Williamsburg to throw all of its resources and energies into finding ways of aiding the large number of its people who depended on formal and informal help to sustain their mostly large families and meet emergencies such as illness. Equally important was the fact that most of them had neither the means nor the resources to start life all over again. Other, lesser leaders might have become frustrated by the overwhelming needs and the size of the problems that evolved as the population of the community doubled and tripled in a few short years because of the continuing influx of newcomers and the high birthrate. Not so the Rebbe of Satmar,[2] who since his earliest years as a leader and community head never faltered in his faith that whenever funds were needed and the cause was a worthy one, divine providence would provide whatever was required. Hence, he never would let the shortage of funds or the lack of prospects of assistance stop him from undertaking new projects or programs he considered vital for the physical or spiritual welfare of his followers. For the same reason he never acceded to turn for help to the usual sources of financial assistance of most organizations and institutions in the broader Jewish community, including the Orthodox, the powerful Jewish federations and philanthropies that have always provided for the financial substructure of the broad spectra of Jewish causes in the U.S. His fierce insistence on total independence would not brook any type of supervision, direction, or ideological bias that come with financial support.

This absolute faith in the help of divine providence and in the loyalty of the masses of his followers in Williasmburg and in other Jewish communities in the U.S. and elsewhere enabled him to carry out his ambitious plans for the rebuilding of his *kehillah* in Williamsburg in spite of the limited resources of his people.[3] But this was the very essence of the charismatic leadership of Rabbi Yoel Teitelbaum, which motivated him and enabled him to marshal the forces to do what was necessary to stop the disintegration of Jewish Williamsburg and transform its then bleak present into a thriving future.

The central strategy of this mobilization of his community was the emphasis on *hesed*, loving-kindness and concern for the well-being of others, as the key to the dynamics of the human interrelations among his *hasidim*. It became the lever of the vital activities that permeated every facet of the hasidic life-style and its underlying ideology, which he preached on all occasions and which his teachers inculcated into their students. The result was and continues to be a massive outpouring of active concern for one's neighbors, which translates into action. Thus was it possible to develop major networks of collective communal and individual projects on such a massive scale. Small wonder that these programs made such an impression on hasidic as well as nonhasidic and even non-Orthodox religious communities, such as *Hatzoloh* or *Bikkur Cholim*, the programs on behalf of patients in the major hospitals in New York.

SOCIAL WELFARE PROGRAMS IN THE HASIDIC COMMUNITY OF WILLIAMSBURG

The discussion of this chapter will analyze the scope and types of charity and social welfare programs, projects, and institutions or organizations that have evolved in response to the physical, economic, and social needs of the residents of the hasidic community of Williamsburg.

It is divided into programs and projects fostered by the community itself, by governmental agencies, by subcommunities, family groups, and individuals. They have become part of the intrinsic texture of the community life of Williamsburg and cover most areas of the life-cycle from birth to death. A good many of these have expanded or were copied by other hasidic and nonhasidic Orthodox communities in the U.S., in Israel, and in other religious centers of the contemporary Jewish world.

Governmental Programs

The first and most significant projects on behalf of the needy were established by the heads of the hasidic community, such as the Rebbe of Satmar and his colleagues, the other Rebbes and leaders of the various groups, in the '40s and '50s. Yet most important for the welfare of the residents are those programs that draw on national, state, and city projects that were established on behalf of the needy of all racial and ethnic minorities in the U.S. As discussed in chapter 8 on political activism it took years and a great deal of effort and intensive political pressure until the most vital of these governmental resources initiated as part of the War on Poverty were made available to the hasidic community as to other minorities, such as the American Indians, Puerto Ricans, and blacks. They were denied to *hasidim* until their recognition as a disadvantaged minority in 1984, after ten years of intensive political struggle and campaigning. Already before achieving the new status as members of a disadvantaged minority, *hasidim* had benefited from such federal programs as food stamps aiding more than 50 percent of the population of Williamsburg who had to depend on official and unofficial assistance to meet their basic needs. Even those who earned a modest income were de facto depending on these programs because of the large size of their households and the high cost of kosher food, clothes, tuition, and medical care. The official recognition under the 1984 charter broadened the availability of vital resources and programs and enabled the hasidic population to meet its most urgent needs.

Perhaps the best known of these projects, which has come to mean so much to the hasidic community's daily life, is the Primary Health Care Center that was established with the help of, and is now run by, the office of the ODA. It is constantly adding new departments to provide for ever more of the medical needs of the entire population. At the end of the '80s the Primary Health Care Center was serving over 50,000 patients of all ages. By the beginning of the '90s it had grown so large that it required a spacious new facility near the headquarter of the ODA, which is offers more and new services to approximately 250 patients per day. Its professional staffs are well equipped to deal with the special problems and considerations of the ultra-Orthodox men, women, and children of Williamsburg. Its valuable services are even available on holidays, which are announced regularly in the *Yid*. Patients are charged minimal fees if they can afford them and they are treated totally free if they cannot pay.

Equally important to the health of the hasidic population of Williamsburg is the WIC program, which is also administered by the office of ODA. It takes up the entire ground floor and parts of the other floors of the ODA building. According to Robert A. Mosbacher, the U.S. Secretary of Commerce, who visited it at the occasion of its fifteenth anniversary, it is "one of the best of the community social organizations in the country." It has a large staff of specialists who take care of the needs of pregnant women and their infants before and after giving birth. The office distributes a great deal of money and directs a basic health and nutritional program that is vital for the hasidic families because of the absence of birth control and abortion.

Another very important division of health services directed by the ODA is that of home care for the elderly and ill. It provides vital care to over one thousand people who are homebound and cannot care for themselves. They reside not only in the immediate vicinity but in the adjoining areas of low-income residents, where there is a high percentage of indigent and aged who would not get proper care if not for the highly competent personnel of the Home Care for the Elderly, administered by the ODA of Williamsburg. Here, too, the attention given to the elderly is particularly vital to the hasidic patients because not all of the home care personnel are aware of or can deal properly with the special needs of their charges.

The importance of food stamps, medicare, and medicaid programs for the needy of Williamsburg becomes evident when one visits the local pharmacies, shoe stores, and children's clothes stores, for example. Almost unanimously their owners assert that as many as 60 percent of their customers depend on these governmental programs in order to be able to take proper care of their usually large families. As they emphasize, most of their customers in need are the elderly or young scholars still engaged in advanced study, or those who have recently embarked on a career and are not yet in the position to meet the heavy burden of their family budget. Said one local druggist:

> Many a time older brothers or sisters of babies come with the prescription or want to pick it up. Their mothers are tied down with the infants and other small children. Often they ask that we wait for the payment, if they don't have the forms for Medicaid. Not infrequently, after our messengers have been in the home and have seen the situation, we give them the medication free. They purchase all the items they need for their babies and children of all ages; and you can see it is a real burden for them. Thank God for the government programs; otherwise, I don't know how many of these women with so many children would be able to manage.

Another man, the owner of a local shoe store, stressed that a high percent of the parents come in with a number of children. Even if he charges them the lowest possible prices, they walk out with bills amounting to hundreds of dollars. Without the government aid they would not be able to keep their children in shoes. "And these are items," he emphasized, "on which you cannot save. Children are growing, and for the holidays once or twice a year they must have proper clothes and shoes." If one adds to these basic needs the cost of providing outfits for the adults as well, one realizes the vital function of financial support even now, when a higher percent of the hasidic population of Williamsburg has at least a moderate income. Only in a community that assumes responsibility for the needy is it possible for them to cope with the constantly rising high costs of living.

Equally important are the programs to alleviate the heavy pressure of inadequate housing in Williamsburg, where rents are high and real estate unaffordable for young people largely because much of the surrounding area is in a poor state. Their houses are vandalized or totally destroyed. Urban renewal, which since 1983 has been clearing large tracts of the dilapidated areas, has eventually made land and funds available for communal and private construction of moderate and low-cost housing. Since the '60s five large public and one privately financed housing project were built to ease the local housing shortage. These did much to benefit the hasidic population as well as the members of racial and ethnic minorities living in Williamsburg and the adjoining areas. Both groups of residents are still vying for their "turf," their fair share of the units, each one claiming the other has improperly managed to gain greater access to housing made available by the government or by privately subsidized construction.

Since 1987, the much touted City Partnership, established by former mayor Ed Koch between the City of New York and the hasidic and the Latino communities, is distributing the rights to construct houses and homes for moderate- and low-income members of both groups of residents with the help of funds made available from the sale of city-owned land in the area. Since one-third of the hasidic community members are still young and have large families but want to remain in the neighborhood close to their families and Rebbes, these strenuous efforts are vital for the stability and future of the community. The leaders, prominent among them the heads of ODA, and others are pouring a great deal of effort into promoting public and private construction, some of which have already borne fruit, and lots are being drawn for new units now under construction, thanks to the help of the City Partnership. By the end of 1991, some of these subsidized projects were nearing completion. In one of these, the so-called Southside Houses, around South Eighth and South Ninth Streets, over 70 hasidic families have been allotted relatively affordable apartments or condominiums, which sell for $45,000 to $65,000, depending on the size and number of bedrooms.

There are also other minor governmental programs, which benefit the most needy, such as the distribution of surplus food or the allotment of funds for heating costs, and other emergency assistance. These are mostly handled by the office of the United Jewish Organizations of Williamsburg.

There is also an active senior citizens' center, which provides regular meals and educational and leisure activities to a large number of elderly men and women. Some of them are members of the old Jewish community of Williamsburg, and other residents of the hasidic community. They are offered regular study classes, taught by volunteers of the neighborhood, and other programs that meet their social and spiritual needs. Although they are ambulatory, these indigent elderly have found a "new home and family," as one of the older men put it when interviewed. He had been one of the active members of the former Orthodox community for many years, but has no one of his family or friends and associates left in the neighborhood. He still lives in his old home, but he appreciates the senior citizens' center because, as he put it, it gives new content to his days, besides providing him with food and physical care.

These types of services and assistance, offered with the help of government funds, are basic to the social welfare of the hasidic community in Williamsburg as in other Jewish and non-Jewish neighborhoods.

Communal and Group Programs

The physical and economic welfare of his *hasidim* was one of, if not *the* most important concern of Rabbi Yoel Teitelbaum, the Rebbe of Satmar, when he started rebuilding his community in Williamsburg. The majority of the newcomers who joined him had been victims of the war, persecution, the Holocaust, and the stressful postwar period. They made it to these shores physically broken, indigent, and without the means to start life again without assistance.

To meet the urgent economic and other basic needs of his hasidim, the Rebbe of Satmar set out to create a network of programs, projects, organizations, and institutions devoted to specific wants of his people. Financial assistance was one of the most urgent. Hence he set up the previously mentioned Million Dollar Revolving Fund, which was provided by some of his more affluent followers among the earlier arrivals in the U.S. and Canada, and other parts of the Jewish world. Many of his *hasidim* required physical care. And above all, they needed jobs in order to acquire the functionality necessary to cope with the realities and difficulties of rebuilding their lives in the radically different environment, but they lacked the basic skills and knowledge to make it on their own. As pointed out throughout, as many as 50 percent of the newcomers were dependent on outside help to be able to sustain their families. Naturally, as the hasidic community concentrated on finding work, it focused on the type of jobs that would allow a maximum of sociocultural isolation, in settings that would not interfere with the requirements of the ultra-Orthodox standards of their life-style.

At the time, it was easier for women to find jobs in such fields as the garment industry, which had traditionally been the salvation of the waves of newcomers in the past hundred years. After all, sewing, cutting, pressing, and other staples of the needle trades required little more than the skills that they had practised in their native countries as homemakers. According to the estimate of the community leaders, as many as half of the women of Hasidic Williamsburg had to leave their homes and children in the morning to travel to the jobs that had provided work for generations of immigrants before and after them. They had no problems if the owners of the factories were observant Jews or if they were willing to have them observe Sabbath and holidays, especially during the winter months. Thus the women were able to contribute much to meeting the budget of their families, while the men were occupied learning trades or seeking opportunities to start out in some phase of business.

Eventually a small number of the newcomers entered the diamond and jewelry trades, which had already been a boon to the newcomers of the post-World-War-II period in the Orthodox community of Williamsburg and elsewhere, quite a few of whom had become diamond cutters and dealers. It was no longer as profitable a trade in the '40s and '50s, when it had contributed much to raise the low standards of life in Williamsburg and elsewhere. Yet, in spite of its highly cyclical and volatile nature, for those fortunate enough to find work and to establish a trade of their own, it was still one of the more lucrative realms open to newcomers. More recently, the jewelry trade has been offering opportunities to capable members of the middle-aged and younger generations of *hasidim*. Quite a few of them work in the uptown centers and in their own and other neighborhoods of Jewish New York. Many of them travel all over the country and seem to have little difficulty dealing with local department and jewelry stores.

Equally important as these determined efforts of the hasidic community to find trade and business openings for their people are the systematic drives of the men's and women's organizations of the various subcommunities in Williamsburg to set up campaigns and projects to raise the vital funds to meet the needs of the constantly growing population. Every issue of the *Yid* is filled with announcements of lunches, auctions, teas, bazaars, *melaveh malkehs*, and banquets run by the various congregational and institutional organizations or by small groups on behalf of institutions, special programs, or projects targeted on some specific need of the population. They range from pregnant women and their infants to widows and orphans, to the indigent and ill in Williamsburg, in the U.S. at large, in Israel, and in other Orthodox centers of the Jewish world. A major portion of these regular and special drives are devoted to help finance the educational systems for boys and girls, for special students, and for the mentally ill or handicapped.

From the plethora of social service and welfare programs that were initiated by the various subcommunities of Williamsburg over the decades, a number have emerged to become hallmarks of the *hesed* orientation of the *hasidim*, though obviously not exclusively theirs. Among the most important of the communal projects that were started by small groups of individuals and that grew to become major organizations are the by now famous *Hatzoloh*, a medical volunteer corps, the *Shomrim*, a volunteer civil patrol, and *Tzedakah Vechesed*, a volunteer organization for the distribution of food to the needy. Above all, there is the broad network of *Bikkur Cholim*, various men's and women's organizations that care for the needs of the ill, at home and in hospitals all over New York, and for the needs of their families.

Teams of volunteers, frequently senior citizens or youngsters, dedicate their spare time to helping patients in such institutions as hospitals for the chronically or terminally ill or nursing homes, whose regular staffs are not always able to cater to the special needs of Orthodox patients. There is also a medical referral service and a host of other services organized by Satmar and other hasidic subcommunities. Then there is also *Pesach Tikvah*, the first institution for Orthodox or hasidic mentally ill or dysfunctional people. Finally, there is *Dor Yeshorim*, an organization for the prevention of genetic diseases, in addition to others that focus on particular needs or problems of the hasidic communities.

One of the first and most important of the organizations that were started in Hasidic Williamsburg is *Hatzoloh*, a medical volunteer emergency corps, which is the largest of its kind in New York State. It was started in response to the crying need for emergency medical help at a time when it became difficult to get professional attention. Physicians were no longer readily available because of shortages of trained personnel to make house calls and offer emergency services, especially at night. Nor were many of the professional and voluntary service staffs able to handle the special needs and requirements of their hasidic patients. It did not take long for the emergency number of *Hatzoloh* to be displayed in every house and home in the neighborhood. The vehicles and crews, which are certified by the state health and police departments, became an integral part of the street life of Williamsburg, as an increasing number of hasidic young men who are well versed in the particular laws and regulations of the *halachah*, the religious prescriptions for dealing with medical emergencies, as with the medical procedures and rules, flocked to join the elite corps of the *Hatzoloh* volunteers. Their efficiency and effectiveness have become recognized by the authorities, as well as the Jewish and non-Jewish communities. To the hasidic ill their very presence means spiritual solace as much as medical help.

It was only a matter of time until other religious neighborhoods of urban and suburban New York asked for help from the Williamsburg *Hatzoloh* to start branches of their own, all of whose activities and services are coordinated by a central office. Under the experienced guidance of Rabbi Edgar Gluck, working from his office in the state police headquarters in the World Trade Center, *Hatzoloh* functions in close coordination and cooperation with the city and state police, and its vehicles are seen and respected everywhere, including in the thickest traffic arteries of mid-Manhattan during the busiest traffic hours. By the middle of the '80s, *Hatzoloh* was handling as many as 25,000 cases annually and established records for the speed of its response time to emergency calls at all hours of the day and the night. Eventually the Jewish communities of Canada, England, and Israel started their own *Hatzoloh* emergency medical volunteer corps patterned after that of Hasidic Williamsburg.

The same readiness to help people in need and to prevent serious problems and tragedies is displayed by the *Shomrim*, the members of the civil emergency patrol. Their vigilance and effective response have contributed much to transform the climate of fear and suspicion in Williamsburg, which had destroyed other similar neighborhoods, into one of the safest in the city. This is true in spite of occasional incidents, such as the murders of a young girl on the way to an early school activity and of a popular rabbi on the way to the early-morning services, both of which were committed by outsiders. Thus, the concern for one's neighbor's welfare is a clear indication of the effectiveness of the *Mobilization for Chesed*, which the Rebbe of Satmar initiated to preserve the neighborhood for his people.

The realm of *hesed* that is most characteristic of the spirit of the hasidic community of Williamsburg is that of *Bikkur Cholim*, the special attention paid to the commandment of visiting sick people and catering to their needs. It has been built into a large network of service organizations, programs, and projects, which were initiated by individuals, family groups, and the men's and women's organizations of the various subcommunities in the neighborhood. Typical of the admiration and recognition which this 36-year-old, multiphased campaign on behalf of the ill and their families receives is the reaction of Rabbi Dr. Charles Spirn, the Jewish Chaplain of Mount Sinai Hospital in Manhattan, who has called *Bikkur Cholim* of Satmar the largest, best, and most effective organization that benefits the patients in his hospital. In his opinion, there has never been such a massive effort made to ease the problems and relieve the concerns of the Jewish sick in this country. This enthusiastic acclaim of *Bikkur Cholim* is highlighted by the fact that as a result of a number of socioeconomic factors the traditional effort of most larger Jewish communities in this country to build and sustain a Jewish hospital in their cities has largely ground to a halt. Mounting costs of hospital care and maintenance have forced most of these Jewish hospitals to become nonsectarian in order to qualify for vital government subsidies. The migration of the Jewish middle- and upper-class communities to the suburbs and exurbia has further decreased this once major effort of the philanthropic Jewish organizations.

In contrast, the *Bikkur Cholim* networks, with their fleets of buses, vans, and teams of volunteers who provide daily help, encouragement, and emotional support not only to the hasidic patients, but to all who request it, are constantly expanding their services and the areas of help commensurate with the growth of the hasidic population. Large numbers of men and women visit hospitals all over Brooklyn and Manhattan to keep the patients company, many of whom have difficulty communicating with the staff, or who do not have family to help them cope not only with the physical, but with the mental anguish and pain. They involve themselves actively in the bureaucratic processes that have become so important in dealing with the governmental and other services, such as Medicare, Medicaid, and various health-care groups and insurances, and are integral concomitants of hospitalization and related care. Three times a day buses, mostly purchased by private donations, leave the hasidic community and, recently, other Orthodox Jewish neighborhoods as well, filled with volunteers going to their assigned stations. Vans pick up sick people from their homes and deliver them to the offices of their doctors or medical institutions, covering vast areas of the city.

Another large group of women has initiated and is sustaining the equally important service of preparing and delivering fresh meals to hasidic and other religious and even nonreligious patients who request them in place of the standard frozen meals whose quality leave much to be desired, according to the testimony of the patients. The large lower floor and basement of a house in the center of Williamsburg, donated by its owner, has been converted into a kitchen facility where the fresh food is prepared every morning. The number of patients receiving this form of *hesed*, of personal care and concern, is growing daily as ever more specially equipped vans expand their daily deliveries of the fresh food to all major hospitals and medical facilities frequented by Jewish patients. A letter in a recent edition of *Der Yid* written by the relative of a patient far from the Jewish community, describes enthusiastically the depth of the services of *Bikkur Cholim*. It did not only deliver tasty fresh food to the patient. A representative first called the family to find out whether there was anything else the patient needed besides food for the regular meals and for snacks for him and his family, plus everything the patient required for Sabbath, such as wine and a *kiddush* cup. All this was in addition to regular visits by members of *Bikkur Cholim*. The writer could not stress enough how this loving care and personal concern helped him and his family to cope with the crisis of hospitalization. This letter is only one of the numerous testimonials received constantly by the offices of *Bikkur Cholim*.

Supplementary services of *Bikkur Cholim*, mentioned before, such as the purchase or leasing of apartments near the hospitals to enable members of the family to remain close to the patients even on Sabbath and holidays, at minimal or no cost, have already been discussed. A more recent addition is the creation of a blood bank at the cost of $60,000, which is staffed and adequately supplied with blood by hasidic volunteers, and which is available to all members of the religious community who require it. Blood mobiles visit the religious communities regularly, to keep the blood bank supplied.

One of the fascinating aspects of the total mobilization for *Bikkur Cholim* has been pointed out in connection with the discussion of the responses of the small survey sample of hasidic women. As attested to by a number of the respondents, the women of Williamsburg have made *Bikkur Cholim*, support for the formal organization and its varied services, as well as of a number of other informal, smaller ones, *their own mitzvah*, their good deed. They take special pride in it even more than in many other *hesed* projects in which they are involved. Small groups or families have made it the target of their personal ambition to find special needs and provide assistance and funding, such as professional and volunteer aid to special types of sick or ailing. The women stress that they join teams that visit hospitals and institutions to help feed or entertain patients, or just to make them feel that they are not alone or abandoned by the world. One of the young, unmarried women in the survey said: "This was perhaps the most impressive learning experience of all the years at school when we went on Friday afternoons to feed some of the old people, some blind, some too sick to feed themselves or to communicate with the staff in the institution. I had to tear myself away from a girl who was lying in a cast, and had no one to come to play with her or read a story to her. There I learned what *hesed* means." Another youngster who visits the Home for the Jewish Incurables expressed the same idea even more dramatically:

> At first it was difficult for me and my friends to help the unfortunate people who are locked in there. Some of them look outright grotesque. But you should see their eyes light up when we come and speak to them, or when we tell them what we are learning in our classes. Nothing we learned in all our *mussar shi'urim*, the lectures on proper moral and ethical behavior, had a deeper impact on us than the gurgling sounds one of the patients makes when he sees us come, when we sit by his bed and just pat his crippled hand, as he reaches out for us. I leave a piece of my heart there every time I must bid him and the other unfortunate patients farewell.

This type of learning by doing is an essential ingredient of the educational approach the Rebbe of Satmar had in mind when he initiated the *Mobilization for Chesed* as the characteristic strategy of coping with the serious obstacles and problems he faced when he started building his community.

The same spirit of selfless devotion to the needs of others resulted in many smaller or larger service groups and organizations initiated by individuals or small groups, such as *Kimpatorin Aid,* assistance to women before and after they give birth, or *Oseh hesed, Yeled shaashuim,* and a number of others dedicated to providing assistance to future mothers, to women before and after birth, and to their infants and families. It motivates the teams of men, women, and single girls who volunteer their services to the aged inmates of *The Aishel Avrohom* nursing home before going to work or in the evening. Only some of the women interviewed, those with large families, did not indicate any form of participation in the work of *Bikkur Cholim* as their favorite social welfare activity. In fact, some of these indicated that once they have more time they, too, would attempt to do their share for the ill, poor, and needy. It did not take long for the women in the other Orthodox Jewish communities, such as Boro Park, Flatbush, or Monsey, to establish branches of *Bikkur Cholim* and the other organizations that provide aid to women and their children.

The second most valuable service organization, next to *Hatzoloh*, is the *Shomrim*, a volunteer civil patrol corps. Like so many of the other services and organizations, it was founded on the initiative of a single *hasid*, a rabbi and store owner. He campaigned for it as a form of self help, in view of the limited control provided by the police, whose district headquarters had been moved from Williamsburg to an area on the other side of Brooklyn Broadway, which is largely occupied by Latinos, blacks, and members of other ethnic or racial groups. The *Shomrim* best represent the spirit of the *hasidim*, discussed before, to refuse to remain passive after the experiences of the Holocaust and the concentration camps. This spirit motivates the *Shomrim* volunteers to make sure that they will never again be subject to the violent attacks and criminal treatment that had plagued this and other older Jewish neighborhoods after the mass influx of members of other minority groups. Its phone number visibly displayed in every house and public facility, the *Shomrim* organization has done an excellent job to control and hold to a minimum the constant attempts at turning Williamsburg into another of the slums ruled by lawlessness and crime.

Other *hesed* organizations that originated in Williamsburg and have found recognition and acclaim, and which have been copied elsewhere, are *Tzedakah Vechesed, Tomche Shabbos*, and similar projects to help the poor and needy. *Tzedakah Vechesed*, charity and kindness, was started by Rabbi Polatchek, a teacher of the yeshivah, in his own home. He solicited help from his family and friends to pack bags of food, and everything else a family requires for the Sabbath meals, on Thursday nights and had them delivered to the doors of the needy before dawn on Friday mornings, so as not to embarrass the recipients. By the end of the '80s *Tzedakah Vechesed* had become a large, citywide organization, with a central office in Manhattan. Large caravans of vans, station wagons, and private cars cross the Jewish neighborhoods, manned by hundreds of volunteers who not only donate funds but their time and personal efforts to ferret out the needy and prepare for them every week, especially on Sabbath and holidays. Yet, it is still Rabbi Polatchek, who in his own inimitable way solicits the necessary funds on special days like Purim. People flock to him, to his customary seat in the *bet hamidrash* of Satmar, to do their share and to provide for his ever expanding project of feeding the hungry and needy who have no one else to care for them.

There are also numerous other, smaller organizations initiated by individuals who target their *hesed* efforts on important causes, such as various *Hachnossas Kalloh* funds, which provide young women from poor families, or orphans, with the necessary money to enable them to get married. In view of the large families of many of the neediest residents of the hasidic community this is a vital project, especially since most of the young girls are intent upon marrying young Torah scholars who will continue their advanced talmudic studies for years after marriage, and even after they have children. And as pointed out throughout, these young *kollel* couples must subsist on minute scholarships and the little that their families can contribute, beyond what the women are able to earn before and between having children. Even if the weddings are kept to a modest minimum, the contributions of the *Hachnossath Kalloh* funds are vital for poor parents who have several daughters to marry off and to set up in their apartments, with the barest minimum of equipment.

In a personal conversation in February 1990, Rabbi Moshe Teitelbaum, the Rebbe of Satmar, remarked that at present there are three hundred of his older *yeshivah* students on his mind for whom the time has come to get married. They are depending on his personal help to find fitting *shidduchim*, brides, to help them get married and set up in their own homes, so that they may be able to continue their studies and qualify for the constantly growing number of religious functionaries' positions, proliferating with the explosion of his community beyond Williamsburg into other urban and suburban neighborhoods. As the Rebbe stressed, these are only his most gifted, most promising young scholars; yet there are so many others who have no one to worry about and for them.

Similarly, there are a number of organizations that focus on such problems as aid to widows and orphans left behind without a provider, of which there are unfortunately a significant number. Other groups are dedicated to helping women get a *get*, the religious divorce document, from the husbands who have deserted them and are using the desperate situation of their former wives to extract large sums of money from their families. Even worse is the situation of wives whose husbands have disappeared without leaving an address, thus making it impossible for them to marry again. As pointed out in the discussion of marriage and divorce, there are significant numbers of such *agunot*, and there are specialists and groups who exclusively devote themselves to the halachic and human aspects of this tragic problem.

One area of major concern that had traditionally not received much attention in the hasidic or in the Orthodox and non-Orthodox communities is that of mental health. Long after the broader community had become open to discussion and the need for confronting the problems of the mentally ill and the emotionally disturbed, Jewish people were still rather reluctant to acknowledge and deal effectively with this realm because of the vestiges of the stigma attached to mental illness. Even after Jews had become prominent in the study and treatment of mental illness in this century, and preeminent in various forms of treatment, and after psychiatry and psychotherapy had emerged as socially acceptable, the hasidic community continued to avoid paying proper attention to this vital area of treatment. Even after the Holocaust and the years of persecution and insecurity had increased the urgent need for help to the victims, they preferred to deal with the normal and extraordinary traumas of the survivors in their traditional fashion, relying on the strength of the family and the help of the Rebbe and his prayers.

The obvious reason for the rejection of psychotherapy, especially psychoanalysis, is, of course, the trend among most mental-health professionals to blame religious restrictions and the observance of the laws of the Torah for various types of complexes, mental disturbances, and emotional traumas, in addition to the resultant disabilities and dysfunctions. Any cure that depends on the relaxing of the religious standards and life-style of the *hasidim* was automatically unacceptable. Fortunately there has been a significant increase of highly qualified mental-health professionals who are themselves products of an intense religious education and who have developed techniques and approaches that enable their patients, including *hasidim*, to cope with their ills and problems. They do not resort to the usual negative attitude toward religion and to cures that would create conflicts with the central values and practices of Orthodox beliefs.[4]

It took extraordinary efforts by Rabbi Chaim Moshe Stauber, one of the community leaders, to overcome the usual stigma of shame and rejection of professional treatment in all but extreme cases of illness to create a more positive attitude. With the approval of the Rebbe of Satmar and other leaders he established proper facilities for the treatment of mental illness. What started as a department in the Primary Health Care Center became *Pesach Tikvah*, the Gate of Hope, a full-fledged institution that soon became recognized as a highly effective health organization not only in Williamsburg, but as a center of treatment for mentally ill of the broader religious community of New York. Working closely with the Woodhull Clinic for the seriously ill, *Pesach Tikvah* has proven remarkably successful in expanding its services and adjusting its treatment to the needs of Orthodox patients with the help of a competent staff of professionals, most of whom are Orthodox themselves. Hence they understand the problems and can gauge the feasibility and effectiveness of various types of treatment. According to the report of Rabbi Stauber, its director, *Pesach Tikvah*, which has moved to large, new quarters at the edge of the Jewish Triangle, works with more than two hundred cases in the clinic, which translates into approximately six hundred visits per month. Its day-care facility was treating forty patients with severe problems of mental and emotional disturbances and different stages of retardation. About fifty patients are receiving some vocational training in the *Pesach Tikvah* workshop shelter, where they learn to handle simple jobs like packaging, which will enable them to gain a feeling of achievement and self-esteem, while earning minimal wages. *Pesach Tikvah* also maintains two community residences. One accommodates twenty-four mentally ill male patients. The other cares for fourteen women, 16 and up, who are moderately functional. Several of the latter receive some education at the Brooklyn School for Special Children.

The most recent program initiated by *Pesach Tikvah* in its new headquarters is devoted to family therapy. Only a short time after its establishment, Rabbi Stauber reports such results as the saving of more than two dozen marriages that had seriously been strained by mental problems. This department has separate facilities with its own entrance to avoid embarrassing its clients.

Thus, *Pesach Tikvah* has become one of the major services of the hasidic community to its residents and, beyond it, to the entire Jewish Orthodox community of New York, which still suffers from the antireligious approach of psychotherapists and the inability of most of the prestigious institutions for the mentally ill to accommodate the needs of strictly observant patients. The growing number of Orthodox psychiatrists and psychologists, graduates from the finest universities, has eased the problems. Yet, it took the initiative of the hasidic community of Williamsburg to pioneer the institutional network of *Pesach Tikvah*, with the full approval of the Rebbe of Satmar and the other Orthodox leaders, to successfully confront one of the most serious problems of the religious community in the post-Holocaust era.

A related area of social welfare to which the hasidic community of Williamsburg has paid attention, especially since the '60s, is the care of their "special children" who require education adjusted to their various types of physical and mental disabilities. Although the emphasis of the hasidic schools' approach is to mainstream as many of their students as possible and as soon as their disabilities do not interfere with their emotional, intellectual, and social growth, it was inevitable for the heads of the hasidic school systems to realize that there are children whose handicaps require special approaches, special equipment, and trained teachers who know how to handle their physical and emotional problems in small group settings that allow for a maximum of individual attention. Fortunately, the heads of the hasidic schools, through their excellent relations with the local school board, have been able to offer such programs, with the help of specialists from the public schools. One large group of severely handicapped children in their early teens meets daily in specially equipped rooms in the local school district building. They are brought there in the morning by buses and returned to their base schools in the afternoon. Other groups are instructed in their own school buildings by specially trained teachers, after an attempt to place classes of handicapped girls in an unused section of the local public school was foiled by the resistance of the P.T.A.

Naturally, the administrators and parents prefer to have the handicapped special children in their own schools for the sake of their self-image and their progress in their Jewish studies, in the atmosphere that is most conducive to their well-being. When we visited one of the school buildings of Satmar, we observed quite a few youngsters in wheelchairs and specially equipped, self-propelled vehicles. Not only did these students get around on their own, they also participated in games with the other students. When questioned about the advisability of exposing both the functional and the handicapped youngsters to the painful contrast, the principal remarked enthusiastically:

> This is as good an opportunity to practice *hesed*, loving care and concern for one's fellow being, as any. They learn to accept each other, to be considerate and as helpful as possible, and to make those less fortunate feel as equals. And the youngsters with handicaps and disabilities learn that their special problems do not isolate them socially and that they can be functional. This is learning by doing and coping with one's challenge.

The easy give-and-take between the students in the large playground substantiated this approach, and the therapeutic value of the mutual exposure and atmosphere of friendship and understanding.

The largest and most important institution created by the hasidic community of Williamsburg for its special children is *Chush*, or *Yeshivas Limudei Hashem*, which in the decade since its founding has proven quite successful in its innovative, creative efforts to work with learning-disabled and handicapped youngsters from preschool age to a post-high-school class. Recently *Chush* added an early childhood division for boys between 3 and 7, which is under the direction of one of its creative teachers. Its staff has designed special equipment, such as computer software for its Hebrew studies, which enables the students to progress and gain self-respect as they learn to master some of the standard texts studied in the hasidic *yeshivot*, and which otherwise would have remained inaccessible to them. They are allowed to work with computers on an individual basis and to develop skills that may come in handy when they leave, after they have mastered what for them is an individually prepared curriculum of Hebrew and secular studies. The teachers of the advanced classes take a great deal of pride in the relatively large number of students whom they have been able to get ready to be mainstreamed in the regular classes of the *yeshivah*.

There are also a number of other programs designed to meet the needs of both male and female youngsters with special physical, mental, and emotional problems. Not only has there been a special school set up for girls, which meanwhile meets in the *Chush* building but which is to move into a special building that is being built in Boro Park by Satmar and other hasidic groups. There is *Eis Laasot*, literally "time to act," the Williamsburg Infant and Early Childhood Development Center, which has already set up branches in other Orthodox communities such as Boro Park, where it has also established a program for children with Downs Syndrome, the only one of its kind in the Orthodox Jewish community. A program for blind children is located in one of the elementary-school buildings in the heart of Williamsburg. *Eis Laasot* also offers clinical therapy for young children, which is directed by the wife of one of the hasidic leaders from one of the famous dynasties in Poland and Hungary.

It is not accidental, in the light of the developments discussed before, that one finds in the *Yid* frequent announcements of special meetings and workshops for mothers of children with learning and emotional problems. They are addressed mostly by Orthodox experts, many of them Orthodox women who have made a name for themselves as counselors, therapists, and family workers. Obviously, there is a great deal of interest, need, and concern among the mothers of the hasidic community who are seeking understanding and proper advice or professional help from competent sources to enable their children to function normally.

Group and Individual Projects

While the large governmental and communal programs and projects, organizations, and institutions have contributed much to the social, physical, mental, and socio-economic welfare of the population, one would be remiss not to mention numerous group and individually generated projects. In the words of one of the spokesmen of Hasidic Williamsburg, they have become more than isolated efforts. They are, as he put it, a hallmark of the general *hesed* orientation of the *hasidim* in the neighborhood. They fill gaps and lags in the broad texture of the services offered by the community on every level of community life. At the same time they reflect the intensity of the mutual concern that has become the strongest force binding the people together in a network of groups and organizations. Each of these small groups has one or more leaders, prominent men or women who make the projects their personal vehicle for contributing to the welfare of others. In turn, this social activism provides them with a chance to make a name for themselves as they run affairs in their own homes or in large places that attract crowds in support of their causes. Every issue of the *Yid* is filled with announcements of various groups, which publicize their luncheons, auctions, bazaars, or teas, not only the stock in trade of fund-raising for specific causes but a major part of the social life, especially of the women in the hasidic community, who combine leisure with fulfilling a *mitzvah*.

One such characteristic *hesed* organization is *Mesamches es Halev*, meaning "making hearts rejoice." Its members and sponsors devote their efforts to easing the plight of widows and orphans. In their latest report, they state that by 1990 they were working with a caseload of about eighty widows, their children, and with orphans who were left in care of strangers. It is typical for a *hesed*-oriented community that in spite of the major foci of the large programs to which the neighborhood devotes its strongest efforts, there will be individuals or small family groups that devote themselves to the "small" problems that mean so much to their unfortunate victims. They focus on the *tza'ar*, pain and suffering, of other human beings whom Providence has deprived of those who mean most to them. Usually in a community that is characterized by strong family ties, such personal needs are best handled by the intimate group. But in a community that is beset by severe socioeconomic problems that require the concerted efforts of the leaders and the people themselves, it takes a great deal of sensitivity and humanity to search out and be supportive to little-known men, women, and children in need. Hence, these small groups serve a vital function, which goes deeper than the broad organizations that work in the limelight. A number of such groups dedicate their efforts to enabling young girls from poor families to get married, providing them with all they need to set up their homes, including the funds for a modest wedding.

Another such organization, which started out small but has expanded to serve a vital function, is *Ezrat Nashim*, which concerns itself with helping married women cope with health, economic, and management problems. Another is *Atzas Sholom*, which, as the name implies, focuses on families with marital problems. Others specifically devote themselves to helping couples in trouble either to work out their problems or to taking care of couples about to be divorced, especially in cases where children are involved or when illness and poverty complicate the already unhappy situations. Several formal and informal family courts have been established by groups or individuals to help settle disputes, serious conflicts, and divorce cases. Since many of the hasidic marriages are entered into at a very young age, and since there is no birth control, undue stress and strain are bound to develop, especially if the husbands are still studying in a *kollel*, or have just embarked on learning a trade or are starting out in business. Hence, it is not surprising that one such family court set up by the rabbi of one of the congregations to saving marriages in trouble reports having dealt with four hundred cases.

Other, similar organizations, discussed in detail in chapter 4, deal with such problems as helping women to obtain a *get*, the divorce document without which she cannot get married again, in cases when husbands refuse or move away without leaving their addresses. One volunteer, who made a name for himself in handling the halachic, legal and technical, problems of difficult divorce cases, and who is called in on divorce proceedings not only in New York, but in other Orthodox Jewish communities throughout the country, indicated that though there is a significant increase in divorces or family breakups among *hasidim* and Orthodox Jews in general, he considers the reports of large numbers grossly exaggerated. According to his estimate, there is no more than a 15 percent divorce rate in Orthodox and hasidic families as of the beginning of the '90s. According to his estimate, there are also not more than a thousand cases of women who are *agunot*, deserted by husbands who are unwilling to give them a *get*, in the U.S. It is, however, no wonder that institutions like *Pesach Tikvah* have set up special services to help families in stress.

Another organization that serves families, in particular, women before and after giving birth, is *Kimpatorin Aid*. It consists of a group of competent women who have years of experience in handling housework and in raising children. They volunteer their services to women after they give birth, are confused, upset, or suffering from postpartum depression and other psychological problems. They stay with them, helping them to organize their old and new chores efficiently until they have recovered sufficiently to resume their duties as mothers and housewives. The annual 1992 report of *Kimpatorin Aid* indicates that in the few years they have been in existence they have already helped over 2,500 such women. They are not professionals, but enthusiastic volunteers who spread the information of their availability to those in need of help 24 hours a day, "just because we care," as one of their leaders said. Another one of these smaller organizations is *Ezrat Nashim*, Women's Help. Yet another offers a broader range of aid and relief projects, especially to women and their families before and after the arrival of a new baby; it is called *Oseh Hesed*, people who want to do *hesed*.

Obviously, the fact that there are so many of these small social welfare organizations founded by members of various hasidic and nonhasidic subcommunities indicates the broad range of the *Mobilization for Chesed*, initiated by the Rebbe of Satmar. It has become a preoccupation of the residents of Williamsburg, and has been taken up by other communities and groups as well.

Finally, one of the most fascinating organizations that evolved in Williamsburg, and which still has its center there although its work has spread far and wide across the broad range of religious Jewish communities in the U.S., is *Dor Yeshorim*, a service dedicated to "healthy future generations." It represents a major effort of the hasidic community to come to grips with the specter of genetic and other crippling diseases, which modern science has studied intensively and which may be prevented if detected early enough. *Dor Yeshorim* devotes itself to spreading valuable information about health and disease to the public. It offers systematic testing programs in the centers of larger Jewish communities, not only in the hasidic neighborhoods. Its volunteers and professionals focus on such sicknesses as Tay-Sachs, which has been found to afflict Jewish people more than other groups. Synagogue bulletin boards everywhere display news items and announcements of dates and locations of semiannual testing programs arranged by *Dor Yeshorim*. Its volunteer physicians give public lectures and their leaflets provide valuable information about vital health problems and diseases that may affect the future generations.

Dor Yeshorim is the type of health organization, like *Pesach Tikvah*, *Hatzoloh*, and *Bikkur Cholim*, that demonstrates the readiness of the hasidic community to make full use of all possible means on behalf of the physical welfare of its people, unlike other extreme fundamentalist churches, which reject the advances of modern medicine as contrary to their religion. These major efforts to safeguard the health of the future of their people with the help of the finest professionals and the most advanced methods of medical science have the wholehearted support of the Rebbe of Satmar and the other heads of the hasidic communities.

Quite in keeping with this approach of the hasidic community is its openness to what may benefit the mental welfare of its young. As one mental-health counselor expressed it, after having directed several workshops for hasidic mothers:

> I was deeply impressed by the seriousness and the openness of these women dressed strictly in line with the hasidic life-style. Contrary to what I had expected, they wanted to know everything I could tell them about the emotional and mental problems their children may encounter, and how to cope with them. This workshop in one of the hasidic girls' schools was one of the most interesting, frank, and valuable experiences I had in years of working with groups of concerned parents.

Hesed Projects for Institutions in Foreign Countries

Jewish Williamsburg, like other American Jewish communities, has always been called upon to support all kinds of causes, especially institutions, Jewish political organizations, and projects in Israel, in Eastern Europe before the Holocaust, and elsewhere. The *Mobilization for Chesed* in the hasidic community is doing equally well on behalf of the needs of the Orthodox and hasidic community in Israel, and in other countries. If anything, it has heightened its intensive work for *yeshivot* and the other religious school systems, and religious and ritual institutions that are proliferating daily in Israel, commensurate with the growing needs of its old and new population of immigrants from the far corners of the world, such as the Ethiopians, Rusians, and Iranian Jews who are flocking there by the thousands.

Hasidic Williamsburg is particularly concerned with the welfare of the institutions of the Old Yishuv, which do not get any support from the state or from the usual American sources and depend solely on their sympathizers among the hasidic groups that follow the ideology of Satmar. Since the Rebbe of Satmar is also the official rabbinic head of the *Aidah Charedit*, the independent community of hasidic and nonhasidic congregations and institutions, which do not accept any support from the Israeli government, they are practically part of the *hesed* campaigns of Williamsburg. Regular and special programs, appeals, and annual campaigns keep them in the forefront of the institutions to which all subcommunities devote their efforts and resources. A constant interchange of the dignitaries of Williamsburg and the leaders of the Old Yishuv and its official bodies keep the populations of both ultra-Orthodox communities well informed and the active support on a high level.

A second type of charity for institutions in foreign countries is devoted to the centers of Satmar and other hasidic movements in England, Belgium, Austria, and Latin America. Frequent articles in the *Yid*, followed by full-page ads, are part of the regular fare of the large readership and keep their interest and readiness to invest in their progress not only because they are part of the same world movement. One of the fascinating outgrowths is the growing trend of the intermarriage of the children of the prominent rabbis, Rebbes, and heads of the institutions, which are featured almost weekly in the ad pages of the *Yid*. Concurrent with this trend is the active exchange of students on the higher levels, which is creating an international community of young scholars who are being groomed to become future rabbis, heads of congregations, institutions, and religious organizations in the expanding hasidic centers. Hence, these hasidic communities in London, Antwerp, Vienna, or Buenos Aires, and so many others, are very much part of Williamsburg. The annual and special affairs run by or for them are regular features of the social calendar of the members of Satmar and the other hasidic groups. Their *pushkes*, collection boxes, are part of the batteries that grace every home in the hasidic neighborhoods throughout the U.S., as in their home countries.

Equally important is the wholehearted support given to the organizations established by the Rebbe of Satmar and other hasidic leaders, such as the Sukulener Rebbe, to provide emergency help to hasidic and nonhasidic populations whose survival is threatened in their native lands, such as Iran, Russia, or Romania. Foremost among these organizations are *Rav Tov* and *Yad L'Ahim*. As stressed before, Satmar and the other Hungarian hasidic movements do not focus on outreach to nonreligious Jews, as do Lubavitch and other hasidic and nonhasidic movements.

Rather, they concentrate on the intensive education of their own youth. Yet when the developments of the post-Holocaust era increasingly threatened the very existence of parts of the Jewish people as in Iran, Russia, and Ethiopia, the Rebbe of Satmar responded by establishing *Rav Tov* and making it a major rescue organization, devoted to the spiritual as well as the physical assistance of Jewish refugees. *Rav Tov* helps them escape, find temporary shelter, and facilitates their eventual permanent immigration and resettlement in the Holy Land or in the U.S.

Founded in 1973, *Rav Tov* grew to become one of the most respected rescue organizations, recognized by the State Department and the Red Cross for its resourceful work. In the two decades of its assistance to the unfortunate victims of persecution in Iran, Russia, and other countries, it has helped over 10,000 men, women, and their families in their escapes. It has built temporary shelters, schools, and training centers in Austria, Italy, and in Israel. It has provided them with food, clothes, and jobs. Its emissaries have established contacts with the authorities in the countries of transit and of resettlement to ease the problems of temporary and permanent immigration. And it continues to work with the new arrivals, helping with their economic and social adjustment in Israel and the U.S. More recently, *Rav Tov* has concentrated on the mass immigration of Russian Jews, as it expanded into a mass exodus, and is working actively with thousands of them, many of whom have no or very little knowledge of the basic facts of their Jewish heritage. Thus, they not only provide for their physical well-being, but pour much effort into their Jewish education. Special funds have been created and are supported by the hasidic communities of Williamsburg and elsewhere, such as the *Keren Lemozon Ulehalboshoh Veshiurei Hatorah*, the fund for food, clothes, and religious instruction, which aids Russian immigrants from the moment of their arrival in the airports, taking over from their emissaries who officially and unofficially help to arrange their emigration. Unlike some of the other, large immigrant aid organizations in Israel and the U.S., they emphasize spiritual as well as physical and economic assistance. Strong efforts are made in the main centers of settlement of the Russian newcomers for their and their children's Jewish education by such organizations as *Hatzoloh* and *Kiruv Ruchanit* in New York and elsewhere.

Another organization that originated in the hasidic community and has made a name for its relief and outreach activities is *Yad L'Ahim*, literally, lending a hand to brothers. It garners a great deal of support among *hasidim* and non-*hasidim* for its programs for needy old-timers and newcomers among the immigrants in Israel. Equally important and famous for its decades of rescue work for Romanian Jews is *Hesed L'Avrohom*, founded by the previous Sukulener Rebbe, Rabbi I. A. Portugal, who was himself incarcerated for his rescue efforts and who, even while he was in prison, nevertheless continued his emergency aid. His *hasidim* and admirers tell legends of his heroic efforts on behalf of others, which he continued and expanded after his release and immigration to the U.S. His son, whose headquarters in the very heart of Williamsburg is a beehive of activity, continues his father's relief and rescue work, as well as the spiritual guidance of his many followers. After the recent revolution in Romania, many of the secret rescue efforts carried out by officials and volunteers upon the initiative of the Sukulener Rebbe and often financed by him and his associates have come to light. His admirers emphasize, however, that much will never be revealed because of the sensitive dealings involving important political figures. And of course many of the benefactors who helped get victims released from prison, or helped to smuggle them out of the country, are no longer alive. They have taken the secret of their rescue with them to their graves in Israel or in the U.S.

These are just a few of the major and minor programs and projects or organizations on behalf of the victims of oppression and misfortune that have originated in

Hasidic Williamsburg and have gained the recognition and full support of the broader hasidic and Orthodox nonhasidic communities. One of the women interviewed about her interest in such *chesed* work said:

> We who have gone through similar experiences not so long ago have been charged by our *Heiliger* Rebbe to show that we have learned our lesson. That it is a privilege, rather than an obligation incumbent upon us, to share with others whatever the Divine Providence has blessed us with. Nothing that we will ever do can measure up to the miracle of our survival from the very fires of *Gehinnom*. We have to show our gratitude by action, by devoting our resources, time, and efforts on behalf of those who are less fortunate and who look to us for help.

This is the spirit of the *Mobilization for Chesed*, which has made the survival and renaissance of the hasidic community of Williamsburg possible, after most observers had considered it doomed, and its glorious history a memory recorded in the annals of contemporary American Jewish life.

SUMMARY

Few of the chapters of this report on the renaissance of the hasidic community of Williamsburg have the dynamic impact of this summary of the formal and informal social services and social welfare programs and projects devoted to the needs of its residents. What makes it so effective is the light it throws on the forces and factors that triggered the amazing survival and growth of this old neighborhood after it had been written off for all practical purposes.

As in most other phases of the community life, the major force was the Rebbe of Satmar, his vision, and his impact on the life of his *hasidim*, as he set out to mobilize them into a task force devoted to the improvement of the standards of life and the welfare of the needy. Even the most sanguine of his followers could not have anticipated the degree or scale of his success in this enterprise. His indomitable faith, which would not brook any compromise in the pursuit of his objectives and goals, regardless of cost and obstacles, provided the impetus to achieve the near impossible. In spite of crises and threats that drove others out of the neighborhood to safer, better communities, he and the leaders of other subcommunities never let up in their determined efforts to overcome a high degree of poverty among their followers, most of whom were survivors from the Holocaust and post-Holocaust traumas.

Rabbi Yoel Teitelbaum initiated major campaigns to create opportunities and develop centers of training for trades and business that allowed his *hasidim* eventually to start life all over again. The practical key to his success was the strategy of mobilizing his people into devoting their best efforts and resources to projects and programs of *chesed*, care and concern, for the physical and mental well-being of their neighbors. It became a central theme of his preaching and teaching, and the focus of the moral education of the thousands of his male and female students in the schools he continued to build and expand. It affected every phase of community life, and it produced a broad network of sociopolitical structures, which opened access to the resources of governmental help, which were to play a major role in the revitalization of the socioeconomic welfare of the hasidic community of Williamsburg.

The result of this multipronged effort was the development of a broad range of social services, organizations, and institutions, which have radically changed the life and life-style of the hasidic community. The most important of the sociopolitical achievements was the breakthrough that allowed the opening of the channels to the vital federal, state, and city programs, the official recognition of the hasidic community as a disadvantaged minority in 1984. Equally important for the welfare of the residents of the neighborhood was the organization of major and minor social services, such as *Hatzoloh, Bikkur Cholim,* the *Shomrim,* and a host of others, to meet specific needs and problems of the population of Williamsburg. Their achievements led to their recognition and acceptance in other hasidic and nonhasidic communities in New York and beyond.

In retrospect, it was the vision, the charisma, and the organizational efforts of the outstanding hasidic leaders, foremost among them Rabbi Yoel Teitelbaum, the Old Rebbe of Satmar, and his successor, which powered the multiphased offensive on the problems of the neighborhood. Eventually, it succeeded in overcoming crises and threats on behalf of a secure present and, hopefully, of a safe and prosperous future for its three-generational community.

❧❧❧❦❦❦

Summary Conclusion

My original report (1961) in this longitudinal study of the Jewish community of Williamsburg since before World War II concluded with somewhat pessimistic questions about the ability of this old Jewish neighborhood to survive in the face of major crises. In contrast, this report on the developments of the last three decades culminates with an optimistic projection of the viability of the three-generational hasidic community of Williamsburg, a quarter of a century after gloomy predictions of its doom.

Essentially, this study has pinpointed the following major factors as having transformed the very foundations of life and created a sound structure for the continuing functionality of this unique community as it enters the last decade of the century with faith in its future, despite ever new problems and threats to its survival.

1. The central role of the religious values and the hasidic ideology in the structure and dynamics of the hasidic community of Williamsburg.
2. The dominant role of the Rebbe of Satmar and other Hungarian hasidic leaders in the life of their followers.
3. The return of the synagogue to its traditional place at the center of the hasidic community and the status of the rabbi to the highest social level by virtue of his scholarship and authority in all matters of ritual and religious law.
4. The crucial role of the demographics, the unflagging population explosion, as the younger generations choose to remain in Williamsburg, despite disadvantages and hardships it imposes on their life-style.
5. The increasing share of middle-aged and young *hasidim* in the conduct of most aspects of the organizational and institutional life of the community.
6. The focus on intensive Jewish education of the young and on lifelong Torah study of the adults.
7. The corollary concentration on careers in business and trades rather than on the higher professions, which require intensive secular education.

259

8. Political activism and involvement in the political processes on the city, state, and federal levels.
9. The continuous intensive efforts of the community to alleviate the critical housing shortage with the help of governmental programs and private investment.
10. The mobilization of the community on behalf of the social welfare of its residents.

These are the factors responsible for the survival and growth of the hasidic community of Williamsburg and for its socioeconomic and sociopolitical strength: they augur well for its future as a unique American hasidic community.

❧❧❧❧❧❧

Appendix A: The Voice of Williamsburg: Mass Media in a Hasidic Community[1]

The editor of *Der Yid*, the voice of Williamsburg Jewry and of Satmar Hasidism and its anti-Zionist stand, would probably agree with the sociological view that the power of a newspaper comes not from the number of people it reaches, but from the role it plays in the communal organization. It is in these terms that the editor of *Der Yid* may be justified in suggesting, as he did in a recent interview, that *"Der Yid* is perhaps the most influential Jewish publication today."

This claim sounds almost ludicrous given a circulation of 30,000, of which 25,000 are sold in Brooklyn's Williamsburg and on 120 newsstands in the rest of Brooklyn and Manhattan.[2] Of the remaining 5,000 copies, 2,000 are shipped to Israel; the rest go to Canada, England, Belgium, France, Austria, Latin America, and the Orthodox Jewish centers of the United States outside of New York. Impressive as these figures are, they do not match the circulation of *The Jewish Press*, for example, with over 100,000 readers, and other Jewish political or regional publications with large readerships, such as the *Hadassah* magazine.

What then is the source of the extraordinary strength of *Der Yid* and its effectiveness as a medium of molding public opinion, verified by this observer in over 250 interviews with men, women, and adolescents of the hasidic community of Williamsburg? The answer lies in the very texture of the social structure and dynamics of the community and its unique life-style. *Der Yid* was founded in 1953 as an offshoot of the venerable Yiddish *Daily Morning Journal* by Dr. Aaron Rosmarin, one of the latter's most prominent writers, after the demise of the *Morning Journal* in the wake of the radical decline in the Yiddish-reading public. A few years later it was chosen by the famous hasidic leader and renowned scholar, the late Satmar Rebbe, Rabbi Yoel Teitelbaum, as the official voice of his *kehillah*, Yetev Lev of Satmar, which he had reestablished in Williamsburg in 1947 after his escape from a concentration camp and a brief sojourn in Palestine. In a relatively short time the founder of a distinctive school of Hungarian Hasidism more than 70 years ago in Satmar (Satu Mare), the Hungarian town that gave his hasidic movement its name, developed the new American Satmar as a center of contemporary Hasidism, with branches in the major communities of the Orthodox Jewish world. True to Rabbi Teitelbaum's ideological commitment, *Der Yid* became the center of the most forceful, outspoken, religious anti-Zionism.

The extraordinary charisma and ideological consistency of this sage of Williamsburg attracted hundreds and thousands of followers, in spite of the strong animosity harbored against him by the broader Jewish public because of his sharp, unmitigated opposition to the secular State of Israel. To the growing flock of his *hasidim*, Rabbi Yoel Teitelbaum was *der Heiliger* Rebbe whose every wish was a command, and whose directions and instructions were accepted without question or doubt. Thus he was able to implant his fervor, zeal, and strong stance in all matters of Jewish ritual, communal, and political affairs in his *hasidim*. At the time of his death in 1979, these numbered close to 40,000 in New York,[3] and many more thousands in the other Orthodox Jewish centers of America, Israel, and the surviving Jewish world. Through the force of his personality and convictions, he created on the unlikely American soil a hasidic community that combines the most rigorous type of Hungarian Hasidism, with its emphasis on cultural otherness and social isolation, with such characteristic American values as pioneering, self-help, and entrepreneurship. Doomsday pundits had thought Hasidism buried with the destruction of its vast population reservoirs during the Holocaust, and denied any future to the attempts of the few surviving leaders to reestablish their movements in America. However, such Rebbes as the Satmarer and the Lubavitcher proved the viability of contemporary Hasidism beyond the gradually vanishing generation of the survivors of the Holocaust in this country.

In fact, the very source of the strength and assurance of the survival of the Satmar community in Williamsburg and Kiryas Joel, its exurban center in Monroe, upstate New York, is the determination of its young to remain there. The children – eight or nine per family of childbearing age[4] – fill old and new school buildings as fast as they are opened. The educational systems for boys and girls, from day-care centers to institutes of advanced study, the *kollelim*, constitute what is probably the largest single Jewish religious school system, adding two new classes per month. According to current figures there are a total of 28,000 boys, girls, and young men and women in Satmar institutions, of whom 15,000 are in Williamsburg, close to 4,000 in Monroe, 1,800 in Monsey, New York, and 4,400 boys and girls in the Boro Park, Brooklyn branches of the system.[5]

The nature of the Satmar *kehillah* and its sociocultural milieu are major factors of the effectiveness of *Der Yid*, substantiating the claim of its editor. Rabbi Yoel Teitelbaum set out to make it the *moreh derech*, a major educational tool to mold the thinking and affect the communal participation of its followers. His absolute authority and forthright espousal of his views in all matters of local, national, and international concern, albeit unpopular in most of the Israel-oriented nonreligious and religious world, were enough to assure the success and effectiveness of *Der Yid*.

There is a still broader and deeper basis for the powerful impact of *Der Yid* beyond the normal range of the media. It, too, originates in the charismatic power of the

Satmar Rebbe to mold the total milieu of his community and its hasidic life-style to such a degree that it makes the impression of an anachronism to an uninitiated observer. The tourists who visit Williamsburg regularly, loaded down with cameras, tape recorders, and gross misconceptions, experience a journey into the exotic East European *shtetl,* romanticized and popularized by the writings of Martin Buber, Abraham Heschel, Elie Wiesel, and the growing scores of interpreters and misinterpreters of the wealth and depths of hasidic lore and legend.

"We are not an exotic lost tribe of Israel," commented a spokesman of Williamsburg and of Satmar recently as we observed a group of curious, kind-hearted tourists. They leisurely walked up and down busy Lee Avenue, dressed in their summer garb that seemed equally exotic in the eyes of the locals in their long, dark hasidic outfits. The visitors were gooing and gawing, patting the cheeks of little boys with dangling blond and black *peyot,* and also asking serious questions. "We are sober, hard-working people who want to live a decent, proper life," he continued, "like our parents and grandparents in Hungary or Poland, a life consistent with our hasidic beliefs, in the midst of a secular world rent by immorality and generation gaps, revolutions, and perversions that threaten the very survival of our Jewish heritage. As you can see, we have no generation gap here. The only missing generation is the one that perished in the concentration camps and the ghettos. If anything, our children are even more enthusiastic in their hasidic beliefs, and have an equal, if not a better and more intensive, Torah education. They are *Bnei Torah* who are successful businessmen, skilled workers, tradesmen, or *melamdim,* teachers on all levels. They are fighting to show that one does not have to yield an iota of one's beliefs and of the hasidic life-style while participating in the opportunities offered in mainstream America." Another Williamsburger emphasized, "This is the great *yerushah,* the charge that we have received from our sainted Rebbe, and that is perpetuated by his successor and the other leaders of our community."

What distinguishes Williamsburg from most other hasidic centers, including those of Boro Park, Monsey, or Israel, is this challenge to maintain, expand, and intensify its life-style of social and cultural isolation from the secular society that engulfs its neighborhood from all sides. The neighbors have come to respect and accept this determination to survive and succeed as one of the many subcultures in pluralistic America.[6]

The features of this hasidic life-style and cultural milieu in particular make it possible for *Der Yid* to exert its powerful influence as the almost exclusive vehicle of ideology, information, and communication in most realms of Williamsburg's religious, social, political, and institutional life. First and foremost is the rejection of the influence of the media that shape so much of American life, including that of an increasing number of Orthodox Jews. Television is almost nonexistent, as evident by the almost total lack of the ubiquitous forest of TV and cable TV antennas. Only a few, mostly from among those who have come from a different background, admit to listening to radio, including the increasing number of Jewish cultural and religious programs. Similarly, secular English literature is almost totally absent from the libraries that take up a prominent place even in the most crowded homes. Instead, shelves are filled with the Hebrew religious, halachic, and hasidic standard books typical of the products of the intensive *yeshivah* education for boys and girls.

Even more important than the conscientious blockage of the influence of the media, especially TV–which they call the *yetzer hara* box, "the instrument of the Evil Instinct," or even more graphically *die shmutzige keili*, "the dirty instrument"–is the almost exclusive emphasis on Jewish religious studies, for boys even more than for girls. Most young students after bar mitzvah spend their entire school day, often from 6:00 A.M. to 10:00 P.M., exclusively on their religious studies. And most subjects taught in the girls' high schools' secular departments, apart from the minimal requirements of social studies, sciences, and health courses, are vocational. The girls are consciously preparing themselves for a trade that will allow them to earn money before their marriage–usually in their late teens–and during the early years of marriage when they will probably have to support their husbands who either will still be engaged in advanced talmudic study or will be trying to establish themselves in a business or trade. Even afterwards, the large size of the typical family of still young couples, by the time they have reached their thirties, makes it mandatory for mothers to work between pregnancies. The women take jobs in bookkeeping, teaching, the needle trades, computer programming, or as sales personnel; if at all possible they prefer to work in companies run by or for the religious community. Few women of Williamsburg will peruse any secular litera- ture, including the growing English literature written for Orthodox Jewish readers. Teachers alone may look for books of stories that will enrich their Hebrew or secular instruction (as one of them told me when I met her in the back room of a Williamsburg bookstore, where the English books are displayed, away from the general buying public).

Because of this double-pronged rejection of the secular media and literature, almost none of the Williamsburg hasidic youngsters qualify for or are even vaguely interested in pursuing professional careers, unlike members of other Orthodox or even hasidic groups elsewhere. "Yet," said one Williamsburg businessman proudly, "many of our *yunge Leit*, our young people, make more money than your college graduates." A typical Williamsburg mother stressed that her five sons-in-law, none of whom had finished high school secular departments, speak English "as well as anyone else, and are highly successful in their trades, which require constant contact with the world of business. Two of them read the *New York Times* in their offices, but they don't bring it home to their wives and children," she emphasized. She herself, being of a nonhasidic background, does listen to the radio and occasionally reads magazines like *Readers' Digest*, but none of her eleven children, of whom ten are married, do so. The youngest, a boy of 14, indignantly rejected the idea of studying secular subjects. He attends a small elite *yeshivah* for intensive talmudic studies from morning till night, and has no interest in anything else. "I read *Der Yid*; that gives me all the news I need to know," he volunteered. Interestingly enough, a recently published survey of the Jewish community of Boro Park, the neighborhood that in some ways most closely resembles the intensively Orthodox life-style of Williamsburg among New York's Orthodox communities, found that almost half, or 46 percent, of the large sample population surveyed read the *New York Times*, 40 percent read the *New York Post*, and 30 percent the *Daily News*.[7]

This rejection of the influence of the general media is the major source of strength of *Der Yid*. It was consciously produced by the Satmar Rebbe in order to preserve the integrity of the intellectual, emotional, moral, and social wholeness and "wholesomeness," as he used to stress in his addresses, of the hasidic life-style he established and cultivated in Williamsburg for over 30 years.

When asked whether he would introduce English columns in *Der Yid* for young people who might like it, the editor stressed, "We have a mandate by our sainted Rebbe to uphold the integrity of our great *yerushah*, our heritage as *hasidim*. English sections would break down the total milieu and the flow of communication that we help to maintain, though, admittedly, there may be some young people who would like to see English articles in *Der Yid*."

The cumulative intrinsic, as well as extrinsic, controls of the intellectual, spiritual, social, and cultural hasidic life of the hasidic community of Williamsburg have thus put *Der Yid* in a unique position to mold the public opinion, and to shape the sociopolitical views, of its reading public. In a sense, it is the most significant indication of the consciously developed total milieu, the wanted otherness and isolation in the midst of the most intensive media blitz of metropolitan New York.

Appendix B: The Saint and Sage of Williamsburg: The Satmar Rebbe זצ"ל

A number of years have already passed since Rabbi Yoel Teitelbaum זצ"ל, the Rebbe of Satmar, returned his holy soul to its Heavenly Maker. The Satmar Rebbe was one of this century's greatest sages. In the nine decades of his life and leadership, he left an indelible imprint on the hasidic world in particular and on the Orthodox Jewish world in general. During his lifetime, he earned the love, respect, and reverence of hundreds and thousands of deeply devoted *hasidim* of his worldwide community.

Reb Yoilish, as the Satmar Rebbe came to be called by his followers, was the son of Rabbi Chananiah Yom Tov Lipa Teitelbaum of Sziget, the illustrious scion of a 200-year-old Hungarian hasidic dynasty. He was descended from Rabbi Moshe of Ujhely, the author of the classic *Yismah Moshe* commentary on the Torah and a disciple of the Chozeh of Lublin. Known as an *iluy* (prodigy) since his early youth, Reb Yoilish began to build a large personal following with his dazzling scholarship and saintly way of life during the short time he served as rabbi in several relatively unknown positions, such as the town of Krule.

In 1928, after his older and equally scholarly brother succeeded to the rabbinate of Sziget, Rabbi Yoel Teitelbaum burst upon the broader world of Hungarian Hasidism when he was chosen rabbi of the then still insignificant town of Satmar (Satu Mare) in Carpatho-Russia, Romania. In a few short years, he managed to transform Satmar into the center of a distinctive, powerful, and aggressive hasidic movement that looked up to their beloved Reb Yoilish with the type of respect and reverence accorded only great masters of the hasidic and nonhasidic communities. In the years immediately preceding the Holocaust, Reb Yoilish put Satmar into the forefront of Hungarian Hasidism and won recognition as one of its most remarkable leaders.

As the persecution by the Nazis and their Romanian collaborators engulfed Hungarian Jewry, he refused to leave his faithful. Consequently, in spite of world-wide efforts to save him, he was seized and taken to the notorious Bergen Belsen concentration camp. He was saved from certain death by superhuman efforts of some of his *hasidim* inside and outside the camp and, eventually, he was freed and allowed to leave on the famous transport arranged by Dr. Kasztner.

After brief stays in Switzerland and Eretz Yisrael, Rabbi Yoel Teitelbaum came to the United States in 1947. He settled in Williamsburg, already one of the largest Orthodox Jewish communities in America, where large numbers of refugees of war, persecution, and the camps had found a haven to rebuild their lives. Among them were many Satmar *hasidim.*

From this strong base, the Rebbe of Satmar reorganized his community and made it one of the most impressive of the contemporary Jewish world. Directly or indirectly, he had a profound influence on the Orthodox Jewish community of Williamsburg, now a predominantly Hungarian-type hasidic center, and those of Boro Park, Flatbush, Monsey, and other communities where Satmar *hasidim* moved in large numbers. Even more important was the creation of a totally new township of Satmar *hasidim* in Upstate New York, outside of Monroe, named Kiryas Joel in honor of the Rebbe, and a second one in Bnei Brak in Eretz Yisrael. Other major Satmar centers sprang up in Antwerp, Canada, London, Vienna, Latin America, Jerusalem and other cities of Eretz Yisrael.

Until the very end of his life, at the age of 93, Rabbi Yoel Teitelbaum kept firm control of every phase of the phenomenal growth of his network of *kehillos,* institutions and organizations in every realm of the religious, educational, social, economic, and political life of his vast followership. Unflinchingly, he accepted challenges from within and without, as he had done since the early years of his leadership in Hungary, challenges that embroiled him in numerous halachic and ideological controversies with some of the most respected scholars and hasidic leaders of his time. Disregarding popular trends in the old and the new world, in the decades prior to and following the Holocaust, he expanded the physical and spiritual bases of his community to build a veritable bulwark of intensive Orthodox Judaism and Hasidism proud of its otherness by design.

To the outside world, his fame rested on his function as the most prominent ideologue and spokesman of anti-Zionism since the earliest days of his Hungarian leadership. Even in the face of the wide acceptance of Zionism in some religious circles, he rejected any form of accommodation with the historical rise of the State of Israel and its claim to a leading role in the post-Holocaust Jewish world. This much maligned "intransigent" attitude was based on his firm belief in the metahistorical, divinely ordained purpose of the physical and spiritual *Galut*, until the Ultimate Redemption through the true *Moshiah.* He spelled out the halachic and aggadic justification of this ideology in his monumental *Vayoel Mosheh* and in numerous *teshuvos* published over the years, particularly in the three essays of *Al Hageulah V'al Hatemurah.*

In his opinion, a national, secular Jewish state contradicted the very spirit and laws of the Torah and halachic tradition. The establishment of the State of Israel and its attitudes toward religious Judaism only confirmed his conviction, and he considered it his sacred duty to pronounce and promulgate his strong criticism of the realities and policies of Israel.

In the '50s, the Satmar Rebbe became the official head of the ultra-Orthodox *Aidah Hachareidis* community of the Old Yishuv of Eretz Yisrael, which had set up a quasistate within the state by its rejection of Jewish secular statehood. Undismayed by worldwide vilification and vehement accusations of *hillul Hashem* and treason flung in his face, the Satmar Rebbe did not hesitate to spread his anti-Zionist stand in the non-Jewish, as well as in the Jewish, world, in mass meetings from Williamsburg to Madison Square Garden, and from his militant papers and magazines, such as *Der Yid*, to the ad pages of the *New York Times*. This persistence irritated the sensitivities of those Jewish people to whom Israel and its historical mission are sacrosanct and all criticism smacked of treason and heresy. Yet, when Rabbi Teitelbaum visited London and Eretz Yisrael in 1956, he was treated like royalty by the huge throngs that turned out to see him, inspired by the boundless reverence of the hundreds and thousands of his followers everywhere.

THE SCHOLAR

Lest there be any mistake about the source of this tremendous impact of the Satmar Rebbe, it must be emphasized that first and foremost it was his stature as a Torah scholar of the highest order that propelled him to the top of the religious world. It won him undisputed recognition in nonhasidic as well as hasidic circles even before his rise to prominence as the Satmar Rebbe. He caused a sensation everywhere he was called to deliver discourses on complex or esoteric issues in talmudic or halachic literature.

On a visit to Eretz Yisrael in 1925, the Satmar Rebbe, then still known as the "Kruler Iluy," astounded the galaxy of scholars who came to listen to the *hasid* at the Etz Chaim Yeshivah, the fortress of nonhasidic scholarship. Many decades later, he similarly stupefied the famous scholars of the Telshe Yeshivah in Cleveland when he visited this foremost institute of advanced rabbinic study and spontaneously delivered an impromptu discourse on a topic they were just then studying, ranging over a vast literature of commentaries and elucidations in great depth.

It has been only recently, especially after his death, that his writings have been published in book form, having previously appeared in numerous *teshuvos* printed elsewhere. They are continuing to pour forth, as hundreds of the manuscripts he has left behind are published by a group of close associates and outstanding scholars.

Most famous among Rabbi Teitelbaum's works is the *Divrei Yoel*, commentaries on the Torah and the Festivals, ten volumes of which have thus far appeared in print. *Vayoel Mosheh* is the Satmar Rebbe's major work outlining his position on the land, laws, language, and people of *Yisrael*, and on *Galus* and *Geulah* in general. Among his earlier collections of important contributions to talmudic scholarship are his five-volume *Kuntres Hidushei Torah* and two-volume *Hidushei Sugyos*. Numerous other large and small books, treatises, and pamphlets espousing his halachic and *hashkafah* writings on specific topics, collections of *teshuvos*, and articles that have previously appeared in various Torah magazines are coming off the presses in a steady stream. They attest to his stature as a supreme scholar in all realms of Torah, *kabbalah*, and *Hasidus*.

Until the very end, even after a stroke and serious illness, he was known to have rarely slept more than 2 to 3 hours a night, except on *Shabbos* and *Yom Tov*. Always expanding his vast knowledge, this exceedingly brilliant master of the *halachah* was forever in a state of growth.

Typical of the respect the world of Torah scholars had for him, even those who disagreed with his positions, is the comment of a famous sage who had come to the Rebbe's "court" on Bedford Avenue to engage him in a discussion on some of the most complex topics of the Talmud. When he walked out several hours later, he is said to have offered the understated but supreme compliment and token of recognition in the world of Torah scholarship, *"Der Yid ken lernen.* (This Jew knows how to learn).*"*

THE LEADER

Of course, among the hundreds and thousands of his followers – to whom Rabbi Yoel Teitelbaum was *"Der Ruv," "Rabbeini Hakudosh,"* or *"der Heiliger* Rebbe" – there was no need for outside accolades of their revered spiritual leader. To them, he had always been the undisputed supreme authority whose very word was command and whose personal conduct and ideology were the unquestioned guide of their individual and collective life.

When he came to the United States and settled in Williamsburg after his liberation and a brief stay in Eretz Yisrael, his world stature was further enhanced as he built his community into a veritable center of contemporary hasidic life. Hundreds of refugees and survivors of the camps had preceded him there, among them famous scholars from the great Eastern European academies and hasidic rabbis and Rebbes. Among them was the Tzelemer Rav, Rabbi Levi Yitzchak Grunwald, who in many ways prepared the climate of Williamsburg for the intensive, uncompromising stand and life-style that have become the mark of Hungarian hasidic communities in general and of Satmar in particular.

In a period of Jewish history said to be devoid of the type of giants of the hasidic world of old, the Satmar Rebbe rebuilt his "hoif," his court, on the unlikely *"treifeneh* soil" of America and expanded it into an empire totally unlike any other in the contemporary Jewish world, perhaps with the exception of the center of the Chabad movement in Crown Heights.

In Williamsburg, he translated his ideology into a strong, independent community life, one which takes pride in maximal guidance and control of the life of its individual and collective activities, organizations, and institutions. This is all the more impressive because, on the surface, the very nature of the Satmar community and its life-style seem totally out of step with the realities of twentieth-century society and culture. Indeed, its rejection of any form of accommodation to modern standards and contemporary values seems unrealistic and anachronistic to outsiders, a throwback to the Dark Ages. Yet, even the most skeptical or unsympathetic visitor who views Satmar in Williamsburg with jaundiced eyes on a first visit, comes away with amazement at the vibrancy of its multifaceted activities.

ESSENTIALS OF THE SATMAR IDEOLOGY

Some people unfamiliar with the underlying ideology of Williamsburg and Boro Park have called these large American hasidic communities reconstructions of the Eastern European *shtetl* that are bound to vanish with the last survivors of their first and second-generation immigrants.

Superficially, this might seem true, because the Satmar Rebbe and others like him insisted on maintaining the traditional East European garb and similar external trappings of a life-style antipathetic to the American environment. Yet a more profound analysis will show that what the Satmar Rebbe built in Williamsburg, Kiryas Joel, Bnei Brak and other centers of Orthodox Jewish life, is something revolutionary and new. It represents his indomitable will to create a total physical, social, and intellectual milieu that preserves its independence and otherness within the very realities of life in the twentieth century.

It is the metahistorical existence of a here-and-now life-style that preserves the eternal Torah values while interacting with the non-Jewish environment in a competent and meaningful way. Williamsburg and Boro Park are not Satmar or Tzelem or Belz, just as the Crown Heights community of the Lubavitcher Rebbe is not Lubavitch or Otwotzk, or even Kfar Chabad in Eretz Yisrael. In the ideology of the Satmar Rebbe, spelled out in the elaborate essays of *Vayoel Mosheh*, these are new, intrinsically American forms of the movable *Mishkan* (the Sanctuary) and the *Mahaneh Yisrael* (the Camp of Israel). Their essential function is to preserve the sanctity of the Jewish individual, family, and community in any *midbar* (figurative wilderness) anywhere in the world. The eternal *Am Yisrael* is guided by the web of divine commandments and guidelines. These apply equally in Williamsburg, Monsey, Eretz Yisrael, or anywhere else at any time in history until the Divine Will decides that the people of Israel are worthy of the Ultimate Redemption.

The essential makeup of the *Mahaneh Yisrael* is not variable by time and place or subject to the vagaries of historical, political, social, or economic circumstances and situations. Each country and culture in which Divine Providence has caused the Jewish people to set up their "tents" on their passage through 2000 years of exile presents a different challenge and a new chance to rise to higher levels. This is the sole *raison d'être* and criterion of the Jewish community in the United States or Eretz Yisrael of today, just as it was in the *shtetl* of Poland, Hungary, or Russia, and just as it was in the medieval or ancient communities of the Near East and Central, Western, and Eastern Europe.

If language or garments, such as Yiddish or the hasidic garb, historically served to provide barriers against assimilation, they have acquired a measure of sanctity and are therefore cultivated for their own sake, regardless of their historical origin and of the change in the settings in which they emerged. But it would be a serious mistake to treat such criteria as essential. Satmar in America or in *Eretz Yisrael,* or Ger, Belz, or Vizhnitz, are re-creating their communities in response to the ever new and different challenges. They are not simply perpetuating the old Eastern European *shtetl,* because it would become dysfunctional in a highly complex urban society with little room for anachronistic sentimentalities. More important, it would represent a serious flaw in the basic Torah perspective whose eternal values apply to the contemporary settings as well as to those of any other place, at any time, before and after.

Against the warp and woof of this thoroughly consistent Torah ideology, one must view the achievements of the Satmar Rebbe who in spite of serious illness and other severe obstacles, produced veritable miracles of organization by the sheer strength of his will, by his superb scholarship, and by his charismatic leadership as a contemporary saint and sage.

THREE PERSONALITY TRAITS

The combination of three traits gave the life and work of the Satmar Rebbe their singular character and force. First and foremost, he was a man of deceivingly simple faith and *bitahon,* absolute trust in the guidance of Divine Providence. Therefore, words such as unrealistic, impossible, or too costly did not exist in his vocabulary. If he perceived a genuine need in the life of his *kehillah,* and there were no prospects of meeting them routinely, he was fully convinced that somehow funds would be forthcoming. This same quality has woven legends about the lives of the very great in the hasidic world, as well as in the nonhasidic world, all the way back to the sages of the Talmud who had absolute faith in divine providence and whose routine or emergency needs were answered unfailingly.

Two examples of this faith come to mind. In 1948, soon after the Rebbe came to Williamsburg, the need for financial support for his *yeshivah* induced him to travel to Chicago to raise funds among his many followers. In a few days he had what was then the large sum of $6,000. On the day he was to return to New York, after visiting the *mikvah,* which he had found in poor condition, he asked why it was not repaired. He was told it was impossible to raise the $5,000 needed to get the job done. At once, the Satmar Rebbe turned to one of his men and told him to give $5,000 to the Rav in charge. "Hashem will help us raise the money for our *yeshivah,*" he said. "This money is needed right here in Chicago."

Another revealing story is taken from his earlier life. As a young married man, the Satmar Rebbe lived in Orshava, a town not far from Sziget. He had no regular income and lived on the little that a few charitable admirers collected for him, so that he could sit and study all day in his small *bet midrash.*

One of the men collecting the money once went on a business trip to Klausenburg. There, one pious man spoke with great admiration about the young Reb Yoilishel in his town Orshava. Once he had been in dire need of the sum of 500 *kronen* to survive a crisis, the man related. Hearing of the power of the young scholar's prayers, he had written to him and asked him to pray for him. Indeed, a week later, the full sum arrived and saved his life.

Angry and upset, the *gabbai* who collected the few pennies for Reb Yoilish every week came home. He had to go to so much effort to collect just enough to sustain the young scholar and here he sent such a "royal" sum, 500 *kronen*, to a complete stranger in Klausenburg. As soon as he arrived, he went over to the young Rebbe and confronted him with the story he had heard. Reb Yoilish looked up, thought for a moment, then a happy smile broke out on his face.

"I can explain it easily," he said. "Just after I received the letter from the *hasid* in Klausenburg, a woman came in crying to me. Her child was sick and she asked me to pray for his recovery. She offered any sum to help her child. I realized that Divine Providence had given me a chance to help both people in such a critical moment. I told the woman that if she sent the 500 *kronen* to the man in Klausenburg, the child would surely be helped by the *Ribbono Shel Olam*. And indeed, the child got well soon. Surely, that money did not belong to me. It was *bashert* for such a great *mitzvah*. Who am I that I deserve it? I was merely the *shliah* at the right moment."

Few people in our generation have personified this character trait and its practical consequences as much as the saintly Rebbe of Satmar. He never abandoned a project, though others would try to dissuade him, as long as he was convinced of its inherent merits. Such persistence added a legendary touch to his ability to overcome obstacles and tread on ground that others cautiously avoided. Ultimately, this quality enabled him to build his farflung network of religious institutions and organizations during an age of cynicism, distrust, and the glorification of materialism.

The second characteristic quality of the Rebbe of Satmar was his consistent refusal to brook any compromise or deviation from the paths of Torah and *halachah*. One of his favorite sayings was that he was a *lehat'hilah-Yid*, a Jew who acted in the preferred rather than the merely acceptable manner. Hence, he rejected any *bedi'eved* accommodation in the life of his community and in all phases of his work for the spreading of Torah and the essential facets of its ideology and practical application in contemporary world Jewish society.

His uncompromising stance, regardless of its unpopularity, was rooted in his belief in the guidance of Divine Providence in all affairs of the collective as well as the individual life, at any time and anywhere in *Galut*, now, as in the past and in the future. If it were the divine will to prolong *Galut* until the coming of *Moshiah*, the Ultimate Redemption, then no secular or religious movement had the right to intervene or act counter to this basic direction as pronounced by the prophets since the beginning of the exile. Hence, the secular State of Israel, established by secular non-Jewish and Jewish authorities, had no place in the ideology and practical realities of the Satmar Rebbe's world.

Eretz Yisrael was never far from his thoughts and prayers, but the state, its ideology, constitution, and policies were to him flagrant violations of the very texture of what he considered the only authentic Torah ideology. Therefore, he could not accept any other opinion, even if it were expressed by other greats of the hasidic and nonhasidic movements. Participation in the political processes of the state, such as voting, was not allowed. Hence, it was rejected by the followers of the Satmar ideology in Eretz Yisrael. This was valid under any circumstances and conditions; even if—*bedi'eved*—it might mean the loss of crucial gains for causes of Torah and *Yiddishkeit*, even physical survival.

Similarly, the use of modern Hebrew outside the classical language of the prayers and Torah literature was to the Rebbe of Satmar profanization—*hill lashon hakodesh*, profaning the holy tongue. Hence, it was also excluded from the studies in his educational systems for boys and girls. Any partnership with Zionist causes and the Israeli government, such as the acceptance of cabinet membership by the Religious Zionist movement and the non-Zionist Agudath Israel world movement, with approval of its *Moetzes Gedolei Hatorah*, its supreme Council of Sages, was wrong, even if this participation produced great gains for the recognition of Torah and *halachah* in the life of the holy land and the official conduct of its government. To the Satmar Rebbe, these gains were expressions of historical *nisyonos*, the temptations of evil, which served to prolong the *Galut* and prevent the coming of *Mashiach* in our days.

The promulgation of this attitude in the publications of the Satmar communities and in the non-Jewish media such as full-page ads in the *New York Times*, in response to specific policies of the Israeli State, triggered a great deal of animosity and vilification. But it did not deter the Satmar Rebbe from the course he had chosen for himself and for his worldwide movement.

This stance, born of his faith in divine guidance and his refusal to compromise under any circumstances, was greatly aided by his third major character trait of fierce independence. This thrust was responsible for a great deal of misunderstanding and maligning. In turn, it produced a measure of aggressiveness in the polemics and controversies that embroiled the Satmar Rebbe's life and work since the earliest years of his leadership and work until the very end of his long life and beyond it. Unfortunately, exaggerated and overexposed recent incidents, such as clashes with the followers of other famous contemporary hasidic leaders such as the Lubavitcher Rebbe and the Belzer Rebbe, are the result of the Satmar community's rejection of any belief, policy, or practical life-style but the one the Rebbe espoused and transmitted to his *hasidim*. This has led to censure and hostility in the most Orthodox circles, frequently because of the excesses of some of the more militant among the young Satmar elements.

Yet, the Satmar Rebbe himself openly disavowed acts of violence and expelled some of the perpetrators from his *kehillah*. He always placed strong emphasis on *midos* (character qualities), humility, gentleness, and most of all, on *hesed* (kindness) in his regular educational meetings with the thousands of his students and *hasidim*. Famous is his constant saying: "One may have learned and mastered many *mesichtos* (volumes of the Talmud) but be ignorant of *mesichtas Midos*."

Indeed, this fierce independence was one of the sources of the Satmar Rebbe's underlying strength and confidence. It enabled him to break down barriers and overcome obstacles no one else in the Jewish world dared tackle. In total disregard of precedents and traditions, he molded the community and the life-style of Williamsburg according to the pattern he had established in the community of Satmar decades earlier.

In the same way, he created Kiryas Joel, his independent, totally hasidic community outside Monroe, New York, as a stronghold of his faith and ideology. In both of these communities, groups of capable, dedicated, and loyal leaders have created compact neighborhoods held together by tight networks of *shuls*, schools, and institutions. It is no exaggeration to credit the Satmar Rebbe with almost single-handedly safeguarding the survival and continued growth of the Jewish community of Williamsburg when most observers had predicted its decline after the construction of the Brooklyn-Queens Expressway made other religious neighborhoods of New York, such as Boro Park, Flatbush, Monsey, and Queens more accessible.

Still more impressive is a trip in one of the special buses that connect Williamsburg to Kiryas Joel, which lies about 90 minutes north of New York. In spite of innumerable economic and political obstacles, this monumental enterprise was conceived, initiated, and developed under the guidance of the Satmar Rebbe in just 7 short years. At this writing, there are already nearly a thousand families living there. Most of the men commute to work in New York. Their simple, tasteful homes are built around the magnificent *bet midrash*, a *yeshivah*, and school system that has over three thousand male and female students on all levels and a *kollel* of young married scholars. It took all the force of the Rebbe's vision and indomitable practical leadership to create this total hasidic community, at a cost of $10 million. Smaller or larger communities of Satmar *hasidim* have since been built, most prominent among them Kiryas Joel in Bnei Brak in Eretz Yisrael.

Obviously, these projects required huge sums of money and the backing of people of means, as well as an efficient, multiphased organization with leaders able to cope with the rough-and-tumble economic, social, and political climate of New York. Fortunately, some of the most successful Orthodox businessmen in the United States, Canada, England, and elsewhere were among the ardent admirers of the Satmar Rebbe. They considered it a privilege to fulfill any request the *Heiliger* Rebbe made of them.

Numerous are the stories of people, *hasidim* as well as non-*hasidim*, who have prospered greatly after generously supporting the Rebbe's continuously expanding network of projects. For example, one young man advanced the funds to establish the stocking factory that produces stocking for hasidic women in keeping with the Rebbe's standards of *tzni'ut* (modesty). Another man, a margarine manufacturer, built a string of houses for the Rebbe's institutions in Williamsburg and in Bnei Brak. Both of these men are known to have become phenomenally successful in their business ventures.

Similarly, when the Brooklyn-Queens Expressway cut a wide swath through the very center of the old religious community of Williamsburg with the approval of the political authorities, the Satmar Rebbe and his community not only held on, they actually rebuilt and further expanded much of the already deteriorating neighborhood. Representatives of the Satmar community became active in most phases of the local communal organizations, projects, and activities. They learned to cope with the problems arising from the influx of other minority groups, particularly in the housing projects erected in the very heart as well as on the fringes of the neighborhood. Consequently, Williamsburg became one of the largest centers of contemporary hasidic life, second only to Jerusalem.

The complexion of the hasidic community of Williamsburg, however, has changed in recent years. The Orthodox Jewish life-style of Williamsburg has been transplanted to Boro Park. It is essentially different from Boro Park, which has replaced much of the old Williamsburg Orthodox Jewish life as ever more Williamsburgers move there and amalgamate their life-style with that of the Boro Park Jewish community.

During the height of Williamsburg's transformation into a Hungarian-type hasidic center, as many as twenty young couples of the Satmar community married in an average week, all intent on remaining in the neighborhood because they wanted to be near the Rebbe. As a result, rents continued to rise steadily, and real estate prices climbed steeply, far above those of similar neighborhoods. Over the decades, the upgrading of the old homes has changed the outer appearance and revitalized much of the declining local street life. This trend continues, though an increasingly large number of the older Williamsburg population has moved to Boro Park, Flatbush, Monsey, Queens, Kiryas Joel, and similar exurban hasidic developments in upstate New York and New Jersey. New high-rise housing projects, both public and private, are largely occupied by hasidic families, even on the higher stories, in spite of the inconvenience of having to walk up fifteen and more flights of stairs with large numbers of children on *Shabbos* and *Yom Tov*.

Unlike the almost total lack of participation of the former Orthodox elements, the hasidic leaders take an active interest and share in the sociopolitical organizational structure of the neighborhood so as to protect their own interests. They have considerable input and growing influence on public affairs, even in realms that are beyond the pale of their own activities. One has only to stroll through the streets of what was once the outer fringe, beyond Bedford Avenue, toward the old navy yard, to see the incredible growth and expansion that is unquestionably due to the efforts of the Satmar Rebbe's community to maintain Williamsburg as a vital hasidic center. This holds true even after the establishment of Kiryas Joel and the Rebbe himself taking up his residence there for a good part of his time during his last years.

Some of the most prominent buildings of old Williamsburg, such as the huge Eastern District High School that covers an entire city block and that had once been one of New York's largest and finest public high schools, has been taken over by the Satmar girls' school system and is a beehive of constant activity, day and night. Similarly, other large buildings in the area, vacated because of population shifts, have been taken over and renovated and are now thriving centers of educational and other institutions of the Satmar community and satellite groups.

EDUCATION

The typical Williamsburg family is large and growing. The average household has at least four children, and a good many have as many as ten or more, for an average of seven to nine children per child-bearing household. The central streets, such as Lee Avenue and Bedford Avenue, are often choked by veritable parades of carriage-pushing young women. Small wonder that as soon as new schools for boys and girls are opened, they are filled. Fleets of buses and vans pick up and deliver large numbers of children at every corner in the morning and the late afternoon from Sunday through Friday. Feeder buses bring additional students from other Orthodox Jewish neighborhoods, such as Boro Park, Flatbush, and Queens, though most of these have growing networks of hasidic *yeshivot* themselves. In Williamsburg, the Satmar schools have approximately six thousand five hundred students in thirteen school buildings. In greater New York they have a total of nine thousand boys and girls on all levels, and twelve thousand in the United States.

In view of the large families and continuously growing school system, the Satmar Rebbe understandably found it necessary to devote his best and most intensive efforts to the building, expansion, and personal guidance of his educational networks. It was here, in the realm of his *hinuch*, that he made special efforts to perpetuate the traditional patterns, standards, and ideological orientation. The curricula here were designed to safeguard the future of the Satmar community in the spirit that he had successfully transplanted to the American soil with the same intensity and consistency as in the old world.

This is evident in any of the Satmar schools. Like the other Hungarian-type *yeshivot*, the emphasis in their *hinuch* is on an early start. Boys and girls begin their actual learning at the time when other schools focus on play, fun activities, and informal social learning in nursery and kindergarten.

The curriculum in the Satmar *yeshivot* is oriented toward mastery of practical *halachah* in content and format of learning. This is in marked contrast to the emphasis of the Litvishe (Lithuanian-type) *yeshivot* whose curricula have little immediate regard for training students in practical, applicable *halachah*.

Litvishe *yeshivot* are oriented toward theoretical scholarship and focus on the mastery of the standard cycle of the *yeshivishe mesichtos*, those tractates most conducive to developing the ability in students for in-depth analysis of the talmudic discussion and the commentaries. A premium is put on prolonged study on the graduate level, sometimes continuing for many years after marriage for their superior students.

Though the standard curriculum of the Litvishe *yeshivot* allots some time for daily study of the *Humash* and the classics of the ethical (*Mussar*) and philosophical (*Hashkafah*) literature, the pursuit of practical *halachah* is not generally emphasized. Only students who intend to pursue a career in the rabbinate and as other religious functionaries devote several years to the study of the tractate of *Chullin* and those parts of the *Shulhan Aruch*, the Code of Jewish Law, that are usually required for *Semichah*, rabbinic ordination. Except for the popular study of the *Mishnah Berurah* (the halachic work of the Chafetz Chaim, one of the greatest sages of this century) the emphasis is on theoretical "learning for learning" as the supreme value.

In contrast, Hungarian-type *yeshivot*, such as Satmar, emphasize early acquaintance with the language and literature of the *Shulhan Aruch* and the related classic commentaries and their application to daily life in a highly technological civilization, as it affects the individual, the family, and the community. One major reason for this early concentration on the study of practical *halachah*, the detailed guide to observant Jewish life, is the fact that the average student is expected to leave the *bet midrash* before or soon after marriage to learn some trade, profession, or business. By focusing early on the practical application of their studies, the students become familiar with the halachic decisions that concern their social, economic, dietary, and ritual life.

In line with the same approach, in the opinion of the Satmar Rebbe, only the top students are encouraged to continue their advanced, in-depth talmudic studies in a *kollel* for an extended period after marriage. This is in stark contrast to the practice in most American *Yeshivos gedolos* which promote advanced talmudic study even for their average students. Indeed, it has become practically a status symbol for parents to have their sons or sons-in-law study a few years at one of the prestigious *kollel* institutes after marriage and to support them financially so that they can devote all their time to talmudic scholarship. In turn, it has become the standard for graduates of Orthodox girls' high schools or seminaries to look for a husband who will learn in a *kollel* while they go to work.

Today, there are large Satmar *kollelim* for superior scholars in Williamsburg and Kiryas Joel, which are expected to produce the future rabbis, *dayanim*, and other religious functionaries. Generally, however, the Satmar Rebbe frowned on the custom of the average *yeshivah* student of marriageable age continuing his advanced studies far beyond the age of 20. Many stories are told about the Satmar Rebbe looking around his *bet midrash* and questioning older students as to why they did not go out to learn some marketable skill or enter a trade or business and get married. In many cases, he personally intervened with established businessmen or professionals among his followers to provide training and job opportunities for his older students when they were ready to get married and had to make a living. Only when the need for highly trained *dayanim* and other rabbinic specialists had become urgent did the Rebbe himself initiate the establishment of *kollelim* that are now training over three hundred future scholars and *poskim* to serve his and other hasidic communities.

Naturally, as pointed out before, all learning at Satmar *yeshivot* and schools is carried on in Yiddish, which for most of the students is their mother tongue – though the members of the younger generation are quite fluent in English. Similarly, the major part of their daily studies is devoted to religious subjects. Only the absolute minimum of time is set aside for secular studies and some skill training.

In spite of this, many students of Satmar *yeshivot* have gone on to become highly successful in business, skilled trades, professions, and communal and organizational work. They are highly respected in a number of manufacturing lines and are prominent in such popular fields of business as the jewelry and diamond trades, real estate, and other lucrative lines, even though they persist in wearing their hasidic garb, beards, and *peyot*.

Almost until the very end, the Satmar Rebbe personally guided the vast educational network he established in this country and elsewhere. All major decisions were made by him, because he was vitally concerned with preserving his high standards which he considered even more important in America because of the greater exposure to corrupting influences. For this reason, he spent much time testing, teaching, directing, and advising the teachers of his schools in regular monthly meetings. He insisted that his *melamdim* and *roshei yeshivah* know what he expected of them, and he addressed the hundreds and thousands of his students in regular meetings, inspiring them and infusing in them his zeal, faith, and ideals.

Little attention was generally paid to accepted patterns such as the school calendar and the hours of instruction. Among other innovations, Satmar schools are in session practically the entire year. During the hot summer months, classes meet in well-equipped summer camps in the Catskill mountains under the guidance and supervision of specially trained teachers and a staff of older counselors. The families of the teachers have proper accommodations and don't need the usual "bungalows in the country" that New Yorkers have to worry about.

One prominent *yeshivah* teacher recently commented:

> If you really want to see the difference between our *yeshivah* and the Satmar *yeshivot,* visit the summer camps. They are a far cry from the primitive bungalows and rough facilities in which we spent our summers as students and counselors, that is, if our parents could afford to send us there. Thus, the students don't mind the year-round sessions, because the camp settings are beautiful. And there is still plenty of time to enjoy swimming and all the other activities we usually associate with camp.

Even more characteristic of the singular nature of the Satmar Rebbe's educational philosophy is his mushrooming Bais Ruchel school system for girls. Classes there range from nursery through post-high-school study programs and are spread throughout the large centers of the Orthodox Jewish community in Brooklyn and elsewhere.

Just recently, a number of smaller Bais Ruchel schools in Williamsburg joined together and took over the huge complex that had housed Eastern District High School in the very center of the neighborhood. All the wings and floors of the building, which takes up a full city square block, are crowded with students, day and night. The halls resound with the typical singsong of girls studying, singing, playing, and learning. Not even 10 years ago, during the peak of expansion, could anyone have anticipated this phenomenal growth of Satmar's Bais Ruchel schools, which have replaced the once dominant Bais Yaakov elementary and high schools in Williamsburg, with a total of three thousand five hundred students.

There is a marked difference in the educational philosophy and programs of the Bais Ruchel schools and the highly respected Bais Yaakov schools. The latter take a great deal of pride in their superior Hebrew and secular departments, both of which have in recent years expanded their range of subjects. The Hebrew curricula include advanced Hebrew, literary, and even talmudic studies, in addition to their emphasis on Hebrew, *Tanach,* Jewish history, and ethics.

In contrast, Bais Ruchel schools live up to the practical "learning for living" educational philosophy of the Satmar boys' and girls' schools. They educate their students for the tasks of future mothers. Much of their learning is of the type that Orthodox girls would have gotten simply by living in the intense atmosphere of the old world setting, in the dynamics of an *"ehrlich heim,"* watching and working with their mothers and helping them care for the usually large families.

At Bais Ruchel, they become thoroughly familiar with the subjects and activities of the traditional Jewish woman's realm, such as *kashrut, tzini'ut* (modesty), the stringent laws of the family life, basic mastery of the *Humash*, and related subjects, all taught in Yiddish. Their secular studies are more extensive than those of the Satmar boys' schools, which are kept to the required minimum. Bais Ruchel students, especially on the high-school level, are trained in home economics, business subjects, sewing, secretarial skills, and some trades. This type of secular and vocational education serves as a practical preparatory for future Orthodox Jewish housewives and mothers who will probably marry early and have large families. A number of these girls will also have to supplement their husbands' limited incomes, especially in the early years of their marriage, in order to sustain a decent standard of living.

Special efforts are also made in the girls' schools of Satmar to limit the influence of the *treifeneh* (general) culture, while preparing the students for a vocation. General literature and most liberal arts courses are banned. Emphasis is on the texts, manuals, and courses that are needed for occupational skills and competency in commercial and other practical professions.

Even in these realms, the Satmar Rebbe went beyond anything previously done. He established a Bais Ruchel publication organization, which prints texts and books that provide a maximum of guidance and knowledge presented in the right spirit and eliminates some of the "harmful" influences that over ten thousand students of the American day-school movement are exposed to in their general studies because there is no alternative available.

Like the Satmar boys' schools, Bais Ruchel schools also have virtual year-round sessions. In their practical approach, Satmar schools also engage in seeking job opportunities for their graduates with firms owned by Orthodox Jews. This helps avoid violations of the laws of modesty, or *yihud*, one male and female working behind closed doors. Not many other firms would permit their office doors to remain ajar so that their employees, graduates of Satmar schools, would be able to observe such stringent requirements.

SOCIAL WELFARE PROGRAMS

The Satmar Rebbe also devoted a great deal of attention to the social welfare programs of this community. With the active participation of the Rebbetzin in many projects, especially those for women, the elderly, and the indigent, the Satmar Rebbe developed a network of organizations, institutions, and programs that cover the economic and social needs of his people. For counter to some misconceptions about the incidence of wealth in Williamsburg, at least 25 percent of the hasidic community is poor due to large families, advancing age, or physical disability.

Long before similar agencies were established in the broader community, the Satmar Rebbe initiated projects for the alleviation of serious problems as they developed and were brought to his attention. Best known among them was his Million Dollar Revolving Fund which aided people in financial stress, widows and orphans, the elderly, and the sick, especially among the newcomers in the years after the Second World War.

The administrators of the Satmar programs worked with other Jewish and public relief organizations and programs. They learned to cultivate good relations with influential political figures in all branches of government. The fame and power of the Satmar Rebbe also opened doors and channels that normally would not have been easily accessible to the hasidic community. In public recognition of the stature of Rabbi Teitelbaum, it was standard practice of candidates for political office, including the presidency, to visit the Rebbe in his residence in Williamsburg and to ask for his blessing and endorsement.

Other important projects that owe their existence to the initiative of the Satmar Rebbe and his community are fleets of *Bikkur Cholim* vans and buses that take volunteers several times a day to visit the sick in various hospitals and nursing homes. They also transport elderly and disabled or handicapped persons to doctor appointments and social services all over Brooklyn and New York. The volunteers feed and help care for disabled and terminally ill patients who otherwise would be dependent on the often inadequate hospital staffs, especially when there is a language barrier. Today, one of the major extracurricular activities of *yeshivah* and Bais Yaakov students is to participate in these and similar *Gemillas Hesed* projects. Satmar deserves a large share of the credit.

Of even greater importance is the *Hatzoloh* organization, an emergency volunteer medical service whose little stickers are prominently displayed in every house and store in Williamsburg and Boro Park. They offer speedy help at all hours of the day and night, with fleets of specially equipped cars, ambulances, and drivers thoroughly trained in paramedical techniques. Over the years, countless people have been saved from death or serious disability by the quick response and expert care of the dedicated *Hatzoloh* volunteers.

There are numerous other services organized by the Satmar *hasidim* to provide a broad range of aid to their own and other people in need, including the distribution of free food to the poor and handicapped every Friday.

Though not publicized, there is also an effective self-help organization of the Satmar and other hasidic communities in Williamsburg. Woe to the would-be attackers when the defense whistles sound or there is a cry of *"Chaptzeh!"* Crowds pour out of their homes all around and immediately overwhem the attackers. Gangs of young toughs and even the occasionally contemptuous officers have learned to respect the wrath and strength of this response of the hasidic community to provocation and attack.

Another effective project organized by the Satmar Rebbe is the *Rav Tov* program to aid Russian and Iranian Jews who choose to immigrate to the United States. *Rav Tov* workers provide them with transportation, the education of their children, and continuous support until they can stand on their own feet. The record of Russian and Iranian newcomers who have gone through this program and are now members of the Torah community speaks for the effectiveness of this large project.

THE REBBE

Last but perhaps most important in the success of the Satmar Rebbe during the decades of his leadership was his close relationship with his followers. To them he was always *der Heiliger* Rebbe. They literally carried him on their hands, treated him like royalty, and revered the very ground he walked on because, first and foremost, he was a personal leader, guide, and teacher to his *hasidim*.

After his *petirah* in 1979, the stewardship of the worldwide Satmar network has passed into the capable hands of the Satmar Rebbe's nephew Rabbi Moshe Teitelbaum, an outstanding scholar and a strong leader in his own right. Yet, the unmistakable impression one gets from Reb Yoilish's *hasidim*, in spite of their tremendous respect and admiration for their new Rebbe, is that their loss will always remain irreparable. The Satmar Rebbe's saintly presence is still very much in the memories and hearts of his faithful followers.

Never again, as one *hasid* put it, will the *tishen*, the *Shabbos* gatherings at the Rebbe's table, have the same special aura of mystic inspiration. The Rebbe taking a few small bites from the heavily laden tray and the hundreds of *hasidim* leaning over the long table, desperately trying to grab some *shirayim*, a morsel of fish or *kigel* over which the Rebbe had pronounced the blessing.

Once, I saw an older *hasid* give a young boy a bite of the *shirayim* he was fortunate to be able to grab with his bare fingers and say, *"Zolst gedaynken, mein kind, di host gegessen fin daym heiligen Rebben's shirayim*. Remember, my child, you have eaten a piece of the food over which the Rebbe has said the blessing." The expression in his eyes and the tone of his voice made the gesture and the memory more precious than if he had handed him a large treasure of gold or silver.

To the Satmar *hasidim* there will never again be such a *davening*, a sacred prayer service, when thousands would crowd into the large *bet midrash* on Bedford Avenue, Keap Street, or in Kiryas Joel, to hear the Rebbe's high, frail voice. Never will there be such a frenzied ecstasy and inspiration in the huge crowd that stayed up all night of Simhat Torah to watch *der Heiliger* Rebbe dance round and round the long, narrow path that opened respectfully before him. Never again would they see him with a small *sefer Torah* held tightly to his body, his eyes looking up to the higher spheres on this night of joy and rejoicing of the Torah.

The rare blend of superior scholarship, faith, piety, and ideology combined with extraordinary leadership qualities and the charisma of a beloved saint and sage enabled Rabbi Yoel Teitelbaum from the small Romanian town of Satmar to build a vast following and a worldwide community of his faithful. In spite of any controversy that surrounded him, he was universally recognized as a giant of our time who taught the contemporary Jewish world the power of faith in Divine

Providence and the strength of a consistent Torah ideology in the face of seemingly insurmountable obstacles. In this sense, the Rebbe of Satmar will forever remain one of the greatest Jewish leaders in modern times, having left his indelible imprint on Jewish history during one of the most tragic yet heroic centuries of *Klal Yisrael* in *Galus*. *Zechuso yagen aleinu*.

Appendix C:
Maps and Tables

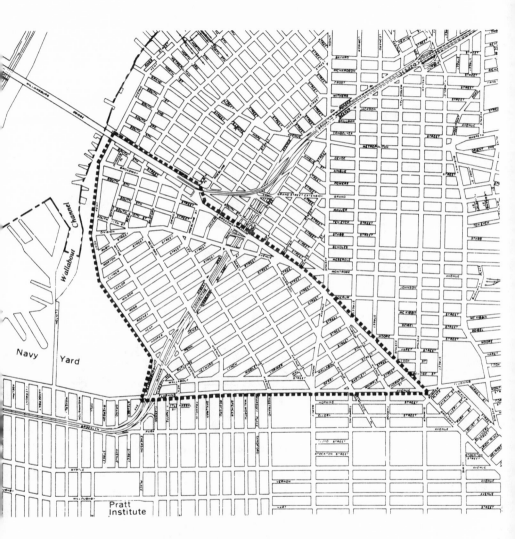

The Study Area: The Jewish Triangle

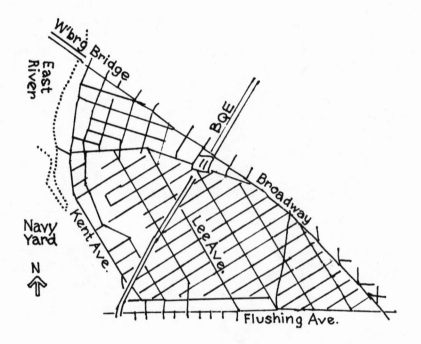

The Residential Core

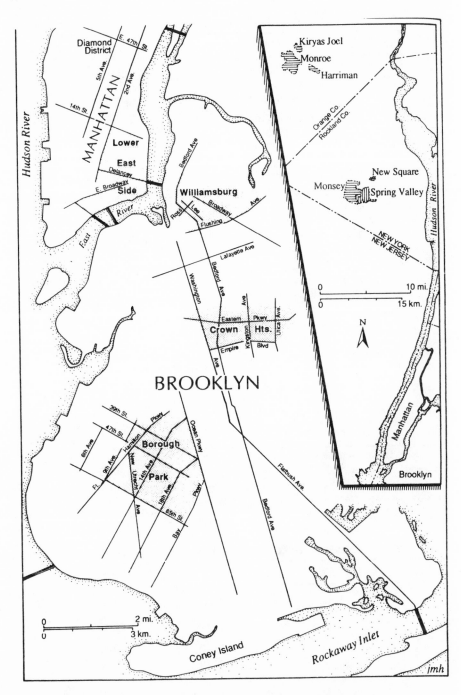

Hasidic Communities in New York City and Suburbs

South Williamsburg Median Family Income: 1970 and 1980 Compared

	South Williamsburg				New York City
Tract	1970 Median	1980 Median	1980 Average Household Size	Percentage NYC Family Median	Median 1980 Family Income of the Five Boroughs
507	$ 4,392	$ 2,969	2.9	18%	$16,818
509	$ 4,865	$ 12,000	3.3	71%	$16,818
525	$ 6,756	$ 9,804	2.9	58%	$16,818
529	$ 6,052	$ 8,290	3.5	49%	$16,818
531	$ 4,867	$ 10,370	3.7	62%	$16,818
533	$ 5,833	$ 8,388	3.8	50%	$16,818
535	$ 6,245	$ 8,160	3.5	49%	$16,818
537	$ 4,517	$ 7,172	4.3	43%	$16,818
539	$ 6,857	$ 9,834	4.4	58%	$16,818
545	$ 7,665	$ 8,995	3.6	53%	$16,818
547	$ 5,618	$ 4,828	3.0	29%	$16,818
549	$ 4,192	$ 10,057	3.1	60%	$16,818
Total	$67,759	$100,869			
Average	$ 5,646	$ 8,406	3.5	50%	$16,818

*Denotes Hasidic Dominant Census Tracts

Source: U.S. Census 1980

NOTE: 1970 N.Y.C. Median Family Income was $9,862. Whereas 1980 is $16,818; this is a 70% increase. The average median family income for South Williamsburg in 1970 was $5,646, and in 1980 was $8,406; a 49% increase. Thus the increase in average family income for South Williamsburg is two-thirds that of New York City.

1982 Poverty Guidelines by Income by Family Size

Number of Persons in the Family Unit	Income Level
1	$ 6,850
2	7,775
3	9,700
4	11,625
5	13,550
6	15,475

Source: N.Y.C. Community Development Agency

Notes

CHAPTER 1

1. See, for example, J. A. Jewel, *History of Williamsburg* (New York, n.d.); Eugene L. Armbruster, *Eastern District of Brooklyn* (New York, 1942); *History of Eastern District of Brooklyn* (New York, 1897); and Henry R. Stiles, *History of Kings County of Brooklyn* (New York, 1884).

2. The Williamsburg with which this study deals does not refer to the entire area that goes officially under this name and includes the territory ranging from the East River and the Brooklyn Navy Yard in the west to Greenpoint in the northeast, Stuyvesant Heights and Willoughby in the south, and Bushwick and Ridgewood in the southeast. This Old Williamsburg, which is the locale of Betty Smith's famous *A Tree Grows in Brooklyn* and of Daniel Fuch's earlier and less popular but brilliant novel, *A Summer in Williamsburg*, was already in the '20s a "gray and dreary slum, the home of the poorest of New York's Jews, a social group even less favored than those who lived in Manhattan's Lower East Side." Irving Howe, "D. Fuchs: Escape from Williamsburg." *Commentary* 6:1 (July 1948).

3. U. S. Census–Williamsburg Study of Jewish Welfare Board, (New York, 1936), p. 57(a).

4. "The top hats, tails and carriages are as plentiful as on Fifth Ave." Unidentified quote in H. Logan's *Williamsburg*.

5. Sam P. Abelow, *History of Brooklyn Jewry* (New York, 1937).

6. Estimated on the basis of the proportion of Jewish children in the local public and parochial schools.

7. The transliteration of Yiddish or Hebrew words, as stated in Zborowsky and Herzog's *Life Is With People* (New York, 1952), is difficult because of the many conflicting methods. Basically this study has tried to adopt the system generally found in the Anglo-Jewish press, rather than the one which uses the scholarly phonetic symbols. Standard terms are italicized, particularly when used the first time. Terms, such as Torah, which have become part of the English language, are used in their common spelling. Generally the Neo-Hebraic Sephardic system of pronunciation has been preferred in the transliteration.

8. "The migration of Jews into Williamsburg and Greenpoint was not received gracefully

291

by the old settlers. The bearded Jew who ventured far from his home was not certain of returning without scars on his face made by rowdies. Nor was the unbearded Jew safe. . . . Lastly the increasing number of Jews and their readiness to give blow for blow cowed the hooligans." Sam P. Abelow, *History of the Jews of Brooklyn,* op. cit., pp. 12, 13.

9. Since the end of Phase I, when the Orthodox elements comprised only about a third of the Jewish community, they have become a good two-thirds of the community because of the departure of the old elements and the increasing number of Orthodox newcomers who settle in Williamsburg.

10. In the spring of 1954 many of the central blocks had been torn down to make way for the Queens Highway project and Williamsburg looks to have been hit by a few bombs. Yet of the approximately five thousand families thus forced to move, most of the Hungarian hasidic elements stayed on because they wanted to live in the neighborhood of their Rebbe and their educational institutions. Other Orthodox elements have mostly moved to Crown Heights or Boro Park. The majority of the non-Orthodox elements moved out to the suburban communities of Long Island.

11. It was only after a few serious incidents, which climaxed in the slaying of the elderly rabbi and the young girl by outside criminals, that the hasidic community once again mounted a strong campaign for more police protection. It culminated in a protest meeting with Mayor Dinkins, to break what Rabbi Hertz Frankel, spokesman of Satmar, called "the stranglehold of crime on the neighborhood."

12. Compare such studies as Ida Susser's *Norman Street: Poverty and Politics in an Urban Neighborhood,* Nathan Glazer and Daniel Patrick Moynihan's *Beyond the Melting Pot,* and the more recent *Canarsie* by Jonathan Riemer, for a more detailed discussion of these issues.

13. See U.S. Dept. of Labor Statistics, *A Socioeconomic Profile of Puerto Rican New Yorkers* (New York Bureau of Labor Statistics: Middle-Atlantic Regional Office, 1975), pp. 31, 39, 44, 73, 74.

CHAPTER 2

1. See the special editions of *ODA Today* published in honor of the visits of U.S. Secretary of Commerce Malcolm Baldridge, November 18, 1986, and his successor.

CHAPTER 3

1. See W. Helmreich, *The World of the Yeshivah* (New York: Free Press, 1982), p. 305.
2. See the discussion of this phase of hasidic education in I. Rubin, *Satmar: Island in the City* (Chicago: Quadrangle Books, 1972), p. 152.

CHAPTER 4

1. See *The Jewish Press,* 9 October 1987.
2. See G. Kranzler, "The Changing Orthodox Family," in *Dimensions of Orthodox Judaism,* ed. R. P. Bulka (New York: Ktav Publishing House, 1983), p. 566.

3. Compare A. Cherlin and Frank F. Furstenberg, Jr., *The New American Grandparent: A Place in the Family, A Life Apart* (New York: Basic Books, 1986).
4. Compare Sidney Hook's comments along these lines in his autobiography, *Out of Step* (New York: Harper & Row, 1987) a typical product of this atmosphere in pre-World-War-I Williamsburg.

CHAPTER 5

1. See Robert and Helen Lynd's *Middletown* (New York. Harcourt, Brace & Co., 1929) and *Middletown in Transition* (New York: Harcourt, Brace & Co., 1937).
2. See my 1961 report for the statistics of the career choices of the graduates of a local *yeshivah* and girls' high school; 67 percent of the young men and 50 percent of the women entered college (p. 101).
3. See in my 1961 study the case of the poor egg-peddler who at a time when most of the large Williamsburg synagogues charged as little as $10 for a seat during the High Holidays featuring well-known cantors and choirs, spent $100 for the privilege of partaking in the services conducted by the *Heiliger* Rebbe himself (p. 75).
4. In 1990 the Old Rebbetzin took steps to sell the mansion and Beth Hamedrash to a group of men led by one of her close associates. They wanted to establish a separate *kollel* in this building located opposite the mansion of the new Rebbe. This led to altercations between hotheaded partisans of the Rebbe and the individuals involved in this deal that was never consummated. As usual, the media played up this incident as indicating dissension and strife in the ranks of Satmar. Barely a year later, things quieted down and the causes of friction were eliminated.)
5. See my *Williamsburg Memories* (Lakewood, NJ: C.I.S., 1989) for representatives of this type of the old community's leaders.
6. Compare W. L. Warner and Leo Srole, *The Social Systems of American Ethnic Groups*, the *Yankee City Series*, vol. 3 (New Haven: Yale University Press, 1945).

CHAPTER 6

1. For details of the court battles initiated by the Latino community which tried to stop the construction, see Jerome Mintz, *Hasidic People* (Cambridge, MA: Harvard University Press, 1992).
2. For a detailed discussion of the problems of contemporary Orthodox rabbis prior to the arrival of the famous *roshei yeshivah* and hasidic rabbis after World War II, see Marvin Schick, "The Legacy of Rav Aharon Kotler," *Jewish Action* (Summer 1988): 77–85.

CHAPTER 7

1. See William M. Kephart, *Extraordinary Groups: Sociology of Unconventional Life Styles* (New York: St. Martin Press, 1976). Also see "A Silence of Sanity," *Commonwealth*, 5 November 1988, 631, which compares *hasidim* to the Amish and emphasizes the higher level of knowledge of the *hasidim* and their education.

CHAPTER 8

1. For details on the feud between Satmar and Lubavitch see Jerome Mintz, *Hasidic People* (Cambridge, MA: Harvard University Press, 1992) chapter 14, p. 154. For details on the altercations and conflict between Satmar and Belz also see Mintz, pp. 135–136. For details on the court battles and friction between the school administration of Kiryas Joel and the local school district, also see Mintz, pp. 310–320. And for details on the court battles for the right to construct the new *yeshivah* building of Satmar on the land cleared by WUR behind the mansion of the Rebbe of Satmar, also see Mintz, pp. 266–268.
2. See Ari Goldman, "Police to Guard Israeli Rabbi Due in New York," *New York Times*, 3 March 1981, 13, for details.
3. On June 27, 1994, the U.S. Supreme Court rejected the legality of the Kiryas Joel School District with a 6:3 majority. Yet even the opinion of the majority expressed sympathy for the vital need of a separate school for the learning-disabled children of the hasidic community and suggested new approaches that would make the establishment of the school district bypass the problem of the separation of church and state.

CHAPTER 9

1. See David Kranzler, *Thy Brother's Blood* (New York: Mesorah Publications, 1987).
2. See my *Williamsburg Memories* (Lakewood, NJ: C.I.S., 1989), p. 193.
3. One has only to think of the most ambitious project he initiated a little more than a decade before his death, the establishment of an exurban branch of his community, Kiryas Joel, which was named in his honor. In the words of his successor, Rabbi Moshe Teitelbaum, it cost $10 million to establish and an additional $10 million annually to maintain and further expand. "Only a man of the stature and near-miraculous power of *der Heiliger Rebbe* could venture to undertake such a momentous giant task and carry it out successfully," responded Rabbi Moshe Teitelbaum, when asked about possible plans for the establishment of other hasidic centers like Kiryas Joel.
4. For a detailed discussion of the attitude of the community and of therapists, see Jerome Mintz, *Hasidic People* (Cambridge, MA: Harvard University Press, 1992) chapter 20, p. 216.

APPENDIX A

1. Most of the facts, figures, and views expressed are based on 270 personal interviews with community officials and members, hasidic and non-hasidic as well as non-Jewish.
2. The figures for *Der Yid* were provided by the managing editor.
3. A study done for *South Williamsburg*, a publication of the Opportunity Development Association, states at the end of its 1982 population analysis: "We estimate the population of the study group (Hasidim of Williamsburg) to be in the range of 47,000–57,000" (p. 15). Most officials use the ball-park figure of 40,000. The reason for the higher estimate is given in the same statement cited before: "The birth rate in the Hasidic Community is among the highest in the nation."
4. The birthrate figures are cited by the heads of the Health Care and WIC programs of the ODA, which provide comprehensive services to women and babies before and after

birth. The same figure of eight to nine children per household of birth-age families was given by the head of *Yeled Sha'ashu'im*, the health facility set up in the villa of the late Satmar Rebbe in Kiryas Joel, Monroe, New York, where the women of this exurban branch of Williamsburg spend 2 weeks after giving birth. "The official figure for the entire community is 6 children per household, but this includes the large number of households after birth age and newly married couples." The number of students in the constantly expanding schools of Kiryas Joel (founded in 1976) is 3,000 for the 1200 families residing there.

5. The figures for the educational network of Satmar *yeshivot* and girls' schools were provided by the coordinator, Rabbi S. Herzog, by several officials, and by the principals of individual institutions.

6. An aerial view of Williamsburg yields a picture that is probably unique in American urban and rural life. In the six census tracts of the core residential area where hasidim concentrate are very few TV antennas. They are only on the five public housing projects, where there is a 55:45 or 60:40 proportion of Jewish to non-Jewish residents. All adjoining areas, like everywhere else in New York (including Boro Park, a neighborhood partially resembling Williamsburg, with an admixture of hasidic and non-hasidic elements) display the usual forest of TV antennas and dishes.

7. *The Boro Park Community Survey, 1982–1983*, by Egon Mayer (The Council of Jewish Organizations of Boro Park), p. 33.

Glossary

Adas Yereim (H) Congregation of the God-fearing.

Agudath Israel (H) World movement of Orthodox Jews, which has national and local branches, synagogues, and women's and youth branches.

Agunah, -ot (H) A wife whose husband's whereabouts is unknown, or who refuses to give his wife the religious divorce document (*get*) she needs to remarry.

Aidah Charedit (H) Community of the strictly observant, name of the ultra-Orthodox community of Jerusalem.

Aishel Avrohom (H) The tree of Abraham; name of the old age home of Williamsburg.

Aishes Chayil (H) A woman of valor; a good wife.

Akeret Habayit (H) The foundation of the home; a good wife.

Aliyah, -ot (H) Going up; used to refer to the honor of being called to the Torah; also name of the pilgrimage to the holy Temple in Jerusalem. In modern times, it refers to immigration to Israel.

Alter Heim (Y) The old home; the native homeland.

Am Ho'oretz (H) An uneducated, ignorant person.

Ashkenazim, -ic (H) Originally referring to Germans, it is the Hebrew name for Jews of Germany and West Europe. Since the sixteenth century it includes Eastern Europe. The Ashkenazim have developed a set of distinctive rituals and customs different from those of Sephardic Jews from the Mediterranean countries and North Africa. Congregations that follow the traditional rites of either of the two are called Ashkenazic or Sephardic, though the original geographic meaning is lost, especially since the hasidic rituals of Eastern Europe are mostly Sephardic.

Atarah -oth (H) A decorative silk or silver band on the *tallit*.

Atzas Sholom (H) Aid to preserve peace; an organization to help families in crisis.

Avoda (H) Work, service to the Lord.

Baal Melachah (H) Worker, tradesman, craftsman.

(H) — Hebrew; (Y) — Yiddish; (G) — German

297

Baal Tefillah (H)   A lay reader who conducts the service, in contrast to a *hazzan*, a professional cantor.

Baal Teshuvah (H)   A nonreligious person turning to the observance of religion and the divine commandments.

Baale-Battim, -ish (H) Baale-Bos (H)   *Baal Habayit*, meaning master of the house, in modern usage the term is applied to the constituent members of a congregation or of an establishment. In a good sense, it refers to someone who maintains socially acceptable standards of living.

Bachur, Bocher (H)   Young boy, single young man, student.

Bar Mitzvah (H)   Son of a commandment; a boy who has reached the age of 13, the age of adulthood, at which he is expected to accept full responsibilities. This coming of age is celebrated in a ritual in the synagogue and usually in an informal festive party.

Baruch Hashem (H)   Thank God.

Batlan, -im (H)   Someone who is not employed; used to refer to people available to establish the required quorum for a service. Traditionally also used to connote a clumsy, impractical person.

Bechinah, -oth (H)   Test, examination.

Behang, -t (Y)   To hang jewelry, or wear a lot of jewelry all over one's body.

Bekeshe (Y)   See *kaftan*, or *kapotte*.

Bekoved (Y)   A proper, honorable person.

Benshen (Y)   Saying of Grace, bless.

Besamim Box (H, Y)   Spice box used for ritual blessing said on Saturday night.

Bet Din (H)   Court.

Bet Hamidrash (H) Batei Midrash, Bet Medrash   House of Study; also used for an informal synagogue, or the study hall attached to a synagogue.

Bet Horo'oh (H)   Court for ritual, religious, and some civil-law decisions, manned by qualified scholars, rabbis.

Bikkur Cholim (H)   Visiting of the sick; name of organization caring for the ill at home or in hospitals.

Bitahon (H)   Faith in divine providence.

Blatt (of Gemara) (Y)   A page; usually used for the two sides of a page of the Talmud.

Bnai Torah (H)   A scholar, student of Torah.

Bnos Agudath Israel (H)   Daughters; used for the junior organization of girls, or women belonging to the Agudah movement.

Bochen (H)   An examiner; one who gives tests.

Bodek, Bodkim (H)   Inspector, checking of kosher food.

Brit Milah (H)   Circumcision.

Bubbeh (Y)   Grandmother; old woman, in general.

Chap (Y)   Grab, seize.

Chaptzeh (Y)   lit. "Grab them!" Call used to alert residents or passersby to help seize would-be attackers or criminals; used to deter crime.

Daf Yomi (H) Daily study of a double page of the Talmud, completing it every 7 years.

Derech Eretz (H) Respect, manners; also the connotation of the study of secular subjects.

Derlangen (Y) To pass, slap, hit.

Der Yid (Y) The Jew, the weekly of Hasidic Williamsburg, published by Satmar.

Dor Yeshorim (H) Institute for the Prevention of Genetic Disorders.

Drashah, -ot (H) Sermon, lecture.

Ehrlich (Y) Sincere, honest, truly pious.

Einikel, -lach (Y) Grandchildren, descendants of a hasidic Rebbe.

Eis Laasot (H) Time to act; early childhood center and organization.

Etrog Box (H) Container, silver box to hold the *etrog* fruit used for the Sukkot service.

Ezrat Nashim (H) Organization to help women cope with their small infants and families.

Farbrengen (Y) Communal meal; see also *tish*, in the residence of the Rebbe.

Farheren (Y) Giving an examination to students.

Farherers (Y) Examiners testing classes.

Farputzen (Y) To dress up.

Frum (Y) Pious.

Frumak (Y) An extremely Orthodox Jew, connotation of being fanatically pious.

Frumkeit (H) Piety.

Gabbai, -o'im (H) Official of a synagogue, usually taking care of the services.

Galut, Galus (H), (Y) Exile.

Gartel (Y) Belt, girdle. A soft, black cotton belt worn by *hasidim* for prayer, to symbolically separate the upper from the lower half of the body.

Gemara (H) See Talmud; a volume of the Talmud.

Geshickt (Y) Skilled, handy.

Geshmack (Y) Tasty, tasteful.

Get (H) Religious divorce document.

Glatt Kosher (Y) See Kosher; *Glatt* literally means smooth, beyond any question. It is usually used in connection with kosher meat. A term introduced by Hungarian *hasidim* to indicate their more stringent requirements for kosher food. Connotation of higher standards of dietary laws.

Green, -er (Y) Referring to greenhorns, a somewhat derogatory term for new immigrants.

Hachnossath Kalloh (H) Providing for the trousseau and other needs of brides.

Hachnossath Orchim (H) A place set aside for poor people or guests to be able to stay in a community overnight.

Haichal Hakodesh (H) Palace of Sanctity (kabbalistic term).

Haichal Haneginah (H) Palace of Melody (said to be next to the Palace of Sanctity in the Heavens), connoting the sacralization of music or of singing as an important element of the religious service.

Hakafah (H) Festive parade around a synagogue on Simhat Torah, carrying the Torah scrolls.

Halachah (H) The ritual laws and religious laws contained in the Codes of Law.

Halat, Chalat (Y) See *Kaftan*.

Hanukkah, Chanukah (H) Feast of Lights, commemorating the victory of the Maccabees over the Greek armies.

Has Vehalilah (H) God forbid.

Hashem (H) The Divine Name, referring to God.

Hashkafah, -oth (H) Outlook, viewpoint, ideas, ideology.

Hasid, Hasidim (H) Hasidism Pious, a godly person: the followers of the Hasidic movement, founded by Rabbi Israel Baal Shem Tov in the eighteenth century, that provided spiritual hope and uplifted the common people; largely based on kabbalistic sources. The hasidic communities are centered about *tzaddikim* or *rebbes*, righteous, saintly leaders, whose prayers and guidance elevate the prayers and service of the masses to higher levels of religiosity. Those who oppose Hasidism and its teachings are called *mitnagdim*, opponents. There were large branches of the hasidic movements and schools throughout Eastern Europe, each following the teachings of famous scholars and thinkers. Their descendants usually head the contemporary movements that have survived the Holocaust. Most have their own customs, rituals, and life-style.

Haskalah (H) Movement of Religious Enlightenment, especially in nineteenth-century Eastern and Central Europe.

Hasseneh, -s (Y) Wedding.

Hatzoloh (H) Rescue; name of the famous volunteer medical corps.

Haver, -im, (H) Comrade, study companion.

Havruta (H) Study companion.

Hazzan, Chazzan (H) Cantor.

Heder, Cheder (H) Room; traditionally the name of traditional schools, usually on an elementary level. In modern times, it was the name for the type of religious schools often ridiculed in the Yiddish literature not doing justice to its crucial role in the perpetuation of knowledge and scholarship among the masses. In the hasidic literature, the term *heder* refers to the study group or the founders of a hasidic school.

Heilig (Y) Holy.

Hesder (H) The *yeshivah* whose students serve in the Israeli Army while remaining *yeshivah* students, alternately being trained, serving, and studying.

Hesed, Chesed (H) Loving-kindness.

Hesed L'Avrohom Organization devoted to helping needy Jews spiritually and physically.

Hevrah (H) A group, a society; used, for example, in *Hevrah Kaddisha*, a burial society, and so forth.

Hillul Hashem (H) Desecration; profanization of the divine name.

Hinuch (H) Education.

Hoben (Y) To have.

Hol Hamoed (H) The semiholidays of Passover and Sukkot.

Hosson, Chosson (H) Bridegroom.

Hozrim Biteshuvah (H) Same as *teshuvah,* Jews who come back to the observance of the Jewish religion.

Humash (H) The Five Books of Moses, the Torah.

Humrah, -oth (H) The more stringent pattern of ritual observance.

Hutzpah, Chutzpah (H) "Nerve."

JAP Jewish American Princess, somewhat derogatory connotation.

Kabbalah, -ist (H) The body of esoteric, mystic knowledge of the Torah, contained in the *Zohar,* or in the teachings of Rabbi Isaac Luria, the Ari on which much of the hasidic teachings are based.

Kaddish (H) A prayer of sanctification recited at certain points in the synagogue service. It is best known as the prayer said by those in mourning.

Kaftan (Y) *Kapotte, Bekeshe,* or *Chalat,* A long, loose black silk or wool gown, held together by a belt, worn by *hasidim,* especially on Sabbath and holidays (from Turkish Oaftan).

Kahal Kehillah (H) A congregation, community; the Jewish community organization managing its affairs.

Kaileh, Keileh (H, Y) A vessel, instrument.

Kallah, -oth (H) Bride.

Kaptzan (H, Y) A poor person.

Kashrut, Kasher, Kosher (H) Something that is proper, usually referring to food prepared according to or meeting the requirements of the Jewish religious dietary laws. It is usually supervised and approved by rabbinic authorities.

Kavvanah (H) Proper devotion; intensive concentration on the meaning of the prayers and texts of the sacred studies, inspiration.

Kibbud (H) An honor.

Kibbud Av va-Eim (H) Honoring father and mother.

Kiddush (H) Prayer of sanctification that ushers in the Sabbath and holidays, usually said over a cup of wine or *hallah,* bread. In folk usage it refers to a festive meal served at celebrations in the synagogue or at home on special occasions.

Kimpatorin, Kimpetuerin (Y) A woman after giving birth.

Kind, -er (Y) Child, children.

Kiruv (H) Outreach, bringing close.

Kiruv Rehokim Outreach programs, efforts to bring nonreligious Jews back to religious observance.

Klal (H) The public, the community.

Klaus, Klois (Y) A small study hall, frequently used for services.

Kollel (H) Institute of advanced talmudic study for young, married scholars.

Kolpik (Y) A high oval fur cap, type of *shtreimel* usually worn by Russian-Polish *hasidim.*

Koved (H, Y) Honor.

L'Haim (H) To life; a toast. Used for the hasidic custom of drinking to each other's well-being on such occasions as the *yahrtzeit,* or on festive occasions.

Licht Benshen (Y) Lighting of the candles for Sabbath or holidays.

Mahmir, Humrah (H)   Deciding in favor of a more stringent interpretation of the law; someone who usually follows the stricter interpretation or application of a law.

Mal'och, -im (H)   An angel; the name of an organization of a young Orthodox American group following the teachings of Rabbi Maloch, who inspired them to a more pious, ultra-Orthodox life-style before the arrival of the hasidic newcomers.

Marsh, -en (G)   Marchlike melodies sung by some groups of *hasidim* in the services or on festive occasions; see *niggunim.*

Matnas Aniyim B'Seter (H)   Charity given anonymously to needy people.

Matnas Chinom (H)   Charity.

Mechalisten (Y)   Followers of Rabbi M. Leibowitz, a former teacher of the Satmar *yeshivah* who started his own group of *Hasidim.*

Mechanech, hinuch (H)   Educator, education.

Mechitzah, -ot   A divider, a wall or curtain that separates the sections reserved for men and women in the synagogue, and at social affairs.

Mehutan, -onim (H)   In-laws.

Melamed, -im (H)   Teacher of children; famous as the instructor of the *heder.* In the folk use this title has a somewhat pathetic connotation of a man who is not able to make a living in a different profession. Still used for a Hebrew teacher in the Yiddish literature.

Melaveh Malkeh (H)   Accompanying the queen; it is the name of a special private or communal meal eaten on *Motzoe Shabbath,* Sabbath night, with special songs and customs. It is a popular communal meal eaten with the Rebbe by his *hasidim,* clothed in a mystic kabbalistic aura and practices.

Menagen, -im (H)   A singer; usually referring to a layman who is able to sing the typical hasidic melodies, *niggunim,* in the services, at festive occasions, or at meals.

Menahel, -im (H)   Head of a school.

Menahel Ruchani (H)   Spiritual head of an institution.

Menaker, -im (H)   A person who prepares meat for kosher use by removing veins or fat, which are not permitted to be eaten by the religious dietary laws.

Mensh, -en (G, Y)   A good human being.

Menshlichkeit (Y)   Decent, ethical, humane behavior.

Menuhah (H)   Rest, peace of mind.

Mesamches es Halev (H)   Making someone's heart rejoice; the name of an organization helping people in trouble.

Mesifta, Mesivta (H)   Name of the higher division of a *yeshivah;* usually the high-school division of an American *yeshivah.*

Mesirat Nefesh (H)   Wholehearted devotion to a cause, even at the risk of life, in extreme cases.

Mezzuzah, -ot (H)   Piece of parchment attached to a doorpost, containing portions of text (Deuteronomy 6:4–9, 11:13–17) rolled up in a container.

Mikvah (H)   The ritual bath, or ritualarium, required for religious purification, especially for the monthly purification of women. Hence it is absolutely mandatory for an Orthodox community. It is customary, especially for *hasidim,* to immerse themselves before the services on Sabbath and holidays.

Minhag, -im (H) A religious custom that may or may not have a basis in the written or oral law; it is made binding by long established use. Many are included in the Codes of Jewish Law.

Minyan, im (H) A quorum of ten men required for the congregational service. In folk use, the term refers to a small congregation that meets in a private place.

Mitnaged, -im (H) An opponent; *mitnagedim* are the opponents to the hasidic movement.

Mizrachi (H) Name of a worldwide Orthodox Zionist organization.

Moetzes Gedolei Hatorah (H) The council of the highest Torah authorities, established by the world movement of Agudath Israel as the supreme authority in questions of Jewish law, life, and policies.

Moshiah (H) Messiah.

Mussar (H) Moral and ethical teachings, a body of classical and contemporary ethical writings.

Nadden (Y) Dowry.

Nahas (H) Pride and joy of parents derived mainly from children.

Nazis (G) National Socialists, followers of Hitler.

Neder, -im (H) Pledge, vow, such as those made by people called up to the reading of the Torah.

Niggun, -im (H) Melody. *Niggunim* are the melodies created by the various hasidic schools and used in the services and at all festive communal and private celebrations.

Nisayon, -oth (H) Tests, temptations of a person's character and faith.

Nisht, Nit (Y) Not.

Nisht Passig (Y) Unbecoming, improper conduct.

Nusach, -a'oth (H) Prayer or ritual order or versions texts; used particularly to describe the texts and rituals of the prayer services of the Ashkenazic or Sephardic congregations.

O(i) berland, -er (G) The upper land of the Austro-Hungarian empire; comprising areas of Czechoslovakia and Moravia; used in distinction from the Unterland, the lower lands of Hungary, especially Carpatho-Russia with their mostly ultra-Orthodox hasidic communities, such as Satmar or Sziged.

Oisher (Y) (H) A rich man.

Oseh hesed (H) Doing acts of loving-kindness. Name of an organization devoted to charity.

Ostjuden (G) Jews from Eastern Europe; a collective term used by Western European Jews for all Jews from Eastern Europe, in a somewhat derogatory manner.

Passover (H) Holiday commemorating the liberation of Israel from Egyptian bondage.

Pesach Tikvah (H) Gate of Hope; name of an institution for the mentally ill.

Petsh (Y) Slaps, a beating.

Peyot (Y) Sideburns or sidelocks worn by Jews, especially *hasidim*, in compliance with the biblical prohibition of Leviticus 19:27.

Pirchim (H) Blossoms, sprouts; name of the youth organization of Agudath Israel.

Poale Agudath Israel (H) Name of the labor movement of Agudath Israel. More militantly pro-Israel than the mother organization.

Pollack, -en (G)   Used somewhat derogatorily for all Jews from East. Europe by Western European Jews.

Purim (H)   Festival of Lots. It commemorates the day on which the Jews of the Persian empire were saved from oppression at the hands of Haman, and is celebrated with much merriment and the reading of the Book of Esther.

Rabbeim, Rebbe, Rebbes, Rabbi, Rabbonim, Rav (H)   Rabbi, master, teacher; used particularly for the charismatic hasidic leaders, in place of rabbis.

Rahamim (H)   Mercy, compassion.

Rahamonim bnai rahamonim (H)   The Jewish people are depicted as "most merciful, compassionate people."

Rav Tov (H)   An abundance of good; name of the relief and rescue organization founded by the Old Rebbe of Satmar for the physical and spiritual rescue of Jewish people, e.g., in Iran, and Russia.

Rebbe (Y)   Head of hasidic communities.

Rebbish (Y)   Belonging to a Rebbe; e.g., a Rebbish Einikel, a grandson or descendant of a Rebbe.

Rishut, Roshoh (H)   Evil deed, of a *roshoh*, an evil doer; name frequently applied to enemies of the Jewish people, anti-Semitism.

Rosh Hashanah (H)   The Jewish new year.

Rosh, -ei Yeshivah (H)   Head of a *yeshivah*, especially on a higher level of advanced study.

Scheirith Israel (H)   Remnant of Israel; frequently used as name of a congregation, especially a congregation of refugees.

Sefer, -orim (H)   Book; used particularly for the sacred books of the religious literature, or for a Torah scroll.

Sephard, -im, -ic (H)   Jews coming from Spain and Portugal; the customs, rituals, and services of the Sephardim differ from those of the Ashkenazim, Jews originating in Germany and Eastern and Central Europe, geographic origins largely lost; hasidic congregations whose rituals and customs are only partially based on those of the Jews from Spain or North Africa, and are based on kabbalistic sources, e.g., the writings of R. Isaac Luria, the ARI, are also called Sephardic.

Seudah Shlishit (H)   The third meal of Sabbath.

Shaaloh, -ot (H)   Ritual or religious question decided by rabbinic authority.

Shadhan (H)   A professional or amateur matchmaker.

Shammes, Shammash (H, Y)   Title of the synagogue sexton; also used for the personal attendant of a Rebbe.

Shehitah, Shohet (H)   Ritual slaughtering, slaughterer of an animal in the manner prescribed by the Jewish Law. A *shohet* must be trained and certified by a rabbinic authority, usually a strictly observant, learned Orthodox Jew. Many Rebbes have their own personal or congregational shohet.

Sheigetz, Shkotzim (Y)   Derogatory term used for non-Jewish rowdies or anti-Semitic hoodlums. Also used for ignorant, less pious Jews by extreme Orthodox Jews.

Sheitel (Y)   A wig covering the hair of married women; now available in modern fashionable styles for Orthodox women.

Shidduch, -im (H) Marriage, matching a young man and woman for eventual marriage.

Shirayim (H) Pieces of food handed by a Rebbe to his *hasidim* during a communal meal.

Shlemiel (Y) An unhandy, unlucky person.

Shmad, Geshmat (H, Y) A Jew who had converted from his religion.

Shofar (H) The curved ram's horn, blown on Rosh Hashanah, as a call to penitence.

Shohet, -im (H) Religious slaughterer.

Shomer, -im (H) A guard, watchman; *Shomrim* is the name of the volunteer civil patrol in Williamsburg

Shtander (Y) A stand or high desk used in study halls for students, or for the reader of a synagogue service.

Shtetl (Y) Small town; usually used to characterize the typical East European community and culture.

Shtiebel, -lach (Y) A small room; name for the small, informal hasidic synagogue in a private or converted private home.

Shtievel (Y) Boots; boots worn by *hasidim*, especially in Poland or Russia.

Shtikel Rebbe (Y) A minor hasidic leader, mostly a descendant of a noted Rebbe.

Shtreimel (Y) High fur cap worn by *hasidim*, especially on Sabbath and holidays.

Shul, -s (Y) School; popular folk term for a synagogue.

Shulhan Aruch (H) A set table; name of the four-volume Code of Law compiled by R. Joseph Karo in the fifteenth century.

Simhat Torah (H) The festive last day of the Sukkot holiday. A joyous holiday on which the last of the weekly portions of the annual Torah cycle is read, and the first of the Torah is begun. It is celebrated by *Hakafot*, festive parades and dancing with Torah scrolls, to symbolize the conclusion of the Torah cycle and the end of the High Holidays.

Smihah (H) The act and certification of a rabbinic scholar's ordination as a rabbi, authorized to decide questions or problems of ritual or religious nature.

Sofer, -im (H) Scribe of Torah and other scrolls.

Sukkah, Sukkot (H) Festival of Booth, eight days, one of the three pilgrimage festivals, concluding the High Holiday season.

Tallit, -im (H) A prayer shawl, usually silk or wool, fringed at each corner in accordance with Numeri 16, 38, worn by the male adult Jew.

Tallit katan (H) Small prayer shawl, worn all day under the shirt, even by a child. *Hasidim* wear the *tallit katan* over the shirt, their long, woolen *tzitzit* dangling visibly as they work in their shirt sleeves.

Talmid, -im (H) Student.

Talmid Hacham, omim (H) A Torah scholar, an authority in the talmudic studies.

Talmud (H) The many-volumed record of the discussions of the Babylonian and Jerusalemite scholars, elaborating on the laws of the Mishnah.

Talmud Torah (H) Popular Hebrew school for Jewish children, organized by a congregation or privately; dominant afternoon Hebrew school in America until the rise of the day schools. Name for the elementary division of a hasidic *yeshivah*.

Tanach (H)   An abbreviation of the names of the three parts of the Bible. Torah *Neviim, Ketubim.*

Tefillin (H)   Phylacteries consisting of two square leather boxes, one worn on the left arm, the other on the forehead, by the male adult Jew.

Tiferet (H)   Glory, magnificence, beautiful in appearance; a concept from the kabbalistic tradition describing the creation. Man is to fulfill the divine commandments in an esthetically beautiful manner.

Tiflut (H)   Immorality.

Tikvah (H)   Hope.

Tish, -en (Y)   A table; usually used by *hasidim* to designate a table round, a communal meal eaten with the Rebbe on Sabbath or holidays or at festive occasions. The Rebbe's participation in the meal, his blessings, and his talks transform the meal into a sacred, inspiring, religious experience.

Tomche Shabbos (H)   Support for Sabbath observance; an organization that provides food for needy people.

Torah (H)   Teaching; originally the name for the Five Books of Moses, it subsequently became the term used to encompass the entire body of the study and literature of the Jewish religion.

Torah im Derech Eretz (H)   Usually denoting a combination of Torah and general, secular studies; the popular formulation of the ideology set forth by Rabbi Samson Raphael Hirsch, the founder of the separatist Orthodox Jewish communities in pre-Hitler Germany, it was largely rejected by most hasidic and nonhasidic communities in Eastern Europe because of its proposed synthesis of intensive Torah study with cultural knowledge especially in the educational philosophy of the Hirschian school.

Treifoh (H, Y)   The opposite of kosher, what is acceptable in the dietary Jewish laws. Used in a broader sense for everything that is not acceptable in the spiritual as well as in the physical realms of Judaism.

Tza'ar (H)   Pain, suffering.

Tzaddik (H)   A righteous, saintly person; often used to describe a scholar and sage, such as a hasidic Rebbe.

Tzedakah (H)   Charity.

Tzitzit (H)   Ritual fringes attached to the four corners of a garment, especially a *tallit*, in accordance with Numeri 16, 38.

Tzni'ut (H)   Modesty, behavior that meets that demands of the moral and ethical teachings proper for men and women, set forth in the Jewish law and tradition.

Vaad Hakehillot (H)   A council of communities, United Jewish Organizations.

Valgern Zich (Y)   To be destitute, homeless, not settled in a place.

Values   Objects of human desires or appreciation. Any objects, conditions, or principles around which meanings have grown up in the course of human experiences. Social values are those objects and activities that have common meanings for the members of a particular group or society.

Verheren, Ferheren (Y)   To give children an examination.

Weltanschauung (G)   A particular philosophy or ideology that provides a systematic perspective or view of the world, a history, or explanation, of the particular functions and phases of the world or of a society.

Yad L'Ahim (H) A hand to brothers; name of a relief organization initiated by the Sukulener Rebbe.

Yahrtzeit (Y) Anniversary date of a person's death, usually observed by close relatives by the saying of *kaddish*, a special prayer in the synagogue, and burning a light in the house for 24 hours. The *yahrtzeit* of a famous sage or scholar, or of a famous Rebbe, is observed by *hasidim* with special customs.

Yahsan (H) A man of *yichus*, noble lineage; used to denote a man of importance, a privileged character.

Yarmulkeh (Y) A skullcap, worn by observant Jews all the time as a token of one's reverence for the omnipresence of the Lord. *Hasidim* wear a *yarmulkeh* under the hat, too.

Yecke (Y) A popular Yiddish name given mostly to German Jews, making light of their supposed inflexibility.

Yeshivah, -ot (H) A school for intensive religious, talmudic, and rabbinic learning. The distinction is made between a *yeshivah ketanah*, the elementary division, and a *yeshivah gedolah*, the higher division of advanced studies.

Yetzer Hara (H) The evil drive or instinct.

Yetzer Hara Box (Y) A derogatory term for TV denoting its bad influence.

Yichus (H, Y) A person of *yichus*, a *yahsan*, is a descendant of noble lineage.

Yid, Der (Y) The Jew, from the German *Jude*; the name of the Yiddish weekly published by Satmar.

Yiddish (Y) The language spoken by Eastern European Jews, which is a mixture of German and Slavic and other languages; it evolved over the centuries of Jewish migration from Western and Central European countries to the East. It was the classic language of the *cheder* and the *yeshivah* world, and also became the language of the secular East European masses, which evolved its own literature. It is still the international language of Jews everywhere after the Holocaust, but is gradually being replaced by modern Hebrew, especially among the younger generations. The hasidic masses are cultivating and perpetuating the speaking of Yiddish as part of their life-style.

Yiddishkeit (Y) Piety, the spirit of Orthodox Judaism and Jews.

Yir'at Shomayim (H) The fear of the Lord, piety.

Yom Kippur (H) The Day of Atonement.

Yomim Noraim (H) The High Holidays.

Yoreh De'ah (H) Part of the Code of Law dealing with ritual commandments and prohibitions.

Yoreh Yoreh, Yodin Yodin (H) The rabbinic ordination, authorizing the scholar to act as judge in cases of religious ritual and civil law.

Yunge Leit (Y) Young people, especially referring to young middle-aged men and women.

Zeideh (Y) Grandfather.

Zeirei Agudath Israel (H) Young people; name of the young men's division of Agudath Israel.

Zula'gen, Zugelagt (Y) Losing, losing out.

References

Abelow, Sam P. *History of Brooklyn Jewry.* New York: Sheba Publishing, 1937.

Anthology of Hasidic Thought. New York, 1923.

Arden, Harvey. "The Pious Ones." *National Geographic* (August 1975): 276–298.

Armbruster, Eugene L. *Brooklyn's Eastern District.* New York, 1942.

Bulka, Reuven P. *Dimensions of Orthodox Judaism.* New York: Ktav Publishing House, 1983.

Caplow, Theodore, et al. *Middletown Families.* Minneapolis: University of Minnesota Press and Bantam Books, 1982.

Carlin, Jerome, and Mendlowitz, Paul H. "The Rabbi." A Sociological Study of a Religious Specialist. In *The Jews.* Ed. Marshall Sklare. Glencoe, IL: Free Press, 1968.

Cherlin, Andrew J., and Furstenberg, Frank F. *The New American Grandparents.* New York: Basic Books, 1986.

Danziger, Herbert. *Returning to Tradition: The Contemporary Revival of Orthodox Judaism.* New Haven: Yale University Press, 1989.

Dicker, Herman. *Piety and Perseverance: Carpatho-Russian Jewry.* New York: Sepher Hermon Press, 1981.

Duncan, Gregory J. "Welfare Use in America." *Winter Bulletin* (University of Michigan, Institute of Social Research) (1986).

Engelman, Uriel. "Education." In *American Jewish Yearbook.* Vol. 44. Philadelphia: Jewish Publication Society, 1944.

_____. *Medurbia.* Contemporary Jewish Record, 1941.

_____. "The Size of Families." In *The Jewish Population of Buffalo.* Vol. 16. Buffalo: University of Buffalo Studies, 1938.

Firey, Walter. *Land Use in Central Boston.* Cambridge: Harvard University Press, 1947.

Fuchs, Daniel. *A Summer in Williamsburg.* New York: Vanguard Press, 1934.

Garvey, John. "Asylums of Sanity." *Commonwealth,* 15 November 1985, 631.

Glazer, Nathan. *American Judaism.* Chicago: University of Chicago Press, 1972.

Glazer, Nathan, and Moynihan, Daniel P. *Beyond the Melting Pot.* Cambridge: M.I.T. Press, 1970.

Goldberg, Nathan. "Occupational Patterns of American Jews." *Jewish Review* 3 (1945).

Goldscheider, Calvin. *The American Jewish Community.* Providence, RI: Brown University Studies, 1986.

Goldscheider, Calvin, and Zuckerman, Alan S. *American Jewish Fertility*. Providence, RI: Brown University Studies, 1986.

———. *Jewish Continuity and Change*. Bloomington, IN: University of Indiana Press, 1986.

———. *The Transformation of the Jews*. Chicago: University of Chicago Press, 1984.

Gordon, Albert I. *Jews in Transition*. Minneapolis: University of Minnesota Press, 1949.

Graeber, Isaque, and Britt, S. H. *Jews in a Gentile World*. New York: Macmillan Co., 1942.

Grinstein, Hyman B. *Rise of the Jewish Community of New York: 1654–1860*. Philadelphia: The Jewish Publication Society, 1945.

Handlin, Oscar. *The Uprooted*. Boston: Little Brown & Co., 1952.

Heilman, Samuel. *Defenders of the Faith: Inside Ultra-Orthodox Jewry*. New York: Schocken Books, 1992.

———. "The Many Faces of Orthodoxy." *Modern Judaism* 2:1 (1988): 23–51.

Helmreich, Wilhelm. *The World of the Yeshiva: An Intimate Portrait of Orthodox Jewry*. New York: Free Press, 1982.

Hook, Sidney. *Out of Step*. New York: Harper and Row, 1987.

Howe, Irving. "Daniel Fuchs: Escape from Williamsburg." *Commentary* (July 1938).

Jewel, J. A. *History of Williamsburg*. New York, n.d.

Jewish Welfare Board. *Study of the Jewish Community of Williamsburg*. New York, 1936.

The Jewish Press. October 9, 1987.

Kephart, William M. *Extraordinary Groups*. New York: St. Martin's Press, 1976.

Kranzler, David. *Thy Brother's Blood: The Orthodox Jewish Response during the Holocaust*. New York: Mesorah Publications, 1987.

Kranzler, George. *Williamsburg: A Jewish Community in Transition*. New York: Feldheim Books, 1961.

———. *Williamsburg Memories*. Lakewood, NJ: C.I.S., 1989.

Kranzler, George, with Herzberg, Irving I. *The Face of Faith*. New York: Ktav Publishing, 1973.

Lamm, Norman. *Torah Umadda*. Northvale, NJ: Jason Aronson Inc., 1989.

Leibler, Isi. *Jewish Religious Extremism*. New York: World Jewish Congress–Australian Institute of Jewish Affairs, 1991.

Logan, Helen. *Williamsburg: A Neighborhood Study*. N. P., 1936.

Lynd, Robert H., and Lynd, Helen. *Middletown*. New York: Harcourt, Brace & Co., 1929.

———. *Middletown in Transition*. New York: Harcourt, Brace & Co., 1937.

MacIver, Robert M. *Community: A Social Study*. New York: Macmillan Co., 1931.

———. *Social Causation*. New York: Ginn & Co., 1942.

———. *Society*. New York: Farrar and Rinehart, 1941.

Maller, Julius B. "A Study of Jewish Neighborhoods of New York." *Jewish Social Service Quarterly* (1934).

Mayer, Egon. *From Suburb to Shtetl*. Philadelphia: Temple University Press, 1979.

Medoff, Raffael. *The Deafening Silence*. New York: Shampolsky, 1987.

Mintz, Jerome R. *Hasidic People: A Place in the New World*. Cambridge: Harvard University Press, 1992.

New York City Housing Authority. *Special Tabulation of Tenant Characteristics. Williamsburg Housing Report*. New York, 1984.

New York City Planning Commission. *Community Planning Handbook*. Rev. ed. New York, 1974.

New York Times. "Birth of a Voting Bloc: The Hasidim and Orthodox Organize." Kifner, John. 2 May 1989, 22.

———. "Brooklyn Project Shatters Hispanics, Hasidim Peace." Goldman, Ari. 1 October 1990, B1.

_____. "Hasidim Navigate Secular Worlds While Living a Life Apart." 4 July 1987, 29, 31.

_____. "Police to Guard Israeli Rabbi in New York." Goldman, Ari. 3 March 1981, 13.

ODA-Opportunity Development Association. *South Williamsburg.* Rev. ed. New York: Newman Assoc., 1982.

ODA Today. 4:1 (Summer 1979).

_____. Special Edition (Spring 1982).

_____. Special 10th Anniversary Issue 1974–1984 (October 24, 1984).

_____. Special Issue in Honor of the Visit of the Secretary of Commerce Malcolm S. Baldridge (November 18, 1986).

Poll, Solomon. *The Hasidic Community of Williamsburg.* New York: Schocken Books, 1961.

Potok, Chaim. *The Chosen.* New York: Simon & Schuster, 1967.

Riemer, Jonathan. *Canarsie.* Cambridge: Harvard University Press, 1985.

Rubin, Israel. *Satmar: Island in the City.* Chicago: Quadrangle Books, 1972.

Sacks, Jonathan, Rabbi. *Traditional Alternatives.* London: Jews College Publications, 1989.

Schick, Marvin. "The Legacy of Rav Aharon Kotler." *Jewish Action* 48:2 (Summer 1988): 77–85.

Schiff, Alvin I. *The Jewish Day School in America.* New York: The Jewish Education Committee Press, 1966.

Silberman, Charles E. *A Certain People: American Jews and Their Lives Today.* New York: Summit Books, 1985.

Sklare, Marshall. *America's Jews.* New York: Random House, 1971.

_____. *Conservative Judaism.* Glencoe, IL: Free Press, 1955.

Sklare, Marshall, and Greenblum, J. *Jewish Identity on the Suburban Frontier.* Lakeville Studies. Chicago: University of Chicago Press, 1979.

Smith, Betty. *A Tree Grows in Brooklyn.* New York: Harper and Bros., 1943.

Srole, Leo, and Warner, W. L. *The Social Systems of American Ethnic Groups.* Yankee City Series. Vol. 3. New Haven: Yale University Press, 1945.

Stiles, Henry R. *History of Kings County of Brooklyn.* New York, 1884.

Sullivan, Donald G. "Great Expectations: Historic Williamsburg." *New York Magazine* (April 1978).

Susser, Ida. *Norman Street: Poverty and Politics in an Urban Neighborhood.* New York: Oxford Press, 1982.

Time magazine. "Dealing with Demography." 7 August 1989, 12.

Tobin, Gary. *The Jewish Communities of Baltimore and Washington DC.* Baltimore: Assoc. Jewish Charities, 1985/1986.

Tovar, Frederick S. *Handbook of the Puerto Rican Community.* San Juan: Plus Ultra Education Press, 1970.

U. S. Bureau of the Census. *Williamsburg: A Study of the Jewish Welfare Board.* New York, 1936.

U. S. Department of Commerce. *Minority Business Today* 4:2 (May 1985).

_____. *1986 Study of Poverty.* Washington, DC, 1986.

U. S. Department of Labor. Bureau of Labor Statistics. *Profile of Puerto Rican New Yorkers.* Washington, DC, 1975.

U. S. Housing Authority. *Williamsburg Houses.* New York, 1951.

Warner, W. Lloyd, and Lund, P. S. *Democracy in Jonesville.* New York: Harper & Bros., 1949.

_____. *The Social Life of a Modern Community.* Yankee City Series. Vol. 1. New Haven: Yale University Press, 1941.

_____. *The Status System of a Modern Community.* Yankee City Series. Vol. 2. New Haven: Yale University Press, 1943.

Washington Post. "Cultures Clash as Hasidic Jews Compete for Turf." Hornblower, Margot. 9 November 1986, A1.

Waxman, Chaim I. *America's Jews in Transition.* Philadelphia: Temple University Press, 1983.

Weld, Ralph Foster. *Brooklyn Is America.* New York: AMS Press, 1967.

Wirth, Louis. *The Ghetto.* Chicago: University of Chicago Press, 1928.

Wyman, David. *Abandonment of the Jews.* New York: Random House–Pantheon Books, 1984.

_____. *Paper Walls.* Amherst, MA: University of Massachusetts Press, 1968.

Der Yid. 28 December 1990.

Zborowsky, Mark, and Herzog, Elizabeth. *Life Is With People.* New York: Schocken Books, 1952.

⇛⇛⇛ ⇚⇚⇚

Acknowledgments

The author gratefully acknowledges permission to quote from the following sources:

"The Women of Williamsburg" by George Gershon Kranzler. Copyright © 1983 by the Rabbinical Council of America. Published in *Tradition* magazine 28:1 (Fall 1983). Used by permission.

"The Voice of Williamsburg" by George Gershon Kranzler. Copyright © 1988 by the Rabbinical Council of America. Published in *Tradition* magazine 23:3 (Spring 1988). Used by permission.

Maps on pages 287, 288, and tables on page 290 are from *South Williamsburg: A Strategy for Preserving a New York Neighborhood,* prepared for Opportunity Development Association by Newman Associates. Copyright © 1977 by Milton R. Newman. Used by permission.

Rendition of The Residential Core map by Shari Stahl.

Map on page 289 reprinted by permission of the publishers from *Hasidic People: A Place in the New World* by Jerome R. Mintz. Cambridge, Mass: Harvard University Press, copyright © 1992 by the President and Fellows of Harvard College.

Williamsburg: A Jewish Community in Transition by George Kranzler. Copyright © 1961 by George Kranzler. Published by Feldheim Publishers. Used by permission.

"The Saint and Sage of Williamsburg" from *Williamsburg Memories* by Gershon Kranzler. Copyright © 1988 by C.I.S. Communications Inc. Published by C.I.S. Publications. Used by permission.

Index

ABOUT THE AUTHOR

George Gershon Kranzler, professor emeritus, received his doctorate from Columbia University. He was a pioneer of Jewish day school education in this country and served as principal of elementary and high schools for over 25 years. From 1966 to 1986 he was professor of sociology at Towson State University and taught at Johns Hopkins University. His *Williamsburg: A Jewish Community in Transition* became a classic of Jewish community research. His *Face of Faith* (photos by I. Herzberg) won the prestigious Seltzer Brodsky Prize of the YIVO Institute for Jewish Research. Dr. Kranzler has written many books of fiction and nonfiction for Jewish juveniles, some of which were translated into Hebrew and Russian. *Hasidic Williamsburg* is the last of his 4-volume longitudinal study of this unique Jewish community in Brooklyn, New York.